A Decade
of Delusions

A Decade
of Delusions

From Speculative Contagion to the Great Recession

Frank K. Martin

WILEY

John Wiley & Sons, Inc.

Published by John Wiley & Sons, Inc., Hoboken, New Jersey.
Published simultaneously in Canada.

Library of Congress Cataloging-in-Publication Data:
Martin, Frank K.
    A decade of delusions : from speculative contagion to the great recession /
Frank K. Martin.
        p. cm.
    Includes index.
    ISBN 978-1-118-00456-2 (cloth); ISBN 978-1-118-07814-3 (ebk);
    ISBN 978-1-118-07815-0 (ebk); ISBN 978-1-118-07816-7 (ebk)
        1. Investments—United States.   2. Finance—United States—History—
21st century.   3. Financial crises—United States.   4. Speculation—United States.
I. Title.
HG4910.M349 2011
332.60973—dc22

                                                                        2011004110

Printed in the United States of America

10 9 8 7 6 5 4 3 2 1

*May the few who profit from this book be
mindful of the many who cannot.*

Contents

Foreword

Frank Martin is one of the wise men of American finance. No, he doesn't have the public profile of the late Benjamin Graham and Peter Bernstein, or Warren Buffett, Paul Volcker, and Henry Kaufman, but he stands firm and tall with them in the pantheon of my heroes and mentors. This book, *A Decade of Delusions*, will make it clear both why I admire Frank and why I commend his wisdom to you.

The first thing you should know is that Frank Martin is the founder (and remains the intellectual leader) of Martin Capital Management, an investment advisory firm established in 1987 and located in Elkhart, Indiana. Yes, he manages "other people's money" (OPM). But what differentiates him from most other advisors (and nearly all advisors to mutual funds) is that he manages the wealth entrusted to his care by his clients under substantially the same investment principles and strategies as he manages his own wealth; he takes essentially the same risks with his clients' money as with his own. Investing under the principle of "my own money" (MOM) makes him more than an advisor to his clients; it makes him their partner in every sense of the word.

Those of us who have been plying the investments trade over the past few decades have been eyewitnesses to one of the most remarkable eras in U.S. financial history. We've seen the bubble in the "New Economy" of 1996 to 2000; the (inevitable) stock market crash that followed; the ensuing (likely inevitable) recovery; the ultra-speculative financial Bubble of 2005 to 2007; and the (again, inevitable) crash of our investment system, our economy, and our society. Frank Martin was one of us, but with a difference. He pondered each event, looked for causes, considered outcomes, contemplated resolutions, and drew both on the wisdom of the ages and on the fundamental mathematics of business and investing, turning information into knowledge, then into his own wisdom.

What was the author thinking and doing during those waves of hope and fear, during that environment of greed and speculation? Happily, we know the answer to that question. For he wrote (and wrote and wrote) about the saga as it unfolded in the markets. An assiduous chronicler of those events, Frank prepared annual reports to his clients that carefully described the thinking, the actions, the policies, and the strategies that drove his and his firm's investment decisions. These annual reports are lengthy and deeply detailed, but they provide precisely the kind of information that intelligent investors have a right to expect—no, to demand—from their own wealth managers. Were I not a financial professional with substantially 100 percent of my wealth invested in the Vanguard funds, that is exactly what I would expect from the manager of my own assets.

Commonsense Wisdom

I've read the Martin Capital Management annual reports for more than a decade now, ever since the 1998 edition. These annual reports, through 2004, were packaged together in Frank's first book, *Speculative Contagion*, published in 2006. Largely an anthology of his earlier reports, the book's publication immediately preceded the financial crisis that would soon unfold. I marveled not only at the book's prescience, but at the commonsense wisdom that helped to cut through the dense fog of infinitely abundant information that, paradoxically, has clouded our vision, and the intensity of emotion that has plagued investor behavior as we act on those eternal enemies of long-term investing—hope, greed, and fear.

Frank's philosophy of long-term investing in companies (not stocks as such, a critical distinction) minimizes such counterproductive behavior. After *Speculative Contagion* was folded into *A Decade of Delusions*, the new material takes us through the rest of the decade just ended. Some of Frank's chapter headings and subheadings will leave you little doubt about the direction and force of his opinions (in the interest of continuity, I'll omit the quotation marks): The Power of Popular Delusions. Only Fools Rush In. The Rogues Gallery. The Great Abdication of Fiduciary Responsibility. S&P 500 Earnings Dissected. Of Pawns, Guinea Pigs, and "Retail Investors." The Mathematics of Patience. The ARM-ed Robber. The Perfect Storm Redux. The Misalignment of Incentives and the Opaque World of High Finance. Back to the Age of Innocence? "This Time Is Different." If these excerpts suggest that Frank is fun to read—as well as stimulating—you understand my point.

But what I like most about Frank Martin's voluminous output is his penchant for quoting the words of others, always spot-on in relevance. Ben Graham and Warren Buffett? You'll meet them inside. Lord Keynes, Cervantes, Bertrand Russell? They're here, too. General Patton and Ted Williams? Sure. Bonhoeffer, Minsky, Leibniz? If you've not known them before (perhaps likely?), you'll meet them here and enjoy their timeliness in our world of today.

A Decade of Delusions is not only a wise book, it is a deep book—deep with sound philosophy—and a fairly long one (except when compared to my own recent tomes!). But all that heavy intellectual baggage—greatly simplified and made relevant to the average investor by Frank's deft touch—is easy reading. To lighten your journey, the book is interspersed with illustrations, cartoons (with biting satire), and charts of the ups and downs in the Standard & Poor's 500 index that show just where "the market" was as Frank was writing and as you are reading—clearly marked "You Are Here."

The Proof of the Pudding

As it is said, "The proof of the pudding is in the eating," and the investment returns earned by Martin Capital Management (MCM) for its clients over the years have been solid.

Especially during this past decade of delusions, MCM's performance record is impressive on balance. But its year-to-year variations have been wide—just what you would expect from a firm holding strong principles and convictions. Frank was among the few advisors who eschewed the euphoric buying frenzies that created recent equity Bubbles. His investors' allocation to equities was 30 percent or less in late 1999 and again in mid-2007. As a result of this flexibility—plus owning shares of corporations for their intrinsic value rather than, say, their price momentum—MCM earned its stripes. A timely and conservative posture offered excellent returns relative to the S&P 500 from 2000 to 2002, then lagged behind the powerful recovery of the index in the ensuing bull market of 2003 to 2007. But in 2008 and 2009, despite the sharp drop in the S&P 500, the MCM return was strongly positive.

There is a message here: Independent-minded money managers don't follow the crowd, aiming at high correlation with the stock market's shorter-term vagaries; they invest with the conviction and boldness required to take "the road less traveled by." Not only MCM but its clients must have the wisdom and the courage and (especially) the patience to focus on durable long-term values rather than fickle short-term stock prices.

No one can forecast with accuracy whether the MCM record will be similar, or better, or worse in the years ahead. But I am fully confident that—especially in the risk-infested world that we now inhabit— Frank Martin's investment principles are sensible principles (however implemented) for investors seeking to capture whatever long-term returns our financial markets are generous enough to provide for us, as well as to offer an anchor to windward against whatever short-term losses may be inflicted on us. I summarize these principles here:

- Performance goal: to maximize long-term portfolio returns, while strenuously avoiding the assumption of risks that might result in permanent loss.
- Investing in the basic asset classes: long-term, common-stock holdings; fixed-income securities; and cash equivalents, seeking the highest possible after-tax, risk-adjusted returns.
- Reasonable expectations: purchasing stocks as if buying into a private business.
- Minimizing risk and eschewing leverage.

- Minimizing conflicts of interest by having the firm's principals invest in substantially the same securities as the firm's clients.
- The firm's principals conducting themselves in their relationships with clients as if the roles could be reversed at any time, the ultimate ethical standard ("Do unto others . . .")—and striving for candor and forthrightness at all times.

So read *A Decade of Delusions* for wisdom, for insight, and for fun. I thoroughly enjoyed it, and I know you will, too.

JOHN C. BOGLE
Valley Forge, Pennsylvania
March 2011

Mr. Bogle, founder and longtime chief of The Vanguard Group, celebrates his sixtieth year in the investment profession on July 7, 2011.

Preface

S*peculative Contagion: An Antidote for Speculative Epidemics* was first published in 2006 and originated from my fascination with and skepticism about the widely embraced "Great Moderation," an economic era of predictable policies, low inflation, and tempered business cycles. The origins of the Great Moderation can be traced back to late 1987, when the economy barely flinched after the shock of the Dow Jones average's unprecedented and infamous 23 percent freefall on October 19. Quick intervention by Alan Greenspan, Federal Reserve chairman, who had been confirmed only two months before, likely stemmed the tide. But in doing so, he established an oft-repeated enabling precedent for what became known as the "Greenspan put," an implicit government guarantee against the consequences of financial and economic crises.

The original *Speculative Contagion*, its title a loud and clear warning bell, was published 18 years into the Great Moderation. Little did we know it was going to be a premonition of what two years later became known as the "Great Recession." During the prolonged spate of generally stable times, apprehensions about risk gradually faded as the economy— along with the market prices of popular asset classes of stocks, bonds, and real estate—continued to trend inexorably upward. The momentum of invincibility was so entrenched in the popular psyche that even the bursting of the "Great Bubble" in 2000–2002 did not restore an abiding respect for risk.

As *Speculative Contagion* was being published in 2006, it became evident that fallout from the Great Bubble's bursting was muted by monetary intervention and by a public all too willing to believe. The decline in stock prices did not rouse an aversion to risk but rather a cocksure belief that the economy and the capital markets were impervious to wealth-threatening, systemic calamities. The antidotes for speculative epidemics fell on deaf ears.

What was happening was fantasy. In 2002, leery of the near-term consequences of a possibly harsh but cathartic recession happening on his watch, the "second most powerful man in the world" once again took the path of least resistance. The Greenspan put was invoked. But it only bought some time—and ultimately at a huge social and economic cost.

The unintended side effect was a blitzkrieg of dubious, and sometimes extreme, financial innovations that became dangerously complex and interdependent. Investment banks, no longer structured as partnerships with open-ended personal liability, ratcheted up financial leverage until it spiraled out of control. This combination gave rise to a financial services sector whose high-octane incentives were so irresistible and so contagious that the epidemic could not be reversed except through self-destruction. The structured-finance products fabricated in this environment begot huge distortions in home prices and, to a lesser extent, those of marketable securities.

Flashing back to the latter half of the 1990s, market commentators more or less arbitrarily and, as it turned out, quite irresponsibly, asserted that a decline of 20 percent would constitute a bear market. This implied that investors and speculators alike need not anticipate anything worse. The approximate total market value of all domestic equity securities reached its apogee of $17 trillion, estimated from Wilshire 5000 data, in the spring of 2000. By the late fall of 2002, approximately $8 trillion of illusory, inflated value—roughly half of which can be attributed to the savaging of stocks making up the Nasdaq index—had disappeared into thin air as the Bubble burst. An antidote for a speculative epidemic? Not on your life. Retail investors' increasing home values soon compensated them for losses of the dot-com days. The financial wounds were salved, and the ever-more-dangerous disregard for risk morphed into a full-blown epidemic.

As a consequence, the bloodletting at the outset of the new millennium was only a prelude to the utter carnage between 2007 and 2009. The market value of U.S. stocks plummeted from $18 trillion to $7.9 trillion, but this time the disease migrated to other asset classes—and then to the economy at large. (Whether sustainable or not, another Fed-induced Bubble has spurred the market to regain 60 percent of the ground lost, and the aggregate value now stands, in November 2010, at $14 trillion.) According to Federal Reserve data, the market value of average Americans' most prized possession, their home, fell dramatically for the first time in modern history, from $22.7 trillion as of year-end 2006 to $17.1 trillion at the end of the second quarter 2010, a jaw-dropping 25 percent.

More worrisome, mortgages and home-equity loans actually increased marginally during the same time frame, from $9.9 trillion to $10.2 trillion. Even though the market value of U.S. stocks has at least partially recovered, the aggregate net worth of American households has sustained the most devastating body blow since the Great Depression. For that reason, the current economic contraction is unlike the typical "inventory" recession of the post-World War II era; in reality, what we are dealing with now is properly known as a "balance sheet" recession, which is significantly more problematic. As the three-year anniversary of the Great Recession approaches, it is becoming more and more apparent that when critical sectors of the economy are consumed with deleveraging their balance sheets, they are stubbornly unresponsive to government stimulus.

■ ■ ■

Speculative Contagion was a compilation of my published annual communiqués from 1998 to 2004. The concluding chapter, the 2004 annual report, left the reader in suspense, warning of an approaching tempest: A financial tropical depression had already formed and was gaining intensity. Two and a half years later, it raged into the worst financial and economic crisis since the 1930s. The prophetic section was titled "Marathon Endurance," the opening paragraph of which follows:

> The message throughout this report, summarized here, is that we are nearer the beginning than the end of the long secular transition from greed to fear, from exhilaratingly high prices to despairingly low ones, from irrational exuberance to level-headed rationality and perhaps (I say irrespective of how remote the possibility) from a financial economy to [a] real economy. Accordingly, we have, out of necessity, a heightened sense of vigilance, a pervasive but hopefully constructive skepticism.

Speculative Contagion was more than simply a chronicle of the first half of a decade of financial and economic reversals. Like the original work, *A Decade of Delusions* (the sequel) is anchored to mainstream historical data, events, and anecdotes that are analyzed and interpreted, real time, in terms of whether they confirm or impugn one of the observer's principal theses: that the foibles and follies of humanity are among our species' irrefutable constants. John Wiley & Sons' editors thought it a helpful study of how one might assemble from available evidence and data, and without benefit of hindsight, an accurate assessment that trouble is on the way. The devastating storm that uprooted our financial system and the economy during the last years of the decade had been visible on radar, but many chose to interpret the ominous blips as false echoes or simply ignore them altogether.

A Decade of Delusions aspires to capture a subtle shift in human behavior that may have undergirded what was outwardly manifested. Beneath what seemed like an increasingly reckless disregard for risk was *moral drift*, which may be remembered as the signature causative force of the "Lost Decade." Though I elaborate further on this important point in Chapter 7, allow me to say this much up front: The term *willful ignorance* is the desire for an action's intended result that is so all-consuming that one largely ignores the unintended effects. Of this transgression, many were conflicted but few convicted. Individuals and boards in positions of power and responsibility the past decade all too often sold their integrity down the river for financial gain.

■ ■ ■

This sequel builds upon the bulwark of the original. The 1998 through 2004 Martin Capital Management annual reports are largely intact. Most additions to the original text are bracketed; a modest number of changes to the original reports were added to improve clarity. In addition, substitutes were inserted without acknowledgment for duplicated pet words, phrases, or aphorisms; and the potentially annoying repetition of a number of key ideas or concepts (as might logically appear in seven discrete reports) was generally left unattended in order to maintain the flow of the text. Every effort was made to avoid omitting anything that might cast the narrative in a more favorable light than it deserves. Each annual report (organized in Chapters 1–7) told, in its own time and in its own way, how it felt to be pulled one way by the temptation to mindlessly join the crowd in its rush for paper gold and the other by the sometimes fragile convictions about what constitutes rational thought and behavior. *Speculative Contagion* concludes in Chapter 8 with insights gleaned from years on the front lines. More Darwinian than prophetic, they were presented as guideposts to help investors adapt to an ever-changing world, rather than predictions about just what those changes might be.

Chapters 9 through 11 draw from 180,000 of my words that were published during the second half of the decade in annual reports to clients, as well as in quarterly communiqués and other writings. I also use one of my FDR-esque "Fireside Chats" as the basis for the Epilogue. *A Decade of Delusions* thus embraces the entirety of 10 years of unrelenting speculative contagion. Chapter 9 includes the annual reports of Martin Capital Management from 2005 and 2006 when fundamental conditions deteriorated, even as housing and security prices continued their upward trend. The 2005 report is significant in its use of "The Perfect Storm" as a descriptive means of alerting clients to the dangers that likely lay ahead. It is a theme repeated and more closely analyzed in the 2006 annual report, culminating in Chapter 10, which is aptly titled "The Tipping Point." It might be said that in the 2007 quarterly communiqués and that year's annual report, the severe storm *watch* issued in preceding years was elevated to a severe storm *warning*. Here in the Midwest, residents of "tornado alley" are all too aware of the significant difference in these terms: A watch means conditions are right for the formation of damaging storms. A warning means the storm has been spotted and its arrival is imminent. Take cover.

Chapter 11 consists of annual reports from 2008 and 2009, which covered the early stages of a nation in the midst of a global financial maelstrom and ensuing meltdown. It was a time, hardly unexpected, of massive governmental intervention. However ill-conceived their actions, however ineffective their experimentations, however costly the ultimate consequences, government officials almost invariably feel compelled to intervene for political and social reasons. Centralization of control has enfeebled the once-free markets. According to the Business Cycle Dating Committee of the National Bureau of Economic Research (NBER), the Great Recession began in December 2007 and, apart from a possible easy-money-inflated bubble in risk assets, the economy remains unresponsive. As time passes, some will argue that if authorities had let the markets clear unimpeded, however terrifying in the short run, the consequences might have been a deeper but far shorter economic V. The point, however, is moot. To quote the chairman of the Federal Reserve Board, "There are no atheists in foxholes and no ideologues in financial crises." Was the massive Keynesian, monetary, and regulatory intervention part of the solution—or part of the problem? In short, were the financial crisis and the Great Recession the end? Or just the beginning?

For the record, on September 20, 2010, NBER determined that the recession ended in June 2009—after 18 months. It has been wrong before.

The Epilogue is intended to leave the reader with the notion that once the catharsis is complete, long-term investment will once again be recognized as the rational course. We won't know until long after the fact whether the speculative contagion has been purged. As baseball legend Yogi Berra once sagely observed, "It ain't over till it's over." Hard to argue with that logic. Consequently, the last word in this volume will undoubtedly disappoint those seeking a detailed and pinpoint forecast. Consistent with the rest of the work contained in *A Decade of Delusions*, the Epilogue represents the musings of an observer examining a single snapshot of the landscape in real time. The next frame in the larger motion picture has yet to be photographed and developed, and that is naturally cause for unease.

As an investment advisor prone to reflect on cause and effect, I came to work in the midst of the grand delusion every day of the past decade. I watched and wondered, sometimes nearly overcome with self-doubt, worrying that we as a firm were out of step with a new-era reality. At other times, I was modestly encouraged by some seemingly insignificant piece of evidence that gave us a sign, often little more than a fleeting assurance, that we had not lost our way, that our sense of historical proportion might eventually validate the vision we were pursuing for our clients and ourselves. It was a grueling experience.

It is hoped that the reader will discover a common thread woven throughout the book: Success is more likely to come to those who have some clue about the counterintuitive way that the thought processes and subsequent behaviors of crowds differ from individuals. There is a sound basis for the famous quote from the poet/dramatist Johann von Schiller, who once said, "Anyone taken as an individual is tolerably sensible and reasonable; as a member of a crowd he at once becomes a blockhead."

If one is to avoid the allure of the majority—or the mythical character "Mr. Market," as defined by Benjamin Graham in the pages that follow—one must have an understanding of the manic-depressive nature of this creature. One also should gain some awareness of an asymmetrical behavioral pattern common to the conduct of crowds as their collective state of mind tends to swing from extreme to extreme. I believe that there's a cyclicality to the world of finance that is more than mere coincidence and makes the study of history relevant. Books like *Extraordinary Popular Delusions and the Madness of Crowds* by Charles Mackay, LLD, put this propensity into a context that leaves the careful reader feeling that delusions are indeed endemic to the human condition.

Taken as a whole, *A Decade of Delusions* serves as my bully pulpit. I found it bordering on the unconscionable to live in close proximity to the latest incarnation of *Den of Thieves* (1992), James Stewart's chronicle of the Wall Street depredations of the 1980s, and not to speak out against the crimes and misdemeanors perpetrated by the "masters of the universe," aptly named by Tom Wolfe in *The Bonfire of the Vanities* (1987). Accordingly, throughout *A Decade of Delusions* the reader will encounter occasional tirades directed at the more flagrant violations of the standards of ethical conduct, rationalizing my outspokenness by turning to no less an authority than eighteenth-century Scottish economist and philosopher Adam Smith. The book that established economics as an autonomous subject and launched the economic doctrine of free enterprise, *An Inquiry into the Nature and Causes of the Wealth of Nations*

(1776), examined in detail the consequences of economic freedom, including the role of self-interest. As a moralist, Smith argued that the system of free enterprise was only as strong as the general ethical character of the society of which it was composed. Egregious ethical breakdowns, particularly the abuses of fiduciary trust and power at the highest ranks of corporate governance, frequently become the weak link in the economic chain. If the chain breaks, chaos is likely to reign. Dare I hold my tongue when the consequences of silence could be so dire?

Acknowledgments

Every tree that withstands tornado-force winds has unseen roots buried deeply in the soil. This book is the tree, but its roots nurture and strengthen it. Countless people are, collectively, the roots. Among those who bent their shoulder to the wheel to get *A Decade of Delusions* rolling, including those who critically read it: Keith Rockey and Bob Ellis; Adam Seessel, Zack Clark, and Jeff Robbins did blue-pencil editing; within my firm, analysts Aaron Kindig and Clint Leman, consummate, selfless team players, were invaluable in too many ways to enumerate, as was Gary Sieber, head of marketing, who, as a broadcast journalist, proved to be a man of letters as well. Kristen Myers-Smith, my assistant, ably played the role of juggler, keeping the pins aloft between and among all parties. Thanks to Lauren Silva, who, because of the high-tech digital world in which we live, provided impressive editing assistance without us ever having met face to face. Dan Shenk, proprietor of CopyProof, has left his indelible mark on every single page of the book: first by editing most of the missives when they were originally written, then proofing this manuscript with his characteristic attention to both detail and the big picture. And the good folks at Wiley demonstrated their professionalism at every turn as they took my sow's ear and turned it into a silk purse.

By chance in 1998 I happened across the work of cartoonist Bill Monroe. He was as pleased as I to have his artwork bring smiles to the faces of readers of a book that sought to treat the subject at hand as more than just the dismal science as it is often characterized. Still drawing at the age of 77, Bill would love to sell you fine art prints. See what he has to offer. His web site: www.monroeartist.com.

So that they aren't forgotten, the following acknowledgments appeared in *Speculative Contagion.*

Al Auxier, Warren Batts, Edward Chancellor, Marks Hinton, Janet Lowe, John Maginn, Merle Mullett, Rich Rockwood, and Shirley Terrass, all of whom provided advice, support, and encouragement along the journey. A special thank you goes to Dennis Rocheleau, Mike Stout, and Larry Crouse who reviewed the manuscript with the same critical eye as if it were their own. Aaron Kindig and Tom Dugan, outstanding junior analysts with our firm, accepted with enthusiasm the many assignments thrown at them and produced results commensurate with their outstanding effort. Kristen Smith, who stepped into the project midstream, did a remarkable job getting up to speed in a heartbeat while assisting with the editing and keeping me focused on the task at hand. Stephanie Malcom, the formatting pro, packaged the prose. Wordsmith Dan Shenk once again helped me look good.

I cannot even imagine what my journey thus far might have been had a few exemplary gentlemen not showered their remarkable favors on one so undeserving as the undersigned. Among them was my dear friend Ted Levitt (1925–2006), the economist and Harvard professor who coined the term "globalization," and Peter Bernstein (1919–2009), known by many as author of *Against the Gods: The Remarkable Story of Risk* and by me as a man whose words of encouragement (and once or twice of richly deserved reproach) will never be forgotten. Jack Bogle, the 82-year-old founder of the $1.4 trillion Vanguard Group, reigns supreme as "Mr. Integrity" in the financial services world. He is the living epitome of what is good in our industry and a fearless critic of what isn't. Few realize that Bogle made a choice in the 1970s between putting the customer first and a personal fortune that likely would have put him on the *Fortune* list. Instinctively, he took the high road. I highly recommend two of Bogle's increasingly relevant books: *Battle for the Soul of Capitalism* and *Enough.* Warren Buffett, 80, with whom I have had the least face-to-face acquaintance of the four (we communicate mainly by letter and e-mail), but whom I most emulate, has cast the longest shadow of anyone I've known in my professional development. Once I realized the extent and durability of Buffett's genius, as both investor and thinker, I studied him with such singular focus that some have called me a sycophant. In relation to the Oracle of Omaha, I could have been called worse! All four men share similar traits, including:

- Intellectual brilliance
- Irrepressible drive and focus (65 was less a speed limit than a speed bump that they hardly noticed)
- Exemplary honesty and integrity, as well as a lifelong passion for learning
- An amazing approachability and likability

They were or still are humble giants. I believe I inherited at least two traits from them: I didn't even feel it when I blew by 65, and if my appetite for food were the equal of that for learning, I'd be 400 pounds and counting. My debt to these masters of my universe knows no bounds.

I have also drawn much strength and wisdom from clients (*friends* is a more fitting descriptor) with whom our relationship in almost all cases has been constructively candid and mutually respectful. Many are older and far more experienced, and their sage advice has often been vitally important, particularly when one's convictions are tested to the core day in and day out. Regular encouragement from virtually every client has kept my spirits high and my desire to persevere undeterred. Those words are not platitudes. There are few men or women alive who reach their potential without the support of caring others.

In the 2001 annual report (Chapter 4), I addressed the matter of attribution as follows:

> Sources for factual matter include the *Wall Street Journal*, *Barron's*, *Fortune* magazine, *Forbes* magazine, various Internet sources, Bloomberg, and others, along with a number of books. Considering the limited audience for whom this report is intended, the abbreviated production window, and the fact that most readers already are familiar with my ideas and writings, my words and those of others are freely mixed, sometimes without formal acknowledgment, particularly in the latter sections of the report. It is not my wish to put forth as original the ideas or words of others. To the contrary, I wish to save them the embarrassment of being associated with me! If you find a really great

idea in these pages, and you're sure it could not have come from my semantically challenged synapses, give me a call, and I'll find the source and give credit where credit is due.

In reading *The Problem of Pain* by C. S. Lewis, I found he expressed the issue much more succinctly: "As this is not a work of erudition, I have taken [few] pains to trace ideas or quotations to their sources when they were not easily recoverable. Any theologian will see easily enough what, and how little, I have read." While I must read to compensate for my incapacity to think and reason (as Lewis did seemingly without effort), and *erudite* would not be the word to describe this far-from-scholarly exposition, I nonetheless have followed Lewis's lead and have not taken pains to trace all "ideas or quotations to their sources" (though permission has been received for the extensive references to copyrighted material from Ben Graham and Warren Buffett). As one observer suggested—with obvious reference to the quality of the effort (and therefore the need for *any* attribution, as well as the reason I sought solace from Lewis's book)—"Don't quit your day job!"

Enough

This book's purpose is not promotional. Rather it is personal. I hope that my experience—and account of events—can help future investors. I am a stickler for documenting in a profession where most people fear having their reputation indicted because of the paper trail. When I finally go to pasture and someone asks me what I did in my work life, I don't want to have to say, "Oh, I made a lot of money." How inconsequential, how pathetic. I've had the luxury of living through some of the most interesting economic times in modern history. And I've had the privilege of being able to record some of what I've observed. I would not be content keeping this exhilarating experience to myself.

As noted in the preceding paragraph, we are *not* soliciting new business through this book nor, accordingly, can we respond to inquiries from readers. Rather, the book is offered as a small contribution to the body of investment knowledge. We encourage readers to apply whatever insights they might glean to the management of their own investment assets or what they might look for in selecting a manager.

In Chapter 11 the reader will find a full account of the firm's investment performance history during the Lost Decade. Its purpose is to authenticate (or perhaps repudiate; be sure to read the fine print!) what might otherwise be perceived as just so many words. Pontifications from pundits are too often taken at face value. Although I'm not sure on which side of the line that separates crudeness from healthy skepticism readers might perceive me to be, it is my nature to discount whatever is said today unless corroborating (or, more often, contradicting) evidence from earlier pronouncements can be found and verified.

A Decade of Delusions, an indelible, and sometimes self-indicting, paper trail, reveals my foibles and fortes—and the investment record that exposes both. Warts and all, it is hoped that the contrast will be refreshing.

Finally, the opportunities for reflection and contemplation abound for a professional investor for whom success is not measured in dollar terms. It would have been a great loss if I had sped through the preceding decade in the pell-mell pursuit of the almighty buck and missed a lifetime of lessons that were there for the taking. Such ineffably sublime gifts are given to those whose senses remain attuned to the juxtaposition of the daily stream of anecdotal tidbits, like so many falling leaves, and the perpetually repetitious nature of the willful human mind. On an even more personal note, in the reckless rush for riches that characterized the Lost Decade, all too many were so consumed by the "more is better" mind-set that they seldom paused long enough to ask: "How much is enough?" I hearken to the thoughtful words of Kahlil Gibran in *The Prophet*: "And what is fear of need but need itself? Is not dread of thirst when your well is full, the thirst that is unquenchable?"

While I confess to being a contrarian, I will never submit to charges of pessimism. The great deleveraging likely ahead will be burdensome, to be sure, but it may yet have a positive outcome: helping Americans rediscover what it means to have—as Jack Bogle stated simply—"enough."

FRANK K. MARTIN
November 2010

A Decade
of Delusions

Chapter 1

Lead Us Not into Temptation*

S&P 500 (SP50)
— Price

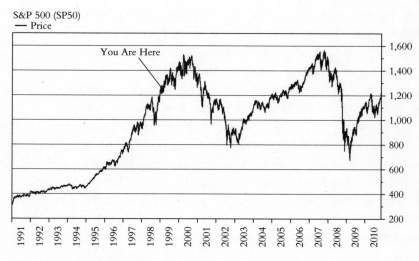

SOURCE: © FactSet Research Systems.

---

*This material is adapted from the 1998 annual report of Martin Capital Management.

Throughout the book, you will see charts that include an arrow indicating "You Are Here." Like the ubiquitous directory map on a shopping mall kiosk, these charts are intended to orient the reader to what was known and what was yet to unfold as I took pen in hand to communicate with clients of Martin Capital Management. Since many chapters are constructed of excerpts from annual reports, the time period being reviewed is the preceding year. In some sections, the focus may be on a particular quarter or may involve a review of events over a long period of history. The first "You Are Here" map shown here, for example, tracks the market's steep ascent as I wrote the first document—the 1998 annual report for Martin Capital Management. The journey through subsequent years takes on the appearance of a rugged and dangerous trek through the Himalayas, but at that moment it looked as if the only direction for the market to go was up, up, up. How could we have known what lay ahead?

For the mathematically inclined, a point of clarification is required. Under most circumstances, we would use logarithmic scales for the vertical (price) y-axis. Logarithmic scales represent an equal amount of percentage change. Arithmetic scales represent an equal amount of numerical change. However, for the time period in question, most of the charts throughout the book reflect stock prices that typically range from flattish to downtrending, often accompanied by atypical volatility. The S&P 500 charts at the beginning of each chapter are a case in point. The arithmetic scales give a more accurate portrayal of the volatility in an environment that lacks no clear trend.

The first eight chapters of *A Decade of Delusions* are taken virtually verbatim from the book *Speculative Contagion* (2006), which, in turn, was based on Martin Capital Management annual reports, 1998–2004. Most of the bracketed material in the first eight chapters was added by the author for *Speculative Contagion* and in a few cases for *A Decade of Delusions*. Brackets are also occasionally used in quoted material for the sake of clarity.

May Reason Prevail

In June 1998 Warren Buffett, in a public-television interview with *Money Line*'s Adam Smith, was asked, "Why do smart people do dumb things?" Buffett opined that greed, fear, envy, and mindless imitation of others are among the factors that mitigate the transfer of the mind's horsepower to the wheels that propel us along the road toward business and invest- ment success. Rather than superior intelligence, Buffett confided, it is the capacity for unconditionally *rational* thought—followed by proportional action—that separates the winners from the also-rans. These qualities have distanced him and Charlie Munger from the pack by such a margin that the multitude is no longer even a speck on the horizon.

While reading for the first time the recently reprinted first edition (1934) of *Security Analysis*, authored by Buffett's mentor, Benjamin Graham, to which much-deserved attention is directed in this report, a similar thread was strikingly evident throughout the 700-page master- piece. Written in the darkest depths of the Depression by a man who personally was not spared its devastation, the volume reveals Graham's genius for almost inhuman objectivity and rationality in the face of a financial and economic storm that wreaked such havoc and mental anguish on a whole generation of investors that most had no stomach for stocks throughout the rest of their lives.

To the extent that the writer is able to view the investment land- scape from a similar frame of reference, this report in its entirety will ideally reflect the ascendancy of reason over emotion and fact over folly.

A Reader's Guide

This year's account is organized by topic, prioritized from most impor- tant to least important based on the presumed breadth of their appeal. Beyond the discussion of issues of immediate relevance, a lengthy essay [beginning a four-year diatribe against willful, and ultimately shame- ful, disregard for the necessity of an honest system of "weights and measures"] in accounting for corporate results follows—the value of which transcends the moment. A magnifying glass is used to exam- ine the relaxation of standards in corporate financial management and reporting that came about when executives put pragmatics before principle in their run for the roses in the earnings-per-share-growth- at-any-cost derby. Readers of corporate annual reports know that this is a time to resurrect the Latin expression *caveat emptor*. [In this chapter, the section "It's a Numbers Game" exposes the progressively widen- ing gap in GAAP (generally accepted accounting principles). By con- trast Chapter 7 wraps up with "Fully Deluded Earnings," the S&P's

initial attempt to put the creative accounting genie back into the bottle. Three accounting sections in other annual reports were omitted to avoid beating a dead horse.]

The Year 1998 in Review

The past year brought to the fore an interesting and challenging—but not unprecedented—dichotomy. The most widely referenced equity-market benchmark, the Standard & Poor's 500 stock index, heavily weighted for the big and the beautiful, rose by 26.7 percent in 1998, achieving in the process a record-setting fourth year in a row of gains in excess of 20 percent. The Nasdaq index, dominated by large-capitalization technology companies, including several that have prominent places in the S&P index, put on an even more impressive show, rising 39.6 percent. Nasdaq volume, we parenthetically note with undisguised amazement (since we are aware that the companies of which it consists are among the least proven), regularly dwarfs that of the New York Stock Exchange (NYSE). During that same interval, the Russell 2000, composed primarily of so-called small-cap stocks, told an entirely different story, actually falling by 3.4 percent for the 12 months.

Surprisingly, despite the handsome showing of most of the major indexes, the majority of stocks suffered a losing year in 1998. Backsliders outpaced winners both on the Big Board and, more dramatically, on Nasdaq, where the 1,690 stocks that registered higher prices for 1998 were handily outnumbered by the 3,351 that fell. The two-tier market that emerged in the spring of 1998 is reminiscent of 1972. We took the "road less traveled."[1]

While the prices of the most favored companies rose farther and farther above what we believe to be their intrinsic worth, several fine businesses (but market wallflowers) presented us with attractive purchase opportunities during the late-summer rout. And while the S&P 500 and the Dow Jones industrial average backtracked by nearly 20 percent from July through August, the three that we purchased in larger quantities

---

[1][2006, *Speculative Contagion*] Just as the "Nifty Fifty" skyrocketed to eventual oblivion beginning in 1972, so did technology and Internet stocks in late 1999 and the spring of 2000. The mundane "Main Street" companies fared far better in both episodes.

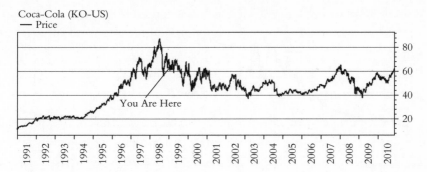

Figure 1.1 Coca-Cola Stock Price History
SOURCE: © FactSet Research Systems.

traded at their lows for prices that were, on average, approximately one-third of their 52-week highs. More importantly, these growing companies were purchased at an average price-earnings ratio of below 10 times trailing earnings. They have since rallied sharply but still trade well below their earlier highs. If we are confident that we (a) understand a business that historically earns high returns on shareholders' capital, (b) feel that its business model is stable enough for us to estimate its intrinsic worth, and (c) conclude that management is both competent and shareholder-oriented, falling prices play to the strength of our business analysis. In each case, our average cost is well below what we think the businesses are worth. If business conditions remain reasonably positive, five-year expected returns for the three companies could average better than 20 percent, compounded annually. Since the mailing list for this report extends beyond our clients, we are not mentioning the companies by name.

We admit to having an abiding interest in the great consumer-products franchises like Coca-Cola and Gillette (stock price performance shown in Figures 1.1 and 1.2), and we would purchase them and others of their ilk if, based on conservative terminal-price assumptions, five-year expected returns approach 15 percent. Based on our work, at current prices, they are likely to earn little more than the yields available on U.S. Treasury securities for the foreseeable future. That's not enough to get us off the dime.[2]

---

[2][2006, *Speculative Contagion*] We often talk about patience, but Coca-Cola and Gillette have tested our limits. After peaking around $90 per share in mid-1998,

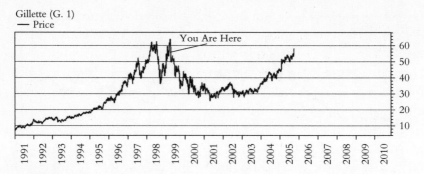

Figure 1.2   Gillette Stock Price History
SOURCE: © FactSet Research Systems.

Patience and Persistence

Short-term market-price volatility is relatively high for mid- and smaller-sized companies found on the road less traveled. While the market prices of the companies we own eclipsed by some margin the performance of the popular averages (and most equity mutual funds) in 1996 and 1997, this past year was a different story. We don't want to appear indifferent to these shorter-term outcomes, be they positive or negative, but our focus remains on the ultimate rationality of markets over time. Today's investor pays a heavy premium for popular big-cap companies. We expect the earnings of the companies we own to grow at a rate no less than the earnings of the S&P 500 index, and yet we acquired them for one-third of the index's price-earnings ratio. To paraphrase Benjamin Graham, in the short run, it's popularity and outward appeal that help a girl win a fellow's attention, but in the long run, it's good cooking that helps her keep it.

We would be less than candid if we didn't admit to coveting the returns that the S&P 500 and Nasdaq 100 have earned during the past

---

Coke began a long stair-stepped descent, hitting $37 in the spring of 2003 and recently traded for $42. In similar fashion, Gillette peaked at $63 at the same time that Coke was reaching for the stars. It hit a low of $27 in the spring of 2001. For whatever strategic reasons, Gillette agreed to surrender its independence (for an 18 percent premium to the prevailing market price) to Procter & Gamble and is currently selling at $55, pending consummation of the merger.

several years. We regret not being able to find ways to fully and prudently share in the explosion of financial wealth that has been created out of thin air. Furthermore, it's a near certainty that if present trends continue, we will lag even farther behind. The high-stakes game of musical chairs that Wall Street has been playing is neither one we understand nor one in which we have any demonstrated competence. In the final analysis, our respect for history's lessons (see "The Dean of Wall Street Revisited" later in this chapter) and our pledge to think and act rationally leave us no choice but to stay our carefully plotted wealth-preservation course.

We have an aversion to investment operations that may lead to permanent loss of capital. In our judgment, permanent loss can result from (a) investment in securities of issuers in which high confidence of their ability to survive particularly adverse economic circumstances is not warranted by the facts and/or (b) an investor becoming so despondent because of the decline in the market value of his or her portfolio that in a moment of all-consuming fear he or she forces the conversion of a paper (and perhaps temporary) loss into a permanent one. We go to great lengths to minimize the likelihood of the first eventuality, a course of action for us that is essentially devoid of emotional forces. The second is more problematic. There is little basis for us to determine in advance how an individual might respond under conditions of such high stress. It has been 25 years since tolerance for wealth-threatening market-price declines was tested in the crucible of high emotion, and there is little precedent, therefore, from which to make such judgments about what form that response might take today should the market fall long and hard. At considerable cost in temporary (if not permanent) loss of opportunity, we have managed portfolios to avoid subjecting our clients to that test.

As we wait (im)patiently for some semblance of order to be restored in equity valuations, the vast majority of the assets over which we have control are invested in the safest-harbor securities available. The money we manage, both yours and ours, that isn't committed to equities is squirreled away in the highest-grade fixed-income securities, including Aaa-rated pre-refunded or escrowed-to-maturity tax-exempt municipal bonds and U.S. Treasury bills and notes. To compromise on credit quality at this juncture in our economic history would be the equivalent of a boat's captain feigning preoccupation with safety as he snugs the vessel alongside the pier. Only he knows that below the waterline the hull is riddled with leaks, and the junk (pun intended) will stay afloat only so long as the bilge pumps keep working. Higher portfolio returns, if they are to be achieved, will be the result of rising interest rates or expanded investment opportunities in equity securities, not compromising on credit quality in fixed-income securities.

Market interest rates fell during 1998. Because we have elected not to expose our clients to the market-price volatility inherent in long-duration bonds (made even longer by lower coupons) as I did in the early 1980s, falling interest rates are anathema to longer-term investors such as ourselves. While short-duration bond prices rise moderately, coupon interest is reinvested at lower rates. The "realized compounded yield," a bond-management term, suffers accordingly. Conveniently, the consumer price index is concurrently wallowing in low single digits, making the yields from fixed-income securities somewhat more palatable. Unfortunately, the bulk of the income and realized gains earned on the wealth we manage is not consumed but reinvested instead. We openly acknowledge the formidable task that lies ahead: We must cope intelligently, on the one hand, with a global deflation that has driven bond-market yields to the lowest levels in a number of years and, on the other, with a virulent price inflation that is sweeping through the U.S. equity markets like a raging inferno. Necessity (with due apologies to Aesop or a lesser-known Latin source) is not the mother of a sound portfolio policy; purchasing quality assets at or below what they are worth is. We can't change the game, but we can determine if and when to play. In all decisions, we pledge to conduct ourselves in a businesslike manner—to be, above all, rational and circumspect. As noted earlier, we will do our best to avoid being held hostage by greed, fear, or the mindless imitation of others.

Analysts, as if there's any doubt, are not always right—even when the logic of our reasoning is theoretically sound. As we ply our trade, modern communications technologies have given us fingertip access to vast amounts of economic, business, and financial information at a somewhat reasonable price. Most of it is reliable. Deliberate falsification, while often sensational, is relatively uncommon. A far more important source for errors is in making judgments about an always

uncertain future. Lacking anything more tangible, we feel compelled to
proceed on the basis that the past is at least a rough guide to what
tomorrow has in store. At times it isn't. Another handicap is the sometimes irrational behavior of market participants, seemingly playing in
concert under the direction of a slightly mad imaginary maestro. We
must rely on this market to ultimately vindicate our judgments. All too
often it is painfully slow in adjusting to our way of thinking! As readers are acutely aware, our contention that there is little or no margin
of safety in the current prices of many common stocks is of little relevance in a market where the players are rhapsodizing to an improvised
tune, the tempo of which is wildly upbeat. Patience and persistence,
we frequently remind ourselves, are virtues, even if they don't feel particularly noble at the time they are called into play. We know all too
well why the head of the tortoise is held low until the hare is in sight.

The Fixed-Income Alternative

Forecasting interest rates is surely the most difficult and error-prone
assignment that a manager who relies on fixed-income securities to
function as portfolio workhorses must accept. Let's begin by examining the bond-yield forecast implicit in the yield curve. The bond
market is huge, global, active, and therefore relatively efficient; it represents a good summary of what institutional fixed-income investors
around the world think about U.S. interest rates. When we observe
that the yield curve is relatively flat, as it is today, in nontechnical
terms we mean that market yields for securities due in 30 years are
not much higher than those due in just one year. For example, the
spread between the 30-year and the one-year yields was 0.58 percent
at year-end. Why, you might wonder, would investors lend money
for 30 years for essentially the same annual amount of interest they
can earn by lending it for one year? The only reasonable conclusion
is that they must think that interest rates will fall and that their total
return over time will be higher if they "lock in" the yields available
on longer-term instruments. If they felt otherwise, surely they ands
other investors of similar persuasion would sell longer-term bonds (at
the margin, causing their prices to fall and their yields to advance)
and purchase short-term bills or notes (resulting in their prices rising

and their yields falling), producing an upward-sloping yield curve that tends to be more understandable.[3]

We don't take exception with the yield curve's forecast. It is reflective of the popular deflationary scenario. However, there are two compelling reasons why we haven't ventured into long-dated bonds. First is the unanimity of bullishness that the yield curve implies. Implicit in bond prices (again assuming the market is quite efficient) is the expectation that prevailing inflation and economic winds will continue to be favorable to bond investors. Little provision is made in today's bond prices for the possibility of reflation, or that the euro will eventually displace the dollar as the world's reserve currency,[4] or any other plausible scenario that might result in rising bond yields.

Second is the matter of duration. *Duration* is a technical bond-management term that quantifies the market-price sensitivity of a fixed-income security to changes in market yields. It makes intuitive sense that the greater the number of years until a bond matures, the more volatile are price changes in response to a given change in market yields. What is less widely understood is that duration is also a function of the size of the bond-interest coupon. The smaller the coupon, holding all other factors constant, the greater the volatility. The roller-coaster amplitude of price fluctuations of zero-coupon bonds, therefore, makes

---

[3][2006, *Speculative Contagion*] Five years later, the forecast implicit in the yield curve proved resoundingly correct. In June 2003 the 30-year Treasury bond yielded 4.17 percent and the five-year, 2.02 percent, while the Fed funds rate was 1 percent. As of June 30, 2005, short-term rates had rebounded from their lows, and the yield curve was nearly as flat as it was in 1998. Currently the 30-year Treasury bond yields 4.30 percent and the 5-year, 3.83 percent, while the Fed funds rate is 3.50 percent. Only time will tell if the bond market has adequately discounted future levels of inflation. [2010 update: Deflation has been a concern for some time now. The 30-year bond yield is 3.65 percent; the 5-year, 1.40 percent; and the Fed funds target rate is 0–0.25 percent.]

[4][2006, *Speculative Contagion*] After its debut on December 31, 1998, at $1.17 per euro, the euro exchange rate sank as low as $.82 in late 2000 and now has recovered and strengthened to $1.20 as of June 30, 2005. The dollar is also weak relative to the yen. The U.S. dollar still reigns supreme as the world's reserve currency, but complacency could eventually topple the mighty buck. [2010 update: At this writing the exchange rate is $1.30. More important, the trade-weighted and the U.S. dollar indexes are still relatively near their lows.]

them the most volatile of all types of fixed-income securities. Since the only cash payment made occurs when the bond is redeemed at par at maturity, duration and the number of years to maturity are one and the same. When I purchased long-term zero-coupon bonds in the early 1980s at market yields in excess of 13 percent, I welcomed the prospect of outsized volatility because I felt it would eventually work in my favor. Conversely, committing capital to 30-year 5.17 percent Treasury bonds today at par borders on speculation, unless it's the investor's intent to hold the security to maturity. If market yields were to increase by 200 points (two percentage points), the bond price would fall nearly 25 percent, in all likelihood foreclosing on the possibility of selling the bond in order to reinvest the proceeds more opportunistically in, say, common stocks.[5]

Finally, a word about bond quality is warranted. As you may not be aware, the yield differential between high- and low-quality bonds widened dramatically during the year when global economic concerns elbowed their way into the headlines. Russia, in particular, shocked selected domestic money-center banks and hedge funds when it effectively defaulted on its sovereign debt. Our stance regarding bond quality remains unchanged. Unless we can find opportunities in investment-grade bonds that compare favorably with those from investment in well-capitalized and reasonably priced common stocks, we will not compromise on credit quality. We feel confident that the creditworthiness of our clients' bond portfolios exceeds that of those managed by any of our regional competitors—by a wide margin.

Sometimes much can be learned by simply stepping back from the hectic pace of business life and asking the question, "Does all of this make sense?" This report, prepared late each year, affords the writer that opportunity. We make every effort to examine all asset classes through the aforementioned paradigm. The combination of OPEC and rising

---

[5][2006, *Speculative Contagion*] While such a bet looked risky in light of historical yields (we have warned against rearview-mirror investing, in which we ourselves have been known to indulge), as noted in a footnote above, the shape of the yield curve indicated lower rates ahead. Committing assets to longer-duration bonds of the highest quality would have resulted in performance that handily beat the S&P 500 since then. Chapter 8 discusses the biases that infect all investors to one degree or another.

inflation sent crude oil prices from as low as $5 in late 1973 to almost $40 in 1980. As the U.S. economy moved from double-digit to low, single-digit inflation during the recession in the early 1980s, the price of a barrel of crude oil fell from its $40 peak to a recent low of around $10. Conversely, the price one must pay to purchase a dollar's worth of bond interest has risen just as sharply as oil prices have fallen. Bond yields, which exceeded 14 percent when oil was peaking, have since declined dramatically to 5 percent. (Bond prices move in the opposite direction of bond yields.) Those who believe that the longest peacetime economic expansion will eventually overheat should be as interested in investments that might benefit from rising oil prices as they are wary of long-term bonds with fixed coupons.[6] To be sure, the highest-quality fixed-income securities, with short durations, will likely remain as portfolio stalwarts so long as they meet our present and well-defined need for preservation of principal. When opportunities for growth in principal appear, without concurrently endangering its safety, the role of fixed-income securities will be greatly diminished. Who knows what will appear in their place?

The Dean of Wall Street Revisited

The reign of Antoninus is marked by the rare advantage of furnishing very few materials for history, which is indeed little more than the register of the crimes, follies, and misfortunes of mankind.

The Decline and Fall of the Roman Empire
(1776) by Edward Gibbon (1737–1794)

---

[6][2006, *Speculative Contagion*] In June 2005 the price of crude oil hit $55.58 per barrel, a handsome advance from the $10 at which it traded when the above comments were made. To be sure, capitalizing on the sixfold increase in the price of crude oil is much harder than participating in a rising stock market. It's difficult to share proportionally in the rising price of crude oil, except in the futures market, and using indirect methods can be problematic since the correlation between the price of crude oil and the stocks of major oil exploration and production companies can be surprisingly tenuous. [2010 update: Oil reached $145 per barrel in mid-2008, then fell to below $40 in early 2009 during the low point to date in the global recession. It now trades in the mid-$80s.]

Gibbon offers a curious reference in the opening quotation regarding the unremarkable reign of Roman Emperor Antoninus (Marcus Aurelius), who ruled in the middle of the second century A.D. It is noteworthy that the events that account for the decline and eventual fall of the Roman Empire, not an insignificant development in the course of world history, was, as noted by Gibbon, "little more than the register of the crimes, follies, and misfortunes of mankind." As you may recall, the book *Extraordinary Popular Delusions and the Madness of Crowds* was of similar persuasion, insofar as the subordination of the rule of law and the follies of man (i.e., often originating from periodic episodes when common sense is almost laughably deficient). With the insights gleaned from the 1934 edition of *Security Analysis* by Benjamin Graham and David Dodd, we should be able to gain a clearer appreciation for the origins of the *follies* of the late 1920s that led to the *unfortunate unintended consequences* (often presented as unexpected or unprovoked tragedy) in the 1930s. Our interest is, however, more than academic. To the extent that follies are as cyclical as human gullibility—in contrast to science, where knowledge is cumulative and where real progress is possible—perhaps we can put history's lessons to practical use to avoid some of the more costly logical consequences that ignorance of the past periodically teaches.

By way of introduction, Benjamin Graham died in 1976 at the age of 82; it wasn't until 1996 that his memoirs, written in his later years, were published. Graham had a prodigious intellect, graduating from Columbia University in two and a half years and having the distinction of being invited to teach in three departments (Literature, Philosophy, and Mathematics) at Columbia. Instead, Wall Street beckoned in 1915. During the 14 years leading up to 1929, young Graham tasted much success, first as an employee and then as a junior partner at a brokerage firm—and finally as head of his own business.

At the quarter-century mark of 1925, the great bull market was under way, and Graham, then 31, developed what he later described as a "bad case of hubris." During an early-1929 conversation with business associate Bernard Baruch (about whom he disparagingly observed, "He had the vanity that attenuates the greatness of some men"), both agreed that the market had advanced to "inordinate heights, that the speculators had gone crazy, that respected investment bankers were indulging in inexcusable high jinks, and that the whole thing would have to end up one day in a major crash." Several years later he lamented, "What seems really strange now is that I could make a prediction of that kind in all seriousness, yet not have the sense to realize the dangers to which I continued to subject the Account's capital" (Benjamin Graham, *Benjamin Graham: The Memoirs of the Dean of Wall Street*, edited by Seymour Chapman [New York: McGraw-Hill, 1996], 259). In mid-1929, the equity in the "Account" was a proud $2,500,000; by the end of 1932, it had shrunk to a mere $375,000. The dismay and apprehension Graham experienced during those three long years he summarized by saying:

> The chief burden on my mind was not so much the actual shrinkage of my fortune as the lengthy attrition, the repeated disappointments after the tide had seemed to turn, the ultimate uncertainty about whether the Depression and the losses would ever come to an end. . . . Add to this the realization that I was responsible for the fortunes of many relatives and friends, that they were as apprehensive and distraught as I myself, and one may understand better the feeling of defeat and near-despair that almost overmastered me towards the end. (Ibid., 259)

What has deeply impressed me about the 1934 edition of *Security Analysis*, which Graham set to work on in 1932 (with publication in May 1934), was his uncanny ability to put mind over matter. He intellectually detached himself from the travails that were wracking his portfolio, his confidence, and his sense of stewardship. While there are a number of hints in the book that tie the author's travails to the text, they are most subtle.

The Rise and Fall of Security Analysis

In the introduction to the scope and limitations of security analysis, Graham described the preceding three decades as a period during which its prestige experienced both a "brilliant rise and an ignominious fall":

> But the "new era" commencing in 1927 involved at bottom the abandonment of the analytical approach; and while emphasis was still seemingly placed on facts and figures, these were manipulated by a sort of pseudo-analysis to support the delusions of the period. The market collapse in October 1929 was no surprise to such analysts as had kept their heads, but the extent of the business collapse which later developed, with its

devastating effects on established earning power, again threw their calculations out of gear. Hence the ultimate result was that serious analysis suffered a double discrediting: the first—prior to the crash—due to the persistence of imaginary values, and the second—after the crash—due to the disappearance of real values. (Benjamin Graham and David T. Dodd, *Security Analysis* [New York and London: Whittlesey House, McGraw-Hill, 1934], 3)

Even an analyst as well-grounded as Graham failed to account for the severe economic contraction that followed the crash. Its causes have been speculated about ever since. Today, concerns about the "reverse wealth effect," thought to be a force that exacerbated the Depression, are clearly on the minds of Alan Greenspan and other policymakers.

The New-Era Hypothesis

During the post-World War I period, and particularly during the latter stage of the bull market culminating in 1929, the public adopted a completely different paradigm toward the investment merits of common stocks. According to Graham, the new-era theory or principle may be reduced to one sentence: *"The value of a common stock depends entirely upon what it will earn in the future"* [emphasis added].

From this dictum, Graham drew the following corollaries:

1. That the dividend rate should have slight bearing upon the value.
2. That since no relationship apparently existed between assets and earning power, the asset value was entirely devoid of importance.
3. That past earnings were significant only to the extent that they indicated what changes in the earnings were likely to take place in the future.

This complete revolution in the philosophy of common-stock investment took place virtually without realization by the stock-buying public and with only the most superficial recognition by financial observers (ibid., 306–307).

Fast-forward 70 years, and a student of history might logically conclude that the investment landscape is eerily similar to that which Graham described in the late 1920s. The current dividend yield on the S&P 500, at 1.34 percent, is one-third the yield on U.S. Treasury bonds and is at its lowest ebb in modern history. When capital gains are plentiful, who cares about dividends? After all, if the surveys are correct and the average mutual-fund investor really believes that stocks will provide total returns exceeding 20 percent annually for the next 10 years, today's minuscule dividends pale in comparison to what the investor must expect from capital appreciation. To be sure, the dividend yield would be higher, although not materially so, were the cash used to fund stock-repurchase programs paid out in dividends instead. In plain English, dividend yields are low because stock prices are high (and bond yields are slightly below their long-term average). The explanation is to be found in the denominator, not the numerator.

Likewise, the price-to-book-value ratio of 6.53 is off the charts. As with dividends, there are plausible explanations. Companies like Microsoft and Dell, S&P 500 heavyweights, are short on physical assets and long on intellectual property. In addition, as discussed elsewhere in the report, corporations have taken massive restructuring charges against shareholders' equity in recent years. The growth in book value has, accordingly, not kept pace with the growth in earnings per share. With regard to earnings, Wall Street has never been more dependent on forward thinking than it is today. And that's in spite of the long-evity of the current expansion that has set peacetime records, plus the reality that Japan and various Asian and Latin American economies are groaning and creaking like the timbers of a wooden ship in stormy seas. Given the uncertainties that abound, we wonder whether Graham would characterize the heavy reliance today on future prospects as spec-ulation and not investment.

While the exponential ascension in stock prices during the late 1920s was in large measure a self-fulfilling prophecy, it was not without scholarly explanation, however tenuous. *Common Stocks as Long Term Investments* by Edgar Lawrence Smith, published in 1924, was often cited as justification for the ownership of common stocks. Unfortunately, the sound premise was rendered unsound by dint of prices escalating to speculative levels in the late 1920s. In practical terms, Smith's supposi-tion was as sensible at 10 times earnings as it was ill-advised at 30 times. Coincidentally, Professor Jeremy Siegel's book, carrying nearly an iden-tical title, *Stocks for the Long Term*, is the contemporary version of the same phenomenon.

Graham asked the rhetorical question, "Why did the *investing* public turn its attention from dividends, from asset values, and from earnings, to transfer it almost exclusively to the earnings *trend*, i.e., to the changes in earnings expected in the future?" He observed that the tempo of economic change made obsolete old standards. At one time, stability was thought to be a function of a business being long-established. Instead, corporations that had been profitable for a decade lost their edge. In their place, other enterprises "which had been small or unsuccessful or of doubtful repute, have just as quickly acquired size, impressive earnings, and the highest rating." The parallels with today are unmistakable. Think of IBM, AT&T, General Motors, Eastman Kodak, and Kellogg (to name a few)[7] and the restructuring charges that have revealed cracks in their heretofore impenetrable armor. On the other hand, we all have witnessed the spectacular ascent of technology stocks that has sent the Nasdaq price-earnings ratio soaring to over 100, as well as the flight of Internet stocks that have modest though rapidly growing sales and often no earnings (ibid., 307–308).

Forgetting to Read Menus from Right to Left

As for the analysis of individual businesses, Graham attached great importance to the purchase price, the only variable over which an investor has control (if he has the discipline to patiently wait, and sometimes forgo purchase altogether, so as to pay no more than a price that affords a satisfactory margin of safety). Graham distinguished between financial reasoning and business reasoning as they relate to purchase price:

> We have here the point that brings home more strikingly perhaps than any other the widened rift between financial thought and ordinary business thought. It is an almost unbelievable fact that Wall Street never asks, "How much is the business selling for?" Yet this should be the first question in considering a stock purchase. If a business man were offered a 5 percent interest in some concern for $10,000, his first mental process would be to multiply the asked price by 20 and thus establish a proposed value of $200,000 for the entire undertaking. The rest of his calculation would turn on the question whether the business was a "good buy" at $200,000. (Ibid., 492)

---

[7][2010] All but IBM are selling at lower prices 12 years later.

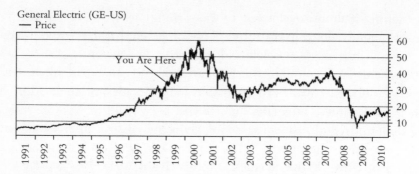

Figure 1.3   General Electric Stock Price History
SOURCE: © FactSet Research Systems.

This elementary and indispensable approach has been practically abandoned by those who purchase stocks. Of the thousands who "invested" in General Electric in 1929–1930 probably only an infinitesimal number had any idea that they were paying on the basis of two and three-quarter billions of dollars for the company, of which over two billions represented a premium above the money actually invested in the business (ibid., 493).

The market value of GE (stock price performance shown in Figure 1.3) has grown to $334.9 billion since then, compounding over the years at an average annual rate of 7.5 percent, plus dividends. The premium above the $37 billion actually invested in the business that an investor pays today is a tidy $298 billion.[8]

Long before modern portfolio theory (MPT) and its mathematical models took root in academia, Graham argued that it was unsound to think that the investment character of an issue was a constant:

> The price is frequently an essential element (of any investment operation), and so that a stock may have investment merit at one price level but not at another. The notion that the desirability

---

[8][2006, *Speculative Contagion*] At the time of this comment, General Electric was selling in the range of $30 (adjusted for a 3:1 stock split in May 2000). It subsequently rose to $60, revealing, as so often happens, investors' misguided affection with the currency equivalent of exchanging two nickels for a dime. Having backtracked to a low of $21 in early 2003, it has subsequently rallied back to a price of $34. Earnings per share were $.95 for 1998 and $1.61 in 2004.

of a common stock was entirely independent of its price seems incredibly absurd. Yet the new-era theory led directly to this thesis. If a . . . stock was selling at 35 times its maximum recorded earnings, instead of 10 times its average earnings, which was the preboom standard, the conclusion to be drawn was not that the stock was now too high but merely that the standard of value had been raised. Instead of judging the market price by established standards of value, the new era based its standards of value upon the market price. Hence all upper limits disappear, not only upon the price at which a stock could sell, but even upon the price at which it would deserve to sell. An alluring corollary of this principle was that making money in the stock market was now the easiest thing in the world. It was only necessary to buy "good" stocks, regardless of price, and then to let nature take her upward course. The results of such a doctrine could not fail to be tragic. Countless people asked themselves, "Why work for a living when a fortune can be made in Wall Street without working?" The ensuing migration from business into the financial district resembled the famous gold rush to the Klondike, with the not unimportant difference that there really was gold in the Klondike. (Ibid., 310)

The Investor's Dilemma

In reflecting on the seven years preceding the publication of *Security Analysis*, Graham pointed out the investor's dilemma brought about by the boom-and-bust market cycles that were emblematic of the most turbulent financial and economic era in the twentieth century.

> The wider the fluctuations of the market, and the longer they persist in one direction, the more difficult it is to preserve the investment viewpoint in dealing with common stocks. The attention is bound to be diverted from the investment question, which is whether the price is attractive or unattractive in relation to value, to the speculative question whether the market is near its low or its high point.
>
> This difficulty was so overshadowing in the years between 1927 and 1933 that common stock investment virtually ceased

to have any sound practical significance during that period. If an investor had sold out his common-stocks early in 1927, because prices had outstripped values, he was almost certain to regret his actions during the ensuing two years of further spectacular advances. Similarly those who hailed the crash of 1929 as opportunity to buy common stocks at reasonable prices were to be confronted by appalling market losses as a result of the subsequent protracted decline. (Ibid., 321–322)

Despite obvious similarities to today, it is virtually impossible to forecast the likelihood that knowledge of history will be of relevance now. Furthermore, in attempting to determine the cause-and-effect correlation between two events, the association can be imaginary. Behavioral scientists call it "illusory correlation." Each reader will have his or her own opinion as to what extent the inferences above are imagined. Nonetheless, wealth management requires that we sacrifice opportunity when its downside, however remote, may be permanent loss of capital (defined in the section titled "The Year 1998 in Review"). The aforementioned conversation Graham had with Baruch, followed later by his words of contrition, are still ringing in our ears.

It's a Numbers Game

In examining the confluence of forces that culminated in the Crash of 1929, Benjamin Graham compared the late stages of the phenomenon with the Alaskan Gold Rush. The blurring of distinctions between Wall Street and Main Street that occurred in the last chimerical years of the 1920s became the fetid bog of exaggerated expectations in which an addictive Gold Rush mentality fermented. The cause-and-effect logic that had throughout history linked effort with reward was thought to be temporarily, if not permanently, suspended. Common-stock paper wealth, gold's modern-day gilt-edged substitute (and lots of it) was to be had by those who simply knew how and where to go to unlock its treasures. Visions of untold riches—made even more seductive because the payoff was far out of proportion to the labor expended to acquire it—transformed plodding and deliberate merchants and manufacturers into wild-eyed prospectors. In their frantic search for the theretofore elusive dream, they gladly swapped their dark suits and conservative ways for a pick and shovel. They abandoned many of the rules of thought and conduct—including reason and common sense—that had governed their lives in what at the time must have seemed like a dull and uninspiring past.

Perhaps Graham's analogy may be applicable 65 years later? What we appear to be witnessing today is a near-universal rush for the gold that common stocks symbolize. A sense of urgency tied to the obsessive belief that the bounty is finite and that a drop-dead point looms out there somewhere has sustained the charge at a fanatical pace. Nowhere in this agitated plot is there a speaking part for the rational man—except as a quiet and skeptical spectator.[9]

The following section examines the lengths to which some corporate executives have gone to massage their corporation's finances and their own compensation programs to seize what they believe to be their share, if not more, of the spoils. All the schemes, however far they stretch credulity, seem to excite little resistance if they are packaged under the pretense of "enhancing shareholder value." The deportment of those who exhibit some or all of the symptoms of Gold Rush fever, when viewed through that fascinating and age-old prism, is made much

---

[9][2006, *Speculative Contagion*] As yet another example of the repetitive nature of history, the eternal gullibility of the "madding (and sometimes mad) crowd," and the parasites who prey on its denizens (see elucidating insights from novelist Ayn Rand in Chapter 7), let's step back in time to the California Gold Rush, which preceded by about 50 years the longer-lived Klondike Gold Rush. It was on John Sutter's expansive property that James Marshall, Sutter's sawmill contractor, discovered gold nuggets in the American River in 1849. Sutter and Marshall suppressed the gold news so as not to cause interruptions with their real estate development. Not surprisingly, it was a San Francisco merchant and master of hype, Sam Brannan, who got wind of the seemingly well-kept secret and subsequently became the richest person in California—but Brannan never mined for gold. When he started racing through the streets yelling, "Gold, gold in the American River," he wasn't planning to dig for it. He was planning to sell shovels. And the first person who sold shovels got a lot more gold than the person who had to dig for it. The laws of supply and demand were not unfamiliar to Brannan. His wild run through San Francisco came just after he had purchased every pickax, pan, and shovel in the region. A metal pan that sold for 20 cents a few days earlier was now available from Brannan for 15 *dollars*. In just nine weeks, he made $36,000. *While there are many stellar exceptions, the sooner one learns that much of Wall Street is actually in the "picks and shovels" business, the better.*

more understandable. Observed under any other construct, such people must appear capricious.

Some years ago, I asked the CFO of a public company what he thought earnings would be for the year. His only somewhat facetious reply: "What would you like them to be?" I wouldn't ask that question today because I'm afraid of what the answer might be.

The Supremacy of Earnings

Somewhere along the road to riches the corporate balance sheet was discarded as having little nutritional value, like yesterday's half-eaten McDonald's hamburger and fries. In its place has arisen "earnings power" (more often than not with substantial justification) as the primary determinant of the intrinsic value of a business. Before we lay to rest this barbaric corporate relic—the balance sheet and in particular the shareholders' equity account—let's say a few kind words in its memory. Shareholders' equity (book value when expressed in per-share terms) represents the shareholders' investment in the business, carried on the corporate books at depreciated cost, after all liabilities have been satisfied. While book value represents a reasonable starting point if liquidation of assets is in prospect, it is otherwise a relatively poor measure of the value of a business. For example, the tangible assets of Coca-Cola and Gillette pale in comparison to the value of their brands. The earnings of both companies are derived more from the market dominance and power of their intangible property than from the physical and financial assets that appear on the balance sheet. Nonetheless, when purchasing a business at a premium price relative to its book value— invariably the case today and frequently with good cause—some awareness of the size of the gap is warranted.

The full measure of the premium is better appreciated when expressed in aggregate terms. Returning to our earlier examples, the market value of Coca-Cola is $171 billion and represents a premium of $164 billion over the $7 billion in net tangible assets. Unconsolidated bottlers are carried at cost on Coke's balance sheet. If the market value of the bottlers is used, the $7 billion would increase to something like $15 billion. The equivalent numbers for Gillette are $52.5 billion in market value of the shareholders' equity and $2.5 billion in net tangible assets. (Excluded is the valuable goodwill associated with the purchase of Duracell.) These financial statistics give credence to the earlier observation that most of the market value of these two businesses is derived from corporate assets that are nowhere to be found on the balance sheet. The not-insignificant premiums that the shares of these companies command in the marketplace are more understandable than many less-established companies in vogue today. There is a possibility, however slim (given the lightning pace of change and the general instability in the Internet world), that Amazon.com and Yahoo! (Figures 1.4 and 1.5) will

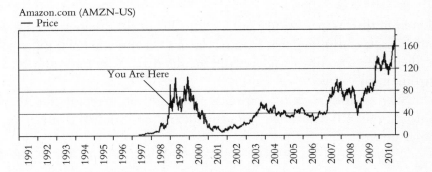

Figure 1.4   Amazon.com Stock Price History
SOURCE: © FactSet Research Systems.

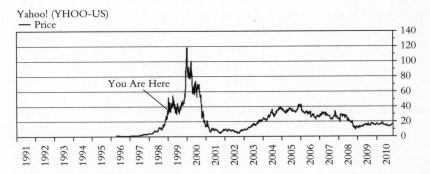

Figure 1.5   Yahoo! Stock Price History
SOURCE: © FactSet Research Systems.

Google (CI A) (GOOG-US)
— Price

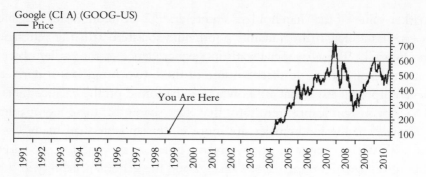

Figure 1.6 Google Stock Price History
SOURCE: © FactSet Research Systems.

dominate their respective markets 10 years hence. But there is relatively little doubt, conversely, that Coca-Cola and Gillette will reign supreme in theirs. He who doesn't understand the difference may ultimately be a victim, not a victor.[10]

Now we turn back to "earnings power." Even here a perfunctory note of caution is justified. Graham offers these thought-provoking observations:

---

[10][2006, *Speculative Contagion*] (Note: All of the following stock prices have been adjusted for splits.) Amazon.com peaked at $110 in late 1999 and cratered at $5 in the fall of 2001, when the market capitalization was approximately $2 billion, which was down from the high of $38 billion. The stock has subsequently rallied back to $33 (a market capitalization of $14 billion) as of June 2005. Sales have grown to $6.9 billion in 2004, from just $600 million in 1998. In 2004 the company earned net income of $589 million. Likewise, Yahoo! skyrocketed to the same lofty price of $110 in early 2000, only to collapse to $4 by the fall of 2001. As of June 2005 it sold for $35. Revenues for 2004 were $3.5 billion, and profits $840 million, or $0.58 a share. The market capitalization as of June 30, 2005, was approximately $48 billion, down from approximately $117 billion at the peak, but still mind-boggling compared with current earnings. Forever chasing the latest great idea, speculators are now ogling Google (Figure 1.6). Amazon was the creation of a young fellow with an audacious idea, whereas Google is the brainchild of two bright young guys with an algorithm. We are addicted to Google as consumers of information, but not to the stock. As of June 30, 2005, its market capitalization was approximately $82 billion, with earnings for the last 12 months of about $1 billion. Seven years later, my skepticism remains unabated. Remember Darwin . . .

In recent years increasing importance has been laid upon the trend of earnings. Needless to say, a record of increasing profits is a favorable sign. Financial theory has gone further, however, and has sought to estimate future earnings by projecting the past trend into the future and then used this projection as the basis for valuing the business. Because figures are used in this process, people mistakenly believe that it is "mathematically sound." But while a trend shown in the past is a fact, a "future trend" is only an assumption. The factors that we mentioned previously as militating against the maintenance of abnormal prosperity or depression are equally opposed to the indefinite continuance of an upward or downward trend. By the time the trend has become clearly noticeable, conditions may well be ripe for a change. (Graham, *Security Analysis*, 36)

The Accountants Are Not to Blame

Accounting is under indictment, in all likelihood unfairly.[11] The task of reducing endless variations of actual business activities to standardized financial reports and protocol is at best not without significant real-life problems. No doubt part of the reason is that accounting is, as it always is destined to be, a step behind an ever-changing business world, the current expression of which is increasingly driven by technology and deal-making. In reality, the Securities & Exchange Commission (SEC) and public accountants are chasing a forever-moving target. It is out of practical necessity that the generally accepted accounting principles (GAAP) allows companies' chief financial officers and their bosses plenty of flexibility or, in Washington jargon, "wiggle room." The rules rely on honesty and integrity—behaviors that are ostensibly encouraged by the presence and watchful eyes of "independent" auditors—to ensure that financial presentations are both "transparent" and "reliable." Lawrence Revsine, a prominent accounting professor at Northwestern's Kellogg Graduate School of Management, sums up the current state of

---

[11][2006, *Speculative Contagion*] Sadly, some accountants and accounting firms succumbed to the temptations of the times. Independence became compromised when shekels trumped scruples. "He who writes my checks calls the tune I sing" is an old adage for an ageless reason.

"TO MAKE A LONG STORY SHORT, THE GENERALLY ACCEPTED ACCOUNTING PRACTICES WEREN'T AS GENERALLY ACCEPTED AS I THOUGHT."

SOURCE: Copyright © 1999 Bill Monroe.

affairs succinctly: "Accounting stinks." It always will, but through no fault of its own.

Let's face it: GAAP will never be a good match for those who are intent on finding a way around the sometimes flimsy roadblocks against misrepresentations and other abuses that the Financial Accounting Standards Board (FASB) erects. Besides, the seemingly ever-evolving boom in financial assets that dates all the way back to 1982 has put a premium on deception because, to put it bluntly, it pays so well. Which brings to mind the pungent pronouncement attributed to Mark Twain (loosely paraphrased) that there are liars, there are abominable liars, and then there are statisticians. The head of auditing at KPMG Peat Marwick, the fourth-largest accounting firm, observes: "There's probably more pressure to achieve results than at any time that I've seen." Earnings growth drives executive bonuses as well as stock options (which of late account for more than 50 percent of executive compensation), and the ability to make accretive acquisitions, raise money, or even survive as an independent entity. Robert Olstein, a fund manager and former coauthor of the respected newsletter *Quality of Earnings Report*, lays part of the blame at the doorstep of security analysts. "Accounting tricks are always going on," he says. "What's changed is that companies are getting away with more now because analysts aren't paying any attention." We agree. Unfortunately, as is human nature, the longer the dry spell, the more likely it is that people will stop carrying umbrellas.

The investor's watchdog, the SEC, has begun to rattle its sabers. This past fall, SEC Chairman Arthur Levitt began a rare series of meetings with top corporate CEOs, accounting analysts from investment houses, the FASB, and the Big Five accounting firms, among others. Not only did the midyear stock market retreat prod normally unflappable Federal Reserve Board Chairman Alan Greenspan into action (reaction?), but the SEC's Levitt openly worried that if accounting problems continue, even more damage could be done to investor confidence. It is probably reasonable, although impolitic, to ask: "If the chairmen of both the SEC and the Federal Reserve take their cues from the stock market, why, pray tell, should the captains of industry do otherwise?" Reasoning further, it appears that people in high places sense that the speculative Bubble is inflated to near the bursting point, and no one wants to be remembered by history as the one holding the hatpin.

What's a Company to Do?

If companies aspire to take full advantage of the fruits that this grand and expansive bull run offers, they must demonstrate earnings momentum. Some, whose businesses are simply not up to the test, have relied instead on extraordinary measures, in desperation turning to "cookin' the books" (in most instances on low heat) in order to remain a player.

Earnings management is the unspoken buzzword among corporate managers as they seek to pull out all stops in responding to the Wall Street edict. For many senior officers of publicly traded companies, the fixation on reporting a steady upward progression in earnings per share is more than academic. The potential for millions of dollars of stock-option profits often hangs in the balance. It is paramount, therefore, that managers win and hold the favor of Wall Street analysts, whose thumbs-down reactions (if managers disappoint by missing their "guided" estimate for quarterly earnings per share by a cent or two) can trigger a flood of sell orders.

The "Big Bath" Restructuring Charge

Corporate America has finally discovered what the 42nd president, Bill Clinton, has long known. If you put the right spin on (corporate) sin, what was once unspeakable among estimable gentlemen seated in dark leather chairs around a heavy mahogany table is now an acceptable, if not actually fashionable, topic for conversation. Forgiveness for these sins of malinvestment comes freely from an ever-more-blasé investing public whose memories are short and who call for neither confession nor contrition. This state of unquestioned forbearance has not gone unnoticed in the corporate boardroom.

The naked truth is that restructuring charges (often announced in oxymoronic terms as "nonrecurring" charges) are management's public admission that earnings in past years were overstated. They are a confirmation that corporate resources had been committed to an investment or investments that ultimately failed to measure up to minimal expectations—and the time has come to stop the hemorrhaging. A charge or debit is made to shareholders' equity, and a liability reserve of equal size is established. Liquidation of unproductive assets and personnel severance costs are among those future expenses for which reserves are instituted. As costs are incurred in untangling yesterday's bright idea, the liability reserve is reduced accordingly. It is noteworthy that those costs do not appear as a line item on the income statement but rather are shuttled directly to the liability side of the balance sheet.

To be sure, humans, even CEOs, make mistakes. After all, investments are made in the present, but returns are subject to the vicissitudes of the future. A lot can happen between now and then. For example, how a customer, or a competitor, might respond to a new product is often little more than conjecture until the jury of the marketplace hands down its verdict. Good managers can reduce investment risk, but they can't eliminate it.

Strangely, it's apparent that investors rarely look back as stock prices often rise when restructuring charges are announced. The rationale? First, the operating-earnings drag of the miscue will cease, and thus future reported earnings, *ceteris paribus*, will increase by the amount of the expenses thereby avoided. Additionally, there is a more subtle gain to be had. As sometimes happens, managers will overestimate the costs to be incurred in the effort to right yesterday's wrong. In fact, since Wall Street is ostensibly impervious to the size of the charge (within reason, of course) and, as noted previously, exacts no immediate market-price penalty, is it not better to be safe than sorry? That's how the so-called "big bath" charge came into being. Here's the benefit: After the damage has been repaired, still undepleted reserves can be used to offset future costs without having those costs leak onto the income statement. In Burger King terms, we think of the twin benefits as a "double whopper" for future earnings. No wonder Wall Street cheers! And it all began with the amputation of a leg or an arm from the body of shareholders' equity. I suppose if anyone ever looked at the restructuring charge for what it is from an accounting point of view— a reduction in assets for which shareholders lay claim—the drum roll announcing the event would be muffled. Main Street investors understand the absurdity of what Wall Street investors apparently thrive on. Think of it as emasculation of the corporate balance sheet; assets only count in liquidation, and who's worried about that?

It gets more troublesome. As hinted above, big charges can become addictive. And don't for a minute think that such chicanery is the exclusive plaything of corporate lowlifes. Such behavior can be found in the best of families. AT&T (Figure 1.7), the company whose sadistic, omnipresent telemarketers invade my home (seemingly once a week and, like clockwork, always at dinnertime), took multiple write-offs totaling $14.2 billion during the decade ending 1994. All the while, its earnings miraculously grew by 10 percent a year, from $1.21 to $3.13. Even magician David Copperfield would find that feat amazing. It was, after all, a financial elephant the size of the Empire State Building that

Figure 1.7 AT&T Stock Price History
Source: © FactSet Research Systems.

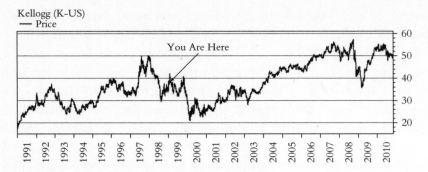

Figure 1.8   Kellogg Stock Price History
SOURCE: © FactSet Research Systems.

AT&T made to disappear in a cloud of accounting mumbo jumbo. The write-offs exceeded by almost $4 billion the $10.3 billion in earnings that the company actually reported. Sometimes it's helpful to compare the growth of a company's earnings over a period of time with the growth in shareholders' equity, before dividends are paid. Don't allow your children to do AT&T calculations unsupervised. We last wrote about AT&T's foibles in the 1995 annual report, and the beat goes on.[12]

Speaking of children, would they clamor for Frosted Flakes if they knew that Battle Creek-based Kellogg Company (Figure 1.8) has taken charges to "streamline operations" in nine of the last 11 quarters through year-end 1997? Real operating earnings for 1997 were more like $1.29 (down 24 percent from the year earlier), compared with

---

[12][2006, *Speculative Contagion*] AT&T continues to be a "poster company" in the numbers game. Following earlier spin-offs of Lucent and NCR, it spun off AT&T Wireless (which was later bought by Cingular in 2004) and Liberty Media in 2001. It discarded AT&T Broadband in a transaction with Comcast in 2002 and announced in mid-2004 that it will be shifting focus from residential services to business services. After reaching $94 in early 1999, the stock fell to a low of $14 in late 2004. Because of the number of spin-offs, the decline in the stock price of AT&T overstates the loss in value for shareholders. In the latest chapter, in early 2005 SBC (one of the "baby Bells" born from the government breakup of AT&T) announced plans to acquire its former parent for $18 per share. But wait, there's more . . . While AT&T no longer exists as a stand-alone operating company, the bloodied but nonetheless venerable AT&T name is likely to survive. In a salute to the power of branding, SBC is considering renaming itself . . . AT&T!

the $1.70 reported. And the company still commands a price-earnings multiple of 31. At what point, it seems reasonable to ask, should such costs be recognized as recurring and thereafter appear as operating expenses in the income statement?[13]

A popular catchall technique, staying with descriptors familiar to children, is the "cookie jar reserve." Companies use unrealistic assumptions to estimate liabilities for such items as sales returns, loan losses, or warranty costs. In effect, they stash accruals in cookie jars during the good times and reach into them when needed in bad times. This practice helps to smooth earnings rather than actually enhance them, as other schemes are able to do.

Some restructuring charges, we hasten to add, actually lead to increased earnings power, thereby enhancing the intrinsic value of the business by pruning dead branches. Our attention here is to the abuses.

Acquisition Reserves

While different in origin, reserves established as a result of acquisitions can serve much the same purpose. SEC Chairman Levitt calls the practice "merger magic." The number of acquisitions taking place each year has skyrocketed, making the issue increasingly relevant. In-process research-and-development write-offs, unknown a decade ago, have soared since IBM (Figure 1.9) used the technique to write off $1.8 billion of the cost of its 1995 acquisition of the spreadsheet creator, Lotus Development. The capitalized expenditure, in-process R&D, is obviously of indeterminate value to the acquirer. It is frequently written off after the acquisition as a "one-time" charge so as to reduce future earnings drag (which, under certain circumstances, we ignore).[14]

---

[13][2006, *Speculative Contagion*] The year 2002 was the first in the last five that Kellogg did not take a line-item restructuring charge. The stock peaked at $50 in early 1998, later falling to $20 in the winter of 2000. It currently sells for around $42, about 20 times earnings, and appears to have cleaned up its act.

[14][2006, *Speculative Contagion*] IBM traded at about $90 when the above comments were made and traded for $75 as of June 2005. It peaked at $135 in 1999 and sank as low as $54 in 2003. In 2002 the company recorded an after-tax charge of $1.8 billion for "extraordinary" items.

International Business Machines (IBM-US)
— Price

Figure 1.9   International Business Machines Stock Price History
SOURCE: © FactSet Research Systems.

WorldCom (WCOM)
— Price

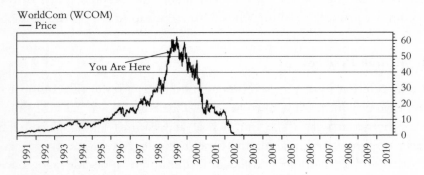

Figure 1.10   WorldCom Stock Price History
SOURCE: © FactSet Research Systems.

WorldCom's $37 billion purchase of MCI Communications is another case in point. WorldCom estimated that at the time of the acquisition MCI had $6 billion to $7 billion in R&D under way but not ready for commercial application, making it the largest in-process R&D charge so far. Since it is possible that WorldCom (Figure 1.10) may never see any benefits from the MCI expenditures, accounting rules allow WorldCom to write them all off at once. Apart from the accounting practice, the Main Street business owner might well wonder why WorldCom paid so much for MCI if there is even a remote possibility that almost $7 billion of acquired assets are worthless. In reality, there is little doubt that WorldCom ascribes great value to MCI's R&D efforts. As WorldCom turns MCI's R&D efforts into salable products, the profits produced will be juicier without the drag

Figure 1.11   Walt Disney Stock Price History
SOURCE: © FactSet Research Systems.

of the amortization of capitalized R&D expenditures. In this instance, expenses and revenues are clearly not properly matched. With regard to the balance sheet, the charges effectively understate the amount of capital invested in the business.[15]

Equally troubling, according to the SEC's Levitt, is the creation of large liabilities for future operating expenses to hype future earnings—all under the guise of an acquisition. Walt Disney (Figure 1.11), in its 1995 purchase of Capital Cities/ABC, wrote off certain of ABC's programming costs at the time of the acquisition, thereby relieving its income statements of three or four years' worth of additional expenses. From this point forward, the company will have to show legitimate earnings growth, not the kind that comes from accounting machinations—unless it can engineer still more deals, as many banks have done.

Pooling versus Purchase Acquisition Accounting

Now we're getting a bit technical. At the risk of missing a subtlety or two, I'll attempt to keep the discussion at the lay level. In the case of an acquisition accounted for as a pooling of interests, the acquired company is absorbed into the parent company. The historical financial statements of the parent are recast so as to portray prior years as if the two had been

---

[15][2006, *Speculative Contagion*] WorldCom filed for bankruptcy in July 2002. It was charged with overstating earnings by more than $11 billion in the largest accounting fraud scandal ever.

a family for a long time. Stringent tests must be passed for pooling to be used. On the other hand, purchase accounting, as the name implies, means that the revenues, expenses, and profits of the acquiree are aggregated with the parent company's income statements from the time of acquisition. If, as is almost always the case, the acquirer pays more than the market value of the net assets of the acquired company, the premium, an asset called "purchased goodwill," must be amortized against earnings for up to 40 years.

The advantage of pooling is that whatever purchase-price premium might have been paid, it is nowhere labeled as such and therefore is not subject to amortization. By way of an analogy, think of pooling as it might apply to a marriage between NBA clotheshorse Dennis Rodman and actress/model Carmen Electra that, hypothetically of course, lasted several years before irreconcilable differences (he never put the cover back on the lipstick) brought an end to the otherwise blissful union. On the date of consummation, Dennis—speaking exclusively in financial terms—may have paid a hefty premium for the 50 percent of his (and soon-to-be-their) marital estate that he effectively surrendered to the comely lass of *Baywatch* fame, if not fortune. (Assuming Nevada's laws on marriage dissolution are typical, Carmen's equity in the marital estate could approximate a shocking 50 percent on that sad day, presuming that the brief time between "Let's get married" and "I do" left no time for a prenuptial.) It is doubtful that their balance sheets or income statements were comparable at the time of the merger of unequals. Poor(er) Dennis surely suffered instantaneous dilution unless he was hedging against a possible seasonless NBA. Because he pooled, rather than purchased, the "goodwill" arising from his impulsiveness need not be officially amortized even though, in reality, a prudent man would do so. Bankers, Dennis should know, are sometimes prudent.

Unless accounting measures can be employed to reduce or eliminate the purchase price paid above the market value of net assets in a purchase transaction (as addressed elsewhere), the premium must be amortized against future earnings. The advantage of purchase accounting is that, depending on how the transaction is financed, a steady stream of acquisitions may result in earnings growth well above that which is organic. Cendant, one of the more celebrated failures of 1998, stumbled badly in executing its strategy of growth by acquisition. For the curious, it's a cautionary tale of a company that camouflaged slow internal growth with a flurry of acquisitions, the last of which turned a formerly *as-cendant* trajectory into an almost fatally *des-cendant* one.[16]

At MCM, we don't quibble with purchased goodwill if it's readily apparent that the premium paid is equal to or less than the value received. As far as we're concerned, companies that go to great lengths to avoid amortization charges are squandering time and money. As a matter of practice, we add back amortization charges to earnings in our valuation work if the usefulness of the goodwill acquired is unlikely to decline over time. In this supercharged acquisition environment, however, we suspect that many acquisitors with voracious appetites have grossly overpaid. Paradoxically, one aftermath of the current binge must inevitably be another wave of aforementioned restructurings, including goodwill write-downs, as a result of overpriced mergers.[17]

With regard to the matter of acquisition accounting, in our financial modeling, we attempt to ferret out economic earnings. Accordingly, we make whatever adjustments we feel are justified—regardless of which method is used to account for an acquisition—to reveal economic

---

[16][2006, *Speculative Contagion*] Within a six-month period during 1998, Cendant stock plunged from $42 to about $7. In the five years since, earnings have been irregular, as the company disgorged itself of hastily conceived acquisitions and reorganized as a global provider of complementary consumer and business services. The stock traded around $22 at the end of June 2005.

[17][2006, *Speculative Contagion*] Until 2002 FASB (Rule 142) mandated amortizing goodwill generally over a 40-year life. In 2002 FASB flip-flopped and relieved companies of the obligation to systematically amortize goodwill. Instead, it now requires that goodwill be reviewed annually for possible impairment in value. If impairment has occurred, the company takes an immediate charge. For the six years prior to the accounting change in 2002, cumulative goodwill amortized for the S&P 500 totaled $3.91 per share. From 2002 to 2004, goodwill-impairment charges totaled $10.36 per share, with $6.91 charged in 2002 alone. The vast majority of these write-offs were related to acquisitions that failed to live up to merger-frenzy expectations, and their carrying value had to be slashed in a more rational environment. To be sure, the old method of amortizing the carrying value of assets that often appreciated in value—and then charging that expense against earnings—made no economic sense. Under the new rule life is different, but not necessarily better. Large one-time impairment charges permit a company to sweep under the carpet prior dissipations of shareholder capital without typically evoking much of a response from Wall Street. Why? Because of the accounting treatment, the action has a salutary effect on earnings, return on equity, etc. . . .

realities. If the analyst community would do likewise, there would be far less use of smoke and mirrors in the practice of financial reporting.

Revenue Recognition

Although we don't encounter this misdemeanor often, in part because of the practical difficulties in identifying it, the SEC has served notice to companies that try to boost earnings by accelerating the recognition of revenue. Think about a bottle of fine wine. It isn't appropriate to pull the cork until the contents are properly aged. But some companies are removing the cork early, recognizing revenues before a sale is truly complete; before the product is delivered to the customer; or when the customer still has options to terminate, void, or delay the sale.

"Stealth Compensation"

The use of stock options as a key component of executive compensation has mushroomed. According to Richard Walker, named SEC director of enforcement last April, stock options outstanding have nearly doubled since 1989, accounting for 13.2 percent of shares outstanding. The *Wall Street Journal* calls them "the steroids that bulk up executive pay . . . the currency of an optimistic and opulent age." From 1992 to 1997, the value of option grants to CEOs and other executives of about 2,000 companies surveyed by Sanford C. Bernstein & Company quintupled to $45.6 billion from $8.9 billion. Also, according to the *Journal*, options-driven CEO compensation has climbed to 200 times the level of the average worker—a fivefold increase from the 1970s. That striking if not unsettling divergence draws little artillery fire during good times, yet the capitalist ideology itself could become the prime target if the cataclysm of serious recession sets in.

With more and more of an executive's pay linked to the upward movement of a company's stock price—in which historically he or she had little cause for direct interest—it's no longer uncommon to see a modern executive preoccupied with financially managing the business for the chief purpose of maximizing the stock price. Such practices may or may not be consistent with the goal of increasing intrinsic value. During a recent analyst conference on another hot topic, fair-value accounting, several participants expressed concern about any changes

Figure 1.12 Microsoft Stock Price History
SOURCE: © FactSet Research Systems.

that would increase earnings volatility. One analyst summed up the
sad state of affairs when he said, "Any [managers] not concerned with
smoothing earnings [are] not doing their job. You need to manage Wall
Street—without being deceptive—while hiding information that could
be used . . . by competitors."

For financial-reporting purposes, option grants are free money,
because in their accounting treatment they are doubly blessed: Options
granted do not appear as an expense on corporate income statements,
yet they are deductible when exercised as a cost for the purpose of tax
reporting.

Microsoft (Figure 1.12) has issued options equal to almost 45 percent of its shares outstanding. Shareholders, including Bill Gates, who
before dilution owns approximately 20 percent of the company, will
suffer massive dilution unless the stock falls to a fraction of its current
price. If the company were to consider repurchasing the shares necessary to fund its options program, they would cost $49 billion at today's
market price. Microsoft has $14 billion in cash. Cash flow for 1998 is
estimated to be $9 billion. Under that hypothetical scenario, the total
of outstanding shares would remain unchanged, but cash on hand and
future cash flow would be depleted for years to come. Regardless of its
name, options are synonymous with dilution.

In 1993, when FASB attempted to rule that the burgeoning use
(and concealed cost) of options should be divulged on corporate income
statements, the agency ran headlong into the lobbying steamroller driven
by the Big Six auditing firms and much of corporate America. Dennis

Beresford, now a professor at the University of Georgia, served as chairman of FASB when the endeavor was flattened. "The argument was: Reduced earnings would translate to reduced stock prices," recalls the then-embattled professor. "People said to me, 'If we have to record a reduction in income by 40 percent, our stock will go down by 40 percent, our options would be worthless, we won't be able to keep employees. It would destroy all American business and Western civilization.'" *Forbes* magazine cynically concluded: "The bull market is more important than accurate financial reporting." Nobody, as noted previously, wants to be caught holding a hatpin should the bubble burst.

Beyond the absurdity of allowing options compensation to escape being treated like any other corporate expense and the possible backlash from eventual exposure of "stealth compensation" (that skews overall compensation in favor of the executive suite at the expense of the factory floor), we have other misgivings about the use of options. A widely cited argument for their use is that they cause managers to think like owners. As owners of the publicly traded shares of businesses, we find it difficult to understand exactly what it is that option holders have in common with us. When we make an investment, our first act is to write a large check. If the stock price subsequently falls—for any of a host of reasons—and we fess up to our mistake and sell, our loss is painfully tangible, and it represents far more than just the loss of an opportunity that the option holder endures. Ever-resourceful "optioneers" have found a remedy for the one downside of options—the opportunity that's lost when the share price heads south. It's increasingly fashionable to restrike options at lower prices should the stock go begging. Who said there wasn't opportunity in adversity?!

As for granting options to the rank and file, sometimes for the purpose of blunting internal criticism of megagrants on Executive Row, the practice is as widespread as it is unproductive in achieving its desired goals. According to a proxy-statement analysis by William M. Mercer, Inc., 35 percent of the 350 major companies tracked by the firm have stock-options programs for all or a majority of their workers. Another source advises that 50 percent of mid-level professionals at major companies receive options. Far from promoting an owner's frame of mind or even inspiring loyalty to the company, the vast majority of recipients treat this form of corporate beneficence as nothing more than a windfall. The Lotto mentality moves up and down the corporate ladder with

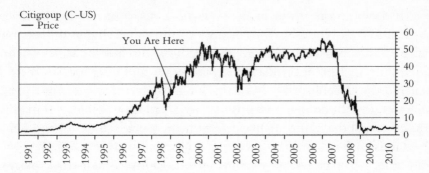

Figure 1.13 Citigroup Stock Price History
SOURCE: © FactSet Research Systems.

surprising ease. When Citicorp (Figure 1.13) Chairman John Reed was asked how he reacted when Traveler's Chairman Sanford Weill first proposed the colossal merger of their huge financial-services firms, he replied: "My instinct was to say, 'Why not?'" In the wake of the surprise announcement, both companies' stock prices surged, as in lockstep did stock-option paper profits for both Reed and Weill, whose one-day windfall was a cool $67 million and $248 million, respectively. Based on what has transpired subsequently, and presuming that Reed was not distracted by visions of sugarplums dancing in his head, "Why?" might have been a more reasoned and less instinctive retort. Boys will be boys, differentiated only by the size of their toys. Our other objections will be saved for another year.

Once again, we acknowledge that option programs have become nearly universal, particularly with technology companies. A company in Silicon Valley, for example, that stands on principle may find it practically impossible to recruit effectively.

In the meantime, rest assured that we comb the footnotes of 10-Ks and proxy statements of every company that we research to unearth stock-option or other abuses that may be tucked away there. Recognizing that stock options in this day and age are nigh unto ubiquitous (yes, rhymes with iniquitous), we don't object to companies that use options sparingly—and, in particular, to companies led by a dominant shareholder who doesn't personally participate in the options program. If the presumably knowledgeable insider is willing to suffer with us the cost of dilution at parity, we see no reason to take issue. As shareholders, we

find repricing proposals to be an even more outrageous example, fancy
explanations notwithstanding, of options simply serving as off-income
statement compensation. Apparently, FASB has reached the same conclusion. Early in 1998 it decided that companies repricing options should
expense the difference between the lower-share price and subsequent
increases. In the end our concerns may be of little consequence. If market
participants of the future are like market participants of the past, and if the
pendulum is freed again to swing, the next pervasive bear market will
close the gap between effort and reward. Options, like stock prices,
will fall—out of favor.

Stock Buybacks

Stock buybacks might well be more appropriately reviewed under a
different banner. Many, if not most, programs evince a prudent use
of shareholder cash. Boards that authorize share-repurchase initiatives
at market prices below what the businesses are intrinsically worth per
share (without forgoing investment in even more compelling growth
opportunities and with due regard for the financial security of remaining shareholders) are clearly putting the shareholders' interests high
on their priority list. While trying not to cast unnecessary aspersions on
the purity of motives, we nonetheless find a curious circularity to the
reasoning behind the calculation of the worth of the business. If
the higher-earnings-per-share growth rate that results from the share
buyback program in turn causes the board's determination of the worth
of the business to be ratcheted up accordingly, where does one get off
the merry-go-round?

Furthermore, and of no pressing concern, it also has occurred to
us that share-repurchase programs are subject to finite limits. There is
conceivably no ceiling on company growth, but a company can retire
no more shares than are outstanding. If there are enough shareholders
who don't comprehend the value of the business and are willing therefore to part with stock at prices well below intrinsic worth, someday
there will be but one shareholder group remaining. That's what we call
an MBO (management buyout)—on the installment plan.

Depending on how they're financed, stock buybacks have the effect
of increasing earnings per share. If the numerator (after-tax earnings
adjusted downward to account for additional interest expense when

money is borrowed to finance the purchase) falls less than the denominator (reduced by virtue of the shares acquired and retired), earnings per
share will rise. In a catch-22 scenario, once a stock-repurchase program
is instituted, discontinuing it becomes problematic. If the stock price
surges in part because of the presumed higher rate of earnings growth,
terminating the buyback plan will remove the growth catalyst that
financial engineering provided, and the share price will likely register
Wall Street's displeasure. Letting the air out of stock prices, as noted
elsewhere, is anathema in modern-day boardrooms. To the extent that
this section addresses techniques by which executives can "manage"
earnings, share repurchases must be included. Such programs—many
of which we applaud, and a few of which we think are blatant, flagrant, and systematic squanderings of shareholder assets—are nothing
more than another arrow in the financial-engineering quiver. Their
only income-statement appearances are through an increase in interest
expense or a decrease in interest income, relating to the means by which
they are financed—and a reduction in the denominator in the earnings-
per-share calculation. They have no effect on operating profits.

As is often the case, the tax code ostensibly forces the corporate
hand. It is reasoned that because dividends to individuals are taxable as
income at rates approaching 40 percent, whereas gains on long-term
capital transactions (including occasions when individual shareholders
sell back to the issuing company) are subject to a maximum 20 percent
tax, the latter distribution option is more tax-efficient.[18] The logic is
not in all instances bulletproof. For starters, shareholders selling to other
investors rather than directly to the company also avail themselves of
the favorable tax rates on long-term capital transactions. The tax differential is admittedly of particular appeal to a taxable shareholder who
sells enough stock each year to equate to a cash dividend, had one been
paid. In effect, he or she creates a synthetic dividend that is taxed at
no more than the 20 percent rate. Tax-exempt shareholders, including
401(k), pension, and other deferred-compensation plans, at least from
a tax perspective, are obviously indifferent to the form of distribution,
whether through dividends or share repurchases.

---

[18][2006, *Speculative Contagion*] The tax on dividends for most shareholders was
reduced to 15 percent as of May 5, 2003.

Finally, little is said about how a company's board of directors views its relationship with passive shareholders. In most instances, it is probably appropriate for the board to think of a shareholder's investment in the company as but one among many similar holdings that make up the shareholder's total portfolio. Such an attitude regarding any obligation that the board might feel toward its constituent shareholders is consistent with the doctrine that holds, "If you don't like what we're doing, you can always sell your stock." This almost universal and impersonal "portfolio of companies" paradigm runs counter to the "partnership" construct that Warren Buffett speaks of in his letters to Berkshire Hathaway shareholders. To be sure, Buffett's ownership structure is as refreshing as it is atypical. His 42 percent stake in Berkshire represents virtually all of his $30 billion net worth.[19] Likewise, for a considerable percentage of the company's outside shareholders, Berkshire also represents a large part of their wealth. Their Berkshire holding is not unlike a beloved lake cottage that becomes a family heirloom. It isn't surprising then that Buffett takes great pride in the low rate of turnover of Berkshire shares. If turnover were to increase appreciably, it might suggest that the lake is going dry.

Conclusion

The increased reliance of companies on accounting practices that are implemented to give the impression of often unwarranted growth, profitability, and stability is a sign of the times. For us, such hocus–pocus (with a bogus focus) simply mandates more thorough "due diligence." We spend extra time these days with financial-statement footnotes, proxy statements, and other disclosure documents. As noted above, when we attempt to determine the true earnings of a company, we often must recast financial statements to more fully reflect economic reality.

---

[19][2006, *Speculative Contagion*] Buffett's investment in Berkshire had appreciated to almost $42 billion as of June 30, 2005.

Chapter 2

Techno Babble,
Techno Bubble*

S&P 500 (SP50)
— Price

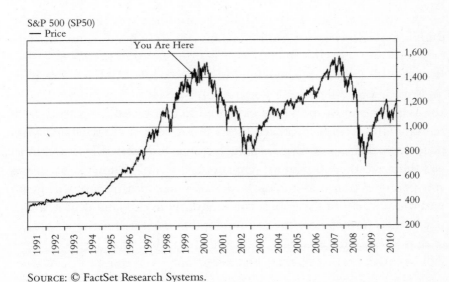

SOURCE: © FactSet Research Systems.

*This material is adapted from the 1999 annual report of Martin Capital Management.

The writing of the annual report is a special privilege for the undersigned. In addition to the opportunity it provides to communicate with a wonderful group of people, it also periodically induces me to step back from the fray and reflect on the nature of the causes of which the capital markets constitute merely the effect. Throughout, an atypical attitude toward risk and opportunity is advocated that may make the journey of wealth management less uncertain if not more productive. Much of what follows, as always, pays due homage to Mark Twain's dictum: "History doesn't repeat itself, but it rhymes." More on that later.

Call it philosophical resonance. At some point in our professional lives, we come to the realization that we can't be all things to all people, that we must choose sides. I had the early-career good fortune of being exposed to the writings of Benjamin Graham well before I was introduced to mainstream thinking. That learning experience proved to be an epiphany. The logic and integrity of Graham's thinking enthralled me. Just as naturally as dessert follows the main course, I later came to embrace the teachings of Warren Buffett, Graham's protégé. Buffett is simply Graham raised to the second power. Such singular focus likewise means there is little room in my intellectual library for the volumes of modern portfolio theory dogma, which governs the thinking of many in our profession. It's not so much a matter of right or wrong that separates the two as it is a difference in time perspective. Buffett thinks in terms of buying businesses, while MPT is about buying stocks. The difference is huge.

While many of the views expressed herein reveal the influence of the opinions of learned others, they cannot be entirely separated from my own evaluation of the prevailing facts and circumstances. Intentional or otherwise, they display my imprimatur, as well as mirror my biases and predispositions. As for the order of things, this report will begin with a discussion of the goings-on in both the equity and debt markets. It will then turn to how the MCM ship has navigated them: where we sought deep water and how we avoided possible shoals. Finally, there will be a section that features heretofore unspoken musings by Warren Buffett on the subject of the outlook for the returns from equities over the next decade or two.

A Tale of Two Markets

The defining characteristic of the markets for U.S. common stocks in 1999 was the divergence in stock price performance between those industries favored by investors and those considered passé. The companies leading the information revolution, broadly defined to include communications equipment (computer hardware, software, and services; electronics; and technology services), turned a trend that was well established in 1998 into a blowout in 1999. The S&P's tech sector jumped 74.7 percent last year, following 1998's 72 percent gain. *Technology issues accounted for about 90 percent of the advance in the overall S&P 500*, which climbed 19.5 percent in 1999. The venerable Dow Jones industrial average, meanwhile, getting a late-year boost from two of its new members, Microsoft and Home Depot, surged ahead 25.2 percent to a record 11497. Reflecting the tidal wave in tech issues, the Nasdaq finished 1999 with a record gain of 85.6 percent. By comparison, the great mass of companies simply languished.

As we are inclined to do, allow us to cast what is happening in the context of both time and space. The 68 companies that comprise the S&P technology index subset accounted for 13.3 percent of the value of the entire capitalization-weighted S&P 500 composite index at year-end 1997. In 24 months, it had tripled to 44.4 percent. The technology-dominated Nasdaq composite index, also capitalization-weighted, has become the market's force *du jour*. (The Internet sideshow is examined elsewhere in this report.) The fact that the companies of which the Nasdaq is constituted are the least seasoned in the American economy does not seem to matter one whit to an investing public whose appetite for technology—or perhaps the rising prices that their shares offer—appears insatiable. The market value of the Nasdaq composite, a mere $220 billion as recently as 1990, has ballooned to an incredible $5.7 trillion. In contrast, the market capitalization of the S&P 500 composite index is about $12 trillion (itself approximately 75 percent of the estimated $16.4 trillion U.S. equity market). Adjusted for the double counting (Nasdaq companies included in the S&P 500 index), the Nasdaq composite looms large indeed next to the sum of the market values of all the other industries that provide the material side of the American dream—industries that build and furnish the homes in which we live; produce, package, and distribute the food we eat and the pharmaceuticals that fill our medicine cabinets; make and retail the clothes we wear; and manufacture and sell the cars we drive and the planes we fly (and the fuel that makes them go). You know, the incidental stuff!

To be sure, the information revolution is the most important growth driver in our economy. Skyrocketing share prices are a testament to the premium that investors are willing to pay for growth or, in the case of the Internet, the distant expectation of it—or to the extent to which investors have taken leave of their senses. Of the three emotions that periodically sweep through the marketplace like a forest fire fanned by high winds—fear, folly, and greed—which might it be? The price-earnings ratio for the Nasdaq composite exceeds an unimaginable 200. Yes, there are two zeros. The off-the-charts trailing, 12-month, 27 to 33 times (depending on how you keep score) price-earnings ratio at which the S&P 500 sells pales by comparison. Indeed, these are the most unusual of times . . .

Growth versus Value

To elaborate a bit more on the subject, it is widely believed that growth investors tend to focus on technology companies and others with rapidly growing profits, while value managers seek undervalued and beaten-down stocks that often have low price-earnings multiples. If we must be categorized as value investors, it's because we only invest in those securities for which we can reasonably estimate their value and only at prices that are less than that value. We prefer growth but understand that it is but one component of a company's value. Reflect for a moment, if you will, on the airline industry and its profitless prosperity.

As for a rough approximation of the growth in the intrinsic value of the S&P 500 index, we estimate it may have increased by a total of 10 to 15 percent over the 1998–1999 period. It was spurred by the 110-basis-points drop in interest rates in 1998 (using the 10-year Treasury note as proxy) in the face of flat operating earnings. The flip side of the coin appeared in 1999 with operating earnings advancing by 16 percent while weathering a 170-basis-points uptick in interest rates. In sum, over the two years, the yield on the 10-year note rose by 60 basis points, and operating earnings for the S&P 500 composite companies advanced at an annual rate of 8.1 percent. The increase in the market value of the index, heavily weighted by technology issues, was more the result of expanding price-earnings ratios than earnings growth. Based on trailing 12-month earnings, from the first day of 1998 to the last day of 1999, the price-earnings ratio of the index advanced from 24 to 33, according to *Barron's*. The S&P value index crept ahead 12 percent in 1998 and 9 percent in 1999, more in keeping with the growth in underlying intrinsic value.

The disparity in performance between growth stocks (including both technology and branded consumer-product stalwarts) and value stocks is most pronounced among the smaller and mid-size companies. Looking beyond the S&P 500, the growth stocks in the Russell 2000 index, the small-cap benchmark, were up more than 40 percent, while value stocks in the index fell 3 percent. That spread is the widest in 20 years.

The growth/value gap was even more pronounced among mid-cap stocks, with the Russell mid-cap growth stocks gaining about 50 percent and value stocks unchanged. In the S&P 500, the gap was narrower. The index's growth stocks rose 27.3 percent last year, and value issues advanced 10.7 percent.

Hedge-fund manager Julian Robertson Jr., writing to the clients of Tiger Management in December, summed up the value manager's dilemma:

> . . . [T]he Internet is a great new technology that will change our lives. But there have been other great developments that created equally important lifestyle changes. In the past, investors overreacted to the promise of these changes. . . . We're in a wild runaway technology frenzy; meanwhile most other stocks are in a state of collapse. I have never seen such a dichotomy. There will be a correction. As to whether or not this correction will take the form of a total market collapse as in 1929, 1973–74, and 1987, I have doubts. Why? The out-of-phase stocks are just too cheap. . . . [T]his would imply a long-term underperformance of technology (believe it or not, it has happened) while the rest of the market continues to advance. Of course, this would be the ideal situation.[1]

---

[1] [2006, *Speculative Contagion*] As events unfolded, Julian Robertson proved to be amazingly prescient. Footnotes 15 and 18 in Chapter 3 tell the rest of this sad but instructive story.

As for the last sentence, Robertson hedges more than just his portfolios.

Zeroing in on one of the two most widely recognized investment styles makes clear the what-price-do-I-pay-for-growth dilemma that a man with money in his pockets faces today. He may be damned if he does and damned if he doesn't. If he forks over an ante that discounts the next hundred years of earnings and something unexpected occurs " 'twixt the cup and the lip," history may reveal him to be a fool—and a much less prosperous one at that. If "Jack" doesn't, and this bean "stock" grows to the sky, his wealth will grow at the pace of a redwood, while everyone else's imitates a rocket. The unwanted consequence of the first choice is that he may find himself absolutely poor and in the second, relatively so. While neither outcome is desirable, the consequences of the first are more severe. We hope you agree.

Another hallmark of the times is the harsh retribution dealt companies that fail to "make their numbers." An interesting ritual has developed between and among corporate America's and Wall Street's *cognoscenti*. Before a company officially announces its quarterly earnings, it is frequently known to "guide" key analysts as they construct their earnings forecasts. So much for independence. Soon a "whisper" estimate mysteriously circulates within the analyst community. Analysts are preconditioned. Understandably, then, when a company's formal release hits the wires, there is precious little tolerance for an earnings shortfall. In the new economy, the element of surprise increasingly has been "managed" out of profits, leaving a smaller portion of the earnings outcome subject to the vagaries of business, at least in the near term. Failure to "make their numbers," therefore, reveals far more about a company's operating results than a penny or two per share would otherwise suggest. If the earnings disappoint, despite the best efforts of the company's managers to massage out imperfections, something must be seriously awry. The palace revolt is as swift as it is sure.

A Study in Contrasts: Debt versus Equity

The two securities that potentially tie up one's capital the longest are common stocks and distant maturity bonds. Ownership can be perpetual, and the return of principal from a bond can be as many as 30 years away. Either, of course, can be sold in the interim under most circumstances.

As noted above, technology stocks have paid off handsomely in the recent past, whether one's investment horizon is near or far. Long-dated bonds (we use the 30-year U.S. Treasury bond as proxy) were the mirror opposite. These "certificates of confiscation," as they are impolitely called, provided a 1999 total return of minus 14.4 percent, far and away the worst calendar-year performance ever.[2] Yields on Treasury bonds began the year at 5.09 percent and finished at 6.48 percent. The Lehman Government/Corporate index suffered a negative return for only the second time (1994 was the first) since it was created back in 1973. The miserable showing of bonds in 1999 might properly be laid at the doorstep of the booming stock market, with investors accelerating a trend that began five years ago of dumping bonds for stocks. An unprecedented development of the late 1990s was that stocks were driving bonds—rather than interest rates influencing equities as they have in the past. The wealth created by the booming stock market is pushing the economy ever higher. Consider that the Conference Board's index of leading economic indicators rose to a 40-year high in November, thanks in part to the sizzling stock market.

Beyond investors' aversion to bonds, other forces had the effect of nudging interest rates higher as well. The economy continued to boil, the Federal Reserve hiked the discount rate three times, and fears of nascent inflation refused to die.

If there were a consensus forecast for interest rates by the end of 2000, it probably would peg the yield on the 30-year bond at 7 percent. In spite of, or perhaps because of, economists' underestimation of economic resiliency in 1999, they are calling for more of the same in 2000. Upward pressures on interest rates will continue to build under that scenario.

---

[2][2006, *Speculative Contagion*] No sooner had the "certificates of confiscation" been spat upon when the worm, as it so often does, turned. From January 1, 2000, through June 30, 2005, the compounded annual total return of the 30-year Treasury bond with interest payments reinvested at 4 percent was approximately 10 percent; the S&P 500, before reinvestment of dividends that would've added a little more than 1 percent to the total return, was −3.7 percent; and the Nasdaq, −11.7 percent. In pretax dollar terms, $10,000 invested in the Treasury bond at the outset would have been worth $17,000 five and a half years later. Sometimes you win by not losing . . .

The wild-card argument for higher yields stems from the uncertainty about how foreign investors will react to any changes in perceptions about the dollar and the attractiveness of the U.S. Treasury market. When the U.S. government borrows money these days, the chances are excellent that foreigners will be the ones writing the checks. Foreign investors— insurance companies, pension funds, central banks, individuals—now own almost $1.3 trillion in U.S. government securities, which is 40 percent of Washington's $3.2 trillion in accumulated marketable debt, according to the latest federal statistics. Five years ago, by contrast, foreigners held $641 billion in Treasuries, just 20 percent of the total at the time. Foreigners, effectively, have helped finance our imports. Princeton economist Alan Blinder, former vice chairman of the Federal Reserve, says there is "an upside and a downside to borrowing money" from abroad: "The upside is you get your hands on the money. The downside is you have to pay it back."

A good case to be made for lower yields is the "flight to safety" proposition. Pronounced stock market weakness could precipitate a scramble for the safe-harbor alternative that high-grade fixed-income securities offer. Any economic weakness that followed also would reduce the demand for money and, *ceteris paribus,* its cost.[3]

How We Managed Risk and Where We Found Opportunity

We believe that if you get the risks right, the returns will take care of themselves. As investors who consider patience a virtue and a prudent purchase price an absolute necessity, we looked for a more favorable mix of risk and opportunity elsewhere, given the considerable danger implicit in paying such extraordinary prices for the immensely popular and impressively growing technology companies. And we found such a mix. In our judgment, it resides in a number of well-capitalized companies whose primary appeal is not that they have a hot-wire connection to the information revolution but that their

---

[3][2006, *Speculative Contagion*] The enigma of lower long-bond yields remains unresolved and inexplicable. The market-clearing yield on the 30-year Treasury bond as of June 2005 was 4.30 percent. We wonder aloud what the yield on the 30-year bond will be in 2010. [2010 update: The yield on the 30-year Treasury was 3.65 percent.]

competitive advantages within their industries are defensible. Their historical earnings-growth rates, as well as longer-term prospective rates, are likely to be several times that of the economy as a whole.

Your portfolio reflects our ongoing reluctance to pay unprecedented premiums to play in a game in which we have no demonstrated competence and no croupier's advantage. We feel like an old hand at Las Vegas; our gut sense of the way things work tells us that the longer we stay at the tables, the more likely it is that we'll walk away empty-handed. Our rational side dominating, we watch and we wonder. To be sure, our reticence to sit for a few hands of blackjack has been costly in terms of lost opportunity, made all the more obvious by the run of good luck the fellow over whose shoulder we're looking is having. Make no mistake, we believe investing is the only game of chance where anybody who is savvy and independent enough can *become* "the house" and set the odds. We abide in that conviction. Our judgment, however, has yet to be confirmed.

According to Ben Graham and Warren Buffett, the three most important words in the serious investor's lexicon are *margin of safety*. In other words, the purchase price of a stock should be sufficiently below the investor's estimate of the company's intrinsic worth—in that if the estimate proves to be low, a cushion in the form of the discounted price still remains. The higher the uncertainty about one's estimate, the greater the margin should be. It's really rather straightforward. How interesting it is that teacher and student *nonpareil* are, above all, concerned with managing risk. In the end, that's where the game is won or lost. In the meantime, rest assured. We will not do things with your money that we won't do with ours, the pressure to keep up with the (Dow) Joneses notwithstanding. That portion of your portfolio committed to well-capitalized, growing businesses that we think we understand and that we purchased on average about 10 times earnings typically did not exceed 30 percent of the portfolio's value at year end.

Fixed-income securities in our clients' portfolios returned less than their coupons. Rising interest rates saw to that. That translates to about a 3.5 percent total return from Treasuries and about 2 percent from municipal bonds. Because of the short durations of our portfolios (average maturities range from one to five years), we were not penalized like long-bond buyers by the rising rates. On the contrary, in 1999 we were able to recycle liquidity at the best yields available in several years. Falling bond prices have actually spelled opportunity for us.

Tax minimization was factored into investment decisions made. For tax-paying investors, the lion's share of the gains realized will be favorably taxed at long-term capital-gains rates, and a varying share of the income earned was from municipal bonds and therefore exempt from state and federal income tax. Interest income from U.S. Treasury securities is also exempt from state income taxes.

As prosaic as this must sound, the 6.5 percent yield available on five-year Treasury notes and the almost 5 percent to be earned from Aaa-rated, pre-refunded municipal bonds of similar maturity may provide ample competition for the broader equity market over the next few years.[4] Despite the goings-on in the broad market, we will continue to buy high-return on equity companies (irrespective of the size of market capitalization) that enjoy solid growth opportunities, are well financed, and are selling at prices that offer an attractive trade-off between risk and opportunity. Our performance-based fee structure means that your portfolio's growth and our revenues are "joined at the hip." [Or, as stated in the MCM Business Principles, "We eat our own cooking."] Moreover, the "high-water mark" proviso checks any urge we might have to overlook risk in the face of the temptations of greed or folly. We appreciate your continued forbearance and hope that in time both of us will be proved wise.

Finally, when you think of common sense ("street smarts" in the jargon of Wall Street), the words of Mark Twain again come to mind. What may surprise you is that the great nineteenth-century skeptic was not in real life the sage that his clever aphorisms would suggest. Twain repeatedly squandered his writing income on questionable investments,

---

[4][2006, *Speculative Contagion*] That is precisely what occurred, with bonds outperforming stocks by an embarrassing margin. Wharton professor Jeremy Siegel, pilloried elsewhere, insists that stocks will outperform bonds in the long run. Roger Ibbotson's voluminous historical account (see reference to Ibbotson elsewhere) lends the weight of historical evidence and precedent to add credence to Siegel's extrapolations. The writer agrees with both. What Siegel, the academic, forgets on occasion is that (to badly paraphrase John Maynard Keynes) while the patient, long-term investor may become "rich" in the long run, if he's foolish he may go broke in the short run!

including a turn-of-the-century version of biotechnology. He appears to have been swayed by investments linked to well-known business-men or politicians. In addition to the biotech fiasco, Twain's losing bets ranged from a health-food company to a new printing process to an Austrian carpet-weaving machine. At least he was able to make light of his losses, and his experiences spawned some classic one-liners. For example: "There are two times in a man's life when he should not spec-ulate," lamented Twain. "When he can't afford it, and when he can." Fortunately, some lessons can be learned vicariously.

Back to the Future?

It is not uncommon for investors to imagine the future as an extension of the immediate past. That is, their vision of tomorrow is wherever a straight line that connects the dots of yesterday takes them. It even has Sir Isaac Newton's physical principles behind it—an object in motion tends to remain in motion. And yet, financial history, with no regard for our forgetfulness, occasionally reminds us of its cyclical (y)earnings. To be sure, few would disagree with the notion that simple extrap-olation of the past is an acceptable beginning point from which to approximate the future—most of the time. But there are moments, inflection points if you will, when and where simply extending the line is a sure prescription for misfortune. It is the line that can be one's undoing. It can lull a person into complacency.

Think of a grandfather clock in slow motion. When gravity gradu-ally and inexorably overcomes momentum, and the pendulum is about to reverse course—when aversion to the mean becomes regression to the mean—linear extrapolation is plainly counterproductive. Periods of linearity are never permanent, any more than are the seasons. In fact, the existence of irregular recurring patterns of events, often well camouflaged by the abstruse symmetry of their ebb and flow (the timing of which can be annoyingly unpredictable) should at least pique one's curiosity about the possible relevance of the study of bygone days.

This cyclical tendency of business and the free markets is such that by the time a trend is most pronounced and thus most widely embraced, it is also most pigheadedly inclined to reverse itself. It is one of life's poetic ironies that in the depth of darkest winter the buds of spring begin to form. The swinging-pendulum metaphor may also help to make the point.

We surely need not be reminded that history is a tool, relevant apart from the classroom setting, that actually has practical utility—like a head is more than just a hat rack. Of equal importance, knowledge of where we've been frees us from the constraints of having to simply take things as they are for lack of anything else to hang onto. Paradoxically, it is a lack of familiarity with, or a general disregard for, history's tutorial that may well exacerbate its repetitious nature. If you don't know history, says the sage, you're condemned to repeat it.

To be sure, history is a teacher in the abstract for those who want to apply it to the future. While, as Twain said, some events of the present indeed "rhyme" with the past, they nonetheless have their own unique rhythm. It is the timing, then, that often proves most nettlesome for those attempting to apply the events of yesterday to make order of today—and to capacitate a clearer vision of tomorrow. Timing errors may humble the prophet, but they needn't necessarily disparage his prophecy. Read on to learn about two modern-day Cassandras whose warnings should not be dismissed simply because they cried "wolf" when none was at the door.

Where's the Wolf?

The date of a most unusual final prospectus was May 9, 1996. The security being initially offered was the new "Class B Common Stock" to be issued by Warren Buffett's Berkshire Hathaway. The relatively small $500 million offering of shares at $1,110 each (the equivalent of one-thirtieth of the Class A shares, the highest-priced stock on the New York Stock Exchange) was solely to forestall promoters from issuing low-priced shares of a unit trust designed to track the performance of Berkshire's Class A shares.

Stated Buffett recently: "Our issuance of the B shares not only arrested the sale of the trusts, they provided a low-cost way for people to invest in Berkshire if they still wished to after hearing the warnings we issued." The timing was thus not of Berkshire's choosing. The following is the impassioned "sales pitch" that Berkshire's chairman provided would-be investors, in full view of even cursory readers, on the cover page of the offering document.

WARREN BUFFETT, AS BERKSHIRE'S CHAIRMAN, AND CHARLES
MUNGER, AS BERKSHIRE'S VICE CHAIRMAN, WANT YOU TO KNOW
THE FOLLOWING (AND URGE YOU TO IGNORE ANYONE TELLING YOU
THAT THESE STATEMENTS ARE "BOILERPLATE" OR UNIMPORTANT):

Mr. Buffett and Mr. Munger believe that Berkshire's Class
A Common Stock is not undervalued at the market price stated
above. Neither Mr. Buffett nor Mr. Munger would currently
buy Berkshire shares at that price, nor would they recommend
that their families or friends do so.

Berkshire's historical rate of growth in per-share book value
is NOT indicative of possible future growth. Because of the
large size of Berkshire's capital base (approximately $17 billion
at December 31, 1995), Berkshire's book value per share cannot
increase in the future at a rate even close to its past rate.

In recent years the market price of Berkshire shares has
increased at a rate exceeding the growth in per-share intrinsic value. Market overperformance of that kind cannot persist
indefinitely. Inevitably, there will also occur periods of under-
performance, perhaps substantial in degree.

Berkshire has attempted to assess the current demand for
Class B shares and has tailored the size of this offering to fully
satisfy that demand. Therefore, buyers hoping to capture quick
profits are almost certain to be disappointed. Shares should be
purchased only by investors who expect to remain holders for
many years.

Buffett, in this instance, was anything but prescient. No sooner had he
given his "not at this price" warning than the stock began a two-year
ascent, during which it more than doubled.[5]

Next we turn to Federal Reserve Chairman Alan Greenspan, the
most powerful appointed official in Washington and the most powerful
person period when it comes to guiding the U.S. economy. Six months

---

[5][2006, *Speculative Contagion*] After reaching a low point of about $1,500—
coincident with the peak in the Nasdaq frenzy—the Class B shares rebounded to
a high of $3,150 in May 2004. Currently they sell for $2,800. Nobody, not even
the most astute and wealthiest diversified investor in the world, is capable of forecasting short-term stock price movements. That's a "tip" worth remembering!

after Buffett pronounced Berkshire stock to be overpriced, the other financial giant of our times, Greenspan, issued his famous "irrational exuberance" statement during a speech to the American Enterprise Institute for Public Policy Research on December 5, 1996. The title of the talk: "The Challenge of Central Banking in a Democratic Society." The chairman of the Federal Reserve Board worried aloud about the economic consequences that might ensue from the collapse of a financial bubble.

> Clearly, sustained low inflation implies less uncertainty about the future, and lower risk premiums imply higher prices of stocks and other earning assets. We can see that in the inverse relationship exhibited by price-earnings ratios and the rate of inflation in the past. But how do we know when *irrational exuberance* [emphasis added] has unduly escalated asset values, which then become subject to unexpected and prolonged contractions as they have in Japan over the past decade? And how do we factor that assessment into monetary policy? We as central bankers need not be concerned if a collapsing financial asset bubble does not threaten to impair the real economy, its production, jobs, and price stability. Indeed, the sharp stock market break of 1987 had few negative consequences for the economy. But we should not underestimate or become complacent about the complexity of the interactions of asset markets and the economy. Thus, evaluating shifts in balance sheets generally, and in asset prices particularly, must be an integral part of the development of monetary policy.

On that date, the Dow Jones industrial average closed at 5178.[6]

Having surveyed the financial-section headlines of major metropolitan newspapers for 1999, it is clear to me that Greenspan's apprehensions about the possibility that the financial markets' collective tail may someday wag the economic dog have not faded in the least. Of particular

---

[6][2006, *Speculative Contagion*] Three years after Greenspan's warning, the Dow reached a peak of 11497.12 on December 31, 1999; it sank to 7591.93 on September 30, 2002, before rallying in the early summer of 2003 to over 9000. The Dow has since lingered around the 10500 mark for many months.

interest is the speech he gave this past October, in which he alluded to the absence of an equity-risk premium that historically has been embedded in stock prices. The word *risk* appears in the text 53 times, as if in Greenspan's tangential way, he was trying to emphasize the point by innuendo so as to avoid the chance of instigating the very event that he clearly fears.

How could these two men, perhaps the most knowledgeable and respected leaders extant in the fields of finance and economics, be so far off on their timing? How could they turn cautious three or more years in advance of a storm that does not yet even loom on the horizon? Unapologetically, Buffett observes matter-of-factly, "Markets behave in ways, sometimes for a long stretch, that are not linked to value. Value, sooner or later, counts."[7] Peter Bernstein [who died in June 2009 at the age of 90] in *Against the Gods: The Remarkable Story of Risk* (1996) identified the phenomenon mathematically as regression to the mean. Dependence on reversion to the mean for forecasting the future, he cautions, tends to be perilous when the mean itself is in flux. And yet, without some regard for the eventual central tendency of stock prices, valuation anomalies like the 200-plus times earnings at which the Nasdaq composite sells are possible. Price fluctuations, however random they appear, must be tied to something more stable than themselves. Indeed, they are accepted with equanimity these days—without triggering cries of alarm much beyond the measured exhortations of the likes of Buffett and Greenspan.

Even the smartest and best-informed economists and investors can't pinpoint the extremes to which crowd psychology—sometimes manic, sometimes depressive—will oscillate (or if and when it will lose its oomph and eventually display its opposite side). Don't lose patience or get distracted, for the race is long. With all of Buffett's "sins" of omission (the most recent being his reluctance to embrace technology or Internet stocks), his net worth is still, shall we say, respectable. Think of him as a $26 billion "loser." But even he admits that his best days may well be behind him, that 15 percent is more achievable. For years

---

[7][2006, *Speculative Contagion*] Once again, the markets have proved the efficacy of Benjamin Graham's adage: "In the short run, the market is a voting machine, but in the long run, it is a weighing machine."

he has warned that size alone militates against the intrinsic value of Berkshire compounding at a rate anywhere near the 23 percent of the last 35 years. By the way, how impressive is that rate?! A college graduation present of $13,600 this spring to a 22-year-old who can match Buffett's after-tax rates of return will have enough seed money to ensure a $100 million nest egg at normal retirement age. Nonetheless, with Berkshire stock down 23 percent in 1999, the first annual decline since 1990, the vultures are beginning to circle. *Forbes* columnist and money manager Martin Sosnoff recently took Buffett to task for being out of touch with the new economy in an article titled "Buffett: What Went Wrong?" The feature article in the December 27 issue of *Barron's* posed a similar rhetorical question: "What's Wrong, Warren?" What if it isn't Buffett who's out of touch?!

Warren Buffett on the Stock Market

Buffett is loath to talk about the stock market, despite his belief in the eventual tendency for prices to converge on value. One would think his confidence in the principle of regression to the mean would have been sufficiently shaken after the ill-timed Berkshire Class B advice and earlier pronouncements that high rates of inflation are endemic to our political economy. And yet, on four occasions in 1999, Buffett felt compelled to speak out, giving extemporaneous talks on the subject to private groups. *Fortune* magazine writer and Berkshire Hathaway annual report editor Carol Loomis distilled the contents of the first and the last in a November 22 article titled "Mr. Buffett on the Stock Market." Buffett then edited Loomis. Most of the observations below have their genesis in the article.

Buffett builds a compelling case that today's investors, prone as they are to look at the future through the rearview mirror, have an unsupportably optimistic view of the returns that common stocks in general can deliver in the years ahead. A PaineWebber and Gallup survey released in July 1999 reveals that the least experienced investors — those who have invested for less than five years — expect annual returns over the next 10 years of 22.6 percent. Even those who have invested for more than 20 years are expecting 12.9 percent. They seem to be able to disconnect themselves from underlying business and economic realities, and that concerns Buffett [not to mention the writer].

Going back 34 years, Buffett overlays a sort of biblical symmetry onto the past to observe the sequential appearance of lean years and fat years. For the first half, from the end of 1964 through 1981, the market's return was indeed lean. The Dow Jones industrial average started at roughly 874 and ended at 875. Observed Buffett wryly, "I'm known as a long-term investor and a patient guy, but that's not my idea of a big move." This anemic outcome was even more curious because of a GDP (gross domestic product) increase of 370 percent over the 17-year span. Two other developments completely negated the upward thrust on equity prices that would logically be expected from a growing economy. First, the market yields on U.S. Treasury bonds rose from just over 4 percent at the end of 1964 to more than 15 percent by late 1981. Since bonds represent direct competition for all other investment assets, the quadrupling of interest rates had the effect of driving bond prices (and therefore the prices of all near substitutes, including equities) sharply downward. Second, after-tax corporate profits as a percentage of GDP—that portion of the total sales of goods and services in the economy that ends up in the coffers of the shareholders of American businesses—tumbled to 3.5 percent, well below the average. So, at that point, investors were looking at two commanding negatives: subpar profits and sky-high interest rates. Looking forward by extrapolating the past, investors were despondent, a state of mind amply reflected in stock prices.

The next 17 years (beginning in 1982) were as fat as their predecessors were lean. The Dow skyrocketed from 875 to 9181, a tenfold increase. Interestingly, GDP grew less than in the first period, but the precipitous fall in bond-market yields to 5 percent and the increase in corporate profits' share of GDP to 6 percent provided much of the impetus for higher stock prices. Long-term bonds rewarded investors with an annual total return of more than 13 percent, but stocks stole the show. Their annual total return, with dividends reinvested, reached an astounding 19 percent. But those two fundamental factors only explain part of the rise. The rest is attributable to the change in investor psychology from the despair of the early 1980s to the exuberance of the 1990s, bordering on the irrational, to which Alan Greenspan alluded. Advancing stock prices soon became a self-fulfilling prophecy. It is from that psychological framework that the current crop of rosy expectations, which the Gallup organization surveyed, has been formed.

What's Ahead?

Staying with the symmetry of the 17-year cycle, what's likely to be in store between now and 2016? Buffett avers emphatically that for an outcome anywhere close to what investors expect—even those with 20 or more years' experience—one or more of the following events must occur. Government-bond yields, now 6.5 percent, must fall farther still. (If one has strong convictions about that, bond options are the purest and most profitable way to capitalize on that scenario.) In addition, the portion of GDP destined for corporate profits must increase. Regression to the mean is a force to be overcome if that assumption is to have merit. For corporate investors to eat an ever-growing slice of the American economic pie, some other groups must eat less. Political pressures, to say nothing of competition, will likely keep a lid on the expansion of corporate profits. Of course, corporate profits could rise to new highs as a percentage of GDP, but they obviously cannot grow faster forever.

What about growth in GDP? The assumption of a 3 percent real growth rate is consistent with historical trends and the expected growth rate in the economy's productive capacity. To that we add inflation of, say, 2 percent, arriving at a 5 percent nominal growth rate. To the extent the rate of inflation changes, so will the nominal growth rate.

So here we are. Profits growth under the above assumptions would approximate 5 percent, to which would be added about 1 percent for dividends in determining the returns investors can reasonably expect. Dividend yields are at record lows, which can largely be attributed to record-high stock prices.[8] Earnings per share would rise faster than profits because of share repurchases, were it not for shares issued in primary offerings and through stock-option plans. They more or less cancel each other out.

If one thinks investors are going to earn 13 percent a year in stocks, one must assume that GDP is going to grow at 12 percent, with another 1 percent coming from dividends. Historical standards, if not the economics of investment, would suggest that little help is going to come from

---

[8][2006, *Speculative Contagion*] The S&P 500 dividend yield has risen to 1.8 percent from a low of 1.1 percent in August 2000, due to a combination of falling stock prices and rising dividends. [2010 update: currently around 1.5 percent.]

expanding price-earnings ratios. On the contrary, one must acknowledge that future returns are always affected by current valuations. The
500 companies that comprise the S&P composite index represent 75 percent of the market value of all U.S. corporations. In the last four quarters, earnings for the S&P 500 companies totaled $403 billion; the
present market value for the index is $11.7 trillion. Current prices in
relationship to earnings are defying history, the laws of economics . . .
and gravity.

Investor expectations are seriously detached from reality today,
according to Buffett, just as they were in the mid to late 1960s in the
final throes of the great postwar bull market. Even though experienced
investors expect annual returns of almost 13 percent over the next 10
years—and novices believe they will get nearly 23 percent—in the opinion of the greatest investor living today, common stocks in the aggregate will be lucky to return 6 percent, or 4 percent after inflation, in the
years ahead.

Investing in Businesses Driving the New Economy?

But, you say, I don't invest in staid old businesses that grow in line
with the underlying economy. I avoid the mundane; I am not broadly
diversified. Perhaps, you argue, there is an alternative to spreading
one's bets all over the board in order to avoid the mediocre returns
from sampling a little bit of everything? Maybe if we concentrate our
portfolios in technology and Internet issues, where growth is sure to
eclipse that of GDP for years to come, we can avoid the curse of the
broader malaise? Read on and decide for yourself.

By way of proper introduction, we begin by noting that the twentieth century has spawned a momentous series of inventions that have
changed forever the way we engage in nearly every aspect of our daily
lives. Think of how far Americans have progressed from the snail's pace
of the horse, buggy, ship, and steam locomotive to the speed, comfort,
and convenience of first the automobile and then the airplane. In communications, we've gone from the Pony Express to the telegraph to
worldwide telecommunications. In media, we've progressed from local
performances to national book chains and "talking color pictures."
Chronicles of the pervasive impact of these marvels of ingenuity on
where we live, work, and play would fill a large library. Imagine how

different home life would be without the telephone, radio, television, and air conditioning—and white-collar workdays without the high-speed elevators and skyscrapers.

Consider some of the following effects of past technological improvements on business. Marketplace opportunities went from being confined to local communities to national and international markets, which gave rise to the notion of "economies of scale" of mass production. National media introduced the concept of "branding." Imagine the process of manufacturing widgets without the ability to constantly communicate with your customer base. And now comes the information revolution whose backbone is the diminutive computer chip. Computers revolutionized the volumes and means by which we manage and transport data. The latest iteration, the Internet, will forever change the conduct of commerce, both retail and business-to-business, and the mechanisms we employ to communicate at all levels. More on that in a moment.

Surprisingly, as awe-inspiring and life-changing as these inventions have been, almost without exception they were a boon to consumers and a disappointment to investors. At the peak of excitement over the prospects for the automobile, there were 2,000 producers in the United States. Now there are three, if you include Chrysler in spite of its recent sale to German carmaker Daimler-Benz. As of year-end 1998 (chosen so that Chrysler would be included), the market value of the domestic automobile companies totaled $118.5 billion. The industry sold $302.9 billion worth of vehicles in 1997 and earned $25 billion, Chrysler included. We can only speculate about the high point in market valuation that the industry excited at the pinnacle of the public's infatuation with the horseless carriage. If it was in the vicinity of $100 million, the average annual increase in market value approximated an unimpressive 7 percent, to which dividends should be added or capital infusions deducted.[9]

---

[9][2006, *Speculative Contagion*] General Motors stock (Figure 2.1) reached a peak of $95 in the spring of 2000. In April 2005, nearing the end of zero percent financed SUV life support, it dipped below $26, its market capitalization around $19 billion at midyear. Ford (Figure 2.2) topped out a little earlier in the spring of 1999 at $37; it reached a low of $7 in early 2003, sporting a recent market capitalization of less than $18 billion. DaimlerChrysler AG followed a descent similar to Ford's,

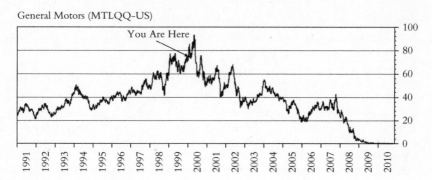

General Motors (MTLQQ-US)

Figure 2.1 General Motors Stock Price History
SOURCE: © FactSet Research Systems.

Widening the scope, there are 230 companies in the FactSet transportation grouping. Included are airlines, air freight/delivery services, railroads, trucking, and marine transportation—the means by which goods sold on the Internet and everywhere else are transported from the manufacturer, through the wholesaler, and ultimately to the consumer. On 1998 sales of $516.6 billion and earnings of $23.3 billion, the mid-December 1998 market capitalization of the industry aggregated $305 billion. Within that segment, the airline and aircraft-manufacturing

rising to $110 per share in early 1999, only to collapse to a price in the high $20s in early 2003. DaimlerChrysler AG was valued in the marketplace at about $40 billion at the end of June 2005. While the shares of all three have recovered modestly from their lows, they are far from firing on all cylinders. The combined market capitalization of the three companies totaled $77 billion, compared with the aforementioned $82.1 billion for Google (Figure 2.3). The three behemoths have 1,072,000 people on their payrolls, whereas Google employs 3,000, less than three-tenths of 1 percent of its gargantuan manufacturing brethren. Of no surprise, brains are going for a premium over brawn in the information economy! It doesn't appear to matter if all the world's auto companies will continue selling 50 million cars a year (something like 100,000,000 tons of steel, rubber, plastic, etc.) if they can't make money doing it. Still, the three companies nominally earned $8.1 billion against Google's $1.2 billion. However, all of their various and sundry liabilities, marked to market, dwarf their consolidated shareholders' equity. I think Google is probably too expensive. I am at a loss to opine on the value of the auto industry. [2010 update: Google has since tripled, and the auto industry, once led by a corporation now known, sadly, as Motors Liquidation Company, well . . .]

Ford (F-US)

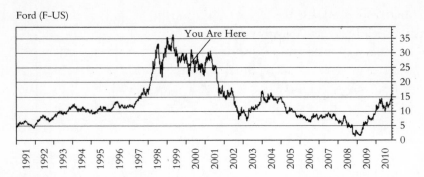

Figure 2.2   Ford Stock Price History

SOURCE: © FactSet Research Systems.

Google (CI A) (GOOG-US)

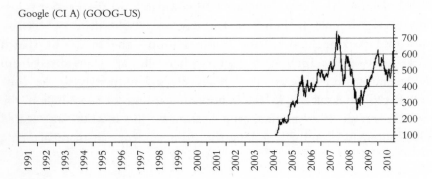

Figure 2.3   Google Stock Price History

SOURCE: © FactSet Research Systems.

industries, which numbered 300 companies in their heyday between 1919 and 1939 (undoubtedly the Silicon Valley of that age), have met an investment fate similar to that of the automobile. If the peak market valuation of the airline industry during that span was $5 billion, its current valuation of $46.7 billion would suggest that investors in the aggregate earned approximately 3 percent before dividends and capital infusions, of which the latter exceeded the former by a huge amount. Further complicating the process, investment in the industry has regularly required special navigational skills as one makes his way through the minefield of business failures. An unnerving 129 airlines have filed for bankruptcy in just the last 20 years [including former industry leaders United, Delta and Northwest].[10]

Moving a little closer to home, if you had invested an equal amount of money in all of the PC manufacturers in the early 1980s, your return would be 4 percent as of the end of 1999.

Is the Internet the Answer?

All of which brings us to technology's *wunderkind,* the Internet. As a firm and as individuals, we at MCM are active consumers of Internet services. While there is little doubt about the expansiveness of its utility in any number of venues, its capacity to generate corresponding profits is not so clear. Regardless, investors have developed a nigh-unto-obsessive fascination with Internet stocks like no craze in modern history (see Nasdaq stock price history in Figure 2.4). In 1996 the fledgling industry, then relatively few in number, sported a market capitalization of $12.9 billion, while losing $134 million on sales of $4.4 billion. By year-end 1998 the number of players had multiplied manyfold, and the industry's market capitalization shot up more than 10 times to $141.9 billion. Sales tripled to $12.4 billion over the two years, yet losses actually expanded, to $2.4 billion. It was throughout 1999 that the Internet fever rose to the point of threatening to shatter the thermometer. For the last four quarters, sales for the 200 public companies that Bloomberg surveys have increased to $21.9 billion, while

---

[10][2006, *Speculative Contagion*] The fallout from the September 11, 2001, tragedy wreaked further havoc on the airline industry. A rough approximation of the market capitalization of the airline industry as of June 30, 2005, was $22 billion (with the industry's anomalous leader, Southwest Airlines, accounting for $10.6 billion of the total!). Anybody want to trade the Big Three automakers—and the entire airline industry thrown in for good measure—for two good geeks and an algorithm? Austrian economist Joseph Schumpeter introduced the concept of "creative destruction" in his 1942 book *Capitalism, Socialism, and Democracy,* a form of industrial mutation that incessantly revolutionizes the economic structure from within, relentlessly destroying the old one, unceasingly creating a new one. Although I read it years ago, its central thesis has not yet fallen victim to "creative destruction"! Great ideas are rather impervious to that sort of obsolescence . . .

Nasdaq Composite Index (COMP)
— Price

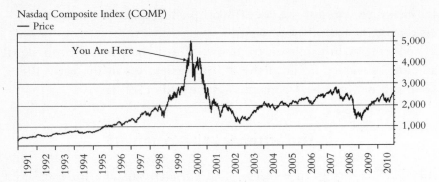

Figure 2.4 Nasdaq Composite Index Stock Price History
SOURCE: © FactSet Research Systems.

losses continue to mushroom—to $4.1 billion. Overlooking the nascent industry's lingering inability to make a buck, all manner of investors and speculators continue to relentlessly clamor for Internet stocks. The market capitalization of the industry reached an astounding $823.1 billion by mid-December 1999. Seizing the opportunity, Internet entrepreneurs and promoters have been quick to satisfy the public's insatiable appetite: Of the record 505 IPOs sold in 1999, more than half derived the lion's share of their revenues from the Net. Together they raised one-third of the past year's $66 billion in dollar volume. As surely as nature abhors a vacuum, supply rushes in to meet demand.

What do the Internet investors expect for an encore? Taking into account the industry's stratospheric valuations, if the Internet industry earns more profits in 2020 than *all* Fortune 500 companies *combined* earn today, or $334 billion—a most improbable outcome—the survivors must command a terminal price-earnings ratio of 20 if investors in the aggregate hope to eke out even a comparatively pedestrian 10 percent average compounded return. In all likelihood, you can't get there from here. We, meanwhile, watch from the sidelines with interest.

As for the investment dilemma posed several paragraphs above, I doubt that the Internet will be the answer. Perhaps what we're witnessing is merely the traditional boom/bust cycle for new technologies . . . at warp—check that—Internet speed.

With the weight of experience behind his arguments, Warren Buffett contends that *the secret to successful investing is not locked up in the knowledge of how much an industry is going to alter the way people live their lives, or even in how much it's going to grow, but rather in determining the competitive advantage of any given company and, above all, the durability of the advantage. Products or services that have wide, sustainable moats around them are the ones that deliver rewards to investors* [emphasis added].

Internet investors, please proceed down the "information super-highway" with caution.[11]

What Buffett Isn't Telling Us

Buffett never spoon-feeds those who dine at his table. He expects his guests to use their intellectual utensils to slice, dice, and then consume and digest the repast he offers. For starters, he does not dwell on the obvious, that the return he expects from common stocks going forward is slightly less than the relatively no-brainer alternative: U.S. Treasury notes and bonds with maturities of two to 30 years offer yields around 6.5 percent today. Of course, taxation of the interest income from bonds is more onerous than capital gains realized from the sale of common stocks. For those investors whose capital is invested in municipal bonds, however, the returns from tax-free interest are comparable to the after-tax returns that Buffett foresees from common stocks.

Equally important, he only indirectly refers to an alternative approach to achieving above-average returns in the future. In all likelihood, the euphoric state of mind that characterizes today's investor will eventually give way to its polar opposite. Persistently high or low valuation markets have never—ever—lingered indefinitely, despite feelings to the contrary at the time they were seducing the investment public at large. Regression to the mean (and often beyond) is likely to manifest itself again . . . and often when least expected. The Dow Jones industrial average will not follow a string from here to 30000 in 2016. (That's where 6 percent a year will take you.) The emotional road that leads from "irrational exuberance" to hard reality will most certainly be rocky. Patiently waiting for market prices of the companies he favors

---

[11][2010] The 1999 annual report, the sum and substance of this chapter, was published one month before the March 10, 2000, peak in the Nasdaq index.

to reflect equanimity, if not despair, rather than unchecked optimism, Buffett will surely again snatch opportunity from the jaws of defeat, just as he did in 1973–1974. He speaks confidently of 15 percent returns for Berkshire shareholders in the future. He will achieve them by buying superior businesses when they sell at prudent prices sometime in the future. And they will, as surely as night follows day. He will avoid the great temptations of the day alluded to above. Meanwhile, he sits on a hoard of cash. Buffett had this to say as part of the chairman's letter in last year's Berkshire Hathaway annual report:

> At year end (1998), we held more than $15 billion in cash equivalents [including high-grade fixed-income securities due in less than one year—$36 billion if you include longer-term fixed-income securities]. Cash never makes us happy. But it's better to have the money burning a hole in Berkshire's pocket than resting comfortably in someone else's. Charlie and I will continue our search for large equity investments or, better yet, a really major business acquisition that would absorb our liquid assets. Currently, however, we see nothing on the horizon.

How's that for a well-articulated strategy?!

What's a Long-Term Investor to Do?

Humankind's recurring propensity to unwittingly fall victim to financial fads, follies, and foibles is like a bad dream that we can't get out of our minds. It's a vague but imposing countervailing force that stands in the way of our unequivocally embracing the new economic and capital-markets paradigm. Add to that the utter absence of anything approaching a healthy respect for risk by a large segment of the investor population, and we have more than enough anecdotal evidence to compel us to fly the caution flag—if we truly believe that preservation of capital comes before all other aspirations. In other words, "To win, first you must not lose." The surest way is to press on toward your destination, while at the same time minimizing the risk of a skyjacking when risks of terrorism are running high, by booking yourself on a train until normalcy returns [little did we know what was to happen 21 months later . . .]. Of course, the train isn't as fast. A less certain but somewhat speedier alternative is to select another airline and a different route. With short- to mid-term U.S. Treasury notes and pre-refunded municipal bonds coupled with high-quality (but presently unglamorous and unloved) equity securities, we are attempting to keep you on your way via both vehicles. If conditions improve—that is, if prices move closer to value—it will be so much easier and less costly to transfer from train to plane.

Investment Redefined

In the depths of the Depression, chastened by his failure to foresee the stock market crash and the enormity of the economic aftershock, Benjamin Graham reflected on the meaning of the term *investment* in the 1934 investment classic, *Security Analysis*. Years before the surreal madness of the late 1920s rendered rationality temporarily AWOL, Graham recalled that an "investor" purchased stocks . . .

> . . . at price levels he considered conservative in the light of experience; he was satisfied, from the knowledge of the institution's resources and earnings power, that he was getting his money's worth in full. If a strong speculative market resulted in advancing the price to a level out of line with the standards of value, he sold the shares and waited for a reasonable price to return before reacquiring them.
>
> Had the same attitude been taken by the purchaser of common stocks in 1928–1929, the term investment would not have been the tragic misnomer that it was. But in proudly applying the designation "blue chips" to the high-priced issues chiefly favored, the public unconsciously revealed the gambling motive at the heart of its supposed investment selections. (Ibid., 54)

Investors' behaviors in the late 1920s differed in one vital respect from earlier practices. The buyer made no attempt to determine whether shares were worth the price paid by the application of firmly established standards of value. The market simply made up new standards as it went along by accepting the current price—however high—as the sole measure of value. Continues Graham: "Any idea of safety based on this uncritical approach was clearly illusory and replete with danger" (ibid., 54). Under that line of reasoning, no price was too high to render a security unsafe.

Now that the 1990s have drawn to a close, I wonder what history's verdict will be of these extraordinary times. Will it remember the last decade of the twentieth century as the beginning of a new era with fresh rules and modernized standards, or will it expose yet another episode of investment metamorphosing [now "morphing"; even language changes and, yes, morphs] slowly but surely into rank and misguided speculation? Will the children of Generation X learn that their Boomer parents were like the rising sun at the dawning of New Age economics? Or, as Jim Grant has suggested, is knowledge in the field of finance cyclical and not cumulative? Why, we ask, hasn't Holland's Tulip Mania of the 1630s slipped quietly into the obscurity of the archives of financial history? Why did Japan repeat in the 1980s the destructive behavior that brought the U.S. financial markets and economy to their knees in the 1930s? Are speculation and its inevitable aftermath unavoidable parts of the human condition? As memories of the lessons of the past fade over time, is each new and uninitiated herd of speculators little more than unsuspecting sheep being driven into the shearing barn to be periodically shorn? [Or worse yet, as the cartoon in Chapter 4 so eloquently illustrates, are the sheep stampeding pell-mell over a cliff?] Is the casino capitalism of today, at rock(y) bottom, simply a new variation on an old theme?

It is to state the obvious that prices, particularly those of companies probing the frontiers of the new tech-based Information Age, have long been detached from traditional benchmarks of value. But it's not just concerns about the relationship between price and value that put a traditionalist on edge. Rather, it's also about how investors attempt to capitalize on what is taking place. Day trading, like Internet pornography, is a diversion with which most of us are unfamiliar. And yet both thrive right under our collective nose—and both with suspect olfactory emanations. Encouraged by the apparent disregard for the nature of the relationship between the price of an asset and its underlying value, day traders provide additional anecdotal evidence of the prevailing atmosphere of speculative promiscuity. It is increasingly common to think of stocks not as fractional ownership pieces of a real business, but rather as pieces of gilt-edged parchment (or, more appropriately, formless entries on a monthly statement) that are to be bought and sold with impunity, much like baseball cards. Casino capitalism may, in fact, be a fitting moniker.

The cynic describes a long-term investment as short-term speculation gone horribly wrong. But, in our belief, *long term* and *investment* are as compatible and as deserving of one another as love and marriage. Instead, the words *short term* and *investment* create the true oxymoron. Confusion about the difference can be dangerous to one's financial health. It is ironic indeed that the Internet has made possible day trading in, as you might guess, the Internet stocks themselves.

The Internet, of course, is reshaping every segment of the economy, but nowhere does that change occur at a greater pace than in the financial-services sector. Specifically, what's happening in the brokerage industry is a preview of things to come in other businesses. It's happening to brokers first because they aren't selling toasters or cars. Their products are intangible, so the transaction can happen purely electronically. When does affection become infatuation? For some, day trading is simply the new game in town. Conditioned by the lottery, the proliferation of gambling casinos, and now such television shows as Regis Philbin's *Who Wants to Be a Millionaire?*, Internet day trading has become the newest "easy money" fad.

SOURCE: Copyright © 1994 Bill Monroe.

The New Tulip Bulbs?

Shortened time horizons have become a fact of investment life. How much has turnover increased? According to *BusinessWeek*, some 76 percent of the shares of the average U.S. company listed on the New York Stock Exchange turned over last year, up from 46 percent in 1990 and only 12 percent in 1960. It was running at 82 percent through May 1999. On the Nasdaq, home of the greatest proportion of high-tech companies, turnover was three times as high. *Time* magazine's 1999 "Person of the Year,"[12] 35-year-old and delightfully affable Jeff Bezos, Amazon.com's founder and CEO, leads a frenetic and exciting life— and so, apparently, do the shareholders of the company leading the e-commerce revolution. The average share in Amazon.com Inc. is now held for *seven* trading days before being sold to someone else. Yahoo! shareholders stick around for all of eight days. As for the more mature technology companies, the holding periods are longer: Dell Computer (3.7 months), Microsoft (6.3 months), and Cisco (8.5 months). Even the consummate hold-it-for-a-lifetime investment, Coca-Cola, sees its ownership turn over every 2.2 years. At the height of Tulip Mania, bulbs were not coveted for the beauty to be derived from their eventual blossoming but to turn a quick profit. Most were never planted. Tulip bulbs were simply the fast-buck medium, incidental to the real objective. They could just as easily have been . . . um . . . Internet stocks!

Of course, most of the churning today can be traced to mutual funds, which own a higher percentage of stock than ever. Constantly under pressure to achieve short-term performance objectives, fund managers are quick to change horses, often midstream. For investors in the highest brackets, taxes on the gains from shares held less than a year are double those held more than 12 months. The shareholders of most mutual funds include individuals whose gains are taxable, as well as tax-deferred entities, such as 401(k) plans. Taxable investors get the short end of the stick in this high-turnover performance derby.

---

[12][2006, *Speculative Contagion*] Telltale signs of exaggerated sentiments were to be found everywhere during the Great Bubble. The "curse of the cover story" befell the enthralled stockholders of Amazon.com and e-commerce wunderkind Jeff Bezos, Amazon.com's founder. (See earlier footnote on Amazon for details.) E-commerce is a small but rapidly growing share of the retail marketplace, but Walmart has yet to be toppled.

More Dollars Than Sense

The "Day Tripper" of Beatles lore could well have been the precursor three decades ago of this era's day trader. In August of 1999, Alan Abelson, the erudite *Barron's* columnist, looked inside the murky world of day trading. He highlighted the findings of the North American Securities Administrators Association (NASAA), which comprises multifarious regulatory bodies that had spent months probing the seams of the "bucket shop" day-trading world, poking into such delicate subjects as commissions, suitability standards, and the whereabouts of the customers' yachts. (Ameritrade, the online broker, recently lost what could prove to be a landmark arbitration case involving an Indianapolis med-school graduate who was trying to speed the payment of his student loans by trading Internet stocks on margin.) One of NASAA's conclusions, which raised many an eyebrow, was that an estimated "70 percent of public traders will not only lose but lose everything they invest." Another of the report's striking revelations concerned the "annualized cost/equity ratio." This neat little number "measures the amount of profit required on average equity just to pay transaction costs and break even." That ratio is an astonishing 56 percent. In other words, on a $100,000 account, you have to make a mere $56,000 just to pay your commissions! Day trading, apparently, is a lot more like gambling than most people think. Fittingly, so are the results.

As long as we're on the subject of illusions, a word or two is in order about the IPO (initial public offering) express train to riches. As anyone who reads the *Wall Street Journal* or watches CNBC is aware, the Boston Chicken–type IPO market is back en masse. You may recall that we expressed our doubts about the Boston Chicken phenomenon in the 1993 annual report. When it debuted in 1993 amid great fanfare, the Chicken's price in the aftermarket rose an unprecedented 150 percent from the offering price. The Ponzi-like[13] capital

---

[13][2006, *Speculative Contagion*] Carlo "Charles" Ponzi emigrated from Italy to the United States in 1903. For the next 14 years, he wandered from city to city holding a variety of jobs, including that of dishwasher. Then he hit upon an idea of arbitraging foreign postal coupons. It was easy money until red tape associated with all the transfers ate away all of Ponzi's imagined profits. That didn't stop Ponzi. The simple scheme that bears his name enjoyed a modest, then rapid, evolution: Ponzi parlayed the original idea into a scam that promised investors would

structure imploded five years later, and the company, like its stepchild, Einstein's Bagels, sunk into the ignominy of bankruptcy. McDonald's recently purchased the remains of the company for pennies on the dollar. This time it is the Internet that is center stage—and the sellers are more clever than ever. In earlier superheated IPO markets, sellers would be suing their underwriters for underpricing the issue if the price in subsequent trading rose by the kind of percentages that are widespread today. This is not so nowadays because by intentionally keeping the initial offering relatively small, in the face of supercharged demand, a scarcity premium is created, and the post-sale price often skyrockets. It is on the strength of that price that real money is raised in a subsequent "secondary" offering. The illusion is that there is lots of easy money to be made by investing in IPOs. In reality, the people who take serious money off the table are the sellers. As for the buyers, recently disclosed secret "pot lists" indicate that institutions, who carry nearly as many sticks as the commission dollars they spread around like so much grease on the wheel, receive 70 to 80 percent of the allocation of the first round. In all probability, many of the retail buyers who bite the bullet in the aftermarket or in a secondary offering will be the first to scramble for a chair once the music stops.

As to the seductive appeal of greed and folly mentioned early in the report, need more be said? Finally, when an epidemic of high-turnover speculation has displaced long-term investment as the standard of conduct in the financial markets, the endgame is almost never pleasant.

---

double their money in 90 days. At the height of his scheme, money was flowing in at $1 million per week. Early winners were paid with the money flowing in from new players. The money distributed far exceeded the earnings power of the underlying activity, which in this instance was nil. Eventually, authorities began investigating the too-good-to-be-true scheme, and the operation began to collapse when the *Boston Post* ran a headline story in July 1920, questioning the legitimacy of Ponzi's devious plan.

Chapter 3

"Pop!!".com*

S&P 500 (SP50)
— Price

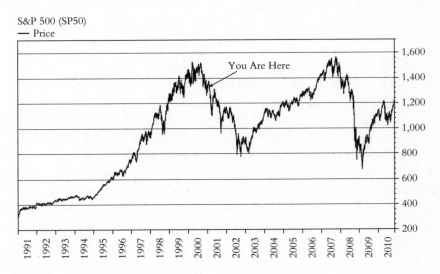

You Are Here

SOURCE: © FactSet Research Systems.

---

*This material is adapted from the 2000 annual report of Martin Capital Management.

The first year of the popularly perceived new millennium began with an ironic twist. The much-ballyhooed and widely feared Y2K computer meltdown will be remembered (assuming the acronym so symbolic of the amorphous outreach of the tentacles of technology has not already been erased from your cranial hard drive) as the ultimate nonevent. Perhaps Y2K's sole redeeming virtue was in once again giving witness to the nearly incomprehensible power of crowd psychology. On the other hand, the largely unexpected and thus not feared disintegration of the technology and Internet stocks was, by chilling contrast, the cataclysmic incident for which the year will not soon be forgotten. The common thread that ties these two incidents together? The willingness of people to submit themselves *en masse* so unquestioningly and with such groundless fear in the first instance and with such "irrational exuberance" in the second. The Internet and computer technology are related ideas from the same school of science: The Internet teems with overcapacity, as the economic efficacy of its many entrants is yet, if ever, to be proved, while most stocks pertaining to computer technology are outrageously overvalued, priced as if endless hypergrowth were assured.

Risk: No Longer an Afterthought

At its most rudimentary level, the featured financial story for 2000 was about speculation in certain favored industries, escalating through the process of contagion to preposterous and ultimately self-defeating extremes. It's a phenomenon that has repeated itself throughout all of human history and which necessarily has been examined in these pages in the past.

If ever-iconoclastic rationalism and uncompromising intellectual independence were called for, the year just past was it. Only you can be the judge as to whether we kept our heads when many about us were losing theirs. Here's the hook: If you expect to make that finding, you'll have to read on!

In the midst of all the wealth-destroying "gore" for which 2000 will be remembered by a horde of sheep shorn naked, we trust that you never lost a night's sleep (or even got "bushed") worrying about the safety and security of your portfolio, about the possibility of a crack that threatens to become a chasm in your nest egg. Wealth management, the markets in their own perverse way occasionally remind us, is not just about eating well, it's also about sleeping well. Perhaps our profession is not unlike amateur tennis: It's usually not the number of winners hit but rather the number of unforced errors that determines the outcome. The rather extraordinary and equally humbling absolute and relative performance of last year was in part the result of good defense—we had only one unforced error—and the concurrent but somewhat unexpected good fortune of the market choosing this particular year to recognize how undervalued some of our companies were, resulting in four outright winners as well.

To be sure, it is not our intent to make light of the breadth of financial trauma suffered in many sectors the past year but simply to remind you of its existence because, like a hurricane in the Caribbean, it rendered its devastation elsewhere. Don't be fooled; the storms may not have passed. And the winds of destruction could reach places heretofore untouched. Though your experience may be vicarious thus far, the lessons learned from the stories that follow should be taken with the highest degree of seriousness. And the word "trauma" may well understate the magnitude of the markets' giant sucking sound, like the enormous and indiscriminate vacuum cleaner mounted on the sleigh of "The Grinch" (the wonderful Christmas movie starring Jim Carrey) as the town of Whoville unwittingly surrendered all its accumulated material gifts to a thief in the still of the night before Christmas. Suddenly, it seems, billionaires have shrunk like cheap cotton to millionaires, millionaires slipped into the ignominy of being merely well-to-do, and all manner of speculators—big fish and minnows alike—were rendered, for lack of a better phrase, acutely *un*rich.

Putting numbers to the diminution of paper profits is telling. Overall, it is estimated that the market capitalization of U.S. equity securities fell some $2.5 trillion over the course of the year, against a start-of-year total of approximately $17.4 trillion. The value of all stocks on the New York Stock Exchange, about $12 trillion, was essentially flat for the year, while the Nasdaq lost approximately $2 trillion, compared with a start-of-year total of an incredible $5.3 trillion. From its peak on March 10, 2000,[1] the Nasdaq Composite fell 39.1 percent. The index

---

[1][2006, *Speculative Contagion*] Unlike the assassination of the Archduke of Sarajevo on June 28, 1914, which was the "tipping point" for the start of World War I, no

itself plummeted from 5049 to 3521 in a matter of 34 days, reaching a low of 2333 on December 20, which translates to a breathtaking peak-to-trough decline of 53.8 percent. In the euphoria of a year ago, a bear market was thought to be a decline of about 20 percent. Who, I wonder, after "tout television" picked up on the 20 percent figure, was originally responsible for suggesting such an arbitrary and foolish metric? The market capitalization of the Dow Jones index of Internet stocks fared even worse. From its peak, also on March 10, the market capitalization declined dramatically from just over $1 trillion to $251 billion on December 21, a shocking 76 percent. The remediation of speculative excess is often as dramatic as it is devastating.[2]

Lest we overlook it, bifurcation was as evident in 2000 as it was the year before, this time in both the equity and the debt markets, as well as between them. With regard to the equity markets, the players simply reversed their roles. While the technology bashing was under way, there was a resurrection of interest of sorts among the old-economy industries. As for bonds, Treasuries prospered, thanks to falling interest rates, while junk simultaneously sank because of worsening credit quality. Finally, while stock prices went down, quality bond prices went up.

Not only was paper wealth greatly diminished as the Bubble began to burst, what wealth remained (of which there is still plenty) was subjected to a winnowing process known as redistribution. In the relative scheme of things, discerning and prudent investors climbed a rung or two on the ladder of wealth preservation and accumulation, while

---

single event triggered the massive and soon-to-be cascading reversal of "fortunes" that began March 10, 2000, of which the Nasdaq index was merely the most illustrative. When someone yells "Fire!" in a crowded theater, it is panic and not rationality that inflames the mind.

[2][2006, *Speculative Contagion*] That was only the beginning. At its low point (thus far), it is estimated that the U.S. equity markets lost more than $8 trillion in value. As if to cushion the effect of the reversal in financial market fortunes over the course of the time span of this book, the estimated value of residential housing in America rose from $8.9 trillion to $17.7 trillion, with estimated owners' equity rising from $5 trillion to $10 trillion. Moreover, the net worth of households and nonprofit organizations, as estimated by the Board of Governors of the Federal Reserve, increased from $33.8 trillion to $48.8 trillion over the same time period, inclusive of losses in the stock market and the $5 trillion gain in homeowners' equity.

those who didn't know any better (or if they did, sacrificed rationality at the altar of momentum investing or its variations) dropped a rung or two . . . or more. As was noted in the 1999 annual report, there are always opportunities, but they are rarely found in the obvious places. As for those who fueled the fires of reckless speculation—the men and women of our profession—we'll have more to say about them later.

In the words of Aristotle, "One swallow does not a summer make." Although the decisions we made during the course of the last year led to above-average equity-investment returns, we view such decision making as but one brief segment in a long-term continuum. Who knows what tomorrow will bring? We draw some solace from the deeply held conviction that the ideological foundation upon which our security selection and portfolio management practices have been painstakingly built will, at the very least, keep you out of harm's way. At the very best, we may surprise a few people who believe that there is always a correlation between risk assumed and return earned—and that *conservative* is invariably synonymous with lackluster results. In the meantime, if we continue to adhere to our principles, we are likely to avoid many of the temptations that come in the form of folly, greed, and (most critical and sometimes most troublesome) fear, which on occasion precipitates the most irrational and destructive of behaviors. Our approach served us well in the final 12 months of the second millennium A.D., but 2001 will be a new odyssey, to be sure. Again, our convictions will undoubtedly be put to the test. As always, we will forsake the lure of so-called opportunity where the flip side of that coin may result in permanent loss of capital.

Equally important is that we provide you with a full explanation of how the investment returns were earned and what risks were incurred with your capital in the process of earning them. First, as has been disclosed on many occasions in the past, it is our contention that there is great virtue in limiting the horses in one's stable to a relatively small number of thoroughbreds. Empirical testing has proved beyond a reasonable doubt that the "riskiness" of a portfolio of 12 to 15 diverse companies is little greater than one loaded with a hundred or more, as is so often the practice among many institutional portfolio managers. In this instance, we define risk as a terribly bad longer-term outcome—and not the extent of annual portfolio price volatility that is the standard by which it is measured according to MPT. We don't subscribe to that popular discipline so much because it is "demented" (in the mince-no-words eloquence of Berkshire Hathaway's Charlie Munger) but rather due to the fact that (1) our investment holding period is ideally very long, and (2) we don't think of ourselves as buying and selling pieces of paper but rather investing in businesses. Modern portfolio theory (MPT) is simply incompatible with our investment style.

It is also important to disclose that we attempt to further ameliorate risks that may be perceived to be associated with a concentrated approach toward investment by (1) selecting only those businesses that pass through our rigorous filters and (2) purchasing such companies at prices that afford us a significant margin of safety, as explained further in "The Art/Science of Managing Risk." We strongly believe that the supply of great businesses is severely limited and to engage in broad diversification (for the often spurious reasons that others offer as rationale) is dilutive to the implicit purpose of earning above-average longer-term returns. Little that is good comes without cost, however. And the cost of a concentrated approach to portfolio management is (1) much greater relative portfolio price volatility and (2) the possibility that we will look like geniuses on one occasion and dolts on another. Neither is an accurate characterization, but if the eventual outcome is superior to the more commonplace practices, we strongly believe that the end justifies the means, despite the exasperation that may occasionally (and, we hope, temporarily) ensue.

To put real numbers to the abstract concept of margin of safety, the weighted-average price-earnings ratios at the time of purchase of the companies we acquired was 9.7 times, compared to a price-earnings ratio for the S&P 500 that averaged in the high 20s during most of 2000. Our weighted-average, estimated five-year earnings-per-share growth rate for those same companies is just under 15 percent, compared with an earnings-per-share growth rate for the S&P 500 of less than half of that.

An additional word on "margin of safety" is warranted here, although it will be discussed in greater detail in "The Art/Science of Managing Risk." Purchasing a business at a price that provides reasonable assurance of a generous margin for error is an erudite way of saying to ourselves, "Buy low, stupid." While intuitively appealing, this is by no means easy to implement. It requires that we step boldly into the lion's den, that we take decisive action at the most unpropitious of times. Backed by extensive research and strong convictions, we must purchase the shares of good businesses in the face of the kind of awful news that forces others to throw in the towel as momentum is turning south or when short-term performance mandates do not permit the luxury of endurance. A significant portion of the favorable outcome achieved in 2000 was due to little more than taking advantage of discarded mainstream companies as the Nasdaq, the presumed ticket to success, sucked money away from everything else while soaring to new highs in the spring. We purchased the castaways you own at deeply depressed prices and then looked on with satisfaction as they surged upward toward intrinsic value and, in a few isolated instances, slightly above—at the very time the Nasdaq index had its comeuppance.

What happens from here on with several of our portfolio holdings may well depend more on the quality of our research and less on our ability to take advantage of a schizophrenic market, though we have identified a number of possible new investees whose depressed market prices would suggest that the "rubber band" effect might be salubrious. If the intrinsic value of the companies we own continues to grow according to our projections—even though the fluctuation in market prices may from time to time suggest otherwise—the market value of the equity portion of your portfolio should follow suit in due course. Buying businesses on the cheap takes chutzpah born of strong convictions. Forecasting future cash flows and discounting them appropriately (the basis for the calculation of intrinsic worth) requires appreciable knowledge and skill—and fair winds. We think we are above average in doing the former; as for the latter, only time will tell. While our aversion to assuming high levels of valuation risk (to say nothing of the difficulty of pushing technology companies through our filters) penalized us in 1997–1999, it had the opposite effect in 2000.

It should be noted that, for most portfolios during the five-year period, the portion allocated to equities rarely if ever exceeded 50 percent, except late in 2000—and that was due largely to the bargains finally found in the spring and the appreciation thereafter. See "Goliaths Slain" if, perchance, you're plagued with lingering regrets for not jumping on the bandwagon in 1998–1999.

Though there were several minor exceptions, generally those few clients who asked that we purchase according to ideas of their own choosing—or who imposed certain moratoriums on equity purchases beyond what their Investment Policy Statement stipulated—fared less well than those clients who left us to our own devices. While we don't necessarily encourage such behaviors, we gladly accommodate them in the name of making the investment experience a personalized one for each client. While it cost them (and us!) money last year, next year may be a different story. In the long run, however, if we become redundant, I'm sure you will let us know! We're working hard to see that this doesn't happen.

In 2000 we continued our practice of investing in only the highest-grade fixed-income securities, despite the ever-widening spreads between U.S. Treasury notes and junk bonds (now an eye-catching 520 basis points). One can buy Amazon.com 4.75 percent convertible debentures due in February 2009 at 35 percent of par for a yield to maturity of 22 percent—if they continue to pay timely interest and are able to return the principal at maturity, a wager we have no interest in taking. If junk bonds, which we defined as a convoluted form of equity with limited upside potential and unlimited downside risk, appear attractive, common stocks are likely to be even more appealing.[3]

While we aren't aggressively active fixed-income security managers, we do try to eke out a better return (than a passively managed laddered portfolio would suggest) by managing duration within the context of a relatively short-term portfolio construct. Where we do get very aggressive is in the selection of the highest-quality tax-exempt bonds we own. If you don't know that market well—and how it differs from the incredibly efficient market for U.S. Treasury securities—you can be made to look a fool without even knowing it. While it's not apparent to the untrained eye, we believe that we add significant value because of our years of experience and daily activity in the specialized market for municipal bonds.

---

[3][2006, *Speculative Contagion*] From a low of about $35 near the end of 2000, the convertible bonds of Amazon.com rallied to near par in early 2003 where they have generally traded since, as concerns about the company's dire financial straits subsided. Junk-bond investors realized a total return of 240 percent (based on coupon payments and bond-price appreciation). Amazon.com's stock reached its low of $5 later in the wake of 9/11. By autumn of 2003 the stock had risen twelvefold to $60. Need more be said about relative upside potential . . . ? The stock settled back to around $35 at midyear 2005.

Another peculiarity of our approach to wealth management is that we see fixed-income securities for the complementary role they play in meeting portfolio objectives and not as a discrete class of security that should be managed by a specialist and measured against a fixed-income benchmark. Our aggregate portfolio benchmark is the S&P 500, irrespective of portfolio-asset class composition, assuming a client has given us discretionary authority to be fully invested in equity securities. In those instances in which a client's Investment Policy Statement specifies a maximum commitment to common stocks of, say, 50 percent, a blended benchmark is obviously used instead. Because of a limited potential for outsized gains, bonds are used primarily for defensive purposes. And yet the crowning indignity for the badly shaken cult of equity worshipers was that stocks in 2000 were left in the dust not only by bonds—the 10-year note was up 16 percent—but also by . . . cash! Sometimes you win by not losing. . . .

Investment Strategy: Is It Time for Technology?

In the 1999 annual report [Chapter 2], we said we had demurred after surveying possible investment possibilities in Internet-related companies. Although it never makes the headlines, sometimes a simple "no" is the best choice. What about technology stocks after the bloodbath? Now that Nasdaq (Figure 3.1) has done its splendid imitation of a swan

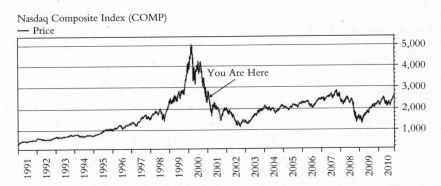

Figure 3.1 Nasdaq Composite Index Stock Price History
SOURCE: © FactSet Research Systems.

in full dive, we wonder where opportunity might be found. We are convinced that, like the Phoenix of ancient lore, some (we sorely wish we knew which ones) will eventually rise in spectacular fashion from the ashes of ignominy. Since few, if any, pass through our filters, let me in this instance defer for a bird's-eye view to an observer whose wise and cryptic insights have intrigued me for more than 15 years.

Marc Faber,[4] a man with a truly global perspective and an uncanny knack for not losing sight of the forest for the trees, has made innumerable appearances in *Barron's*, where he first came to my attention. In a recent piece, Faber addresses the question of whether Nasdaq, which is dominated by technology companies, is overvalued and, if so, by how much. The answer to the first part of the question (it won't come as a shock to you) is yes. To get a fix on just how overvalued that wild-and-woolly market is, he recited a little history.

Launched in 1971 with a value of 100, the composite index, he recounts, never topped 200 until 1982. By 1990 it was still below 500. In 1995 it eclipsed 1000 for the first time and, three years later, reached 2000. After that, it really went stratospheric, soaring above 5000 this past March.

"Never before in the history of financial markets," notes Faber with a touch of awe, "has there been such a highly priced large market as the Nasdaq."

Okay, after that quick background sketch he gets down to the nitty-gritty of determining what a proper valuation would be for Nasdaq. Based on current earnings of something in the neighborhood of $25 billion, he reckons the index should be valued between 800 and 1500. Faber explains that his forecast assumes that earnings either linger around where they are (which would drop the index to 800) or

---

[4][2006, *Speculative Contagion*] Dr. Marc Faber was born in Zurich, Switzerland. He was schooled in Geneva and Zurich and finished high school with the Matura (a small group that tested as gifted). He studied economics at the University of Zurich and, at age 24, obtained his PhD in economics *magna cum laude*. Since 1973 he has lived in Hong Kong. From 1978 to February 1990, he was managing director of Drexel Burnham Lambert (HK) Ltd. In June 1990 he set up his own business, Marc Faber Limited, which acts as an investment advisor, fund manager, and broker/dealer. He is well known for his *Gloom Boom & Doom Report*.

rise to around $40 billion before suffering some major disappointments (which means Nasdaq would be cut "only" in half from present levels).

Another way to assess the future of Nasdaq, he adds, is to assume that it will give back all the gains garnered in the previous five years. That, as it happens, is the average experience of U.S. stocks in [secular] bear markets. If the past is a prologue for Nasdaq, Faber figures, the index eventually will drop to around 1000.[5] In sum, by any sensible yardstick, Nasdaq remains incredibly inflated and has light-years to go before it bottoms out. To be sure, the Internet and all that it means in the new millennium is a great aphrodisiac for many investors—and Nasdaq, the Viagra of the financial world, may well stay up longer than it has any right to. "Yours till Viagra falls" could well become the updated inscription of choice in yearbooks as high school seniors "anticipate" their senior years.

While Faber's perspective is top-down—and is helpful to us in framing our investment decisions—at the end of the day, we're still most at home in our bottom-up price-in-relationship-to-value paradigm. If we don't know what something is worth, how can we possibly determine whether the price is expensive or cheap? Is Microsoft a long-term-investment candidate at its current price of $44, down from a high of $119 in 1999? It sells for 27 times earnings, though as the section on accounting explains [omitted from *Speculative Contagion* and *A Decade of Delusions*], those numbers contain both fire and smoke. We ask ourselves, particularly in view of the maturation of the PC market, what will be the growth drivers for the company five or 10 years from now? More fundamentally, will its energizing options-based compensation culture implode, with some lag, along with the share price? Will

---

[5][2006, *Speculative Contagion*] The Nasdaq index hit 1114 on October 9, 2002, a 78 percent decline from its high in March 2000. It had since rebounded to the 2056 level as of the end of June 2005. This is still 59 percent below its high reached more than five years earlier. If that same metric was applied to the S&P 500, it would have to plunge to a devastating, and eerily coincidental, 500 to retrace its steps from where it began five years before the peak. In very approximate dollars, that would imply a drop in the aggregate market value of U.S. equity securities from the current $17 trillion to around $7 trillion. We are not prepared to comment on the consequences of such an occurrence except to say they would almost certainly be calamitous.

Bill Gates & Co. be able to acquire and hold the talent that has made them a stunning success story in the information revolution as their industry matures and their rewards systems regress toward the mean? Will they be able to monopolize the new venues, into which they are forced to migrate to sustain their growth, as they have the market for operating-systems software?[6]

There is no doubt in our thinking that information technology will remain the fastest-growing segment of the U.S. economy *until* overwhelmed by genetic technology, which is nipping at its heels. Growth, however, is but one component of the value equation. Capitalizing on rapid-growth industries, as the Internet speculators have so painfully discovered, is often fraught with more peril than prize. Easy money is an oxymoron. It is most unlikely that we, as wealth managers, will be placing big bets on little companies attempting to find their niche along the frontiers of science. We think hitting a homer once every hundred times at bat, with dozens of strikeouts in between, will not get us an invitation to the Hall of Fame. We're content to concentrate on singles and doubles. Mixing metaphors (although staying with sports), it's analogous to golfers "driving for show, putting for dough."

Many "Internet" businesses are much closer to traditional media and distribution businesses than their staunchest supporters were willing to admit only months ago. In this context, we may be searching the trash heap for viable business models. In most cases, however, we are increasingly finding "old economy" companies dominating the so-called

---

[6][2006, *Speculative Contagion*] All market prices that follow reflect Microsoft's two-for-one stock split in February 2003. Microsoft now trades around $26, down from its high of $60 and up from a low of $22, compared with $22 when this footnote was originally written in late 2000. With a mountain of cash building and few opportunities to reinvest it all in businesses that enjoy economics even close to the 40 percent operating margins of the Windows/Office juggernaut, Microsoft decided to repatriate some of the spoils of its enormous success. In mid-2004 Microsoft announced a payout of $75 billion to shareholders over the next four years through stock repurchases ($30 billion), a special dividend ($32 billion), and an increased annual dividend ($3.5 billion). Parenthetically, the Bill and Melinda Gates Foundation had a net worth of $27 billion at the end of 2004 and paid out $1.5 billion in grants to charities during the year. The foundation focuses on leveling the playing field, in both global health and education, among other endeavors. The aging prodigy, now 50 years old, continues to distinguish himself inside and outside the business world.

"Internet space." It seems that having an established customer base, a brand name, a physical infrastructure, and an old-fashioned know-how are still of use in the twenty-first century.

Is There a Snowball Rolling Our Way, Gathering Mass and Speed?

Of more immediate concern is the possibility that the massive erosion of wealth that has occurred in the last nine months will precipitate an unexpected economic slowdown or worse after this longest of peace-time expansions. The plethora of recent earnings downgrades from companies representing a broad cross-section of corporate America gives us pause. The acid test will be how the stock market, and later the economy, will respond to what surely will be a kinder, gentler Federal Reserve policy in the months ahead.[7] While we haven't seen it mentioned in print, we don't rule out the possibility that the Fed may find itself pushing on a string. Make no mistake about it, what may be transpiring is as much about the endgame of a once-in-a-generation speculative orgy as it is about the reverse wealth effect. Katie, bar the door if they complement one another. Serious investors would do well to ponder the wisdom of Benjamin Graham as excerpted from a 1934 edition of *Security Analysis* and Graham's memoirs. The speculative pendulum is clearly swinging back toward sanity. How far and how long it swings remains the pertinent question. While the catharsis is under way, capital preservation must take precedence over capital enhancement.

Accordingly, despite lower market yields, we will not depart from our practice of owning only the highest-grade fixed-income securities of relatively short duration. We will venture forth from that safe harbor, as we did last year, only when compelling opportunities appear in equity-type investments in which we can reasonably expect to earn considerably higher returns, consistent with our aversion to assuming anything more than moderate risk, as we define it. We will look forward with one eye and backward with the other, keeping close watch on the

---

[7][2006, *Speculative Contagion*] Greenspan & Co. and company cut the Fed funds rate 13 times since then, to 1 percent, the lowest since 1958. Fiscal policy has been complementary in the extreme. June 2004 started a round of rate increases that bumped the rate up to 3.25 percent as of midyear 2005.

path and size of the snowball rolling toward us, a metaphor on which we expand as we attempt to debunk the "Baby Boomer" myth in the section titled "Baby Boomers: Whither Goest Thou?" Lest we forget, there *is* a contraposition to the aphorism, "A rising tide lifts all ships."

The Art/Science of Managing Risk

Before we can attempt to argue that we are capable of managing risk, we must first define it. As you will see, there are two conspicuously different definitions in use today. First, *Webster's New World Dictionary* renders precise the meaning of risk as a noun meaning "the chance of injury, damage, or loss; dangerous chance, hazard," and as a verb, "to expose to the chance of injury, damage, or loss." Second, MPT, which emerged out of academia in the 1950s and is highly quantitative in its approach to portfolio management, defines risk as "relative market-price volatility." It presumes that markets are efficient and that investors respond rationally to various stimuli; thus greater company-specific uncertainty (returning to the *Webster's* definition) will be reflected in greater market-price volatility than the norm. The term MPT practitioners use to quantify such volatility is *beta*. The S&P 500, the benchmark, has a *beta* of one. Stocks with *betas* greater than one are considered riskier than those with *betas* less than one. Obviously, the greater the variance, the greater the risk.

At first glance, reconciling the two perspectives does not appear to be overly difficult. However, upon closer inspection, serious questions arise. First, *beta* is deemed to be a constant, regardless of price. Because MPT advocates believe that markets are largely efficient—that is, the current price is an accurate reflection of the value of the business based on all available information—risk should not be price-related. Speaking of price, in other words, on March 10 when Priceline.com (Figure 3.2) peaked at $162 per share, it was no more risky than it is at its current price of $1.50.[8] That's where they lost us! To be sure, such

---

[8][2006, *Speculative Contagion*] Priceline.com effected a "smoke and mirrors" one-for-six reverse stock split in 2003. As a result, it currently trades for $21, compared with a split-adjusted high of $975 in May 1999 and a low of $7 in December 2000 and October 2002 (a decrease of 99 percent from high to low!). Priceline delivered its first net profit in 2003 of $12 million on revenues of $850 million.

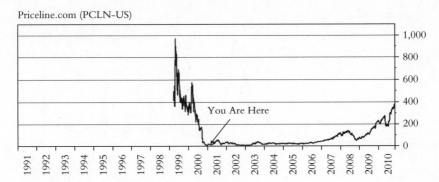

Priceline.com (PCLN–US)

You Are Here

Figure 3.2 Priceline.com Stock Price History
SOURCE: © FactSet Research Systems.

extreme volatility leads one to wonder about the presumed rationality of the investors whose buying and selling in the marketplace set the market-clearing price at both extremes and at all prices in between. Is it possible that a company's fortunes can change so drastically in such a short period of time? Or, heaven forbid, are investors inclined to act irrationally on occasion, thus casting doubts about the efficacy of market efficiency as a primary tenet of the widely embraced MPT?

The "chance of loss" can be broken down further into semidiscrete elements. First, there is business risk, which is largely a function of our free-enterprise system. Our economy is designed to compete away excess profits, usually via lower prices and/or product innovation. Mismanagement also can bring no end of trouble to otherwise fine businesses. Further, there is financial risk, the often catastrophic downside of the excessive use of borrowed money to fund the purchase of assets. And there is valuation risk. Realistically, there is absolutely no way that the future growth prospects of EMC (Figure 3.3) justify a price-earnings ratio of 125. Period.[9] On the other hand, if you pay too much for Coca-Cola, the longer you hold it, the less you

---

[9][2006, *Speculative Contagion*] After eclipsing $100 in the fall of 2000, EMC swooned to $3 and change in the fall of 2002. It currently trades around $14, and with the return of positive earnings in late 2003, the stock still trades at a relatively robust P/E multiple of 34.

EMC (EMC-US)

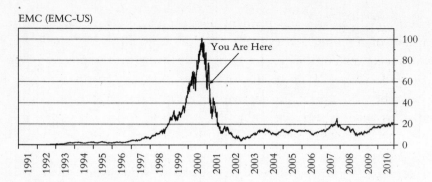

Figure 3.3   EMC Stock Price History

SOURCE: © FactSet Research Systems.

will be penalized for being impetuous.[10] Ultimately, earnings-per-share growth will make you look smart.

The diagram in Figure 3.4 helps to graphically illustrate essential elements of our argument. The left-to-right, upward-sloping, solid linear curve—our approximation of a point value for intrinsic worth over time—is what differentiates our investment approach from those who are inclined toward MPT. It assumes, almost presumptuously, that the marketplace is not the final arbiter of value but that we, and

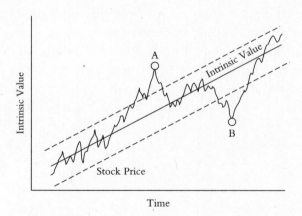

Figure 3.4   MCM Hypothetical Valuation Risk Illustration

---

[10][2010] Refer to Coca-Cola's price chart in Chapter 1, Figure 1.1.

others of a similarly independent and presumably rational bent, are
capable of reaching a reasonable conclusion about a company's value
without the market's help. To be sure, this is the most critical element
of our decision-making model, upon which everything else hinges. It
should be no surprise that deriving it places more rigorous demands
on us as analysts than any other of our activities or, for that matter,
any other analytical approaches should we choose to pursue them. The
gaps between the "value line"—a representation that in reality is never
linear—and the dashed lines on either side are known as the "confidence interval." The wider the gap, the more uncertain we are about
our estimate of intrinsic value; in like manner, the narrower the gap,
the more confident we are of such estimates. Most companies with
high levels of business or financial risk simply don't make it through
our rather exacting filters. The confidence interval would be too wide
for us to find any practical utility in the idea.

Valuation risk, as implied above, is more problematic. The more
linear and upward-sloping the intrinsic-value line, the greater the degree
of confidence in extrapolating it well into the future; the tightness of
the confidence interval around it mitigates valuation risk for long-term
investors. But few businesses offer that optimal package of investment
attributes. In reality, most lines are not nearly so straight or steep in
slope—nor is the future so certain or the confidence interval so tight.
Only government bonds provide similar certainty, and they yield 5.1
percent, well below our threshold of required rate of return for equities.
Working under those conditions of more frequently encountered uncertainty is not without its justification and rewards (as described in the
following paragraph). That's where the concept of "margin of safety"
comes into play. You'll notice that point B on the diagram is well below
the intrinsic-value line immediately above. The spread between what
we think a business is worth and the price at which it sells in the marketplace constitutes what might also be called a "margin for error." If
our analysis of business, financial, or valuation risk proves to be optimistic, and it becomes necessary to shift the intrinsic-value line downward
or flatten its slope (or both), the discounted purchase price gives us a
safety cushion to minimize the consequences of our error. Conversely,
point A, purchasing a company when it is wildly popular, affords none
of the advantages implicit in point B.

There is a corollary to the preceding thesis that appears to us to be
entirely logical but puts us at risk of being called heretics. If the corollary

is to be believed, it turns on its head the tenet that high risk is the only means to high return. In other words, from our perspective, the world is no longer flat! For the long-term investor who is sensitive to the relationship between price and value, point B affords not only a margin of safety (i.e., lower risk), but the holding-period total return is likely to be greater than the growth rate in intrinsic value as well. As I hope is clear by now, point A promises above-average risk and below-average expected return, unless heroic assumptions are made about an upward shift in the value line. That's what we meant when we said, "If we carefully manage risk, the returns will take care of themselves." Comfortable now in our role as nonconformists, we must confess that MPT's use of price volatility as a measure of risk can be for us, as long-term investors, a measure of opportunity. The greater the volatility, the wider the vertical spread between points A and B is likely to be. If we insist on a significant margin of safety at the time of purchase, above-average volatility may well provide above-average returns. Rather simple, when you ponder it awhile.

Those engaged in investment activities more closely associated with shorter-term speculation are well advised to operate under the high-risk/high-return paradigm. Of course, last year's aberration in technology and Internet issues proves that it is possible from time to time to have the deadly combination of high risk and low return.

A significant portion of whatever advantage we gained over mainstream thinking last year arose because we were able to buy the businesses we longed to own below their intrinsic value. That doesn't happen every year. As with the CEOs of the businesses we own, we cannot escape the reality that capital allocation is a critical and unavoidable responsibility. If long-term returns are determined by the long-term performance of the asset, then we can logically expect to enjoy above-average returns by allocating capital to businesses that earn superior returns on capital, provided we are careful not to be goaded by the seductiveness of popular sentiment into paying too high a price.

Capital Markets in a Larger Perspective

With the proliferation of media sources for financial and market information, rather than regurgitate what has already been digested, in this section we will devote more space to our assessment of the *whys* than the *whats*.

It is a generally accepted orthodoxy within the profession of money management to categorize firms as specialists in this or that, like so many different toy soldiers, some with torch to cannons' wicks and others with bayonets in place, some on horseback, others afoot. The list of possible subsets of investment specialists must number in the hundreds. Those who control the distribution channels to individual and institutional investors alike call the tune, and it's a medley of choices, enough to boggle the mind. It has been a burgeoning market. We hope the investors themselves ultimately prosper to the same extent as the promoters.

Our inclination is to look at all the pieces as parts of a bigger puzzle. As has been argued on these pages in the past, a bond is nothing more in its essential form than a stock with a fixed dividend and a specified maturity date and price. Accordingly, as wealth managers, we view stocks and bonds as interchangeable. Since relatively short-term, highest-grade, fixed-income securities are, as risk is defined elsewhere, the safest marketable securities available to us, we treat them as the "default class." Nonetheless yielding, with some reluctance, to convention, we will discuss the debt and equity market separately.

Fixed-Income Securities Telling One Story . . .

Despite a similarity in form with common stocks, a bond's designated purpose is to protect capital and produce income. Keeping things simple for the moment, a bond purchased at par promises no chance for profit beyond the coupon earned. Of course, we understand that fluctuations in interest rates or upgrades or downgrades in the credit quality of the instrument will affect the market price, and profitable (or unprofitable) trades can be made to capitalize on those changes. In point of fact, declining interest rates in 2000 resulted in rising prices for fixed-income securities, precisely the opposite outcome experienced in 1999. The interest-rate forecasting record of economists has been so abysmal over the years that we deem it unwise to make big interest-rate bets. In addition, there are esoteric fixed-income, security-management techniques designed to juice out a slightly higher total return or meet a defined purpose. We have created synthetic annuities where the fit was ideal, but generally we leave the exotic stuff to others.

The long-term investor might be well advised to think of a bond as a security that offers no upside (assuming it's not a convertible bond) and unlimited downside. The best a bond can do is provide timely interest and principal payments; at its worst, it can default and leave you with little or nothing (long after the courts and the attorneys are through). To realize the full benefit of the semiannual coupon and the ultimate redemption at par—all that the bond indenture promises— we make no compromise on credit quality. Almost without exception, every fixed-income security we have purchased is either a direct obligation to the U.S. Treasury or, in the case of pre-refunded or escrowed-to-maturity municipal bonds, it is backed by U.S. Treasuries. If we should choose to compromise on credit quality, we (in effect) would be taking equity-type risks with little chance of a big payoff that common stocks have the potential of providing. When we assume equity-type risks, we do so in equity-type securities.

Falling interest rates were especially kind to the owners of the highest-quality fixed-income securities in 2000, as the total returns from your U.S. Treasury and pre-refunded or escrowed-to-maturity municipal bonds exceeded their coupon income. Despite the more favorable interest-rate environment, owners of instruments of lower quality were rendered a cruel judgment by the markets, with prices reacting negatively to deteriorating credit quality. As evidence of another market dichotomy, market yields on junk bonds rose while prices fell when, simultaneously, Treasury securities yields and prices were marching in precisely the opposite direction.

The creditworthiness of U.S. corporations has been in nearly as steep a free fall as the Nasdaq—and for much the same reason: earnings that have failed to meet investors' previous heady expectations. That points to a rising tide of defaults, especially among junk companies. "We've seen a notable decline in credit quality and an excess of downgrades versus upgrades in the last couple of years," says economist John Puchalla, one of the authors of a new report from Moody's Investors Service. The report adds that even better-rated companies have become vulnerable, having borrowed heavily for equity buybacks, mergers and acquisitions, and capital spending.

Barron's Editor Alan Abelson makes these observations, with more than a dollop of satire:

As it happens, corporate buybacks lagged as the year wore on, but that's easily explainable: Companies like to buy back stock only when its price is soaring. Otherwise, the reminder of how the value of their options is shrinking is too painful for the sensitive officers and directors to bear. That billions of dollars of earlier buybacks they authorized are now underwater may have had something to do with the reduced pace of repurchasing, too, although such picayune considerations never stopped them before.

Default rates are in fact rising, and there has been no sign of a letup this year, especially from shakier issuers that sold debt in the more relaxed credit environment of 1997 and 1998. By the end of 2001, Moody's predicts, 8.4 percent of the junk debt now outstanding will default.

Standard & Poor's also has issued a report forecasting record corporate defaults this year. "Due to the volume of outstanding debt by financially weak companies, we expect defaults to remain high for the next year and the best part of 2002," the company says. So far, $37.7 billion of debt is affected, and S&P expects the total to grow.[11]

The junk-bond market, accordingly, calls for issuers to cough up roughly 13 percent on their new offerings, as well as throw in equity kickers composed of units with warrants for the issuing company. Even investment-grade companies have found borrowing more expensive. The Morgan Stanley Dean Witter Industrials index, which tracks spreads on 5-, 10-, and 30-year investment-grade bonds, stood at 2.17 percentage points over Treasuries in the latest week, up from 2.10 percentage points the previous week. The index is now well above the 1.80 percentage-point spread evident during the 1998 global financial crisis. At year-end the 10-year Treasury note yielded 5.11 percent.

Risk tolerance by investors is wearing thin. An extreme example of the current travails is NorthPoint Communications Group, whose acquisition by Verizon was canceled last week after the DSL provider

---

[11][2006, *Speculative Contagion*] According to Moody's Investors Services, global bond defaults peaked in 2002 at $100 billion. From there, defaults declined sharply to a still high $16 billion in 2004. [2010 update: Global bond defaults reached a record $328 billion in 2009.]

had to restate its third–quarter earnings to reflect nonpayment by its cus-tomers. As part of the deal agreed to on August 7, Verizon was to make an $800 million cash investment in NorthPoint, of which it has already made $150 million. With that no longer happening, NorthPoint's $400 million of 12⅞ percent senior notes due 2010 plunged 52 points last week to just 10.5 cents on the dollar. As recently as the end of October, NorthPoint's junk bonds were quoted at 94. (There are similar horror stories in the low–grade sector of the municipal-bond market as well.)

. . . and Common Stocks Telling Another

For the year, the Dow Jones industrial average was down 6.2 percent, its biggest drop since 1981. For all the volatility in other markets, the average actually traded in a fairly narrow band between 10000 and 11000 for much of the year 2000. The Standard & Poor's 500 stock index dropped 10.1 percent, its greatest swoon since 1977's 11.5 percent decline. Microsoft's impact on the S&P was huge last year. The stock's 63 percent plunge accounted for nearly 30 percent of the index's decline, owing to its market-leading weighting at the start of 2000. Despite the S&P's loss last year, some 249 out of 444 stocks that were in the index at the start of 2000 had actually advanced through December 27, according to analysts at Ned Davis Research in Venice, Florida. The Ned Davis calculations don't include the 56 stocks added to the index this year. Excluding technology stocks, the S&P was down just 0.3 per-cent through December 27, and the median stock gained 10.2 percent. And the Nasdaq composite index fell 39.1 percent in 2000 to end the year at 2470, less than half of its March 10 high of 5049—and its worst showing ever since the index's founding in 1971. At its low of 2333, the Nasdaq had given back most of its prodigious gains achieved over the last two years (it had closed 1998 at 2193).

The market action last year amounted to the reverse of what hap-pened in 1999, when the Nasdaq soared 85 percent, and technology was about the only place to be. During 1999 the S&P 500 rose 19.5 percent but was up just 4 percent when tech issues were excluded, says Ned Davis Research. And despite the index's strong performance, the breadth in the S&P was worse in 1999 than 2000: Fewer than half the stocks in the index rose during 1999, while the median stock fell 2.1 percent.

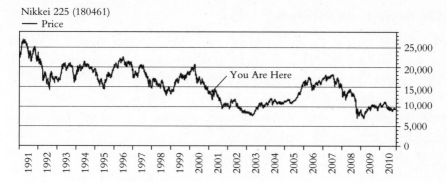

Figure 3.5   Nikkei 225 Stock Price History
Source: © FactSet Research Systems.

Foreign stocks, long ballyhooed by financial intermediaries as an essential ingredient for diversified portfolios, did little to further that argument in 2000. As a representative of Latin America, Mexico's Bolsa index declined 21.5 percent in dollars. As for Europe, Bloomberg's European 500 index fell 10.2 percent in dollars and 17 percent in the faltering Euro. The Pacific Rim's largest market, Japan, saw its Nikkei 225 index (Figure 3.5) plunge 27.2 percent in dollars, 34.7 percent in yen, to 13785.[12] Those with long memories will recall that the Nikkei peaked in 1989 at 39000. We've always been homebodies—and find life easier and our wallets thicker as a result. Besides, mindless imitation of others has never been our style.

The relationship between the total market value of all U.S. common stocks and GDP, until recently, was off the charts, paralleling the Japanese stock market and underlying economy in the late 1980s. Such extreme valuations cause us to shiver just a little. What the data tell us is that despite the great damage done to numerous sectors, this American market by any historical or rational yardstick is still no bargain.

---

[12][2006, *Speculative Contagion*] The Nikkei 225 hit a low of 7607 on April 28, 2003. As of June 30, 2005, it had rebounded to 11584.

The Stock/Bond Dichotomy

We simply can't shake ourselves of the compulsion to view the capital markets as a whole. The corporate-bond market is pricing in a rather high probability that companies will default. The stock market, despite its recent slide, continues to boast historically high valuations. Something doesn't compute here, obviously, since the same earnings that go to equity holders can be used to service debt payments. The quixotic differences in the actions of stocks and bonds tell very different stories.

But it also occurs to us that some of the most robust performers in the equity markets are not overly burdened with earnings either, so their high valuations may be accompanied by equally high probability that they'll default on their obligations. Bridgewater Associates, a highly regarded research firm that invariably asks "why," recently cited Amazon.com as an example of a company on which the stock and bond markets awarded strikingly different valuations. The company had a market cap of some $10 billion ($6.4 billion at year end), down from $50 billion but still quite noteworthy.

Amazon had around $2 billion in corporate debt outstanding. Of that tidy sum, its nonconvertible obligations due in 2008 were trading at nearly 50 cents on the dollar, offering a yield of over 16.5 percent (which, as noted above, is somewhat above that on the 10-year Treasury yield).

Observes Bridgewater: "The bond market is saying, in effect, that there's a 54 percent chance 'the company goes belly-up.' Which isn't exactly consonant with the stock market's insistence that Amazon.com is worth $10 billion." In a sense, Bridgewater commented, in seeking to explicate the paradox of such contradictory valuations, Amazon is a "microcosm of what's happening in the overall equity and debt markets. The debt markets are pricing in significantly high probabilities of default, while the equity markets show little concern." As the year wore on, the equity markets became a little more observant![13]

---

[13][2006, *Speculative Contagion*] Amazon.com has expanded its merchandising from books to almost everything else. In a sense, it is a proxy for the efficacy of online retailing, which commanded 2.2 percent of retail sales by midyear 2005 versus 0.9 percent in 2000. A shockingly low conversion rate of 4.9 percent—the ratio of visitors to a site who will actually make a purchase—continues to be problematic

Baby Boomers: Whither Goest Thou?

Undoubtedly, the most common and adamantly expressed argument I have heard over the last several years in justification of a perpetual cornucopia of stock market riches has as its central thesis the ever-expanding flood of money from the coffers of the Baby Boomers flowing into the stock market. While generally considered even-tempered and understanding, I found that the absurdity of that notion was usually enough to get my juices flowing. First, it focused entirely on demand, with no regard for supply. That most elementary of economic equations, as apparently was overlooked, has two sides. It is price that reconciles the two. Second, and a bit more subtle, is that, metaphorically speaking, in pushing an ever-growing snowball up a hill, it takes more and more muscle for each inch of new territory gained. At some point, the snowball's mass is greater than the muscle behind it. If new muscle doesn't arrive soon, the monstrous snowball may, well, snowball, and start rolling back down the hill. That, perhaps, is the question of the moment. Early returns would suggest that you stay out of its path. [This brings to mind the fate of poor Sisyphus of Greek mythology who was eternally condemned to push a rock up a hill, only to have it roll back down before ever reaching the top. Maybe it's the metaphorical Boomer snowball/rock . . . and Generation X just may end up being Sisyphus.]

According to the *Wall Street Journal* articles, new cash flowing into stock mutual funds dropped 54 percent in November—the biggest monthly decline in nearly two years—as investors, stung by falling stock prices, started voting with their wallets. The decline in new stock-fund money was the steepest since February 1999, when the market was still recovering from the global financial crisis.

The preference for safety was underscored by investors' growing attraction to money-market funds, conservative vehicles that gain about 5 percent or 6 percent a year, regardless of gyrations in the stock market. That is especially appealing this year with the average stock fund

---

for the industry. Moreover, traditional store-based and catalog retailers are providing intense competition for the virtual stores. [2010 update: Please refer to Amazon's price chart in Chapter 1, Figure 1.4.]

down 5.8 percent, according to Morningstar, Inc., the Chicago fund tracker. In November, for the second month in a row, investors stuffed more money into the cashlike funds than they put into stock portfolios. The final figure came out to $56.19 billion, more than double October's $26 billion total and the highest intake for money-market funds since January 1999.

Indeed, enthusiasm for the stock market appeared to be fading fast in December, too. "We're ending the year on a low-key note," said Steve Norwitz, a spokesman for T. Rowe Price Associates, Inc., a Baltimore fund firm. In both November and December, he said, the pace of new money coming into the company's stock funds had slowed to a crawl. The firm expected the figures to end December flat, meaning that no net new money will have come into the stock funds.

One area out of favor and staying that way is international funds. Stock funds that invest abroad lost $2.88 billion to investor desertions in November, up from $206 million in October, according to the ICI (Investment Company Institute).

What about the "Smart" Money?

Steve Leuthold, sage of the Leuthold Group, reports that through July 2000, insider selling of big blocks of stock, which he defines as at least $1 million worth (or 100,000 shares or more), weighed in at $43.1 billion. That's twice as much as sold in the comparable time spans of 1998 and 1999. As a matter of fact, Leuthold notes, this year's insider dumping in the first half tops the record $39 billion similarly disposed of in all of 1999. And, he warns, judging by filings with the SEC, there's plenty more where that came from: "Mother always told us, 'Don't fight the Fed or bearish insiders.'"

The Internet and IPO Frenzy

Internet analysts were the newest masters of Wall Street's universe. With stunning regularity, they would make an outrageous prediction that, within a year, a stock would double or triple or better—and watch gleefully as the stock sometimes did that in a month. This encouraged the analysts to make even more eye-popping forecasts, which many did (to their great embarrassment today, as most of those stocks now sell for a tiny fraction of the price when the predictions were made).

Then there was the great IPO frenzy. Despite warnings that initial public offerings are risky by their very nature because most IPO companies are so new, investors clamored for them—not just some IPOs but almost all of them. And why not, given that many were doubling on their first day? Many of those highfliers have since imploded, with about two-thirds trading below their offering price—and lots of them way below. Many doubled or tripled or more from the offering price as neophyte investors jumped aboard the train pulling rapidly out of the station. The overall losses, therefore, were far greater.[14]

Fool's Gold

Last year, taking stock for payment from dot-com start-ups seemed like the path to Internet riches. Maybe it wasn't so brilliant after all. Not long ago, Web designers, lawyers, executive recruiters, landlords, celebrities, professional athletes, and others with goods or services to offer technology start-ups were accepting—in some cases demanding—stock in lieu of, or on top of, cash for their services to up-and-coming companies. It turns out that many ended up with fool's gold. This and the two paragraphs above remind us of two things: (1) that memories are short and (2) an axiom as old and inviolable as the inevitability of death and taxes: "There is no free lunch."

---

[14][2006, *Speculative Contagion*] The supercharged and frenetic IPO market was a symptom of the speculative Bubble. Its absence from the investment landscape is likewise indicative of the ever-swinging pendulum of investor sentiment. According to available records, bankers priced 543 IPOs in 1999. During 2000, 2001, and 2002, a total of 431, 96, and 85 IPOs, respectively, were brought to market. Seven IPOs had been priced from January 1 through June 6, 2003. The pace picked up after the first half of 2003 as a total of 79 companies went public for the full year. There were 233 IPOs in 2004. The lyrics of Willie Nelson's "On the Road Again" are ringing in my ears. . . . The IPO gang is once again on tour, providing disquieting anecdotal evidence (like mutual-fund cash ratios discussed later) that all is not well with the investor who prefers to buy low so that he might sell high.

Are There Underwater Mines Everywhere?

In a word, no. We were able to find opportunities, or perhaps it was their falling prices that found us during a year with more crosscurrents than a competitive kayaking course. We believe that generally it will be the headwinds that will prevail, and we will respond accordingly. In the discussion on investment strategy that follows, we will explain how we hope to tack gingerly and cautiously upwind. We would prefer a howling broad reach, but the winds have shifted. We can't control the gales, but we can trim the sails.

Goliaths Slain

Many shall be restored that now are fallen, and many shall fall that now are in honor.

Horace in *Ars Poetica*

Thus appeared the prophetic keynote quotation on the first page of the first edition of the investment classic, *Security Analysis*, published in the darkest depths of the Depression in 1934. The following contemporary eulogy is brimming with insights about how money has been managed—or mismanaged—by the biggest and most prestigious hedge funds in the world. It is also a cautionary tale of the rise and fall of two famed financial-market luminaries.

To begin, these two men—Julian Robertson Jr. and George Soros—are not contemporary scoundrels, nor were they poured from the same mold as the robber barons of old. To be sure, they were major league speculators, both as bright as they were bold and sometimes brash, yet not so superhuman in the end as to be invulnerable to the risks inherent in those high-stakes and even higher-profile games of chance for which they were so well known.

Julian Robertson Jr.

Value manager Julian Robertson Jr., the courtly 67-year-old North Carolinian, guided Tiger Management to resounding success since its inception in 1980. Twelve months ago, we had this to say about the

value manager's dilemma, quoting from his December 1998 letter to the
clients of Tiger Management:

> . . . [T]he Internet is a great new technology that will change
> our lives. But there have been other great developments that
> created equally important lifestyle changes. In the past, inves-
> tors overreacted to the promise of these changes. . . . We're in a
> wild, runaway technology frenzy; meantime most other stocks
> are in the state of collapse. I have never seen such a dichotomy.
> There will be a correction. As to whether or not this correc-
> tion will take the form of a total market collapse as in 1929,
> 1973–1974, and 1987, I have doubts. Why? The out-of-phase
> stocks are just too cheap. . . . [T]his would imply a long-term
> underperformance of technology (believe it or not, it has hap-
> pened) while the rest of the market continues to advance. Of
> course, this would be the ideal situation.

A few momentous months later, on March 30, 2000, the same
week the market sounded the death knell for DrKoop.com, Robertson
shocked the investment world as he closed down his hedge funds after
18 years of stellar returns and two years of disaster. His lifetime record
will always be remembered with awe. Robertson turned his original
grubstake of $8 million in 1980 into a personal fortune estimated at
a billion dollars, even after the April setbacks. His investors reputedly
enjoyed annual returns over that period of 25 percent (or so he says).
Then, in the 18 months preceding his announcement—an agonizing
time for value investors—Tiger proceeded to give back half of the gains
it had built up over the previous 18 years. While Wall Street neophytes
and veterans alike cleaned up in technology issues, Tiger shunned
the Internet and stuck largely to old-economy stocks such as General
Motors, Unisys, and US Airways.[15]

His decision to close up shop has occasioned a great outpouring
of commentary, much of it finding fault with one thing or another.

---

[15][2006, *Speculative Contagion*] Unfortunately, Robertson's old-economy largest
stock picks didn't fare well either. General Motors travails were described in an
earlier footnote. US Airways emerged from Chapter 11 bankruptcy in March
2003, only to reenter bankruptcy in September 2004 with hopes of a reemer-
gence in the fall of 2005. Unisys fell from $50 in 2000 to a current low of $6.

Nobody, though, seems to find fault with his indignant refusal to participate in the bull market for technology stocks. Rather, he has been treated as a tragic hero because his adherence to the "value" rule went unrewarded, while money managers who shamelessly chased tech stocks were treated to vast returns. Instead, he is castigated for letting his $23 billion fund get too big to move in and out of companies without roiling the share price, for neglecting good opportunities because they were too small to make a difference, for forsaking stocks to dabble in the occasional bet on interest rates or currencies . . . though his "macro" performance was no less mixed than the other victim of whom I write shortly.

In announcing that he would liquidate his funds and give back his investors' money, Robertson admitted that he is "out of step with a world in which Palm, the maker of the handheld Palm Pilot, is valued at more than GM and in which Priceline.com, which sells airline tickets but has neither earnings nor planes, was valued at more than US Airways [a company that brought Berkshire Hathaway acute, although ultimately temporary, pain and in which he held a commanding 22 percent interest] and most of the other publicly traded airlines combined."

Sadly, for those investors who embraced the Priceline.com story as evidence of both the despair and disillusionment that had overcome Robertson at that moment, the prophetic insights that he so often exhibited were disregarded. The price line that Priceline.com stock tracked has not been unlike the attitude of a plane before and after it "stalls." The stratosphere-bound shares of the popular and creative auctioneer of airline tickets, hawked on television by celebrity spokesman William Shatner, perhaps selected because of the public's familiarity with him as an icon from the era of science-fiction fascination, in the end proved that some ideas are, indeed, more fiction than fact when profitability is used as the standard of measure. During the very same week that a disheartened Robertson capitulated and bemoaned the irrationality of the market, Priceline.com stock's exponential ascent finally slowed to stall speed at the altitude of $163. From there, in little over a year's time, it sped toward Earth in a death spiral, currently languishing around $2 per share, $22.5 billion in market value simply disappearing into thin air during the tailspin.[16]

---

[16][2006, *Speculative Contagion*] Priceline's market price and market penetration problems are mentioned in an earlier footnote. Palm Inc., early leader in the PDA

"DUE TO CUTBACKS AND DOWNSIZING, WE HAVE
TURNED OFF THE LIGHT AT THE END OF THE TUNNEL."

SOURCE: Copyright © 1998 Bill Monroe.

"There is no point in subjecting our investors to risk in a market which I frankly do not understand," Robertson wrote. What's more, he went on, "there is no quick end in sight . . . of the bear market

---

(personal digital assistant) market, currently sells for around $12, but only after a one-for-twenty reverse stock split necessary to artificially lift the stock price out of the "penny stock" category and avoid the limitations on ownership by certain institutions when the stock falls below a specified price. That equates to $.60 per share when compared with the price noted above. Adjusted for the split, the stock exceeded $3,000 in 2000. PDAs are falling prey to such competition as "smart telephones" or converged devices. Palm has since split itself into two operating companies. PalmOne is the maker of the PDA or hardware, while PalmSource makes the software that goes into the PDA device. Adjusting for this spin-off, the two companies' shares have rebounded to approximately a $38.25 value for the holder of both companies after the spin-off. There is now a rumor that Palm may be interested in acquiring PalmSource. [2010 update: On July 1, 2010, Hewlett-Packard Company announced it completed its acquisition of Palm, Inc., at a price of $5.70 per share of the company's common stock in cash.]

in value stocks." That conclusion, sadly for Julian Robertson, was not prophetic.

At the end of 1996, Tiger had roughly $8 billion in capital, 1,000 times its initial outlay but still a manageable pool of money. Then, in 1997, Tiger had its best year ever—up 70 percent. Overnight, Tiger became Wall Street's sensation—just as Long-Term Capital was . . . and just as high-tech funds are today. Tiger's gaudy results attracted billions of dollars from new disciples. "It was fickle money," according to a spokesman for Tiger. "You could say hot money." By August 1998, Tiger's capital had burgeoned to $22.8 billion.

Perhaps intoxicated by his record, Robertson allowed the fund's leverage to balloon to three to one, meaning total assets topped $60 billion. (Of course, leverage also had helped inflate returns on the way up.) With such a bloated portfolio, Robertson knew, as he admitted to a *Wall Street Journal* reporter, that some of his biggest holdings were illiquid. He learned of the terrifying capital erosion at Long-Term Capital, which blew up just as Tiger began to run into trouble. Nonetheless, Robertson apparently was surprised by how fast his fund came undone.

In the fall of 1998, he dropped $2 billion on Japanese yen—a misplaced speculation—and then $600 million more on Russian treasury bonds. Meanwhile, Robertson's cheap stocks kept getting cheaper. In 1999 Tiger had its worst year, losing 19 percent. In the first two months of 2000, it fell another 14 percent. The hot money that had so recently pursued Tiger took a flying leap. Some of its old money followed suit. In a relatively brief span, Tiger was forced to redeem $7.7 billion— roughly equal to its total investment and retained profits over its first 16 years. With money running for the exits and losses compounding due to leverage, Tiger had no choice but to sell favored stocks at depressed prices.

Tiger made three mistakes, dangerous in isolation and fatal in combination: It got too big, it got too exposed to withdrawals from hot-money investors, and it got too leveraged. Despite Robertson's miscalculations, his final letter proved prescient: "The current technology, Internet and telecom craze, fueled by the performance desires of investors, money managers and even financial buyers, is unwittingly creating a Ponzi pyramid destined for collapse."

Value investing never becomes irrelevant; it merely goes out of fashion from time to time. Price and value are ultimately reconciled, so the principal attribute required is patience. The flip side of adversity is opportunity. Value investing is more than just purchasing low price-to-earnings stocks as it is conventionally defined; it is also purchasing low price-to-value stocks (a big difference). If properly employed, it also imposes a longer time horizon on the investor's expectations for rewards. Julian Robertson grossly abused the value concept by piling on leverage and by not discouraging hot money from investing in his so-called value-based hedge fund. Robertson's excessive use of leverage as a value strategy was, in a business sense, a contradiction in terms. Robertson gave the impression of a conservative, vaunting his "value" approach, but in fact was a speculator because of the use of leverage and taking large bets in marginal companies or macro ideas. In the wake of the disaster, there have been some long faces lately in Mister Robertson's neighborhood.

Last year, two of the same factors (leverage and size), coupled with intellectual arrogance, felled another storied hedge fund—the aforementioned Long-Term Capital Management—whose collapse seemed on the verge of toppling all of Wall Street until the Federal Reserve hastily organized a private bailout. To be sure, there are vast differences between the two funds. Long-Term's equity was virtually wiped out, though the fund sputtered on after getting an emergency injection of capital. Tiger is liquidating at its leisure. Even with its losses, a dollar invested at Tiger's inception has grown to a total of $82 (after fees), a sensational compound rate of 25 percent a year, according to the firm. Robertson's funds are currently so far underwater that it would likely be years before he would exceed the high-water mark and earn performance fees again. His high-overhead operation would surely have exhausted his personal fortune before that day arrived.

Tiger's recent meteoric growth and subsequent implosion harbor a dire warning for today's investors, especially momentum-following mutual-fund investors who are crowding into ever-fewer, high-tech growth funds. If you think your favorite dot-com-laden mutual fund is immune, thanks to the new money that continues to pour into its coffers, remember that a short time ago Tiger was all the rage—and that was precisely its problem.

Where does this lethal combination of sizzling profits, followed by astronomical fund flows and huge, concentrated holdings exist today? For many months, tech-heavy mutual funds have been using their outsized

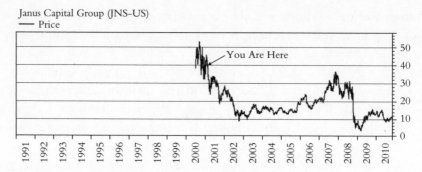

Figure 3.6 Janus Capital Group Stock Price History
SOURCE: © FactSet Research Systems.

gains to attract new money that they promptly reinvest to drive up portfolios and attract still more new money. To cite one example, Janus Capital (Figure 3.6) collected $10 billion (one-fourth of the industry total) in February alone, managing $229 billion by year end, up from $80 billion at the start of 1999. Unlike Tiger's limited partners, who could take money out only every quarter, thus facilitating an orderly closeout, mutual-fund shareholders are free to sell every day. Will these turnstile investors be any slower to exit than Tiger's were restricted to do, once the performance of growth funds inevitably cools? Put it this way: When it happens, I wouldn't want to be standing in the doorway. For an investor in inflated new-economy issues, bailing out will be the only logical move, because once momentum isn't there to hold these issues up, nothing else—surely not earnings or revenues or even voodoo bewitchment—will be. Janus, despite poor performance this year, is still sticking to its guns. As recently as October, its average price-earnings ratio was 48. We'll revisit this evolving story next year.[17]

---

[17][2006, *Speculative Contagion*] As of June 2005, Janus assets had shrunk to $130 billion, owing to stock market depreciation and heavy net redemptions by investors. Janus, whose logo is ironically the Roman god most often depicted with two faces, lived up to its namesake. Implicated in the mutual-fund trading scandals, Janus reached an agreement with regulators, setting aside $100 million to be available to compensate investors. In addition, Janus agreed to reduce its management fees by $25 million per year over the next five years.

George Soros

If Julian Robertson is the Sammy Sosa of hedge-fund managers, George Soros is the Mark McGwire. No pedestal was higher than that of Mr. Soros. A Hungarian refugee from the Holocaust, Soros, now 70 years old, started as a stock-picker in the late 1960s, moving on to "macro" investing—or betting on the broad trends that move stocks, bonds, and currencies around the globe. His style was to wait for big changes in the markets, then take advantage with aggressive moves. Although he turned over the reins of Soros Fund Management to Stanley Druckenmiller in 1989 to concentrate on philanthropy, he continued to keep close tabs on the funds. The firm kept racking up huge gains, creating amazement, even awe, among competitors. Its funds grew so powerful, using borrowed money to magnify their results that their investments moved markets, and their giant bets could be self-fulfilling. For example, in the summer of 1992, it became known that Soros funds were selling the British pound short, betting on a decline. Hearing this, other investors quickly started doing the same. The short-selling foray in the pound earned Soros the label of "the man who broke the Bank of England." He profited greatly from buying Peru's currency and from selling the Malaysian ringgit, which prompted the most insulting of political outcries from none other than the prime minister himself. Paradoxically, Druckenmiller has since said that the Soros funds actually were buying, not selling, Malaysia's currency during that time. Beginning a couple of years ago, though, this outsized influence began to wane. As global markets swelled, Soros assets—even at the $22 billion they then totaled—no longer could move markets so easily, nor necessarily give the firm access to the best information. Power shifted toward money managers, such as the previously noted Janus Capital, once a third-tier mutual-fund group but now a huge one because of its hot performance in technology stocks.

To be sure, the Soros funds had some fumbles and stumbles. They lost more than $1 billion in 1998–1999 betting that Europe's new common currency would rise. Instead, the euro has fallen 24 percent since its introduction on January 1, 1999. In addition, despite their big-picture focus, the Soros funds haven't profited from the doubling of world oil prices over the past year or so. Out of necessity, Soros migrated to the newest hot game in town, the venue that catapulted Janus into the big leagues: technology and the Internet.

In spite of larger-than-life images and egos to match, the intrigue surrounding the goings-on within the offices of the great hedge funds was almost palpable—and, at root, most predictably human. Desire for the power and prestige that massive wealth confers can quickly transmogrify into the fear from which no one, no matter how high or low his or her station, is immune. According to the *Wall Street Journal*:

> For months, through late 1999 and early 2000, the Monday afternoon research meetings at George Soros's hedge-fund firm centered on a single theme: how to prepare for the inevitable sell off of technology stocks. Druckenmiller, in charge of the celebrated funds, sat at the head of a long table in a room overlooking Central Park. Almost as if reading from a script, he would begin the weekly meetings with a warning that the sell-off could be near and could be brutal. For the next hour, the group would debate what signs to look for, what stocks to sell, how fast to sell them. "I don't like this market. I think we should probably lighten up. I don't want to go out like Steinhardt," Mr. Druckenmiller said in early March as the market soared, according to people present at the time. He was referring to Michael Steinhardt, who ended an illustrious hedge-fund career in 1995, a year after suffering big losses.

Soros himself, often traveling abroad on philanthropic endeavors, would regularly phone his top lieutenants, warning that tech stocks were a Bubble set to burst. For all the months of hand-wringing, when the sell-off finally did start in mid-March, Soros Fund Management wasn't ready for it. Still loaded with high-tech and biotechnology stocks and still betting against the so-called old economy, Soros traders watched in horror when the tech-heavy Nasdaq composite index plunged 124 points on March 15 to 4583 (that, of course, was only the beginning; by year end, it had fallen nearly 2,000 more points to close at 2634), while the once quiescent Dow Jones industrial average, also on March 15, leaped 320 points. In just five subsequent days, the Soros firm's flagship Quantum Fund saw what had been a 2 percent year-to-date gain turn into an 11 percent loss.

Continued the *Journal*: " 'Can you believe this? This is what we talked about!' cried a senior trader amid the carnage. Others on the firm's gloomy trading floor busied themselves calculating how much they had lost by aping Soros investments in their own accounts."

Soros pressed Druckenmiller to bail out of some swooning Internet stocks before they sank even farther, while Druckenmiller insisted that the funds hold on.

By the end of April, the Quantum Fund was down 22 percent since the start of the year, and the smaller Quota Fund was down 32 percent. Soros had stated in a 1995 autobiography that he was "up there" with the world's greatest money managers, but he added, "How long I will stay there is another question." Now came an answer. Both Druckenmiller and Quota Fund chief Nicholas Roditi resigned. Soros unveiled a new, lower-risk investing style—completely out of character for him—and conceded that even he found it hard to navigate today's murky markets. "Maybe I don't understand the market," a reflective Soros said at an April 28 news conference (using words of bewilderment similar to those uttered by Robertson just four weeks earlier). "Maybe the music has stopped, but people are still dancing." Soros may have exhausted his supply of useful insight when he wrote: "I used to get particularly excited when I picked up the scent of an initially self-reinforcing but eventually self-defeating process. My mouth began to water . . ."

It is paradoxical that neither of these hedge-fund giants were able to capitalize on the most spectacular speculative Bubble in modern market history. Ironically, Julian Robertson's principle-based and disciplined reluctance to participate in the public's fascination with technology did as much to savage his fund as Druckenmiller's reluctance to withdraw from the same high-tech game before it was too late.[18]

---

[18][2006, *Speculative Contagion*] As a postscript, according to TheStreet.com, George Soros's flagship Quantum Fund was 90 percent in cash by May 15, 2000, and has subsequently been reorganized to reflect a lower-risk profile. Several years ago it was reported that Soros still had $4 billion invested in the fund. The 75-year-old Soros remains ever the outspoken political and social activist. GeorgeSoros.com was established in the months leading up to the 2004 election as part of Soros's campaign to urge his fellow citizens not to reelect President Bush. In addition to the web site, Soros mailed a personal appeal to 2 million voters, purchased advertisements in more than 50 newspapers (including the *Wall Street Journal*), undertook a 12-city speaking tour, and published his views in his book *The Bubble of American Supremacy: The Cost of Bush's War in Iraq*.

According to a *U.S. News & World Report* article dated November 8, 2004, Julian Robertson has "retired" to a palatial estate on the coast of New Zealand's north island where he's planning to build a luxury lodge. The development, which features a sunset room tunneled into a nearby cliff and 24 matching chalets, is causing local birdwatchers to squawk. As luck would again have it for the former Wall Street hedge-fund manager, the lodge is apparently too close to the cliff-top sanctuary of the world's largest colony of Australasian gannets (fish-eating seabirds). For a second time he may have to say: "This nonsense is for the birds." Since his Tiger Management fund group returned its money to investors (it still exists to manage Robertson's $850 million fortune and advise other fund managers), Robertson, now 72, has put considerable time and money into the land of the kiwis. His latest passions: golf courses and vineyards.

Chapter 4

Swimming against the Current*

S&P 500 (SP50)
— Price

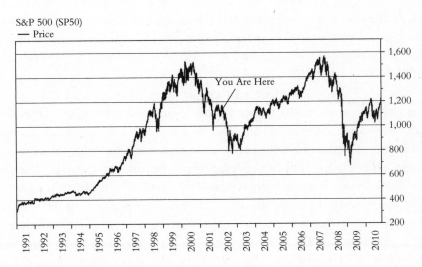

Source: © FactSet Research Systems.

---

*This material is adapted from the 2001 annual report of Martin Capital Management.

We have all made it through the minefields of the last two years looking much more gifted than we actually are, waving aside both pans and plaudits as a matter of course, taking neither seriously.

We must admit that we find it easier to seize an opportunity in the face of generalized fear than to resist temptation while under the seductive and almost irresistible forces of unsubstantiated and illogical greed fomented out of fear of falling behind the pack. The consequences of miscalculations or emotions run amok in the first instance are far less significant than those associated with the latter, as a surfeit of baneful evidence has made abundantly clear in this increasingly pervasive downcycle of the markets. We tend to frame such judgments in mathematical terms. Even though there is only one correct answer, some wrong answers are closer to being correct than others. Nonetheless, running counter to the majority is a day-in, day-out test of will, determination, and convictions.

Gazing backward even farther than a year for a moment, 1999 was particularly hard for us to comprehend or endure because of the unconscious allure of the rampant speculative contagion, the clamor from every direction for action, the epidemic of euphoria over ever-rising prices in already grossly overpriced technology and dot-com shares, the rallying cry that everyone jump aboard the bandwagon or look like a fool. To our good fortune, the latter was shouted by nearly everybody *but* our clients. Suffice it to say, the noise was deafening in the face of all that we knew to be true and conservative. There is an expression that gave some credence to our stand: "Someone who thinks logically provides a nice contrast to the real world." We would agree, though we know the injunction is grossly oversimplified. Since the outcome is never certain, the extent of the logic of one's thinking really isn't known until well after it's too late to reverse one's course. Besides, it's particularly lonely without the comfort and encouragement of the crowd. In truth, investment as we practice it is emotionally taxing: In the course of doing what we think is right, we find ourselves stepping into the fray when the current news is awful and the outlook worse, then doing an about-face and exiting when the sky seems to be the limit. This approach can feel contrary to human nature—that is, until we engage our rational mind and seek solace in the wisdom of its ways. . . .

More significant than the numbers themselves is how they were achieved. If the means we employ are irreducible elements of our philosophy, the results will have more weight, possibly more staying power than the will-o'-the-wisp approach practiced by some. While we claimed that 2000 was an aberration, we weren't motivated by some sense of false modesty to make such an assertion. We make the same claim about 2001. We aren't like "Chicken Little" football coach Lou Holtz: Give us enough time, and the full meaning of those words of caution will be known. However, if we stick to the basic elements of rational investing, it is our hope—nay, our expectation—that we won't stray too far from delivering on our goals . . . over the long haul. As our record indicates, we take "down" years in stride, so long as our longer-term compounded returns are satisfactory. You should know that no sleight of hand, IPOs, or any other tricks of the trade were used to bulk up our results.

SOURCE: Deb Leighty.

Prelude to Our Investment "Strategy"

Two and a half years ago, following a July 1999 speech by Warren Buffett on the stock market—a rarity for the Oracle of Omaha, who is far more interested in companies than composites—*Fortune* magazine (on November 22, 1999) ran what he had to say under the title "Mr. Buffett on the Stock Market." His logic confirmed mine, and so the self-edited speech was profiled in the 1999 annual report. He must have thought the *Fortune* article worth repeating because he attached it to the 2000 Berkshire Hathaway annual report. In July 2001 he gave a second speech at the same site at which, again with the help of *Fortune's* Carol Loomis (who also edits his annual report), he updated his reasoning from two years before. Don't get too excited; Buffett's "updating" is measured in centimeters, not kilometers.

As you may recall, Buffett identified two 17-year periods—first, the lean years and the second, the fat. The first began at the end of 1964 and concluded at the close of 1981; the second was 1981 to 1998. In the first, the Dow Jones industrial average ended within a fraction of a point of where it began, 875, prompting Buffett to grouse that though he is a patient fellow, *that* tested his limits. In the second span, by contrast, it closed at 9181, almost a tenfold increase. Paradoxically, during the lean years, GDP grew by 373 percent, whereas during the fat years, it rose only 177 percent. But, as you know, stock prices are influenced by variables other than just economic growth. Corporate profits, a residual, have generally ranged in the neighborhood of 4 to 6.5 percent of GDP over the last 50 years. Additionally, prevailing interest rates are part of the discounting mechanism that reduces future income to present value. They tell a story that runs counter to the impetus of the economic-growth data. Interest rates on long-term government bonds at year-end 1964, 1981, and 1998 were, respectively, 4.20 percent, 13.65 percent, and 5.09 percent.

There is a fourth variable—besides economic growth, corporate profits as a proportion of GDP, and interest rates—that holds significant sway over the course of stock prices: the aggregate psychological frame of mind of investors.

So, despite robust GDP growth during the lean market years of 1964–1981, interest rates rose dramatically, and corporate profits as a percentage of the GDP pie fell to the low end of their historical range. Investors became increasingly despondent over these double negatives and voted with their feet. The opposite proved to be true from 1981 to 1998. While economic growth was less than half the rate of the first 17-year period, corporate profit margins widened, and interest rates moved sharply lower.

Finally, despondency gave way to euphoria through the process known as contagion (see the section later in this chapter titled "Why History Repeats Itself"), which mutated into an ultimately self-destructive speculative orgy, fueled in its latter stages by little more than rising prices themselves. In my judgment, we are in the midst of hearing the air hissing out of the pricked Bubble. In an analogous reference (mine) to the late 1920s, Buffett observed about the era, "What the few bought for the right reason in 1925, the many bought for the wrong reason in 1929."

Buffett went on to examine the relationship of the economy to the market over the entire twentieth century as a harbinger of things to come. Mind you, his view is *gestalt*: Over and over again, he admonishes investors for looking into the rearview mirror to see what's ahead. We call it the "availability bias," which is simple extrapolation of the immediate past to forecast the future. Surprisingly, over most 10-year periods in the past century, the economy grew rather steadily at an inflation-adjusted 2 to 3 percent compounded annual rate. The Dow Jones industrial average, however, told an entirely different story. During the twentieth century, there were three huge, secular bull markets that covered about 44 years, during which the Dow gained more than 11,000 points. Yet there were three long periods of stagnation, covering some 56 years, during which the Dow actually lost 292 points in the face of the country's solid economic progress. From 1900 to 1920, new innovations in electricity, automobiles, and the telephone formed the backbone of solid economic growth, and yet the market moved at a snail's pace: 0.4 percent per year, compounded, closing in 1920 at 71.95. The market exploded upward during the 1920s, advancing 430 percent to 381 in September 1929. Nineteen years later, the Dow stood at half of its 1929 highs, despite record-setting per-capita economic growth of 50 percent during the 1940s. For the next 17 years, coincidentally (the Baby Boom years of 1947–1964), the Dow advanced fivefold, a nice move but not "fat" by later standards. That brings us to the 17 lean years, followed by the 17 fat years (as detailed above).

How can one explain these anomalies? According to Buffett (whose conclusions largely coincide with my own independent study of the history of investor behavior), investors' perceptions of the future are most heavily influenced by their most immediate past experience—"rearview mirror" investing, as he dubs it. Buffett asserts that a book written by Edgar Lawrence Smith, titled *Common Stocks as Long Term Investments*, contains a watershed development in investment theory.

Based on historical data for the 56 years ending in 1922, Smith hypothesized that stocks do better in times of inflation, while bonds do better in times of deflation. It was his reasoning, later confirmed and therefore consecrated and expanded upon in 1925 by none other than John Maynard Keynes, however, that was most intriguing. Begins Keynes: "These studies are the record of a failure—the failure of facts to sustain a preconceived theory." He concludes: "The facts assembled, however, seem worthy of further examination. If they would not prove what we had hoped to have them prove, it seemed desirable to turn them loose and to follow them to wherever they might lead."

While Smith's conclusions about the future of common stocks have been credited with providing academia's blessing, helping to fuel the ever-growing speculative Bubble in the late 1920s, his "thinking-outside-the-box" contribution was quite impressive in and of itself—and more so in that it was entirely contrary to the way most investors viewed the future.

When Smith's book hit the streets in 1922, bond-interest coupons yielded less than stock dividends (a relationship that prevailed throughout most of the next 30 to 35 years). Keynes rationalized that, since a portion of the company's earnings was retained in the business and therefore reinvested, an element of compound interest existed in common-stock investing, whereas it was absent in the ownership of bonds. The double whammy of a higher-dividend yield at the outset, with the likelihood that it would grow as well, lent credence to the idea of common-stock investing and later stoked the fires of speculative desire. Keynes anticipated in 1925 the potential perversity of carrying this reasoning to extremes: "It is dangerous . . . to apply to the future inductive arguments based on past experience, unless one can distinguish the broad reasons why past experience was what it was."

Buffett concludes that simple extrapolation of the past is the principal instigator of most investment follies. Smith's study covered a half-century during which stocks generally yielded more than high-grade bonds. The relationship between bond and stock yields on which Smith's theory was predicated has been turned on its ear since the mid-1950s. Even though conditions nearly identical to those on which Smith built his case existed in the late 1940s, investors were so hamstrung by their horrible memories of the 1930s that they were blind to the opportunity that lay at their feet. Those conditions have never existed since. We note anecdotally that, according to studies, most investors today assume that bonds have always yielded more than stocks.

Buffett then at length makes the case that such rearview-mirror investing is not merely the asininity of the small investor. He demonstrates convincingly that the great company pension-fund sponsors, actuaries, and portfolio managers repeatedly fall victim to the same malady. [Rearview-mirror investing has nothing to do with the study of history and of similar events (such investors generally reject or ignore such information as irrelevant). Rather, the rearview guys look almost exclusively to their immediate past emotional experience. If it was good—a rising market—they are happy. If it was bad—the Lost Decade—they don't feel so good. But seldom are they encumbered with the broad and intriguing sweep of history.]

More to our immediate interest, and in the midst of castigating large corporations for being no more astute than the man on the street, Buffett refers to an article he wrote in 1979 in which he made the case that stocks were at that time a better investment than bonds. Bonds were then yielding 9.5 percent, and the Dow was selling below book value while earning 13 percent on its equity capital (known as book value, when reduced to a per-share basis). As we have mentioned many times in the past, common stocks are in many respects similar to bonds—and therefore sometimes interchangeable—differing in that their coupons are variable and that there is no set maturity date. Despite these similarities, which are more form than substance, Wall Street, much to Buffett's amusement (and ours), treats them as discrete securities. Admittedly, the amount of the Dow "coupon" is far from fixed, unlike that of a high-grade bond. Still, the opportunity to purchase the Dow below "par" with a variable coupon that had a reasonable chance of averaging 13 percent over the years had to be conspicuously preferential to owning a bond with a fixed 9.5 percent coupon. Referring once again to Keynes, Buffett reminds us that the superiority of stocks isn't inevitable: "They own the advantage only when certain conditions prevail."

This entire exercise helps to make the case that markets are capable of acting irrationally in the extreme from time to time, and the investor who is forewarned is thus forearmed. Buffett and his alter ego, Charlie Munger, have characterized the widely practiced modern portfolio theory (MPT) as laughable. Though MPT isn't mentioned by name in the *Fortune* article, it is damned by implication in the first sentence of this paragraph. Buffett concludes by offering a simple quantitative antidote that investors can administer to neutralize their often emotional "availability bias" assessment of the future. Referring to the 80-year graph depicting the relationship between GDP and the market value of all publicly traded securities (Figure 4.1), Buffett suggests that when the ratio falls to the 70 percent or 80 percent area, "buying stocks is likely to work very well for you. If the ratio approaches 200 percent—as it did in 1999 and a part of 2000—you are playing with fire."

You will observe that the ratio frequently bottomed out at 50 percent or below. For those ideal bet-the-ranch conditions to exist there

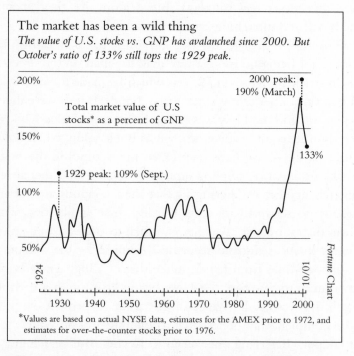

Figure 4.1 Total Stock Market Value to GDP
DATA SOURCE: *Fortune.*

must be a confluence of at least several of the key wet-blanket variables: slow GDP growth, skimpy profit margins, skyrocketing interest rates, and/or pervasive investor despair. Taking a cue from Buffett's behavior in 1973–1974, a rational man, who *by virtue of his lack of time, skill, or experience has no prudent alternative but to be broadly diversified,* begins buying when the ratio falls to 70 percent or 80 percent and, if he is lucky, still has a little money left to invest when it hits 50 percent. Since the "bottom" is only declared in retrospect, those who wait for it almost always go away empty-handed. According to our calculus, the aforementioned rational diversified investor would be far better off owning a fully invested portfolio with an average cost of 60 percent or 70 percent of GDP than the fellow whose congenital state of agitation and anxiety caused by the presence or imminence of real or imagined danger cannot, in the end, pull the trigger, regardless of price. Invariably, he ends up owning nothing but regrets when the ratio returns to 80 percent or more. No man is more entitled to buy at the bottom than Buffett, and yet no man is more aware of the foolishness in trying.

The ratio was 133 percent as recently as October (see preceding graph).[1] Buffett admits that the simple measure has certain minor weaknesses and is hardly precise in terms of timing. But, as a rule of thumb, it's pretty handy. In the long run, if the GDP grows at 5 percent annually, and you expect the 10 percent returns from common stocks, then the corporate-profit share of GDP must go off the chart. "That won't happen," says Buffett.

Finally, referring back to his November 1999 *Fortune* article, Buffett ventures that the investing public should expect total annual equity returns (dividends plus price appreciation) over the next decade or two of about 6 percent, net of frictional costs (such as commissions and fees) of about 1 percent, along with inflation at 2 percent. A year later, stock prices are lower and the economy has grown, so he has raised his estimate, accordingly, to approximately 7 percent for long-term returns. Concludes Buffett: "Not bad at all—that is, unless you're still deriving your expectations from the 1990s."

---

[1][2001, original] The ratio was approximately 120 percent as of June 2005. [2010 update: The ratio was approximately 95 percent as of September 2010. See footnote 2 in Chapter 7 for further details.]

"Mr. Buffett on the Stock Market"— Or Making Headway in Headwinds

This exercise in rationality, for which Buffett is renowned and which we also embrace dispassionately, is more than helpful in framing our day-to-day decision making in the context of the prevailing winds. So often investors suffer great anguish and disillusionment because, unlike the seasoned golfer, they don't bother to toss a few blades of grass into the air before choosing a club. This process of adapting to a new paradigm is evolutionary, not revolutionary. Those most firmly anchored in the immediate past are likely to be among the last to come to terms with the new reality.

Of one thing we are quite certain. Marching headlong, with your bets well spread, into headwinds is certain to result in outcomes similar to what Buffett expects. Broad diversification, use of index funds that replicate some measurement standard (such as the S&P 500), or other similar so-called risk-management mechanisms simply cannot buck the forces of nature. Those who fathom the shifting secular trend and who correspondingly downsize their expectations will find the broad diversification exercise "not bad at all."

Our inquiry into the nature of markets is based on logical reasoning and has resulted in a style that has been different and will continue to be so. We have set our sights higher, and that requires a different approach to solving the headwind problem. Before an individual company qualifies for purchase by MCM, its five-year expected return[2] must exceed 15 percent. As the past two years have given ample witness, it can be relatively and absolutely productive. No course of action, however, is without trade-offs. The attendant cost of our nondiversified style is greater inherent portfolio-price volatility. While volatility has been in our favor most recently, we can say with near certitude that it will run against our interests at times in the future—some of them likely to be agonizingly protracted. Ever iconoclastic, we do not

---

[2][2001, original] The expected return is the internal rate of return that reconciles the current price with the estimated future value. The future value, in turn, is the end product of the analyst's estimate of normalized earnings five years hence, multiplied by a terminal price-earnings ratio that itself takes into account an estimate of the earnings growth rate going forward from there.

subscribe to MPT's reliance upon market-price volatility as a proxy for risk. Rather, we measure risk more like a businessman who owns a private enterprise, whose firm is not "marked to market" on a daily basis. Because there is no group of outsiders valuing his business on a day-to-day basis, and therefore no *beta* (MPT's quantitative measure of risk, i.e., relative price volatility) to numerically approximate business risk, the owner must default to a more Main Street definition: the possibility of an outcome detrimental to his best interests—or at least a result that is less than his expectations at the outset.

But, you say, are you not exposing me to inordinate risks, however they might be defined, by limiting my portfolio holdings to 12 to 15 issues? For that question we have two answers, the first of which is straightforward. Most clients come to us having sold a single business that represented a significant part of their net worth. If we propose an investment policy that expands the universe of holdings to the aforementioned number, and if we assume those businesses are at least as inherently profitable and well managed as the one sold (and are purchased at a price that implies a significant margin of safety), does this scheme not represent a significant reduction in risk?

As introduced in the prior part, the second answer is not so self-evident and may need to be read two or three times to get its full meaning. It is further complicated by the conditional relationship among several variables; for it to bring about the desired result, it relies on the successful execution of certain key activities. Instead of comparing our nondiversified portfolio strategy, at least as conventionally defined, with a single business, we will in this instance contrast it with the S&P 500, which is roughly made up of the 500 most valuable businesses in America, at least in the market's collective judgment.

For purposes of this argument, let's assume that, by number, 75 percent of the companies that constitute the capitalization-weighted index are average or better businesses, worth owning if purchased at a price discounted from intrinsic value that appropriately accounts for the differences in quality, and that 25 percent of them are not worth buying at any price above a token amount. That last group would include airlines, steel companies, automobile manufacturers, and the like. Here's where the case could break down. Let's assume that of the 15 businesses that we might select, two-thirds, or 10, prove over time to be well above average and that they were initially purchased at prudent prices.

Admittedly, those assumptions are at least moderately heroic! Putting that premise aside for the sake of completing the line of reasoning, were you really more secure in the spring of 2000 buying an S&P 500 index fund at 32 times earnings or the handful of companies we bought at 12 times?

Thus the question becomes: Do you feel safer—are you safer—with two-thirds of the companies in your portfolio being above average, or with 25 percent (if you purchase an index fund that replicates the S&P 500) regardless of whether the number of companies is 15 or 500? Needless to say, if you accept the proposition, you might logically conclude that not only are you safer in the first instance, but your chances for better-than-mediocre results also are greatly improved. That has been our experience in recent years, but we can give you no binding assurance that it will be replicated in the future. Sometimes small is better—and, yes, safer.

More relevant to a discussion of investment strategy, can this approach be repeated time and again in the future? A simple "yes" or "no" answer will not suffice.

First, change, particularly in the fastest-growing industries (such as technology), seems to be happening at an ever-increasing rate. Many of the companies we examine have wonderful records of profitability, but we have no idea what they will be doing five years from now, let alone next year. Even in the more easily understood and less-glamorous industries, countless problems can occur. Competitive rivalries heat up, managers lose sight of their loyalties . . . the list is as long as the imagination is fertile.

Second, even if we find them, can we purchase them at prices low enough to make it possible for the full benefits of ownership of the asset to actually flow through to us as shareholders? You see, while the market is occasionally wacko in the valuation of businesses, more times than not it is quite efficient, pricing them close to their intrinsic worth, leaving us with little or no margin of safety in the event we are wrong in our estimate of their value. In point of fact, we rarely get to seize a true opportunity unless it appears to be just the opposite, forcing us to act precisely at the moment our peers can't seem to unload it fast enough. For instance, just when the technology and dot-com favorites were reaching for the sky in the spring of 2000, many of the companies that we had long wished to own were carelessly discarded as worthless deuces and treys in the frenetic, high-stakes game then under way. Those that were cast aside we picked up at bargain prices. In September 2001, the emotional selling that followed the attacks on the World Trade Center provided similar opportunities, despite the fact that we experienced the same feelings and sensibilities as most other Americans.

Our whole investment life is living the antithesis of the lyrics to Debby Boone's hit tune of the 1980s: "It can't be wrong when it feels so right." Running against the herd makes easy copy, but you need only imagine how frightened you would feel if, instead of "running *with* the bulls" in Pamplona, Spain, you were forced to reverse your direction. Indeed, the Wall Street equivalent of this metaphor has occurred to us more than once [see again the brave, against-the-tide example of the sheep at the outset of this chapter]. All of us are comforted by the affirmation of others. We at MCM, on the other hand, must conjure up our own sense of well-being. Our "buy low, sell high" credo certainly helps. The job we do also is made somewhat easier because we enjoy a significant advantage: Our clients allow us to be patient in the search for ideas, whereas many of our colleagues live in a pressure cooker, enjoying no such luxury of *seeming* lethargy. To quote seventeenth-century French mathematician and philosopher Blaise Pascal, most human misfortune stems from "man's inability to sit still in a room."

So, you see, it really isn't a grand strategy at all that we follow but rather a simple pattern of behavior analogous to an imaginary game of baseball. We spend most of our time waiting patiently for pitches that cross the plate precisely at our particular sweet spot. In this fictive sport, we can let pitch after pitch whisk by with no penalty for failing to take a cut at a ball in the strike zone, nor will we be forced to take a base on balls if the bat rarely leaves our shoulder. Sometimes the lumber gets a little heavy, and every now and then, we get an itch to take a swing. But most of the time when we get restless, we just step back from the plate, stretch a little, tap the dirt off our cleats, then step back into the box. To be candid, this is a heck of a lot more boring than regular baseball. But the good news is that by changing the rules to our liking, even a minor leaguer can achieve batting averages similar to those that put Ted Williams in the record book.

Our allocation to equities is not dictated by some arbitrary formula, despite the popularity of the practice, but rather by the arrival of the transcendent pitch. While one might apply the maxim [as we have before] "a rising tide lifts all ships"—and its obvious corollary to the buying and selling of stocks—it's rarely that simple. As noted in our discussion on performance, we purchased the castaways precisely as the Nasdaq index was peaking in the spring of 2000. We are far less concerned about a protracted bear market than we are about our ability to identify great businesses and to exercise the patience necessary to purchase them at prices well below what they're worth. Of course, many of the companies we have bought in the last two years have appreciated smartly, effectively closing the "margin of safety" gap between the original purchase price and intrinsic value. Increasingly, the market price, absent market inefficiencies, will depend on growth in intrinsic value. With many of our holdings, the so-called "easy money" has been made.

We are decidedly agnostic when it comes to acting on the majority forecasts for the economy—in part because prognosticators are, at least in the short run, not paid according to the accuracy of their pronouncements. If they were, there would be no economists. To the point, the "recovery beginning in midyear 2002" consensus scenario is, if our memories serve us correctly, simply the reincarnation of the "recovery beginning in midyear 2001." Accordingly, we think it appropriate to partially hedge our portfolios against the possibility, however remote, that the forecasting errors of the last two years will not be the last in this atypical business cycle, if that's what it turns out to be. Rather than cementing our considerable gains by selling companies that no longer go begging for buyers at bargain prices—and in the process incur short-term capital-gains taxes—we will buy long-term put options on the S&P 100 or another more appropriate index. The insurance purchased will not be used to moderate the impact of minor fluctuations in the value of your portfolio. Those "quotational losses" go hand in hand with investing in marketable securities and are of no concern to us. Rather, we will attempt to partially protect your portfolio from, in the vernacular of the reinsurance industry, "super cat" losses. Think of it as earthquake insurance. For your sake and ours, we hope the options expire worthless.[3]

---

[3][2001, original] Try as we might, we could never purchase the put options at premiums that effectively made the insurance a good value. Such an outcome did not come as a big surprise.

Interest Rates: It Had Better Be Uphill from Here

Late in November, two "marker buoys" in the financial history of the United States were passed, collectively signifying where our economy stands in the grand flow of things.

In September 2001 the United States retired a group of Treasury bonds issued in 1981. The bonds carried an interest rate of 15¾ percent, the highest the government had ever paid on long-term borrowing. It was a nostalgic moment for the undersigned, recalling the 14 percent *tax-exempt* participation certificates, a hybrid form of municipal bond that we underwrote for the Concord School Corp. of Elkhart, Indiana. The choice between equity and tax-exempt debt securities was not an easy one.

A month later, on October 31, 2001, with long-term borrowing costs the lowest in a generation, Washington announced that it would "suspend" its issuance of 30-year bonds. Interest rates plummeted, with the yield on 30-year bonds dropping the next day to 4.80 percent (compared to approximately 5.50 percent at the end of last year), while the yield on the benchmark 10-year note slid to 4.24 percent from the 5 percent range. It seemed that the market was suddenly anticipating the Federal Reserve's decision to lower the federal fund's rate by half a percentage point, to 2 percent, which actually would come to pass the following week.

After 20 years of declining interest rates (dating back to the afore-mentioned 15¾ percent coupon issued in 1981), we have in this country reached the point where we can't reasonably expect rates to fall lower. It's true that the United States is in a recession, and rates tend to decline during periods of retrenchment. But for rates to fall from their current level would suggest the darkest of scenarios. The macro-policy authorities are applying fiscal and monetary stimuli like a drunken sailor buying rounds of drinks for every other inebriate at the bar. This combination has never failed to ignite a rebound in the past—but is the past prologue in 2001–2002?

We won't dwell excessively on the possibility that the cyclical recession in which we find ourselves will not be arrested by the application of traditional palliatives, that it will disintegrate (in the face of repeated denials from economists of all stripes and from far and wide) into something more serious. We are loath to draw parallels with

Japan because the dissimilarities are as striking as the similarities. Most important, while our readings in classical economic theory would suggest that the possibility for an apocalyptic event is perhaps more likely now than at any time since the Great Depression, there are simply too many variables to assimilate, most of which are unknowable as to the likelihood of their occurrence, to say nothing of how they might interact with other equally unknowable variables. The best minds in the world cannot put this puzzle together; we will not attempt to give you a false impression of our acumen, which could lead to either complacency or fear. Neither is warranted.

Rather, in the face of this shadowy threat, we will respond in the only rational way we know how: with an extra degree of caution. As for fixed-income securities, we will continue our long-standing practice of owning only the best—direct obligations of the U.S. Treasury or tax-exempt municipal securities backed by similar Treasury obligations (pre-refunded or escrowed-to-maturity bonds). We will not even think about junk bonds. If the yield spreads get to be so great that they make the headlines, chances are that equity securities will be even cheaper. Because bond yields are relatively low, particularly when compared to the five-year expected returns from some high-grade common stocks, we will rarely extend maturities beyond five years in this environment for fear of getting "locked in" to a security we would prefer not owning for a long period of time.

We read extensively on the bond market. What we find is that most specialists in this area are merely splitting hairs, an exercise we find unproductive. Whether the benchmark 10-year-bond yields eclipse the lows of 4.16 percent (hit at the depths of 1998's global financial crisis) by a few basis points strikes us as utterly irrelevant, akin to speculating about how many *prima donnas* can dance on the head of a pin.

Still, we shall flavor these pages with a bit of history about the bond cycles, largely for the purpose of venturing a guess as to their future course, not so much because we are likely to buy long-term bonds but, rather, because of the effect of interest rates on the valuation of equities.

In a November article in *Barron's,* Richard Sylla, professor of financial history at New York University's Stern School of Business and coauthor with the late Sidney Homer of *A History of Interest Rates,* says the market's actions suggest that the two-decade decline in long-term rates may have run its course.

Another self-proclaimed expert and CNBC commentator, Larry Kudlow, head of Kudlow & Co., thinks that if the Fed were to explicitly target the market indicators—commodity prices, the dollar, the slope of the yield curve, and changes in the 10-year Treasury yield—yields could fall back to the 3½ to 4 percent range. But absent a change in the mind-set of Greenspan & Co., a deeper recession, or a Japanese-style asset deflation (none of which Kudlow sees on the horizon), the benchmark note likely will trade between 4½ and 6½ percent "over the next bunch of years."

Martin Barnes, editor of the *Bank Credit Analyst* whose service we have read for many years, thinks 4 to 5 percent on the 10-year Treasury seems "reasonable." But Barnes believes that corporate-bond yields are likely to remain far higher. "Don't expect corporates to return to their old [historical] average" of around 4 percent and change in the 1960s, he says. Top-grade corporate bonds, which now yield around 7 percent, are back near where they stood three decades ago. Lending credence to our concerns about credit risk, Barnes comments: "Corporate balance sheets are much worse today, requiring the greater risk premium that has been evident since 1998 and limiting the scope for corporate yields to fall."

Neither is it only corporate America's balance sheet that is less than rock-solid. Northern Trust's Kasriel sends a cold chill up my spine when he notes that the federal government faces huge unfunded liabilities. "Whatever happened to the debate over Social Security?" he asks. "It's gone the way of the Chandra Levy story." Paying those future obligations will mean either higher taxes or increased borrowing (most likely the latter). And Ed Yardeni, chief investment strategist of Deutsche Banc Alex Brown, who made his mark in the early 1980s by predicting "hat size" bond yields (7 to 8 percent) when they were nearly twice as high, thinks the long slide in rates is "pretty close to over."

With the overall economy (current-dollar gross domestic product) on a long-run growth path of around 4 to 5 percent a year (3 percent real growth and 1 to 2 percent inflation), 10-year Treasury notes should approximate the same. That leaves scant room for long yields to decline. Indeed, Yardeni uses a 5 percent 10-year Treasury rate in his long-term stock market valuation model.

Turning more to the anecdotal, if you believe that markets know better than government bureaucrats, there's another clear sign that interest rates have bottomed out: By issuing bonds 20 years ago, Uncle

Sam locked in the highest-cost debt in the nation's history; today, Washington eschews borrowing long term, even though rates are the lowest in a generation.

One observer in the *Wall Street Journal* (October 14, 2001) also offered this oversimplified analogy:

> To understand the movement of interest rates over the decades, it's important to note that long-term market trends are defined by a series of cycles with ascending (or descending) peaks and troughs. Think of it as a shoreline. Tides go in and out each day. But if the high-water marks move farther and farther up the beach, there is a definite trend. If the high-water marks start moving down the beach, that trend has reversed. It now appears that the trend of the past 20 years of the tide going out has reversed with a low tide higher than the last.

As for the bottom line, we would be somewhat surprised if interest rates moved dramatically either upward or downward over the immediate future from where they are today. Longer term, we are not so sanguine about subdued rates, more the result of a gut feeling than something concrete we can point to. Accordingly, while we feel reasonably confident that we have a temporary respite from concerns about rising interest rates impacting our earnings-discounting model, that specter may be a reality with which we must deal in the years ahead.[4]

Why History Repeats Itself

History is a perplexing teacher; its lessons often are obtuse, bewilderingly intricate, and complicated. Were they otherwise, the mistakes in the past would not repeat themselves so irritatingly often. And yet, there is much to take away from this school of "hard knocks" for the student who is able to organize the lessons into a variety of models that can be applied in general to events of the future. Unfortunately, what you learn will be of little use tomorrow—or even next year. No

---

[4][2006, *Speculative Contagion*] As of midyear 2005, short-term interest rates had increased on the three-month T-bill from 1.8 to 3 percent, while the 10-year government yield fell from 5.1 to 4 percent. [2010 update: As of September 30, 2010, the three-month T-bill yield was 0.16 percent, and the 10-year was 2.5 percent.]

sinner is more repentant than one whose transgression is fresh in his or her mind. This is a variation of the "availability bias," the penchant to be disproportionately influenced by more recent events as one gazes too raptly into the rearview mirror.

What we write, therefore, has about the same immediate value as closing the barn door after the horses are already out. Be that as it may, we record the lessons so that you might file them away for future reference in times of recurring grand delusions, recognizing that there is nothing really new in the world of economics and finance. The dismal science is inherently cyclical, bound to repeat itself again and again, with the span between episodes a simple function of the length of memories. By contrast, in scientific endeavors, knowledge is cumulative. Think only of the evolution of the personal computer to gain some appreciation of the difference.

The Power of Popular Delusions

Nothing is more central to the dissection of investment manias than to study those human proclivities common to them all. The capacity for human beings to be readily deluded, to be made to look the fool, is the point of origin from which every seeming behavioral absurdity, at least with the benefit of hindsight, naturally follows.

One of the endlessly fascinating aspects of our participation in the capital markets is the opportunity to witness human behavior in a highly charged environment, under conditions that would make a social scientist salivate. On Wall Street one can readily observe individuals whose actions are often the result of especially powerful motivators, such as greed and fear. Further, the abundance of data collected on the transactions that take place permits relatively thorough analysis of those behaviors. While we find the study academically intriguing, our interest relates more to how we can use the information as we ply our trade. We simply think an attempt at understanding the psychology of the marketplace will give us a competitive edge.

Quite pragmatically, much of the practice of psychology is directed toward serving the emotional needs of the individual. Years ago, having read *Moral Man and Immoral Society* by theologian Reinhold Niebuhr, my interest was captured by Niebuhr's different perspective on the study of human behavior. Instead of examining the individual in isolation, he looked at a gathering of individuals and the peculiar impact the group had on the thinking and behavior of its individual members. This was predicated in no small measure by his experience of living through World War II. The general idea certainly is not new. What has great relevance to us as investors, however, is the special nature of that transformation.

Years later, in a search for information on the legendary investor and statesman, Bernard Baruch, I came across the book *Extraordinary Popular Delusions and the Madness of Crowds* by Charles Mackay, LLD; the book was originally published in 1841. Baruch wrote the foreword to a reprinted edition in 1932, as the country reached the depths of the Great Depression. Mackay gives an excellent account of many of history's extraordinary delusions, from the Mississippi Scheme that swept France in 1720 . . . to the South Sea Bubble that ruined thousands in England at the same time . . . to the Tulip Mania of Holland when fortunes were made and lost on single tulip bulbs. On the other hand, *The Crowd*, penned by a Frenchman, Gustave Le Bon, in 1895, delves into the nature of a crowd that makes human beings vulnerable to its powers. According to the authoritative *Handbook of Social Psychology* (published in 1954), *The Crowd* is "perhaps the most influential book ever written on social psychology."

Of what significance is all of this to us? In 1932 Baruch observed in his foreword:

> Some years ago a friend gave me a copy of *Extraordinary Popular Delusions*. In a vague way I had been familiar with the stark facts of these events, as who is not? But I did not know . . . the astonishing circumstances of each of the greater delusions of earlier eras. I have always thought that if in 1929 we had all continuously repeated "two and two still make four," much of the evil would have been averted.

But still one is likely to question the relevance, arguing that 1929 was truly an exceptional period, one not likely to be repeated during our lifetime. And in fact, much to our good fortune and to the preservation of our capital, most popular delusions of the financial variety never reach the pervasiveness of the spectacle in common stocks that ran rampant in the late 1920s. It is interesting to note, however, that

Mackay offered in the preface to the 1841 edition the observation that "popular delusions began so early (in recorded history), spread so widely, and have lasted so long, that instead of two or three volumes, 50 would scarcely suffice to detail their history." We have taken the position that if we become the victim of a lesser-known delusion, we'll feel not one whit better than if we were swept up in the folly of one of extraordinary notoriety. (One bolt of lightning is of no great national consequence, but it may more than command your personal attention if you are directly between it and the ground!)

In 2000 a week's worth of evenings was consumed reading Robert J. Shiller's just-released and well-written book *Irrational Exuberance*, its title lifted from a phrase for which Alan Greenspan was roundly castigated until eventually a crashing market silenced his critics. Were the Fed chairman to author a book, it might be titled *From Castigation to Vindication*. Shiller, an economics professor at Yale and author of *Market Volatility* and *Macro Markets*, which won the 1996 Paul A. Samuelson Award, was generally right—and for the right reasons. I commend him for his scholarly and timely work. The final sentence on the inside cover of the book contains both an admonition and a note of uneasiness; it reveals a shadow of doubt about a future that is never certain: "It will be studied by policymakers and anyone from Wall Street to Main Street who doesn't want to be caught sitting on the speculative bubble if (*or when* [emphasis added]) it bursts." In truth, we never know, but we do become more confident as the weight of evidence gets heavier and heavier.

An Ounce of Prevention . . .

[Acquiring knowledge of the psychology of crowds not only teaches one about the beguiling and insidious dangers of embracing crowd-think—sometimes termed groupthink—but, forewarned and thus forearmed, the *erudite* investor is less likely to succumb to its often ruinous reasoning.] Because of the incredible gains in communications technology in the latter part of the twentieth century, individuals no longer need to enjoy physical proximity to function as a crowd. Despite their disparate locations, investors around the world can become, thanks to modern technology, an instantaneous and homogenous lot, to which October 19, 1987 (and, more recently, 1998, 2000, and 2001!), painfully attests. Our past and our future have been and will be filled with popular delusions to which many will fall victim, ranging from the inconsequential to the extraordinary; the challenge to us is to learn more about how people become such unwitting victims. Indeed, "An ounce of prevention is worth a pound of cure."

Before turning to the "how" and "why" of our apparent capacity to be collectively deluded, let's recall several episodes from the recent past in the security and commodity markets. Such an exercise should lead us to the obvious conclusion: We are as susceptible as our forefathers were (and our children will be) to the suggestions, however reasonable or unreasonable, of the crowds with which we allow ourselves to become joined at the "lip." Each new generation throughout history, armed as it is with more accumulated knowledge than any generation before it, proves with the same certainty as the march of time itself that knowledge is not necessarily wisdom.

During the summer of 1987, the stock market was on a roll, having built a strong base in the second half of the 1970s and having been further stimulated by an injection of easy money in the fall of 1982. The popular averages were assaulting new highs with reckless abandon, with stock prices advancing almost exponentially. The market prices of companies seemed gloriously uncoupled from the plodding performances of the underlying businesses themselves. The Dow Jones industrial average reached its zenith of nearly 2750, and Bob Prechter, author of a popular investment letter that had captured the imagination of Wall Street during the 1980s much the same as Joe Granville did some years before, confidently declared that the Dow would finally peak at 3600 before the party ended. (See Table 4.1.)

Table 4.1   Standard & Poor's 400 Stock Industrial Index

Measurement	Average (annual) (1950–1987)	High (1987)
P/E	11.90–14.90*	19.4
Price/Book	1.66	2.93
Yield	3.54–4.43%*	2.20% (low)
T–Bond Yield	6.28%	10.50%

*Average of annual lows and highs.

The stark reality of the fundamentals permitted only one rational conclusion, but the steamroller of sentiment, unmindful of the quiet warnings that history had to offer, crushed under its weight and momentum the logic and reason that stood in its path. While we're aware that averages, particularly in this instance, can be deceiving, examine the following statistics and see if the message that the fundamentals told should not have at least raised some serious questions.

One must wonder why most participants did not seek a safe harbor when the storm flags flew. Or why so many allowed themselves to get caught up in the riptide of popular sentiment that carried them to a turbulent sea when surely they must have known better . . .

More Fool's Gold

In the late 1970s and early 1980s, there were two popular delusions that grew, at least in part, out of the virulent inflation of that period: gold and oil. Gold, which traded as low as $100 per ounce in 1976, skyrocketed to $850 by January 1980. Except for an aborted rally in late 1980, it fell relentlessly to $300 by the summer of 1982 and currently trades around $360. Rereading popular periodicals of the era helps one gain a sense of time-and-place perspective. *U.S. News & World Report* carried an article on October 8, 1979, titled "Gold Craze—It Sweeps the Country." The author wrote, "Modern day gold fever is gripping the nation as jittery Americans grope for ways to beat inflation. Every day, thousands of people are flocking to coin shops, jewelry stores, and gold dealers to put their cash in precious metals. Consumers who waited in gas lines only months ago are now in line to buy gold coins, bullion, and bracelets in hopes of protecting their savings." And: "This is the biggest gold rush since 1931," said the president of one of the largest gold dealerships in New York, whose "customers have lately been overflowing into the hallways of the Empire State Building."

The speculation in gold in the late 1970s is an interesting case study. The yellow metal is difficult to intrinsically value (and in that respect is similar to collectibles) since it does not grow internally as a business might nor does it provide any current cash return to its owners. Conveniently, the very absence of a benchmark freed the speculators from having to deal with an ever-present fundamental reality. Many elements of crowd psychology can be found in the study of that modern Gold Rush.

Oil Slicks and Beyond . . . ?

Oil, which itself rose in price 1,500 percent from late 1973 to 1981, was an even more interesting and economically widespread delusion. In February 1980 *Forbes* magazine carried an interview with Kenneth Arrow, Stanford economist and Nobel Prize winner, who confidently predicted, "We are heading into a world of higher [oil] prices. It will have a major impact on housing by 1983, and I'd be surprised if gasoline is less than $2 per gallon plus whatever inflation adds . . . Whether Saudi Arabia will be around in four years I can't predict. It is a very uncertain world."

The oil-rig count, according to Hughes Tool, was up to a record 2,600 at Christmastime in 1979. "Just about everywhere you go you stumble over someone pushing a drilling rig," said the senior vice president for land and production at Chevron USA, who went on to observe that Chevron had not been this busy since the great Texas oil boom in the 1950s. The fever was not confined to Texas. Penn State's petroleum engineering classes saw their enrollment surge from 65 to 220 in three years. Most of the major companies in the industry were optimistic, some forecasting the price would hit $90 per barrel by 1990. Why, even conservative Standard Oil of Indiana raised its exploration budget three times in 1979. Money-center banks, active in financing the exploration, were no less upbeat. Chase Manhattan estimated domestic exploration at $15 billion for 1977, $28 billion for 1980, and a whopping $60 billion for 1985. Unfortunately, the widespread bullishness quickly gave way to despair. By 1986, the price of crude had fallen below $10 — to less than 25 percent of its high. Idle rigs and befuddled oil industry executives (including a Texan named George W. Bush), investors, and bankers were more plentiful than politicians at a pig roast.[5]

Fast-forward to the late 1990s. The mania in technology and Internet stocks is simply the latest iteration of this timeless phenomenon. The exponential price curve of the Nasdaq index leading up to its peak

---

[5][2006, *Speculative Contagion*] In Chapter 1 (1998 report) we alluded to the possibility that the lack of interest in oil at $10 per barrel might present investment opportunities. Out of the ashes of despair and indifference, opportunity, like the crocus beneath a blanket of snow, irrepressibly grows . . .

in March 2000 was a near carbon copy of those for gold and oil two decades earlier.

We may be witnessing today a number of delusions that have not run their course. The takeover mania will surely go down as one of the great delusions of the twentieth century. It could even prove to be the ultimate financial excess—making for a dramatic, if not tragic, end to the great post–World War II credit boom. When we finally conclude that the old rules no longer apply, they invariably do! In the same vein, one wonders whether a $50 million price tag for a splash of paint on a piece of canvas will not be remembered as a flight of fancy . . .

The Blockhead

Let's turn now to the somewhat surprising metamorphosis we experience as we become one with a crowd. The poet/dramatist Johann von Schiller once said, "Anyone taken as an individual is tolerably sensible and reasonable—as a member of a crowd he at once becomes a blockhead." That is a provocative statement, one that Le Bon examined with great clarity in *The Crowd*. He suggested that the most striking peculiarity presented psychologically by a crowd is the following: "Whoever be the individuals that compose it, however like or unlike be their mode of life, their occupations, their character, or their intelligence, the fact that they have been transformed into a crowd puts them in possession of a sort of collective mind which makes them feel, think, and act in a manner quite different from that in which each individual of them would feel, think, and act were he in a state of isolation."

Le Bon further observes, as does Schiller (though Le Bon stated it more delicately), that we are likely to function at a lower level—intellectually, morally, and emotionally as a result of submission to the will of the crowd. "Men the most unlike in the matter of their intelligence possess instincts, passions, and feelings that are very similar. From the intellectual point of view an abyss may exist between a great mathematician and his bootmaker, but from the point of view of character the difference is most often slight or nonexistent."

Membership in the crowd brings an egalitarian leveling to the ignorant and educated alike, largely because of the substitution of the unconscious behavior of crowds for the conscious activity of individuals in isolation. Le Bon also describes crowds as emotional and says that, when in them, the individual begins to feel and express the emotions of a "primitive being." [Think lynch mobs at various points in this country's history, and you realize that Le Bon's insights are not confined to any particular time or place.]

The Monster with the Pea Brain

Individuals often become "lost" in crowds and perform acts they wouldn't perform were they alone. In addition to having a collective mind, a crowd is irrational. Moreover, it is worth repeating that the process of capitulation downgrades an individual's capability for intellectual processing to the diminished level of the crowd, effectively the lowest common denominator. The crowd is a mighty monster—usually with a pea brain!

According to Le Bon, three mechanisms are responsible for creating this monster. First, because the individual is anonymous, he or she loses the sense of individual responsibility and thus participates in acts in which he or she would not normally engage. Second, the process known as contagion leads to the reduction of an individual's inhibitions, making it acceptable to behave as a role model behaves. And third, people become more susceptible to suggestion in crowds; the crowd effectively hypnotizes the individual, who then follows the suggestions of other members or the crowd's leader. Behaviors become impulsive, emotional, and difficult to terminate. Simplicity of suggestion is mandatory and paves the way for exaggeration of the sentiments; the throngs are burdened neither by doubt nor uncertainty (at least till later, at which point some members of the crowd begin to wonder "what happened").

Deindividualization

The process known by contemporary social scientists as "deindividualization" takes place, partly because of the aforementioned group anonymity and a heightened state of arousal. (Remember China's Tiananmen Square in 1989?) These conditions lead individuals to become submerged in the group, losing their own sense of identity. When this loss occurs, people no longer feel responsible for their behavior; their attention is drawn to the group and behavior becomes regulated by fleeting cues in the immediate situation.

The Mind of Crowds

A crowd thinks in images. It accepts as real the images evoked in its collective mind, though these images generally have only a very distant connection to the observed fact. Bob Prechter unintentionally encouraged the easily grasped and seemingly boundless image of vast riches with his prognostication of 3600 for the Dow during the summer of 1987. The collective observations of the crowd frequently are erroneous and most often merely represent the illusions of an individual who, by the process of contagion, has influenced his fellows.

Another example of the difference between image and reality can be found in the proposed acquisition of United Airlines, Inc. Do we for a minute think the United Airlines pilots see anything beyond images of great wealth as they assume the awesome responsibility of repaying $7 billion in debt? Marvin Davis, Carl Icahn, and others have created the appearance of a fantasy from a very serious business. The pilots show every sign of being caught up in the crowd. They have risked much—their pension assets, salary cuts, and no-strike clauses. The risks that these people have assumed, we fear, are more foolish than calculated. The pilots have no doubt allowed themselves to believe that the transaction has been legitimized by the presence of Citibank and Chase, who have committed to lend $3 billion and have promised to raise another $4.2 million from others. But some of us remain skeptical. For the pilots' sake, we hope the bankers know more about the airline business than they did about oil, real estate, and Latin America. Some of us can still recall when the airline business was considered cyclical.

As a postscript, after three failed efforts (beginning in 1987), the employee unions of United Airlines finally gained ownership control on July 12, 1994. Despite smatterings of dissenters among sectors of each of the unions, the employee stock-ownership plan was pushed through and approved by shareholders. *Employees* received 55 percent of United Airlines' stock in exchange for $4.9 billion in wage and benefit concessions. The *buyout* was aimed at enabling United, which lost $50 million in 1993, to better compete with lower-cost airlines.

After two and a half years, the transaction seemed to be a success. Adjusting for stock splits, shares had risen from $22 to nearly $60, but it appeared as though the honeymoon was over. In early 1997 pilots voted down a contract offer and demanded a 10 percent wage increase over four years. Similar deals also were rejected by other United Airlines unions. As is the case with most deals made under financial duress, all parties seemed to regret concessions they made under pressure. It seems as though the pay cuts employees agreed to while they were deindividualized in the group became quite personalized when the new compensation program came home to roost, so to speak.

United Airlines stock began to steadily fall in the fourth quarter of 1997. While the stock has languished around $10 following the tragic events of September 11, 2001, terrorist activity is not the only factor that has contributed to United Airlines' downfall. The U.S. Department of Transportation (DOT) ranked United last in service in 1999 and second to last in 2000. Due to ongoing labor disputes with its pilots, mechanics, and flight attendants, United had the worst on-time arrival percentage in 2000: a dismal 61 percent. United Airlines' three biggest rivals—American Airlines, Delta, and Northwest—all ranged from 73 to 77 percent. United was next to worst in mishandled baggage and in customer complaints filed with the DOT. Perhaps the shared imagery of impending riches that spurred on the union members in the early going grudgingly caved in under the weight of reality: Collective dreams turned to individual despair, and group enthusiasm fizzled into apathy.[6]

Might May Not Be Right

If we subscribe to Le Bon's findings and conclusions, we can see the crowd for what it is, rather than for what it appears to be. Despite the persuasiveness inherent in numbers and the implied power of size, the crowd may be a toothless tiger when it comes to certain tasks that require something other than brute force. Le Bon leads us to believe that as individuals we may in fact be functionally superior in many important

---

[6][2006, *Speculative Contagion*] United Airlines, another victim of the "stadium-naming jinx," filed for Chapter 11 bankruptcy protection in December 2002. Almost three years later (after successfully *jett*isoning its pension obligations, ultimately dumping them into the collective lap of U.S. taxpayers, who will see their obligation deferred when, in all probability, the U.S. Treasury will sell more bonds to foreign entities to fund the shortfall . . . !), United is hoping to emerge from Chapter 11 in the autumn of 2005. The loss for all shareholders will be total.

respects to the collective mind of the crowd. We are apt to think on a higher plane (no pun intended in light of the previous section)—and to do so more logically. We are likely to weigh with greater care the consequences of our actions. Our problem-solving capabilities will no doubt be at their best, leading to decisions that reflect our optimal level of reasoning. We will operate more on the conscious level, being better able to control our emotions. Facts, not images, will tend to take precedence as we problem-solve.

To be sure, we're quick to acknowledge that separation from the crowd does not protect us from thinking and acting quite stupidly. However, as part of a crowd, we have little or no opportunity to be the best we can be. We need not be intimidated by crowds if we only understand the transformation that takes place in the functioning of the individuals that compose them. Indeed, crowds have their rightful place in history—and they are capable of incredibly heroic deeds, as the young Chinese students at Tiananmen Square demonstrated. However, investing is a cerebral endeavor, dependent on intellect and not force, reason and not impulse, self-control and not high emotion.

Sometimes when we observe uncharacteristic behavior from someone with whom we're acquainted, we say, "He's just not himself." When we see people we respect taking on the telltale behavior patterns of a crowd, we are probably justified in reaching a similar conclusion. They may be particularly competent when functioning as individuals, but as members of the crowd, they may become . . . well, blockheads, a state of mind to be avoided, not admired.

During the second half of the 1980s, the junk-bond scam reached a fever pitch. The takeover crowd was populated with grand and powerful names, busily, if not blindly, leveraging everything in sight. The end to that unfortunate debacle was as predictable as rain in April. Because of the crudeness and undisguised greed for which it will be remembered—from big cigars to puffed-up egos—and because the episode is relatively fresh in our memory, as are its trademark characters Michael Milken, Ivan Boesky, and a host of other "barbarians at the gate" [see Chapter 6], we won't rehash that disgraceful moment in economic history here. Those who would not have done it were it not "the thing to do" were likely its hapless victims. We may be no smarter than they—except that we possess a little knowledge about "The Power of Popular Delusions"!

Investment Consultants:
The Great Middleman Myth

Turning now from the abstract to the concrete, we see how crowd theory applies to everyday activities.

Not beholden to anyone but our clients, we can utter heretical declarations with equanimity and without fear of reprisal. One of the great myths born of the long bull market is that middlemen—in their many iterations, from financial planners to the institutional consultancies—actually add value in the aggregate. What they add, without a scintilla of equivocation, is another layer of costs. Even investment managers, among whom we must be counted, in total are more of a cost than a benefit. Referring once again to the section on investment strategy, if Warren Buffett's prognosis of 7 percent returns from equities over the next decade or two proves correct the overhead burden of 2 to 3 percent in frictional costs will soon gleam brightly on investors' radar screens. During the 1990s, that cost, while still considerable in an absolute sense, was more easily buried in the aberrant and therefore unsustainable performance results of that decade.

There are, of course, exceptions to the rule that costs exceed benefits up and down the entire food chain; otherwise, the mean, median, and mode would be one and the same. For our sake, I hope you conclude that a bell curve exists and that we are an "outlier"! If we expect to continue to hold our position, we must be vigilant in avoiding mechanistic imitation of others. We must always think counterintuitively, as we again do in the paragraph immediately following.

The middlemen helped create another myth that "more is better." The proliferation of mutual funds of every imaginable stripe and the bewildering boardroom rationale to "downstream" decision making regarding retirement-plan investments to those least qualified is part of the grand masquerade. Again, you will find our challenge to the popular custom of diversification among asset classes, styles, and stocks of so many varieties that they defy description in an essay of this length. We have never understood the truism that most first-generation wealth is created on the strength of one idea or company, and then concludes with the dubious (in our judgment) assumption that in order to preserve it, it must be spread among a thousand other companies. There's more money than truth in that widespread practice. Compelling financial motives for freeloaders (feeloaders?) up and down the food chain, coupled with often gullible investors, make for a most profitable exchange, at least for one of the parties. If you've been in the game for more than five minutes and haven't yet identified the patsy . . . guess what? You're it.

Perhaps most grating to us is the issue of accountability. Because we're investment managers, that subset of our services falling under the quantitative descriptor, investment performance is incontrovertible in its factuality. It is what it is, and that's that. Not so with the fuzzy notion of value added by the middlemen. Playing adroitly to the well-cultivated illusion that safety is found in the sampling of a smorgasbord of choices, the middlemen cleverly avoid being accountable for anything beyond taking the naive and hungry client to the table spread with enough variety to choke a horse. To be sure, justice may not be swift, but it is sure. If the tide continues to ebb, they will in due course be exposed as an unnecessary cost for which the value is *de minimus*.

Surprisingly, those who appear to be most astute are equally eager to embrace this negative-value-added proposition. Almost every endowment fund for a college, university, or community foundation within range of our offices (to say nothing of other pools of organizational money, big and small) uses the consultancy model. The common denominator is the committee structure. As indicated above in the section titled "The Power of Popular Delusions," a committee is an odd potpourri of people whose collaborative idiosyncratic behavior is often in no way reflective of the brilliance or sagacity of any of the individuals of which it is made. A person's capacity changes, and usually not for the better, when he or she submits to the will of a group. Thus what is said below applies only to committees and not to those of whom it is composed. The problem is structural, not personal.

Continuing in this vein, after years of firsthand observation, I am convinced beyond a shadow of doubt of the counterintuitive notion that one astute individual has five times the investment decision-making capacity of a committee of five persons who, individually, are equally endowed intellectually. This metamorphosis—from incisive, decisive individual to mealy-mouthed group member—is not without explanation. No single member shoulders the ultimate responsibility, so a CYP (cover your posterior!) decision-making cloud hovers over the group and often disrupts collective clear-headed thinking.

The lowest-common-denominator syndrome, given enough time, will assert itself. The meeting rarely begins before the last and most harried member arrives, and the tenor of the deliberations is usually established by the member who is both least knowledgeable and most vocal! The group, rarely self-selected and ever-changing, is often so diverse as to talent, level of interest, and amount of experience that effective decision making is rendered nearly impossible. The idea of laying off responsibility to a third party as an antidote to the inherent structural ineptitude of a group of individuals (attempting to carry on business as a unit) often gains respectability by default. Add to that the obligatory consultant's flippant use of the vernacular of MPT, dropping such terms as negative covariance, the efficient frontier, *beta*, and the esoteric math that ties it all together (none of which most consultants could explain with much lucidity), and you have the perfect prescription for a group that looks and functions more like the Three Stooges than what the grand theoretical design would have you believe. What more susceptible prey could a consultant hope for!

Pay close attention to the next consultant's presentation. The charts and occasional histrionics aside, consultants are in the business of collating and cataloguing massive quantities of historical data and trying hard, sometimes almost desperately, to impart some sort of unique spin to other consultants' warmed-over and rehashed verbiage. The sheer amount of material is intended to convey an image of the consultant's facility for thought and reason—and the committee frequently finds the comfort it needs buried in those numbers. Conspicuous by its absence, though, is any subjective reference to the future. Most consultants have a propensity for looking backward, citing the performance of yesterday's darlings who, by the very nature of the ebb and flow of investment fashion, are likely to be tomorrow's dogs. In so doing, they do little more than perpetuate the herd mentality.

While some of the above may seem unkind, you need only hear Charlie Munger rant on the subject to realize that we are in fact falling all over ourselves trying not to offend!

Chapter 5

The "Greenspan Put". . . Again[*]

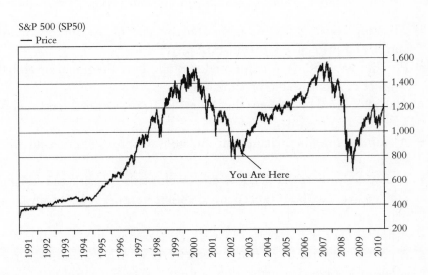

S&P 500 (SP50)
— Price

You Are Here

SOURCE: © FactSet Research Systems.

[*]This material is adapted from the 2002 annual report of Martin Capital Management.

This year's truncated offering is respectful of Einstein's admonition: "Make everything as simple as possible, but no simpler." Accordingly, you will find this report a little light on numbers and a little long on opinion. Reasoned judgment has been in short supply in recent years, and this monograph may be a (subconscious?) attempt to help fill the void. All of us are inundated with information about recent events or happenings, especially as reported by newspapers, periodicals, radio, or television. Regurgitating the facts of yesterday may bring a form of catharsis, but it adds little value. On the other hand, reactions to essays that challenge conformist thought might well run the gamut from raising the reader's ire to piquing his or her curiosity.

Investment Strategy

Although this report is annual, the formidable task of formulating a rational investment strategy in a chaotic world is like warily tiptoeing back and forth along a gymnast's five-meter balance beam. Forces from all sides persistently threaten to knock you off your perch. They include:

- The ongoing nightmare, aggravated by fear of the unknown, of another surprise attack by fanatical terrorists.
- Possible war with Iraq that could explode into a regional or global conflict of unknowable proportions.
- A schizophrenic economy that seems to defy diagnosis (and therefore effective treatment).
- A global economic malaise that threatens to spread like a pandemic disease.
- A destructive bear market, savaging stock market wealth and leaving policymakers without precedent to anticipate its effect on consumer behavior.
- A dollar that has rested on its laurels far too long.
- A political environment that, at least in terms of a coherent macro-economic policy, has yet to define itself.

The ledger of "macro maladies" continues to grow. Moreover, the prices of businesses, on average, still seem rich relative to the plethora of ambiguities, real and imagined—and respected investors, not the least of whom is Warren Buffett, have made broad-brush prognostications about the relatively anemic performances to be expected from the popular averages for some years to come.

Every business day we face the daunting task of enhancing the value of your capital without putting it in harm's way. In so doing, however, we are fortified by the simple wisdom of John Maynard Keynes: "It is better to be generally right than precisely wrong."

Dow 36000: New Strategy for Profiting from Coming Rise in Stock Market

By way of backdrop, a sea change in a deeply ingrained perception about what constitutes investment is upon us. The profound catharsis, deleteriously reversing the treacherous and insidious transition from investment to speculation (and all the accoutrements that distinguished the capital markets and its various links to the economy during the 1990s) is firmly under way.

To begin, let me set the scene in 1998–1999. Following are a few symptomatic indications of the pervasive susceptibility and concomitant euphoria that led to the emergence of "irrational exuberance" in many popular industries, stealthily and progressively biasing the reasoning of the horde of investors who, "at the margin" (those actually doing the buying and selling and therefore setting prices), pushed prices higher and higher as the bull market of the 1990s reached full flower, surging relentlessly toward its own demise. A crowd, as we have often written in the past, is amenable to suggestion, the simpler (and often the more preposterous) the better. What stage-whispered prompting could be more explicit, understandable, and forceful to a layperson than the title of the book by James K. Glassman and Kevin A. Hassett, coauthors of *Dow 36,000: The New Strategy for Profiting from the Coming Rise in the Stock Market*, which hit the bookstands in September 1999, just months before the wild-eyed ride ended in stunning collapse. *Dow 40,000: Strategies for Profiting from the Greatest Bull Market in History*, hurriedly penned by money manager David Elias, trumped the Glassman and Hassett effort, only to be overtrumped by Charles Kadlec, chief investment strategist for Seligman Advisors, Inc., who wrote *Dow 100,000: Fact or Fiction*.

The latter two expect their Dow targets to be met in 2016 and 2020, respectively, implying historically palatable compounded annual returns of 9 percent and 11.1 percent. The latter authors' analytical methodology is fairly standard. On the other hand, Glassman, a *Washington Post* columnist, and Hassett, an economist and resident scholar at the American Enterprise Institute (AEI) where Glassman is also a fellow, must have roundly embarrassed AEI—and possibly herded gullible investors by the thousands to their financial slaughter—because of impossible forecasts supported by cockeyed reasoning. Straining investors' credulity to the limit, they foresaw the Dow reaching 36000 in three to five years, implying ludicrous annual rates of return of 52 percent and 28 percent, respectively. Among other transgressions, they coined a new acronym (that perfectly symbolized the absurdity of the times): "PRP"—a "perfectly reasonable price."

As for the investment eggheads, a conference was conducted in Palm Beach, Florida, in December 2000 for the senior executives of investment advisory firms (where, because of some breakdown in the screening process, I found myself in attendance). One would be quite right in concluding that such an august gathering would insist on more substance than the so-called investor who gets his tips from CNBC's boundlessly blathering broadcasters. Among the featured presenters at the conference was the obligatorily upbeat Jeremy Siegel, professor of finance at the Wharton School of the University of Pennsylvania and author of the much-hyped book *Stocks for the Long Term*. As you may recall, we took Siegel to task in the 1998 annual report [Chapter 1] for repackaging the generally sound concept that Edgar Lawrence Smith introduced in 1924, under the nearly identical title, *Common Stocks as Long-term Investments*, and (disregarding Keynes' admonition) for trumpeting the virtues of common stock investing *at precisely the wrong time*. This atrocity of timing was not unlike the Ford Foundation–funded, well-reasoned, and scholarly study persuasively endorsing the concept of "total return" investing, maladroitly rolled out on the eve of the 1973–1974 bear market. While Siegel's demeanor was a little less ebullient because of the Nasdaq's eight-month plunge leading up to the conference, he remained the prancing Pollyanna that December in Florida.

As a postscript and with the benefit of hindsight, Siegel just didn't get it, as Table 5.1 reveals. Ironically, though, in the long run Siegel will be right, just as Edgar Lawrence Smith was. For many of his fans, however, the reality of greatly diminished wealth in the meantime is proving nettlesome if not downright troublesome.

Table 5.1 Stock Prices in Decline

	12/29/00	10/9/02
S&P 500	1,320.28	776.76
Dow Jones Industrials	10,786.85	7,286.27
Nasdaq Composite Index	2,470.52	1,114.11

Such was the mind-set of both the small and the mighty as we approached the precipice in the late winter of 2000. The signature mental attitude or disposition that predetermines a person's responses to and interpretations of any monumental speculative bubble is a compulsive preoccupation with a fixed idea. For the soon-to-be-humbled investment professional, the polite word was *return*, whereas for the untutored, the bourgeois word *greed* was operative. Both manifested symptoms of restlessness and irritability. Conspicuous by its absence was any awareness of the storm cloud of mushrooming risk looming ever larger on the horizon. In reality, a form of unabashed envy, the thought of being left behind as the freight train of unimaginable riches pulled out of the station, was more than many investors could stomach. Where it was going, or how it might get there, was of little importance. The fact that it was leaving the station was all that mattered.

Remember how CNBC, the continually televised "tout sheet," whose commercial commission (ethical standards were generally suspended wherever a buck could be made) was to opine on whatever investors were craving to hear, came out of nowhere to remorselessly cater to such copycat speculating? Nature abhors a vacuum. The CNBC of today, its programming milieu exuding a reactive case of economic self-righteousness—always solicitous of the viewers' mood—seems more contrite than it did two years ago and will likely, in this writer's opinion, be a shadow of its former self five years hence. That said, CNBC, like a chainsaw, can be a useful tool in the right hands.

The Reckoning

As night follows day, a speculative binge, like a drunken spree, must come to an end—and for many of the same reasons. Overnight exhilaration gives way to disillusionment and despair. The investor who had asked, "How much *will* I make" now, with an anxious look in his eyes, nervously poses the question, "How much *can* I lose?" *Risk* replaces *return* as the operative word. Preservation of capital displaces enhancement of wealth as the prevailing objective. Focusing on our ever-aging population, according to surveys by the American Association of Retired Persons, a Washington advocacy group for people age 50 and older, the universe of affected investors is surprisingly large. The portion of people ages 55–64 who invest in stocks climbed to 58 percent in 1998 from 28 percent in 1989. "Where you once had home value as the largest asset for many people, now it's often stock value." Among investors surveyed between the ages of 50 and 70, fully 77 percent said their holdings have dropped in the last two years, with 37 percent losing between 10 and 25 percent, and 25 percent losing between one-quarter and one-half. About one in five older Americans who lost money in the stock market during the past two years has postponed his or her retirement date, and 10 percent of those already retired are at work again because of stock market losses. Overall, two-thirds of older investors with losses, including those who haven't retired at all, say they are making lifestyle adjustments—from budgeting more carefully (59 percent) to taking fewer vacations (34 percent) to postponing a major purchase (30 percent). And 43 percent worry that, in the future, they will be

"APPARENTLY YOU HAVEN'T BEEN RETIRED AS LONG AS I HAVE"

SOURCE: Copyright © 1993 Bill Monroe.

less comfortable in retirement than they previously had expected. One in five fears that he or she may have trouble paying for healthcare and prescription drugs. Whether it's the AARP—or, perhaps more fittingly, the *urp* generation [see the next section, "Sober in the Morning"]—or the Internet day trader, the relentless erosion in wealth is not a trifling matter, and, as noted below, the full extent of its economic repercussions is yet to be known. Will Rogers' famous dictum will once again be resurrected: "I'm more concerned about the return *of* my principal than the return *on* my principal." This change in general psychology will occur, as always, long after its relevance has peaked.

Sober in the Morning

Among Warren Buffett's pithy sayings, the following is particularly *apropos*: "We are fearful when others are greedy, and greedy when others are fearful." Having generally avoided the epidemic of excessive or uncontrolled speculative indulgence, we, unlike the hungover party animal who is likely to upchuck at the mere offer of another drink, have a relatively clearheaded thirst for opportunity. Moreover, and equally important, in contrast to party surroundings where liquor flows freely, no one is shoving a drink into our hand every time we turn around. We are liberated not only from libations but from the crowd's bothersome banter, freed from the urge to mindlessly imitate others, as we go about our business. If one is to have any hope of making headway in the emotional-roller-coaster world of investment, one must avoid distractions that will get in the way of keeping an even temperament, thereby truncating both the highs and the lows. Investment teetotalers that we are, there will be no "bellying up to the bar" on our watch.

Micro versus Macro

The title of this section refers to our preoccupation with microeconomics (a focus on the firm) rather than macroeconomics (concentration on the system) as we attempt to rationally find our way through the maze that will lead us to durable investment success. Our first turn in the labyrinth—and one that separates us from much of the crowd—is that we spend the great portion of our time and energy studying businesses as opposed to the myriad forces that constitute the external environment in which those businesses operate. Admittedly, businesses do not function in a vacuum. It's just that we're inclined to stick with the knowable and avoid spending too much of our time speculating about what is unknowable. For example, we have absolutely no idea whether, when, where, or how another terrorist attack might be launched in America. No amount of rumination will add one percentage point to the probability that we can pinpoint such an event. Not to downplay the tragedy of 9/11, which affected us as it surely affected you . . . but (for the most part) it was "business as usual" within days of the attack.

Every single business we own kept running as usual, right through the maelstrom. None, to our knowledge, ever considered closing up shop. Berkshire Hathaway, the only one affected in a meaningful way, took a $2.5 billion hit (against a start-of-year equity capital base of $61.7 billion) as the insurer of several of the assets that were destroyed and due to the workers' compensation claims that arose. The record shows that well-managed and well-capitalized businesses with durable competitive advantages, like the seaworthy ship mentioned earlier, survive—and often thrive vis-à-vis their weaker competition—in environments of manifold uncertainty. This kind of information is most valuable because it is in the realm of the knowable.

The "macro trap," because it is so generalized and nonspecific, helps to agitate our anxieties, which is precisely why we don't let it dominate our thinking. Various sectors of the economy were directly affected by 9/11, of course. Commercial airline travel was sharply curtailed in a knee-jerk reaction. Again, truly hoping not to appear callous in my attempt to be coolly analytical, the "rearview mirror" mentality helped fly United Airlines right into bankruptcy court. Fears notwithstanding, in all likelihood the safest time in years to fly commercially was immediately after the attacks when vigilance at all levels was at its peak—and yet the airports were empty. More important, having expended the critical element of surprise in one venue, the terrorists would surely have chosen another if subsequent attacks were in the offing. But the public reaction was indicative of human nature in times of crisis. We "fight the last war" because our vision of the past is always clearer than our foggy notions of the future. That propensity is, as discussed above, at work in the capital markets today.

The Margin-of-Safety Paradox

Not wanting to appear nonchalant, we must face up to some hard decisions in this possibly atypical but not unprecedented economic environment. Remaining rational and circumspect in the months, if not years, ahead will largely determine how well we fulfill our mission to our clients. Are we in a cyclical economic contraction from which we will soon emerge or are we experiencing something more insidious and protracted? A quote from Benjamin Graham is indelibly imprinted on my mind:

> But the "new era" commencing in 1927 involved at bottom the abandonment of the analytical approach; and while emphasis was still seemingly placed on facts and figures, these were manipulated by a sort of pseudoanalysis to support the delusions of the period. The market collapse in October 1929 was no surprise to such analysts as had kept their heads, but the extent of the business collapse which later developed, with its devastating effects on established earning power, again threw their calculations out of gear. Hence the ultimate result was that serious analysis suffered a double discrediting: the first—prior to the crash—due to the persistence of imaginary values, and the second—after the crash—due to the disappearance of real values. (Graham, *Security Analysis*, 31–32)

Parallels with the malaise that has garroted Japan since 1989, not so much the means but the end, cannot be dismissed out of hand, even though we realize that the "availability bias" (the tendency to give disproportionate weight to more recent or readily available experiences or events) is at work here. Listening to Alan Greenspan's words, as well as being very attentive to his inflections, we find it clear that he wonders and worries about whether he has inadvertently taken us to the economic precipice.

If "real values" disappear, how does an analyst get a handle on the intrinsic worth of a business if his "confidence interval" for that swing variable is a mile wide after allowing for the possibility, however unlikely, that "the extent of the business collapse which later developed, with its devastating effects on established earning power, again threw their calculations out of gear"? If the estimation of intrinsic value is deemed substantially unreliable, there is simply no way to determine the extent to which the current market price affords a margin of safety.

Countless technology and dot-com companies serve as vivid contemporary examples of the valuation conundrum that Ben Graham described 70 years ago. Even today, after stocks of many companies of that ilk have withered to less than 10 percent of their highs, we still cannot determine whether they are cheap or dear. But do not despair, for that example is of limited utility. Companies in those industries were just as difficult to value in the best of times. The dilemma was captured in a Christmas cartoon picturing a frustrated reindeer complaining to one of the elves: "We give away all our products. We don't make a dime. I'm telling you, Santa runs this place like a dot-com."

Waiting Patiently for Those Hanging Curves

We at MCM are ever mindful that the size of our paycheck is in direct proportion to the amount of increase in your wealth above and beyond that pesky but ethically critical high-water-mark hurdle, which is also a convenient daily reminder that "in order to win, the first thing you must do is not lose."

Returning to our well-worn (think of your favorite glove) baseball metaphor, there is little to be gained—if the economic contraction proves to be persistent—by going after every pitch. It's in your best interest, as well as ours, to wait patiently for the sweet pitch, refusing to swing at anything else. Thanks to the forbearance of our clients, in this game we'll never lose our place at the plate by being forced to take a base on balls. How simple, you say. But we would beg to differ. Even if the game of baseball were scored this way, batters' egos would soon take over, and they'd flail away. After all, the athlete who is paid to swing, "wood." Steely self-control is the operative phrase in times like these. Patience is the order of the day. To be sure, if this contraction transcends the cyclical, it will be much more difficult to tell the slider from a fastball headed for our sweet spot. And yet it isn't impossible. There are many hard-to-read pitches—and a few juicy ones, the hanging curves, that leave the pitcher's hand destined for solid contact with the bat. Those are the ones we wait for. The many pitches we can't clearly decipher we let pass without regret.

Returning to the task at hand, the economic environment forces us to narrow our focus to those companies that are easy to understand and *relatively* simple to value and whose competitive advantages, including a rock-solid capital structure and level-headed yet opportunistic corporate leadership, enhance their chances of coming out on top whenever the contraction ends and the next expansion begins, even if it's some years away.

Let's Get Mathematical

The value of any stock, bond, or business today is determined by the cash inflows and outflows—discounted at an appropriate interest rate—that can be expected to occur *during the remaining life of the asset* [emphasis added]. That foundational one-size-fits-all investment maxim is older than Methuselah. Please note that this valuation model applies to all investments. The pricing of common stocks, of course, is less exact than bonds: Their "coupons" are variable, and there is no predetermined maturity date or price. Let's frame the challenge investors face in terms of the mathematics of finance, using the above present-value model. Several assumptions, however, must be made (prior to concluding with an obvious question). The assumptions are:

- An investment is made in a first-class company that has earned 15 percent on its unleveraged equity capital, approximating the long-term American industry average.
- Economic hard times exacted their toll, resulting in the company losing money for three years and causing its net worth to shrink by a third.
- The stock was purchased at 15 times earnings and subsequently falls by 50 percent.
- After the storm has passed, the company returns to its historical profitability ratios, and 10 years later the stock sells for 15 times earnings.

Now, the question: "What was the holding-period return during those turbulent times?" The answer, for which we will happily provide details for those who are interested: 7.9 percent. For the mathematically challenged, a simpler example would be if we assume that the economic hard times were such that the company earned a lower-than-historical average return on its unleveraged equity capital of 12 percent over the 13 years. If we argue that, at the end of the period, the stock again sells for 15 times earnings, the annual return rises to 12 percent (the same return as the underlying business earned on its equity capital). Regardless of the example, the investment return hinges on the earnings power of the business and the price the market is willing to pay for those earnings at the beginning and the end. If our ship is seaworthy, we can take each storm as it comes with equanimity, never losing sight of our destination.

Warren Buffett, after a long hiatus following the liquidation of his partnerships in 1969–1970, came back in 1973–1974 with a vengeance. He summarized his enthusiasm, rather impolitely we must admit, for the bargain-priced equities he was gobbling up. Said he: "I feel like a sex-starved man in a harem." What few people know is that at the time the market reached its low point, Buffett's holdings were a full 50 percent underwater.

Sometimes percentages can distort an investor's perception of reality. The following is a theoretical example: Let's say a stock falls 50 percent in year one, from $10 to $5. (Let's assume intrinsic worth was able to be approximated and was constant over the three years at $5.) The next year it declines another 50 percent to $2.50. Finally, after another 50 percent decline in the third year, it reaches $1.25, a decline of 87.5 percent from its first-year high, similar (though not so orderly) to the Dow Jones industrial average during the crash and subsequent bear market of 1929–1932 or the Nasdaq's total reversal of fortunes from 5050 in March 2000 to just over 1100 this past October as indicated in the earlier table. Using the example to hypothetically and approximately index Buffett's experience, after avoiding the lion's share of the 1973–1974 bloodbath, he missed what turned out to be the bottom by a mere $1.25, and, undaunted by his paper losses, he kept making purchases.

How would you judge Buffett's overall perspicacity? First, and most important in this writer's judgment, his initial stroke of genius was in doing nothing when there was nothing to do—that is, committing capital to the folly at $10 . . . or *$12 or $15 or whatever price at which the stock eventually peaked*. He just stood there flat-footed, with the bat on his shoulder, watching pitches whiz by. Admittedly, those times are rare when the pitcher is throwing you nothing but junk. Mind you, Mr. Buffett wasn't asleep; he was simply thinking instead of swinging.

As important as that decision was, because no transaction took place, *it was never even recorded*. And yet it counted—avoiding impossible pitches or knucklehead pitchers plays a huge role in the pursuit of investment success. Likewise, his brilliance was not diminished whatsoever because he didn't pick the exact bottom. Those who unrealistically aspire to the impossible, a la Don Quixote, inevitably go away empty-handed, as we noted previously. In fact, Buffett's genius was confirmed again when he persistently took advantage of the ever-widening gap between the market price and intrinsic value.

There is little doubt in my mind that, had the market continued to fall beyond its eventual 1974 lows of 62.28, for the S&P 500, Buffett would have stayed at the plate, the same gleeful look on his face as a kid in a candy store. Each new low would undoubtedly represent opportunities to add to his existing holdings at even more attractive prices, as well as to make initial purchases of new ones that appeared on his radar screen for the first time as their prices fell. *Although the percentage decline was identical three years running, its investment consequences in absolute dollar terms diminished with each successive year.* If the preceding statement troubles you, test it with your trusty calculator. While we hope not to find ourselves in this position, if we do, count on us not to forget what we are here to do: namely, to honor our responsibility to you.

The Bottom Line for Equities

There are purposes served by these two examples. First, remember the Keynesian quote in the third paragraph of this section. Like Buffett from 1965 to 1972 (and later in 1973–1974), we believe we have been "generally right" about what brought us to this time and place, and we will conscientiously apply our best efforts to stay ahead of the curve as we look through the windshield and not at the rearview mirror. In the abstract sense, if we are any more precise than Buffett in our timing, it will be more coincidental than intentional. The cost of obsessing on precision is to often miss the forest for the trees. Second, we will always try to look across the valley to the foothills beyond, to visualize our destination. At last we can say to long-chastised Jeremy Siegel, this may be your moment, the time to "stock" the bookshelves at Barnes & Noble with *Stocks for the Long Term*. Predictably, if none is to be found, it wouldn't be audacious to surmise that one would be "generally right" buying "stocks for the long term"! Sometimes one's trust in the basic precepts of investing seems foolhardy, only to be proved prudent some years hence. As Blaise Pascal said in another context about the ever-present dilemma with which the opportunistic investor must live: "Too much to deny and too little to be sure." Nobody shoots a gun to start this race.[1]

As for the tangible, the mathematics of finance bridges the gap between conjecture and reality, putting meat on the bones of the theoretical skeletal framework. We know there is much uncertainty we must accept with a wary eye—and yet also with educated equanimity if we expect to earn acceptable returns from the asset class with the most productive history and, in all likelihood, the most productive "long term" future. Ultimately, the "bottom line" for equities must be the "bottom-up" orientation.

---

[1][2006, *Speculative Contagion*] This statement was written at the lowest point in the market over the last seven or eight years. As for Jeremy Siegel, we searched for words of encouragement from him, but none were found. In a November 30, 2004, interview with *Money* magazine he remained the unrepentant optimist. Siegel has always navigated the investment highways and byways while looking backward—to wit, his latest revelation: "My research finds that investors consistently overpay for growth. I want people to think about investing this way: The great growing companies are not often the ones that give you the best returns. The tried and true triumph over the bold and new."

Chapter 6

Only Fools Rush In*

S&P 500 (SP50)
— Price

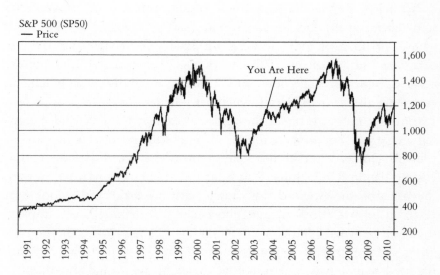

SOURCE: © FactSet Research Systems.

---

*This material is adapted from the 2003 annual report of Martin Capital Management.

The Rogues Gallery, 2003 Vintage

Early 2003 provided a somewhat unexpected respite from the plethora of deplorable corporate disclosures in 2002, which included the WorldCom debacle, where megalomaniac Bernie Ebbers and his apparently dumbstruck board recklessly leveraged WorldCom into the largest bankruptcy in American history. In the professional service sector, the once proud but ultimately disgraceful bust of Arthur Andersen was beheaded by its own sword. These are but two of the more conspicuously reprehensible examples. Momentarily taking center stage, the public relations and military buildup preceding the blitzkrieg in Iraq on March 19, 2003, commandeered the headlines during the first quarter.

Wall Street was back in the limelight on April 28, when a historic $1.4 billion settlement was reached between the Securities & Exchange Commission and 10 Wall Street firms for their fiduciary misconduct during the Bubble days when business ethics were conveniently suspended and the lust for fool's gold made a mockery of morals. Of course, no firm or individual has admitted guilt, continuing a ritualistic dance of "repentance" that takes place between the SEC and the accused, wherein the "not guilty" parties are more than willing to cough up the cash to burnish their tarnished reputations—or at least sweep their misdeeds under the carpet in exchange for the judge turning a deaf ear. For aspiring felons, we note offhandedly, "white collar" crimes stand head and shoulders above most others, without much bothersome dandruff. On June 4 aspiring near-billionaire Martha Stewart, the "diva of domesticity," was caught with her hand in the cookie jar reaching for a chump-change "chocolate *tip*." Reports have estimated she saved between $40,000 and $57,000 by selling prior to the Food & Drug Administration announcement. Five days later Freddie Mac reported that it had underreported earnings and would thus have to restate the previous three years' earnings. While underreporting clearly is better than the alternative, earnings squirreled away today will propitiously reappear when Freddie "Kruger-rand" Mac is money-hungry to shore up results in the future. The rub: The slippery slope of earnings management can easily morph into flat-out misrepresentation where the numbers and reality take divergent paths.

On September 3 New York Attorney General Eliot Spitzer announced evidence of widespread illegal trading in the hedge-fund and mutual-fund industry that proved to be the first volley in a legal/ political battle that continued to rage at year end. On September 10 former Enron treasurer Ben Glisan pleaded guilty to a single count of criminal conspiracy and was sentenced to five years in a federal minimum-security prison. Oh, how slowly turn the wheels of justice. Former Enron chairman and CEO Ken is still *Lay*ing low more than two years after the news broke, thus far untouched by the rubble that continues to cascade down around him.[1]

Only weeks later, on September 17, Dick Grasso, chairman of that bastion of free enterprise, the New York Stock Exchange (the roots of which date back to a first meeting beneath a Wall Street buttonwood tree), resigned amid protests that his $140 million pay package was generous to a fault. Not coincidentally, on September 16 the not-for-profit NYSE had reported "earnings" for the first half of 2003 of $27 million on revenues of $540 million. Graciously, Grasso abstained from pressing for the $48 million still owed him. Truth be known, Grasso was merely the fall guy, though with his golden parachute the landing will be pillow soft. What, we might legitimately ask, was the NYSE's 27-member board—which includes executives from listed companies, Wall Street brokerages, and specialist firms—thinking when the proposed looting came to a vote? If this doesn't reek of all manner of conflicts of interest, your olfactory sensors may have become desensitized by the repugnant, pungent odor endlessly emanating from bored (yes, the spelling is correct!) rooms across the country. As you will read later, the widespread abdication of fiduciary duty by those who

---

[1][2006, *Speculative Contagion*] As of June 2005, Ken Lay and former Enron CEO Jeffrey Skilling had been ordered to stand trial on conspiracy and fraud charges. The trial is set for January 2006, more than four years after Enron collapsed in the fall of 2001. [2010 update: Ken Lay died of a heart attack while vacationing on July 5, 2006, about three months before his scheduled sentencing. Skilling was convicted of 18 counts of fraud and conspiracy and one count of insider trading; he was sentenced in May 2006 to 24 years and four months in prison. As of September 2010, Skilling's appeal was in the U.S. Court of Appeals for the Fifth Circuit awaiting a decision concerning "honest-services fraud."]

hold the highest seats of power in corporate America is, in this writer's judgment, ground zero for much that is out of whack with this otherwise wonderful economic system of ours. As to who put these board members in office in the first place, we'll attend to that later. With the exception of the Martha Stewart fiasco, it seems unlikely that any of the ships mentioned above would have run aground had a qualified and diligent board been on watch.

On September 29 jury selection finally began for former Tyco CEO Dennis Kozlowski and sidekick, CFO Mark Swartz. They have been charged with grand larceny, enterprise corruption, conspiracy, and falsifying business records. Altogether they stand accused of pilfering a measly $600 million from Tyco shareholders. Kozlowski, with his outlandish purchases of $6,000 shower curtains and a $2.1 million birthday

Source: Copyright © 1997 Bill Monroe.

bash for his wife (half of which was paid for by Tyco and its shareholders), may retain the distinction of being appointed the poster child for
this generation of rogues. At Kozlowski's party in Sardinia, a "stream-
ing" knockoff of Michelangelo's David—a statue of limitations if ever
there was one—is a metaphor for much of corporate America: Too
many CEOs go through investors' money like water (or, in this case,
vodka). That may not be urinalysis, but it's my analysis. The long and
the short of it? I hope there's no statute of limitations for prosecuting
people like Koz-*louse*-ski. As with Martha Stewart, he was exposed for
a "relatively" minor misdemeanor: evading roughly $1 million in sales
taxes on art he purchased for his New York City digs. Psychologists
doubtless have an explanation as to why, despite the consequences,
those who are apparently pathologically predisposed to larcenous urg-
ings seem indifferent as to whether their crimes are grand or petty.

As is readily apparent, the 2003 chapter in the "book" on capitalism reads like a litany of woes. The chronology above is perhaps most
appropriately described as a *Who's Who of Robber Barons*, reminiscent
of the stories of the venal vipers of old who are remembered by the
same name: the American industrial or financial magnates of the latter half of the nineteenth century who became wealthy by unethical
means, in those days engaging in questionable stock-market operations
and exploiting labor. Even though the base of their fortunes was the railroad industry, they were (for the most part) more manipulators of finance
than builders of new track. They also were, with few exceptions,
ruthless and corrupt, as was the system in which they were embedded.
Although the term *robber barons* is barely a century old, their *modus
operandi* is as endemic to the human condition as the lust for money
and power. Long before capitalism, a feudal lord who exacted stiff lev-
ies on travelers passing through his domain was known by the name
"baron" [not entirely unlike the local constable who sets a ridiculously
low speed limit in his somnolent hamlet, lies in wait behind some
shrubbery for unsuspecting out-of-town motorists, and then rakes in
the revenues]. In reality, the barons of yesteryear were not much different from the contemporary class of charlatans mentioned above,
who themselves resemble a slightly different iteration of the characters
depicted in the best seller *Barbarians at the Gate: The Fall of RJR Nabisco*,
originally published in 1992.

Making Progress in the
Post-Bubble Environment

There's a trade-off associated with our relatively concentrated approach to portfolio management (versus spreading our bets all over the board, as is the more common practice). Keep in mind that our implicit goal is long-term safety of principal and above-average returns. The trade-off, of course, is often above-average portfolio price volatility. Modern portfolio theorists associate higher volatility with greater risk, and apply *beta* as their quantitative measuring shtick—to individual securities and portfolios alike. In regard to a single security, we obviously have observed heightened relative volatility in the shares of unproven companies. Likewise, in the portfolio context, the day-in and day-out price volatility of an aggregation of 12 holdings is certain to be more pronounced than an array of 250, *even* if the average established quality of the 12 companies is greater than the 250. The inverse relationship between the number of issues in a portfolio and its volatility, assuming comparable quality, is simply a derivative of the law of large numbers.

If you believe, as we do (and on the strength of compelling back-tested evidence), that the random "bad apple" risk against which broad diversification is designed to provide protection can be 90 to 95 percent alleviated with the smaller number of dissimilar issues, then we notice another countervailing trade-off that is rarely factored into the investor's calculus. With the risk of an unpredictable outcome—say the unexpected bankruptcy of a company in your portfolio that you presumed solvent—minimized within prudent limits by a relatively nondiversified portfolio, then you stand a chance, at least in theory, of reducing your exposure to another peril: market risk. A broadly diversified portfolio will tend to mirror the "market," replicating its performance up or down with minimal tracking error. Specifically, the risk that a broadly diversified portfolio would lose half its value from peak to trough in the 2000–2002 bear market's 50 percent retrenchment was as close to a near-certainty as you can get. Here's where the two approaches to diversification part company. Beyond differences in short-term volatility, divergence in the dollar value of the two portfolios, accentuated by the passage of time, is highly likely. Obviously, this divergence can be either negative or positive. For example, consider the difference between MCM's nondiversified portfolio performance and that of the broadly diversified S&P 500, particularly in 2000 and 2001. That outcome could not have occurred *had we been broadly diversified*, we state emphatically. What about the probability that the difference would have been negative? If we thought the probability to be 50 percent, a "random walk," we wouldn't go there. We believe that by confining ourselves to way-above-average businesses and purchasing them at prices that imply a significant margin of safety, we expect more positive differences than negative ones. It also implies that we count on doing better than "the market" over the long haul. Those statements are consistent with our past record and, we trust, will not be invalidated by our future results.

We also seek to objectively reduce the surfeit of frequently conflicting market information bombarding us from all sides to something that is useful and practical. Specifically, we hope to very roughly approximate where we are along the continuum from investment bliss (where value grows solidly and prices are low relative to value, both implying high expected returns and lower risks) to the other extreme: investment misery and agony, the woeful state of affairs in 2000–2002.

You may recall in the 1999 annual report [Chapter 2] that considerable attention was directed to Warren Buffett's well-reasoned macroeconomic market analysis as published in *Fortune*, in part because he has historically redirected questions of that sort, declaring himself an agnostic on the market in general. His tone was uncompromising as he warned investors to downsize their expectations, arguing that earnings growth is not likely to exceed 3 percent (to which we add 2 percent for inflation) unless one uses heroic and historically unsupportable assumptions about interest rates, GDP growth, and expanding profit margins. To that we add a 1 percent dividend yield and arrive at a nominal 6 percent total return from a broadly diversified portfolio of common stocks well into the future. Buffett revisited the subject in July 2001, which we again summarized in our 2001 annual report, incrementally raising his hypothetical expected return to 7 percent because stock prices were lower and the economy had grown. With the S&P 500 finishing 2003 some 28.7 percent ahead of the preceding year's close, it's no wonder that in a *Barron's* October 27 article a patient Buffett admitted he is sitting on an enormous cash hoard—more than $24 billion—awaiting investment opportunities in the stock and bond markets. In the wide-ranging interview, Buffett said he's "not finding anything" in the stock market and isn't enamored with Treasury bonds or junk debt. His market-related comments are consistent with those made in Berkshire's 2002 annual report, which was released in March 2003, and at Berkshire's annual meeting in early May. In the annual report Buffett wrote that "despite three years of falling prices, which have significantly improved the attractiveness of common stocks, we still find very few that even mildly interest us."

While this writer's unabashed admiration for Warren Buffett is manifestly evident, it is not obsequious. Since Berkshire's annual report is published several months after MCM's, I critically review his chairman's letter to make sure his thinking is straight! *This* report takes a look at the "where we are on the continuum" issue from a perspective somewhat different from Buffett's.

There is no more comfortable place to start than with the long-term relationship between price and value. Parenthetically, we would have preferred to begin with a forecast of the future prospects for growth in the underlying value of American industry but found that daunting task well beyond our, or for that matter anyone else's, capabilities.

The first S&P 500 chart in Figure 6.1 presents earnings per share going back almost 50 years. It's very important that you notice the legend is logarithmic, where the value assigned to each equally spaced point on the vertical axis is 10 times the numerical value of the one below it. Compared with the arithmetical grid scale (1, 2, 3 . . . and so on), which is most commonly used, the logarithmic scale is better for showing percentage changes over time, with a straight line representing a constant rate of change. We calculated the trendline—or average compounded rate of earnings-per-share growth—over the 47 years to be approximately 6 percent. Using this method of presentation, and viewing a half-century of progress from our bird's-eye vantage point, one should get a sense of the relative linearity of the overall trend, at least until 2001. In retrospect, the carnage of 1973–1974, for those who take the long view, doesn't seem to be an event worth losing sleep over. As an aside, from 1957 until 1985 dividends yielded 4 percent on average, which, when added to the growth rate in earnings, equaled the oft-referred-to 10 percent total return from common stocks from 1926 through 1985.

Though one can make a science of trying to precisely explain the drop in earnings in 2001 and 2002, we'll attempt a simple explanation.

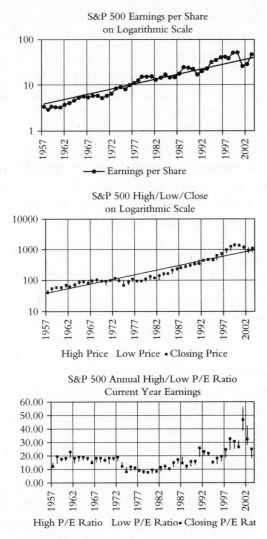

Figure 6.1   S&P 500 Metrics since 1957

DATA SOURCE: S&P 500.

Here we aren't trying to make points; we're trying to make *a* point. Beyond the obvious effects of the recession, it is our general view that in many instances earnings were overstated for any number of years, depending on the company, leading up through 2000. The last seven years' worth of MCM annual reports discussed in great detail the pre-occupation of a number of companies with managing earnings. Many of the sins of the past were recognized with goodwill impairment and a host of other charges in 2001 and 2002. We have no idea how much of the dirty laundry has been aired, but we would hazard a guess that what is hanging on the line represents the majority of it. The reader should be reminded that many companies toed the mark during the period of great temptation, thus ameliorating the repercussions of the most egregious offenders.

So, using S&P data, and relying on an earnings forecast for 2004 of $46.50, which is estimated by fitting a linear trendline to the earnings-per-share chart, is probably a reasonable place to start analyzing to what extent the market is generally cheap or dear in terms of the relationship between price and "trendline" earnings. The S&P index closed 2003 at 1112, resulting in a price-earnings ratio of 24 on 2004 estimated earnings. You'll notice from the price-earnings ratio chart that numbers in the mid- to upper teens prevailed between 1957 and 1973 when interest rates and inflation were relatively low and earnings growth slightly above average. The period from 1975 through 1990 was marked by higher-than-average interest rates and lower-than-average growth rates in earnings.

Next examine the relationship between the S&P 500 index, the index's annual earnings, and the index's annual high/low price-earnings ratio on the charts provided (Figure 6.1). As you can see, the spike in the price-earnings ratio around the turn of the century is partially explained by the doubling of the index (numerator) and the sharp drop in earnings (denominator).

Since today's stock prices are an approximation of the discounted present value of future cash flows, there are three unknowns that must be estimated: (1) cash flows many years hence, (2) the estimated cost of money (the underlying Treasury bond interest) over that same time frame as one component of the discount rate, and (3) the equity–risk premium added to the underlying cost of money to arrive at the total discount rate to be applied to reducing the future cash flows to present value. By comparison, a Treasury bond (currently considered to be the highest-quality, fixed-income instrument available) is priced using the same methodology, though all variables are known. Assuming a bond currently trades at par, only future fluctuations in market interest rates will cause its price to deviate from par.

Returning to the pricing of common stocks, as for the first and very important variable, we are at a loss to forecast the growth rate in earnings (a rough but convenient proxy for cash flow) years into the future with any degree of confidence. Precision is difficult to achieve even in the near term. In a recent *Barron's* poll of 12 Wall Street analysts, S&P 500 earnings growth forecasts for 2004 were as high as 16 percent and as low as 9 percent, in part because of differing earnings measurement metrics. Beyond telling us that the sheep rarely wander far from the flock, we can say the above numbers don't allow much to hang your hat on. And yet the long-term forecast, where the potential for the most uncertainty exists, is usually based on the simple extrapolation of historical growth rates—and generally for good reason. Sometimes, though, as was the case during the Great Bubble, the extrapolation of wildly optimistic (and ultimately fanciful) distant growth rates for many historically high-growth-rate companies led to extreme overvaluation. When visions seen through rose-colored glasses collided with reality, the stocks plummeted.

Looking back at the 47-year history of S&P 500 earnings, simple extrapolation was undoubtedly the most accurate forecasting methodology. While we can think of a number of major evolving forces that could knock the extrapolation train off the tracks, we're inclined to stay with the average 6 percent growth rates for the time being. Nonetheless, we offer a serious note of caution here. In testimony before Congress during the second half of 2003, Alan Greenspan added a new wrinkle to his macroeconomic management formula that looks a lot like "Pascal's Wager."[2] In justifying maintaining the discount rate at the 1 percent level, he admitted that he would rather err

---

[2] [2003, original] Blaise Pascal, the great seventeenth-century French philosopher and mathematician, became a devout Christian in his later years. As one of the original probability theorists, he rationally explained the pious life using mathematics rather than simple faith. He argued that if heaven and hell exist as discrete outcomes in the afterlife and that the probability of each was arbitrarily assigned to be 50 percent, one must still choose the virtuous life. His rationale rested on the difference in the severity of the outcomes: He reasoned that an eternity of heavenly bliss was infinitely preferable to one of never-ending damnation. That, in a nutshell, is Pascal's Wager.

on the side of being too easy than too tight, because the consequences of the latter are much more dire than the former. Thus, even though he assigns a relatively low probability to the deflationary scenario, its consequences are so grave as to cause him to "overweight" that possibility in his policy calculus. And so it is with us. However remote the likelihood of an economic meltdown might be, we, as stewards of your wealth, must overweight it in our portfolio decision making because of the extreme and unacceptable severity of the fallout should it by chance occur. Over the years, we have always positioned ourselves so that if we err, it will generally be on the side of excessive conservatism, otherwise known as forgoing opportunities. Generally, we have compensated by limiting ourselves to good businesses purchased at reasonable prices.

Finally, we turn to the cost of money and the premium in return that one should expect from investment in common stocks vis-à-vis the more predictable U.S. Treasury security. If you view the chart of U.S. government bond yields (Figure 6.2), it's hard to draw a conclusion about what is normal. If you were to overlay a Consumer Price Index (CPI) chart, you would see the logical connection between the rate at which the purchasing power of the currency is being debased through inflation and the rate of interest lenders demand for the rental of their money. Once again, we are at a loss. Intuitively, if we expect

Figure 6.2   20-Year Government Bond Yield History

NOTE: 10-year Treasury post 1953.

DATA SOURCE: www.econ.yale.edu/~shiller/data.htm.

trendline economic growth and take into account anecdotal indicators like the price of gold and the exchange rate of the dollar, inflation should rise, perhaps significantly, over time, from current levels. While there is no direct connection, interest rates should follow—or even lead—the rate of change in prices. As for the equity-risk premium, we feel qualified to prognosticate with more conviction. As we have so often written, investors are inclined to view the world through the rearview mirror. The rocky recent past and the widespread distrust of those who used to report but now manage earnings tarnished the image of equities as the sure-bet road to riches. The equity-risk premium, thought to be largely irrelevant a few years ago, should regain its lost credibility, if not actually overcompensate.

Taking all of the above into account, we must conclude that common stocks, *in general*, as measured by the S&P 500, which tends to somewhat overstate the results because of the survivor's bias mentioned earlier, are at the high end of the valuation continuum. How or when they regress to an approximate mean of, say, 15 times earnings is unknowable. So long as earnings stick reasonably close to their historical trendline growth rates, we believe that the best-case scenario is lumpy total returns from equities that average little more than the underlying earnings growth rate. The likely price-earnings ratio compression may be offset by an ever-rising dividend yield.

From the risk perspective, the most optimistic observation we can offer about the margin of safety is that it is razor-thin. Likewise, the key impetus behind stock prices going forward must be earnings growth since the probability of a significant expansion in earnings multiples is slight at best. In summary, even the best-case scenario is not particularly appealing. No wonder we're finding it difficult to identify companies that meet our threshold return requirement.

How Did We Get Here in the First Place?

Robert Shiller, Yale professor, seasoned market observer, and author of the prescient and timely book *Irrational Exuberance*, published in March 2000, the very month the Nasdaq Bubble burst, offered a number of "structural" causes in explaining how natural exuberance eventually became irrational. By dissecting those causal forces, perhaps we can speculate as to whether their power remains potent or whether it is on the wane.

He begins with the invasion of the Internet, delivering leading-edge technology (and presumably serving as confirming evidence of the "new era" in prosperity led by America's worldwide technological dominance) right into our homes in the second half of the 1990s. Visions of sugarplums, however unfounded, danced in just about everyone's heads. Merrill Lynch's slogan "We're bullish on America" symbolized the triumph of capitalism over other less-effective economic ideologies, the fall of the former Soviet Union being the quintessential case study. Shiller points out that materialism reemerged and business success, measured most conveniently in dollars, gave rise to the proliferation and eventual abuse of stock options as the quickest road to preeminence. Instead of being embarrassed by the polarities brought into bas-relief by their wealth, the newly ascended super-rich scrambled to the newsstands, like students to the bulletin board after final-exam results are posted, to see if their name had shown up on the *Forbes* list of the 400 wealthiest families in America. How much our values have changed from the wisdom of Ralph Waldo Emerson: "Great men are they who see that spiritual is stronger than any material force, that thoughts rule the world."

Tax cuts and the latter expectation of further cuts on earned income, capital gains, dividends, and estates provided encouraging and tangible evidence of a pro-business attitude within the Republican-dominated Congress. The powerful Baby Boomer myth, which was more about public perceptions than demographic logic, gained increasing credence during the decade of the 1990s. Proliferating media coverage of the financial markets only fanned the flames of exuberance, transforming once bland business periodicals into televised tout sheets. Who would have imagined broadcasted stock tips, 24 hours a day? After reading the above, again turn to the S&P 500 earnings-per-share chart to see how much, if any, of all this fanfare percolated through to affect higher rates of earnings growth over the past five years.

Wall Street's *modus operandi* adapted easily—and in fact far too effortlessly—to the times. The independence of analysts was compromised with the crumbling of the "Chinese wall," the imaginary barrier that in theory but rarely in practice separated researchers from investment bankers. Power gradually shifted from the analysts to the chief financial officers of corporations, whose profitable investment banking business was doled out with obvious partiality.

The growth in popularity of the defined-contribution pension plan since 1981—when the 401(k) plan came into existence—greatly increased the public's awareness about stocks, even if indirectly through mutual funds. The short- and long-term consequences of the transfer of decision-making authority to the employee, the emergence of the mutual-fund family that offered a cornucopia of investment alternatives, and the relative decline in the traditional defined-benefit plan are examined later in this report.

Returning to Shiller, the decline in inflation in the 1990s to levels not thought possible in the early 1980s bolstered investor confidence since steady prices are perceived by the public as a sign of economic stability and social health. Declining nominal interest rates added to investors' sense of economic well-being, irrespective of whether the more relevant but harder to understand "real" (inflation-adjusted) rates were relatively high or low.

Gambling has prospered in its many other forms over the past 20 years. For example, in 1975, only 13 states permitted lotteries; the number had increased to 37 by 1999. Until 1990 casinos were legalized in Nevada and Atlantic City only. By 1999 riverboat and dockside casinos numbered over 360, according to Shiller's research. Cable and the Internet have piped gambling right into our homes, and the waiting lines at local convenience stores to buy lottery tickets speak volumes about the mesmerizing hold "easy money" has on the popular imagination. Shiller makes a strong case that gambling fosters an inflated estimate of one's own potential for good luck that may well spill over to its more upscale form, speculation in securities.

Trading volume nearly doubled between 1982 and 1999, with annual turnover exploding from 42 percent to 78 percent, as casino capitalism stormed the barricades of rationality. The groundwork was laid on a memorable day in May 1975 when fixed commission rates were at long last forbidden by the SEC, as deregulation fought its way through heavy resistance to Wall Street. Trading costs stair-stepped down only to collapse like toy soldiers as online trading took *people* out of the process. Discount brokers and day trading proliferated as the speculative mania, like machine-gun fire, indiscriminately hit more and more targets, ranging from the vulnerable and vigilant to the vile and villainous. Dramatic changes in the volume of trading are almost always positively correlated with major bull and bear markets.

The Complementary Role of Behavioral Economics

From the structural changes that were foundational to the Great Bubble, we must look further to behavioral economics to understand how those forces were amplified and exaggerated in the minds of investors. In prior annual reports we have devoted discussion to individual and social psychology as a means of attempting to explain the seemingly irrational behavior of investors from time to time. More than that, we have relied on it heavily in our decision making. The subject of *behavioral economics* has, in the academic world where change is a lagging indicator, gained ground grudgingly as its struggle to obtain acceptability is symbolized by the oil-and-water character of the words themselves, conveying as they do two different strains of ideology. The science of psychology is as soft as economics is concrete. By way of illustration, it's the rare engineer whose library is filled with books on philosophy. Nonetheless, this cross-thinking is gaining credence in leading academic institutions like Harvard and Yale, the latter where Robert Shiller preaches this gospel, in large measure because . . . it works!

Shiller does a masterful job of blending the two sciences in explaining the energy that gave rise to irrational exuberance, not coincidentally the title of his 2000 book. The subject is far too comprehensive to be covered other than superficially here, and we therefore strongly encourage you to purchase the book if you find your appetite sufficiently whetted to induce you to venture out onto the frontiers of economic thought. While the boundaries of the discipline are not well defined, and perhaps never will be, for the sake of expediency I'll boil them in the same pot, though I won't necessarily toss the ingredients into the stew in the same order he did.

Shiller refers to the herd instinct and naturally occurring Ponzi processes as "amplification mechanisms," often causing the pendulum of investment sentiment to swing to extremes not remotely justified by rational analysis. Ponzi schemes, in one form or another, have been around and will be around forever because of (1) their simplicity and (2) the natural instinct (gullibility?) of groups of people all too willing to embrace the improbable. Generally, they are launched with a promoter

putting forth a plausible, although usually improbable, proposition that
large gains can be had from investing in the venture being hyped. In
fact, there is rarely little if any investment merit behind a promoter's
assertions. In reality, once the idea gains a toehold of credence, "feedback" mechanisms pour fuel on the fire of desire and the money flows
in, motivated almost entirely by the prospect for riches, the "investors"
having long forgotten whether or not the original investment thesis was
efficacious. Since there is no underlying asset truly capable of generating
the earnings at the rate promised, new-money inflows are the primary
means of making good on promises to earlier investors. The scheme
must come to an end and does so when exposed, often unexpectedly, but
certainly no later than when the inflows slow to a point that they don't
cover the promised outflows. The whole charade then inevitably collapses like a house of cards.

In its advanced stages, the market (especially Nasdaq) in Internet,
technology, and Telcom stocks took on the characteristics of a classic
Ponzi process. The underlying earnings power of the companies that
made up the industries was minuscule compared with the astronomical
valuations placed on them in the mad scramble for paper gold. As with
all Ponzi schemes, the first sellers are almost always the most fortunate.
And as discussed in the 2002 annual report [Chapter 5], the conspiracy (I don't think that's too harsh a word) to optimize the "rake" for
insiders became perniciously more refined with each new IPO (initial
public offering). In virtually any other venue, such behavior would be
considered criminal.

The *Zeitgeist*, the spirit of the times, can and often does become
irrational because of herd behavior, epidemics, and "information cascades," as Shiller explains. "Groupthink" frequently causes an individual to capitulate to crowd thinking simply because he or she finds it
difficult to believe that such a large group of people could be wrong,
particularly when an authoritative figure lends his or her stature to the
proposition. Shiller argues that the behavior of such individuals may in
fact be predominantly rational and intelligent, even when the views to
which they subscribe conflict with their own matter-of-fact judgment.
The reason: the lasting lessons learned from past errors when going
against the majority view. The spread of epidemics and information
cascades—where a faulty thesis proliferates by word of mouth like a
forest fire leaping from tree to tree, without the validity of the original

thesis again being contested—further explains the suppression of the constraints of rational and independent thought.

Shiller also discusses the psychological factor of "anchoring," a behavioral response that would not be possible if the markets were truly rational (and, by inference, efficient). Anchoring is not so much the result of ignorance but is more attributable to how the human mind works. For example, most of us are quantitatively anchored in the present; in making judgments about the level of a stock's price, the anchor is likely to be yesterday's price. In the qualitative dimension, anchoring takes the form of "storytelling and justification," both of which defy quantification. Liken it if you will to the growing fascination with gambling mentioned above: The vocabulary makes the subtle shift to vague expressions like *lucky day* compared with far more precise terms like *probability*. The emphasis gradually migrates from logical analysis to intuition.

Hand in glove with the above is what we have described in the past as the *overconfidence bias*, the near-universal human tendency toward excessive and unjustified confidence in one's beliefs. While the association is a bit tenuous, overconfidence has been deemed a force in promoting the high volume of trading that is indigenous to speculative markets. A companion affinity is the *hindsight bias* that causes one to see the world as far more predictable than it actually is.

By now you must feel a little overwhelmed by all this soft-science stuff and are no doubt wondering the point of it all. Well, it comes full circle to the centrality of the efficient-market thesis to mainstream investment thinking. For if what is commonly believed in academia is in fact true, much of this report is poppycock, worthless nonsense. "Might does not make right," and we're thusly inclined to resist the temptation to blindly take any thesis at face value, no matter how many Nobel laureates plaques are hanging on the office wall. Does it not stand to reason that if indeed the markets are efficient, and all information publicly known is imputed in current market prices, then markets must be immune from excessive exhilaration, of which bubbles are the end product? As a sidebar, it is presumed that one also can infer that people who have differing abilities cannot produce dissimilar investment results, since the superior understanding of some is already incorporated in share prices. What about Warren Buffett? The authorities have pronounced him an aberration. Without belaboring the point, to my knowledge, no modern portfolio theorists have yet to venture forth to argue that the overblown market boom/bust cycle that began in the late 1990s in any way confirms the validity of the efficient-market thesis. All we hear is silence. To this writer, the thesis is damned by faint praise . . .

To such practitioners as your servants at MCM, we admonish ourselves to never say "never." Despite the intimidating mathematics of modern portfolio theory, of which the efficient market thesis is an essential building block, real-life experience teaches us that free markets have always shown a disposition toward irrational behavior when the stars of exaggerated sentiment are in alignment. Being aware that the market price pendulum can swing—in both directions—to extremes well beyond what our "anchored" thinking would deem possible, we must remain steadfastly independent and rational in our thinking. No mean feat . . . certainly in 1999 . . . and perhaps no less so today.

Back to the Future Redux

Thus armed with additional data, we return to the original question: Where are we on the continuum between exuberance and despair? Turning first to Robert Shiller's structural factors, let's highlight a few in the order they appeared in the earlier section titled "How Did We Get Here in the First Place?"

The public has always been justifiably enamored with new technologies, as was the case with radio, television, and the personal computer in their respective heydays. It's hard to believe that on the twentieth anniversary of the revolutionary technology that became the personal computer, the *wunderkind* is past its prime, relegated to the characterization of technologically passé. Once yesterday's remarkable innovations became commonplace, they understandably lost their luster as the "new and unusual," a fate that will surely befall the Internet. We need only recall that the productivity enhancements that followed the introduction of the PC in the early to mid-1980s economically benefited the user far more than the producer. Despite the impressive 2003 rallies in the stocks of a number of the leading Internet companies, the earnings power of the industry—compared with early projections and because of the industry's competitive construct—remains suspect.

Of course, we must make full allowance for the likelihood of some new technology piggybacking on existing scientific developments, which may go from obscurity to near universal acceptance in less than 10 years, just as the Internet rode into town on the PC infrastructure horse. Highly regarded futurist John Naisbitt opines in the well-documented, insightful, and cautionary book *High Tech / High Touch* that genetic technologies will overwhelm all other technologies in the twenty-first century. He reminds us that all of our technological innovations appeared on the scene long before a full attempt was made to understand their ethical and social consequences. Like the Internet, the economics of genetic engineering are not as compelling as they first might seem. Moreover, ethical dilemmas may, and perhaps should, impede the progress of otherwise unbridled scientific zeal. In sum, in this writer's judgment the Internet was a great catalyst only because it worked well in conjunction with other complementary factors, including earnings growth, managed or otherwise. As we look forward five years into the nascent economic recovery's clouded crystal ball, the list of key macro earnings drivers is indeed short enough that the forces that may cause another contraction not too far down the road should be of greater concern.

Another structural factor that gave rise to the Bubble has not abated to any noticeable extent. Worship at the altar of materialism seems rather deeply embedded in our culture. Spiritually uncomfortable allusions notwithstanding, the production and accumulation of *stuff* is, after all, the practical end objective of our capitalist system. And it is unlikely that materialism will be dislodged except under the most economically discouraging of circumstances. Should the tide turn, there is a higher order always beckoning us (the calling of most religious groups from time immemorial), as Emerson affirmed above.

As for macro policy, it's hard to imagine a fiscal/monetary policy mix more supportive of investment than is currently in place. Barring the unexpected, fiscal policy should be a plus for at least another five years.

Although Shiller's earlier discussion of the vaunted demographic shift was comprehensive, as it should have been, we'll summarize its current relevance in one sentence. The Baby Boom stimulus (a fallacious, one-sided equation, we would argue) is a little long in the tooth anyway, and in less than a decade, it may be the Baby Bust (that began soon after the development of the birth-control pill in the mid-1960s) that will impregnate the collective consciousness of editorial writers.

Turning to investment analysis—on the assumption that the cathartic process (a thorough cleansing of the pervasive, speculative inclination) is not complete—we envision a long period of involuntary contrition that should linger until the speculative sap begins to flow freely again. It might even be possible that respectability may once again become, shall we say, respectable, at least for a time. As for the Chinese wall, count us among the diehard cynics. It is built of beach sand and will always crumble when the waves of greed roll in.

Regarding the continuation of economic utopia (a flat Consumer Price Index and a Fed funds rate of 1 percent), we state emphatically that it will not persist and can present a host of reasons why, but we can't offer a scintilla of evidence in support of precisely when or how the state of affairs might change. We all know the antonyms for the word utopia. To that we can add nothing more.[3]

With respect to Shiller's comprehensive examination of the contribution from the media to the exuberance, as a bold prophecy in the 2002 annual report, the undersigned suggested that in due time CNBC will be a shadow of its current self. It has been a child of the 20-year bull market that culminated in the bulimic disgorgement beginning in March 2000, and its ratings will move in lockstep with stock prices, which, we need not remind our readers, fluctuate! The good news is that the fair-weather financial media, the existence of which is dependent on rising prices and whose emergence was celebrated with such fanfare during the bull market, will die a quiet death. Nielsen ratings will see to that. Don't, however, sell the Dow Jones company short!

Another structural factor is likely to turn from a positive to a negative. The huge spike in overall trading volume is both cause and effect

---

[3][2006, *Speculative Contagion*] Inflation has remained relatively tame. For the year ending June 30, 2005, consumer prices increased 2.5 percent. The Fed, however, backed away from its open-the-floodgates "accommodative" policy, boosting the Fed funds rate by 200 basis points. [2010 update: Over the past five years, ending September 30, 2010, consumer price inflation has averaged 1.9 percent. Through the first eight months of 2010 the CPI had slowed to 1 percent. In an effort to boost demand throughout the "Great Recession," the Fed maintained a target range for the Fed funds rate at 0 to 25 basis points.]

of rising stock prices. Parenthetically, it's a common occurrence in the shares of individual companies, with above-average trading volume most often associated with high and rising prices, when broad attention is drawn to the stock (at least partly due to the self-reinforcing mechanism of the rising price itself). After stocks have cratered—at the very time when some offer the most inviting profile of risk and return—trading volume invariably becomes lethargic. This common phenomenon has not escaped our attention.

That aside notwithstanding, low commission rates and Internet-enabled day trading promote the erroneous perception of easy money. Evidence abounds to the contrary. Frenetic trading, made more risky by the fulcrum of financial leverage, is, for the vast majority of players, a devastating loser's game. As volume slows and price volatility follows suit, the speculators at the margin will gradually drift away. "The lottery" and other forms of gambling may moderate, at least in terms of how we know them today. To be sure, human nature's mostly futile propensity to defy the odds will never, and should never, go away. Some of the greatest innovations in history have come from the minds of such nonconformists. Gambling at its current pace, though, is a social sickness that may have reached epidemic proportions. Eventually all epidemics subside, each for reasons unique to itself.

Because of the relative importance of what follows as a potent swing variable, lengthy ensuing discourse is devoted to the interconnected maze of mutual funds, defined-contribution plans, and corporate governance, after which we'll attempt to answer the question posed at the beginning of this section. (Are you intrigued by the suspense?!)

Sensing the Winds of Change

The subsequent commentary is longer, more taxing, and more controversial than the relatively superficial survey of the structural factors immediately preceding, with the writer begging your indulgence in hopes that the end will justify the means. To begin, certain elements of the capital markets and all their assorted subsets are woven together like the tapestry of a finely crafted Persian rug. The attempt will be to unravel some of the mystery of this complex entity so that several potentially radical hypotheses can be presented that may be relevant to the central issue of this essay. The tentative and untested explanation that accounts for the facts selectively presented below—my theory, if you will—does not necessarily reflect the opinions of my partners and associates.

The Apogee of the Mutual-Fund Boom

Where the process of unraveling begins is itself subject to debate. Exercising the writer's prerogative, I'll start with investment companies if for no other reason than their relative mass and resilience, like the cat with nine lives. Mutual funds in one form or another have been fixtures on the investment landscape since the early 1800s, far longer than most of us would have imagined, anchored as we are in the present. Despite mutual funds' dramatic growth in popularity since the early 1980s, the public's interest in them has historically waxed and waned concurrent with major bull and bear markets. Investment trusts proliferated in the 1920s, only to fall into disrepute during the 1930s because of disastrous investment results and disingenuous promoters whose blatant acts of self-enrichment took precedence over their fiduciary obligation to shareholders (deeds more reprehensible, to be sure, than the malfeasance for which the industry is currently being castigated, as noted below).

The Investment Company Act of 1940 helped to legitimize what became known as mutual funds and, along with the passage of time, to restore investor confidence. Laws are rarely a leading indicator! The Employment Retirement Income Security Act of 1974 (ERISA), which gave birth to the Individual Retirement Account (IRA), paved the way for investing tax-deferred dollars in mutual funds, only to be delayed by another episode of mutual-fund misconduct and the bear market of 1973–1974. The net exodus from mutual funds lingered well into the 1980s until awareness of the rising market spread to the backwaters of investor consciousness. The impetus that mutual funds received from the declining relative importance of the defined-benefit pension plan as money flowed into the defined-contribution 401(k) pension plan in the early 1980s belatedly, but undeniably, took root in the great bull market that followed. Although the vast majority of equity mutual funds failed to match the performance of passive indices (according to Lipper data, over the 30 years through December 2002, diversified U.S. stock funds returned an average of 9.5 percent per year compared with 10.7 percent for the S&P 500), aggressive advertising and more than a tenfold increase in the Dow during the next 18 years helped polish the image, even if largely undeserved, of "experts" at the helm.

To put the last 22 years in perspective, in 1980 a comparatively minuscule 4.6 million U.S. households owned mutual funds, a 5.7 percent penetration rate. By 2002 these funds had become well-nigh-ubiquitous, owned in one form or another by nearly 50 percent of all households, or 54.2 million families. Nature, or in this case mutual-fund sponsors, abhors a vacuum. No surprise then, like the proliferation of pesky dandelions in the spring, 4,682 equity mutual funds (8,231 funds of all types) sprouted in the ensuing years, as tallied in the current Investment Company Institute (ICI) Fact Sheet, a twelvefold increase since 1982. (ICI is the chief advocacy organization of the mutual-fund industry.) In 1982 equity mutual-fund assets totaled $53.7 billion, a mere 2 percent of the $2.7 trillion at year-end 2002. The peak was reached in 1999 when equity funds exceeded $4 trillion. In the aggregate, funds of all stripes—equity, hybrid, bond, and taxable and tax-exempt money market—grew from $297 billion in 1982 to $6.4 trillion by December 31, 2002. No less telling with regard to the pervasiveness of the mutual-fund phenomenon in actual interrelations or comparative importance is the following fact: The number of mutual funds eclipses the total number of individual companies listed on the New York Stock Exchange. Does not the phrase "absurd redundancy" come to mind? When the middlemen outnumber the largest grouping of stocks they ostensibly manage, something, to understate the point, is askew.

On the heels of a bear market that lasted from 2000 to 2002, mutual-fund ownership declined only slightly. In all, a July 2003 ICI survey found 53.3 million households, or 47.9 percent, owned mutual funds. That's down slightly from 54.2 million households, or 49.6 percent, in July 2002. The survey reported that the total number of individual investors owning mutual funds declined to 91.2 million in the 2003 survey from 94.9 million in the 2002 survey. At the same time, the survey found that a record number of households, 36.4 million, owned mutual funds inside employer-sponsored retirement plans. That figure represents 32.7 percent of all U.S. households.

"The harsh financial environment and weak performance in equity markets starting in 2000 contributed to the decline in overall household fund ownership," says Matthew P. Fink, ICI president. "Despite difficult equity markets, ownership of mutual funds within employer-sponsored retirement plans increased to record numbers" (more on this development below). On the surface, the turnover rate in stock funds indicates feverish activity, but the data are likely to mislead. Annual redemptions and redemption exchanges, as a percentage of average net assets, reached 43.9 percent for the 12 months ending October 2002 and 34.8 percent for the year ending September 2003. Most of this is believed to be attributable to a small but frenetic subset of the mutual-fund shareholder population who turned their funds seven times a year on average, as well as a steady departure from foreign funds since 1993. The heavily promoted illusion of limitless riches begging to be mined within the lesser-developed countries was demythologized by the earlier Asian and other foreign bear markets. In point of fact, the vast majority of shareholders rarely alter their portfolio allocations. Institute research confirms that shareholder response to long-term declines in stock prices has been "measured and gradual." Gradual, yes, but measured . . . hardly the word to describe often simple reactive behavior that, by virtue of its momentum, changes course with the quickness of a battleship under full power.

Fund-Owner Demographics

Who are these people who have embraced the mutual fund as the means of realizing the American dream? Most mutual-fund-owning households have moderate incomes and, as you might expect, fund ownership increases with income. As of July 2003, according to ICI statistics, 28 percent of households with income less than $50,000 owned mutual funds, compared with 70 percent with incomes of $50,000 or more.

The vast majority (83 percent) of mutual-fund households are headed by individuals age 25 to 64 years; with 52 percent of all mutual-fund households from the Baby Boomer generation (those born between 1947 and 1964), 23 percent from the "silent" generation (pre-1946, which includes the undersigned, who has been referred to by many names, none of which even resembled "silent"!), and 25 percent from the post-1965 Generation Xers. Thirteen percent of households owning funds are headed by individuals age 65 or older; 4 percent are headed by individuals younger than age 25. A broadly based, middle-class, younger- to middle-aged demographic if I ever saw one . . .

Fink recites the mutual-fund sponsor's mantra on the ICI web site: "Mutual funds offer investors an unparalleled combination of benefits, including professional management, diversification, strict regulations and affordability." Adds Fink: "Funds play a prominent role in helping Americans achieve their significant long-term financial goals, including financing education and retirement."

Disquieting Changes in the Distribution Channel

Beneath the surface of the burgeoning, decade-long surge in mutual-fund sales, subtle changes have been taking place that may well have wide-ranging, long-term ramifications. Direct sales of new funds to individual investors declined from 23 percent in 1990 to 13 percent in 2002. The traditional brokers' share of the shrinking direct-sales channel has dropped from 50 percent to 25 percent over that same time span. Indirect sales through company-sponsored plans have filled the gap. All the while the power has been shifting to the bigger organizations that enjoy economies of scale and the competitive edge of a panoply of product offerings. The top 25 mutual-fund complexes have consistently controlled about 75 percent of the assets over the last five years. The top 10 declined from 56 percent to 46 percent, owing to the fact that the larger fund complexes have a preponderance of equity offerings that fared poorly from 2000 to 2002 compared with the smaller fund families, which are more heavily weighted toward fixed-income products. In this writer's judgment the distribution mechanism, for the reasons mentioned above, has become more automatic and impersonal, rendering it ill-equipped to stem the tide of disillusionment should mutual funds continue to fail to meet investor expectations, which likely remain higher than what might be thought justified, buoyed by the lingering belief that whatever goes down must come back up—reinforced once again in 2003. When an investor's confidence flags, and when there is no human being whose name you know on the other end of the phone line to reassure, emotions sometimes overcome the rational decision-making process. Additionally, as for direct sales, it has long been understood that mutual funds are not bought, they are sold. Direct-sale distribution is the costliest alternative, and pricing pressures mentioned below play havoc with this important, albeit shrinking, channel.

More "Barbarians at the Gate"

Not altogether unlike the 1920s or the 1960s, the mutual-fund barbarians are once again storming the gate—in the historical context an ominous sign indeed. (The apparent 40-year cycles are no doubt coincidental, unless four decades represents the time span required for a new generation of sheep, heedless of history's tutorial, to huddle together in a stupor, ready to be shorn.) Scandalous behavior, likely to be emblematic of the naughty 1990s, metastasized to the mutual-fund industry, which has been largely without blemish since the late 1920s, as the malfeasance witch-hunt continues. Let us not overlook, simply because of the order of magnitude (or insult the memories of old-timers such as the writer), the "go-go" 1960s when Bernie Cornfeld and the other mendacious mutual-fund managers ran recklessly wild, and sullied, with understandable consequences, the industry's good name.

Parenthetically, *Barron's* learned and lettered editor, Alan Abelson, opined recently on the oxymoronic self-righteous political response as big and small funds alike were

> splattered by scandal, featuring fine, upright fiduciaries who scalped an eighth here and an eighth there from their own shareholders. And politics was transformed from a cruddy business into a poisonous one. Congress, whose resemblance to a deliberative body has always been accidental, more and more has come to resemble a sack of spitting cats.

An investigation carried out ostensibly to uncover unethical or even illegal activities, but actually used to further political agendas, can become uncontrollably ugly—like some episodes of aggravated crowd behavior. Joining the chorus with moral indignation and a proposal for swift justice, the Investment Company Institute president in November "Fink-ed" on his minions, whom he legitimized with lavish praise only a few paragraphs above, as he doubtless feigned disgust, admonishing his wards with these whimsical words: ". . . I am outraged by the shocking betrayal of trust exhibited by some in the mutual-fund industry" and those who have violated criminal laws ". . . should be sent to prison."

He went on to caw in testimony before the U.S. Senate Banking, Housing, and Urban Affairs Committee, "I am appalled by the circumstances that caused you to convene this hearing. Like you—and the constituents you serve." [This fellow can patronize with the best of them, demonstrating also that he is at least loyal to a pet phrase, to wit . . .] "I am outraged by the shocking betrayal of trust exhibited by some in the mutual-fund industry." Yes, Mr. Fink repeated himself, word for word.

While on the surface the magnitude of the malfeasance seems to pale by comparison to Enronitis, the public reaction seems to run parallel. Pushing the limits of fiduciary etiquette, so-called investment professionals in positions of power and trust have come to treat the individual investor as the hapless stooge. Any fermenting backlash—lest we forget, there is plenty of yeast in the pot—against the very institution of capitalism, as happened during the 1930s, could have grave and irreversible consequences. As Franklin D. Roosevelt put it rather bluntly in the 1930s, "The money changers were cast down from their high place in the temple of our civilization." A more immediate concern is that fund shareholders, apparently the last to get the word, could, in keeping with their typical delayed-reaction response, vote with their feet.

The Witch-Hunt Disposition and Crowd Psychology

Alan Abelson's observations above speak to the legislative overreaction that sometimes escalates into a sordid cycle. A lawyer friend took careful notes in early December during consecutive programs sponsored by the Investment Companies and Investment Advisors Subcommittee at the fall meeting of the ABA (American Bar Association) Committee on Federal Regulation of Securities. The first topic was the rule-making decisions rendered by the SEC the prior week. The new rules (most of them like Sarbanes-Oxley) offer, by the SEC's own admission, a very mixed bag of trade-offs for investors—much like chemotherapy: If it doesn't kill you, it may be worth the suffering. The extra-strength dose of regulatory medicine, with history as our guide, is generally the wrong remedy to restore the patient to good health. The SEC contends that the rules must be inviolate in order to restore investor confidence that mutual funds are operating in a "fail-safe" environment, justifying the heavy-handedness with the following inflammatory language: "The pervasiveness of prohibited practices within the mutual-fund industry emphasizes the need to adopt extraordinary measures."

The second topic—the proposed rules and even more onerous regulations still on the docket—look like the snarl of a rabid dog. The third topic of discussion was the ongoing litany of enforcement cases. The recent Morgan Stanley settlement was characterized by Mike Eisenberg, the SEC's deputy general counsel, as the most important case, comparing the Canary Capital settlement with the New York attorney general's office as a "wake-up" call similar to the fraudulent behavior at, perish the thought, WorldCom. Mr. Eisenberg, according to my friend's notes, remarked that the SEC commissioners were "shocked, angered, and surprised" at the depth and breadth of venality in the mutual-fund industry. Posturing? Perhaps . . .

What's Next?

By now you may be wondering about the purpose behind the preceding history lesson. For most of the past 20 years the mutual-fund industry has been the ever-burgeoning channel through which billions (and later several trillions) of dollars have found their way from the savings accounts and the money-market funds of individual investors into the equity markets, many of them from the much-ballyhooed Baby Boomers. As entrenched as this phenomenon is, nothing in the business and financial annals would suggest that it cannot be slowed or even reversed. In fact, in this writer's opinion the burden of proof rests with the naysayers. Affection with the stock market that rising prices propagate, as expressed by the weed-like growth of mutual funds, is often followed by disaffection when prices retrench.

Not only are investors likely to exit, but close on their heels will be the funds themselves. Recently the spotlight of regulatory revulsion has focused on the heretofore well-camouflaged and lucrative economics of the mutual-fund industry. Unbeknownst to most lay investors, fees average about 1.48 percent of assets on stock funds, according to Lipper. While Eliot Spitzer and the SEC are squabbling about whether fees should be reduced by edict or market forces, respectively, the near certainty of increased fee transparency in a possible low-return environment is likely to give rise to aggressive price competition as fund-management companies grapple with one another to hang onto the assets of disenchanted investors.[4] Fund misconduct and performance results that have left disillusioned investors wondering what happened to the "experts" who are going to lead them to the Promised Land may be the big first step toward commoditizing the industry. Under that scenario, deteriorating economics will drive the weaker players out of an industry teeming with overcapacity. As for the pace, "batten down the hatches" if the ride we're experiencing is not a new bull market. Later you'll read that one man's bust is another's bonanza. Disaffection with mutual funds may well provide MCM with the best risk-adjusted investment environment we've seen in years.

The Great Abdication of Fiduciary Responsibility: The Defined-Contribution Plan

Mutual funds, possibly unwittingly but nonetheless concurrently, have played an important role in another subtler, and therefore less-publicized (but no less ignoble), activity. The proliferation of funds coincided neatly with what this writer considers an abdication of corporate fiduciary responsibility by shifting investment retirement plan decision making from the knaves in the boardroom to the naive on the factory floor—a.k.a. the "dumbing down" of the investment process. To be sure, most boards simply went along with the crowd, as unacceptable an excuse as that given by the funds that chased the *dot.con* (a book worth reading, by the way) craze right into ethereal cyberspace. If corporate boards of directors cannot be expected to lead rather than follow, who, pray tell, will be the keeper of the gate? Is there a higher corporate authority of which we're unaware? Perhaps with malice aforethought, mutual-fund promoters trumpeted the illusory

---

[4][2006, *Speculative Contagion* footnote] The first shot in a potential management-fee price war was fired by industry behemoth Fidelity in August 2004. Acknowledging that equity index funds are a commodity, Fidelity lowered fees on the $40 billion invested in its equity index funds to 0.10 percent, down from a range of 0.19 to 0.47 percent. This salvo was aimed squarely at Vanguard, the reigning index fund king with around $300 billion invested in index funds alone. Surprisingly, Vanguard has not returned fire. The flagship Vanguard 500 Index Fund has held its management fee at 0.18 percent, almost double Fidelity's fee.

virtues of the opportunity to control one's own destiny when surely those who were of sound mind must have known it was doomed from the start. Having been listening and watching for 35-plus years, the undersigned is convinced that the vast majority of participants in company-sponsored 401(k) plans are not, and likely will not be, prepared to make informed judgments about how their retirement assets should be allocated. Furthermore, there doesn't appear to be a practical and realistic solution to the problem.

Before the 401(k) plan came along, the corporate pension plan, aided by Social Security since the 1930s, was the primary means by which corporations did their patriarchal, post-retirement duty toward those employees who had served their companies long and well. Defined-benefit plans, like Social Security or an extra blanket on a cold night, helped reduce the anxiety about how employees were going to maintain some semblance of their former standard of living after the Friday paychecks stopped. The companies met their contractual obligation to dedicated workers by segregating and investing funds from operations. In a not entirely ironic twist, poorer-than-expected investment performance obligated many companies to cough up more money to meet their contractual commitments. The pension system was slow in reacting to the inflationary debasing of the purchasing power of the dollar in the 1960s and 1970s. In all likelihood, the seed of the defined-contribution plan was planted and grew out of the stark realization that corporations would have to bear much more of the cost of maintaining viable defined-benefit plans than they had originally anticipated. The twofold culprit: overestimating investment returns and underestimating the escalation in wage and benefit costs. Defined-contribution plans, whereby the corporation's responsibility is front-end-loaded, assuaged the nervous Nellies and corporate executives of the fear of a large and unknown future pension-fund liability, as well as the continual embarrassment of looking like wet-behind-the-ears participants themselves. In all fairness, they also underestimated the mushrooming future costs of healthcare benefits that were promised to retirees. Clearly it's a catch-22 situation. The industries with the greatest liability are, more often than not, the manufacturers of durable goods; their ability to pass on these costs to their customers through price increases is severely limited in the competitive marketplace. Regardless, in a very literal sense, and with empty pretense, boards passed the buck and the liability appurtenant thereto. Harry Truman, known for placing a plaque on his desk in the Oval Office that said, "The buck stops here," must be revolving rapidly in his grave.

From 1990 through 2002 corporate defined-contribution plan assets have grown fourfold from $637 billion to $2.333 trillion, net of the boost of a steady stream of contributions and diluted by the stock market losses from 2000 through 2002, while corporate defined-benefit plans grew by little more than half during the same 12 years: from $924 billion to $1.642 trillion. Moreover, that number is down more than $500 billion from a high of $2.150 trillion in 1999, leaving many pension funds underfunded. Recently General Motors borrowed $14 billion to shore up its underfunded plan and, with adroit accounting gimmickry, made the transaction appear accretive to both earnings and shareholders' equity.[5] An apparent babe in the woods myself, I stopped ranting about accounting gambits when I concluded that, once doused by the spotlight of public opinion, they would soon shrink like un-Sanforized fabric. Again a voice is heard, "Yeah, right . . ."

---

[5][2006, *Speculative Contagion*] General Motors' pension fund, the nation's largest corporate fund, became also the largest underfunded plan in 2002 largely because of stock market losses totaling almost $10 billion in 2001 and 2002. Robbing Peter to pay Paul, the company issued $14 billion in debt in June 2003 to prop up its plan that provides retirement benefits for 452,000 retired U.S. workers. While the additional funding and strong equity returns in 2003 helped restore the U.S. pension plan, the non-U.S. plan still carries a shortfall of $9 billion as of year-end 2004. In a case of bad news first, GM's large and growing unfunded retiree medical plan totaled $61.5 billion as of year-end 2004. As a benchmark that might give you pause, GM's highly leveraged shareholders' equity totals a paltry $27.7 billion. An assembler of millions of rearview mirrors, the company's decision makers looked squarely into one in fashioning their future investment policy. But let's lend an ear to GM itself: "GM also plans to expand its investment strategy to include increased allocation to asset classes, such as emerging market debt, high-yield bonds and real estate, which should diversify its pension portfolio while reducing global equity allocation to less than 50 percent. The Company believes these actions will reduce the volatility of annual asset returns and still achieve its targeted return of 9 percent." This, believe it or not, is a true story. Some things never change . . . [2010 update: On June 1, 2009, GM filed for Chapter 11 bankruptcy. As of December 2009 and after a nearly $50 billion investment made by the U.S. Treasury through TARP (Troubled Asset Relief Program), the reorganized GM maintained a pension plan with an unfunded status of $27.4 billion.

Pension funds—and GM is far from alone—do not have stellar investment records. That is a board problem and, given GM's "expanded investment strategy" as thumbnailed in the footnote, is likely to remain one. If that's the case, then at the end of the road it's actually the board that's the problem. We address this dilemma below. Investment-savvy boards or otherwise, the defined-benefit-plan obligation ostensibly has corporate muscle and goodwill behind it. The defined-contribution plan has neither. One of the arguments in favor of the defined-contribution plan is its portability. It doesn't strike me as a Herculean undertaking to find a way to make the funded portion of defined-benefit plans transferable as well. If the idea ever gets a toehold, competition will ensure that it spreads rapidly. Of course, retirement benefits will differ from company to company, but that's the kind of choice a prospective employee is reasonably well equipped to make. How this affects the future growth of the 401(k) plan and the mutual funds through which much of the money is invested is anybody's guess.

Minus Two Plus Minus Two Equals . . . ?

The use of double negatives is considered bad form in the King's English. In the world of money, the math of double minuses is straightforward, and it sums up to bad business. What do we make of the likely slow but relentless reversal of fortunes that may lie in waiting for the mutual-fund industry? Already individual investors are beginning to exit, though the institutionalized momentum of company-sponsored plans continues, albeit at a slowing pace. What if the popularity of mutual funds subsides even more, tracing a pattern from the past? What if the number of households that own mutual funds keeps shrinking, retracing its steps from the current record 50 percent penetration rate

---

Shareholder equity totaled $20.8 billion, following the aforementioned $50 billion infusion made by the government. In its November 2010 IPO priced at $33 per common share, GM raised a record $23.1 billion in common and preferred stock. The U.S. Treasury was able to reduce its ownership stake from roughly 60 percent to approximately 33 percent. Refer to Chapter 2 for a price chart of the former GM, now known as Motors Liquidation Company. The new company, General Motors Corporation, today trades around $33. Despite the initial enthusiasm for the resurrected GM, its success is anything but assured. While the parallels are not precise, hearken back to the story of United Airlines.]

(almost 55 million households) in the direction of the under 5 percent of 20 years ago? Stranger things have happened . . .

Where the Buck Really Stops

The defined-contribution/defined-benefit conundrum is no less perplexing as noted above—and goes begging for a workable solution. In my opinion, Social(istic) Security as it exists today can and should be nothing more than an income supplement and a diminishing one at that, despite its utility as a powerful political tool to extract votes from senior citizens. Privatizing Social Security, a contradiction in terms as proposed, does not, nor did it ever, strike this writer as anything more than a harebrained scheme. The Social Security transfer tax exacted from today's workers, given the drag of an aging population, will make it increasingly difficult for them to afford to single-handedly bear the burden of funding the retirement of the multiple taxpayers who go to pasture before them. Speaking of stretching, there also are practical limits as to how far the age for Social Security eligibility can be extended, the older folks busing tables at McDonald's or serving samplers at Sam's Club notwithstanding. Governmental decrees postponing retirement, coupled with a shrinking standard of living, does not make for a happy electorate.

The owners of American industry (you and I), for whom millions of Americans labor for a working lifetime, must insist that the boards we elect discharge their duties to this worthy and dependent population forthrightly, honestly, and with the intelligence and collective wisdom that is to be expected from such an august body. We shareholders are ultimately where this buck stops. Collectively, we have been grossly negligent. Paraphrasing a quote about democratic governments, the corporate electorate gets the leadership it deserves. Let there be no mistake about it, we have come to know many boards whose conduct is exemplary, whose stewardship is beyond reproach in virtually every regard. Often these corporations are governed by small boards whose ownership stakes are large. Their passion for the business, their integrity, and their sense of personal accountability are not at all unlike the hallmark of many small privately owned businesses. These are not the people at whom we are pointing the accusatory finger.

As a close-to-home example, we (as most readers know) owned a substantial stake in Clayton Homes before it was recently acquired by Berkshire Hathaway for $12.50 per share. There was loud and flamboyant debate, with lawsuits flying like paper in a hurricane, about whether the price was fair to the selling shareholders. I was astounded by the absurdity of the demonstration. Founder Jim Clayton, his now-CEO son Kevin, and the board of directors—the first two of whom I know personally—were, in my judgment, not only eminently qualified to make an informed decision, they also had more financial incentive than any other shareholder to negotiate the highest selling price possible: The board owned 39.7 million of the 138.6 million shares outstanding; 95 percent of shares owned by the board were in the hands of Jim Clayton alone. While Ken Lay was looting Enron and Dennis Kozlowski was stealing the Tyco shareholders blind, a band of misguided malcontents were trying to take Clayton to task. Folks, when the savvy founder's masterpiece, reputation, and considerable net worth are on the line, second-guessing his judgment is not only an insult to him but an utterly unproductive use of everyone's time as well. Critics, with the full benefit of hindsight, have claimed parliamentary procedure improprieties as the Claytons scrambled to consummate the transaction with Berkshire. There is little doubt in my mind that in the heat of the battle to defend their beliefs and with the outcome uncertain, natural instinctive reactions, resulting from a sudden urge or feelings not governed by reason, may well have occurred. I have found myself in that situation more than once. Regardless, none of the faultfinders' critiques I have read has put forth plausible ulterior motives that would explain why the Clayton board's decision was for any other purposes than to meet its fiduciary obligation to shareholders. We hold companies like Clayton in high esteem.

The process to which we are referring is evolutionary. Everything, it seems, has trade-offs—including business growth. When the founder's stake is whittled down because the company needs additional equity capital to support its enlarging asset base, or the founder or heirs sell stock for a host of personal reasons, a subtle metamorphosis often takes place. In time, those who govern the corporation move away from the wealth creator toward the so-called professional manager. Sometimes that's a good idea, particularly when the progenitor is better at originating ideas than managing people. But often the successor, frequently well educated but rarely from the school of hard knocks and betting with someone else's chips, has aspirations and a propensity to assume risks that are different than if the money on the line were the product of his or her own business acumen. This will certainly come as no revelation to the reader.

Concurrently, the size and composition of the board of directors is often gradually transformed, generally a function of the company's size, age, and absence of a dominant personality or owner—an unwieldy organizational construct for which a logical explanation is not immediately transparent to most observers. The conspicuous political correctness and politely perfunctory deliberations are often little more than empty pretense at some Fortune 500 companies—fertile ground, it would appear, for corruption to take root. A domineering CEO sometimes emerges when the system of checks and balances is structurally weak. In the *Essays on Freedom and Power*, Lord Acton wrote late in the nineteenth century that "Those in possession of absolute power can not only prophesy and make their prophecies come true, but they can also lie and make their lies come true." He is better known for his maxims on the abuse of power largely within the realm of politics, though it seems reasonable to apply them to concentrations of power in business as well: "Power tends to corrupt, and absolute power corrupts absolutely." Although the thought does not end there, that's where the quotation is usually concluded, and perhaps for good reason . . . What remains is provocative and leaves us feeling a bit uneasy: "Great men are almost always bad men, even when they exercise influence and not authority: still more when you superadd the tendency or the certainty of corruption by authority." The quote was included not because I submit it as an incontrovertible truth, but because it just might simulate some interesting dinner-table conversation!

Needless to say, the kind of company described immediately above where accountability is questionable is where the risks of mismanagement, and perhaps corporate misconduct, are the greatest. Where necessary, we shareholders must redefine how and for whom our boards work, which will initially entail purging the deadbeats and deadwood from the boardrooms. I would be so bold as to conjecture that more than half the people who fill board seats at America's public corporations add only one thing: extra expense with no offsetting contribution.

Worse even than that, a few bad apples can have a deleterious effect on the whole bunch.

If you find this subject interesting, I strongly suggest you download the 2002 Berkshire Hathaway (www.berkshirehathaway.com) annual report's 20-page chairman's letter and read pages 15–18. Granted, Berkshire may be the gold standard, but by grasping the meaning of the company's 2002 chairman's letter you will have some idea of how far off course much of U.S. corporate culture has strayed. Warren Buffett has served on many boards over the years and offers a disconcertingly frank assessment of how they function in real life. Stealing some of Buffett's thunder, other corporations could follow Berkshire's lead and make the strongest statement possible about their attitude toward corporate integrity by simply doing away with directors' and officers' liability insurance. Under that scenario, those left standing—surely small in number—would be standing tall. It'll never happen because there are at least 20 parasites with nefarious conflicts to every Hank Reardon (the capitalist's capitalist from Ayn Rand's *Atlas Shrugged*). If it did, we could say *sayonara* to Sarbanes-Oxley and a truckload of other burdensome and ill-conceived laws, rules, and regulations . . .

Concluding Thoughts at This Point on the Continuum

Despite the wandering nature of this dissertation, the hoped-for result is that the conclusion would have become self-evident by now. The confluence of structural forces that gave rise to the great bull market did not appear overnight and their unwinding, unless we're in a most unlikely "new era" where prices remain permanently elevated above value, will likely be prolonged as well. The behavioral forces that amplified the advance are apt to cause the pendulum to swing farther than it might have under that scenario. We have no rational choice but to conclude, therefore, that we are dangerously far from investment bliss on the aforementioned continuum.

Lest you throw up your hands in dismay, please be comforted in the knowledge that through the interaction of supply and demand, the free markets are a self-correcting mechanism, constantly adjusting to new realities. Just as mushrooming demand begat an ever-increasing supply that in its own time helped sound the death knell for the Bubble, shrinking demand will just as surely quell supply. The next chapter in the ever-changing book on the history of capital markets may be the emergence of a recycled class of assets that will temporarily dethrone equities as the king of the hill (if you doubt this is possible, see footnote 5 in this chapter, outlining General Motors' prospective investment strategy), and another middleman, perhaps the next iteration of the investment company, will make a buck wedging itself in between the investment idea and the individual investor. Under that admittedly out-of-the-box sequence of events—and so far as capitalism survives the slings and arrows almost certainly to be hurled its way—the ownership of American business and industry will remain safely in the hands of individuals and institutions, and the stock market may be healthier, albeit far less popular, than it is today.

Common stocks, alive and well but no longer the talk of the town, may then sell at compellingly attractive prices relative to intrinsic worth rather than at the premium they have gradually but undeservedly come to enjoy. Assuming we can get there without too much travail for our portfolios, such an environment is nirvana for investors like us. The margin of safety is almost sure to be increasingly generous. If corporate earnings make a respectable long-term showing, it could be the best of investment worlds. We are in agreement with Sir John Templeton, who used to say he liked pessimism because of the prices it produced.

Finally, a nondiversified approach to portfolio management, with its unavoidable (and, we might add, largely irrelevant) volatility, has the potential of working particularly well if the popular averages are either marking time or giving ground. Make no mistake about it, the strategy is sound, but the implementation is the equivalent of driving between the potholes that pepper a poorly maintained northern Indiana road come late winter. We shall do our best to make our way prudently down that treacherous road, knowing that, when least expected, springtime arrives.

Chapter 7

Expanding Concern: A Bigger Bubble?*

S&P 500 (SP50)
— Price

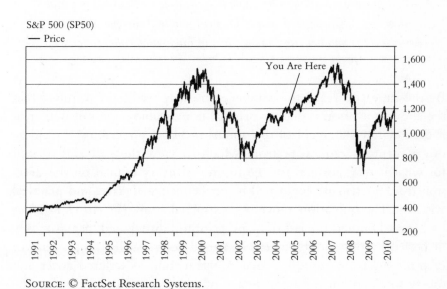

---

*This material is adapted in abridged form from the 2004 annual report of Martin Capital Management.

What is it that characterizes the thinker? First of all, and obviously, vision. . . . The thinker is pre-eminently a man who sees where others do not. The novelty of what he says, its character as a sort of revelation, the charm that attaches to it, all come from the fact that he sees. He seems to be head and shoulders above the crowd, or to be walking on the ridge-way while others trudge at the bottom. Independence is the word which describes the moral aspect of this capacity for vision. Nothing is more striking than the absence of intellectual independence in most human beings: They conform in opinion, as they do in manners, and are perfectly content with repeating formulas. While they do so, the thinker calmly looks around, giving full play to his mental freedom. He may agree with the consensus *known as public opinion, but it will not be because it is a universal opinion. Even the sacrosanct thing called plain commonsense is not enough to intimidate him into conformity. What could seem nearer to insanity, in the sixteenth century, than the denial of the fact—for it was a fact—that the sun revolves around the earth? Galileo did not mind: his intellectual bravery should be even more surprising to us than his physical courage. . . . Einstein's denial of the principle that two parallels can never meet is another stupendous proof of intellectual independence.*

By the time you reach this sentence you may well have surmised that the above quotation is neither original nor autobiographical! Rather, it is the keynote statement of this annual message, prescribing the rigorous perceptual framework from which to view the past and present for what it may portend for the future. At every branch on the decision tree, doctrinaire logic will be challenged with facts and practical wisdom. The quotation above was extracted from *The Art of Thinking* by Ernest Dimnet, the last of many printings distributed, paradoxically or perhaps prophetically, in 1929. A used copy—it has long been out of print—was procured through Amazon.com, its tattered cover and musty smell conjuring up an image of an amended title more appropriate to commemorating that year, with the noun "Art" preceded by the adjective "Lost." Who would've guessed that the book should've been a bestseller 70 years later? It's obvious the publishers weren't thinking, either. British philosopher Bertrand Russell summed up the nature of humankind rather well: "Most men would rather die than think. Many do."

And while on the subject of thinking, another feature of this annual labor of love is the intention to make every effort to present facts as the primary raw material for thought. Accordingly, now that nearly four years have come and gone since the speculative fabric began to unravel and the famous millennium Bubble started to split at the seams, a number of scholarly books have been written on the subject, several of which I have voraciously consumed. Repeated reference will be made to several of them for the factual backdrop they'll provide in assisting the writer's attempt to "see where others do not see." It is hoped the reader will conclude that the outcome reflects a sincere preference for truth over opinion.

Gilbert Chesterton, biographer for Dickens, argued that the French Revolution was predicated on a false notion of "new ideas":

> It was not the introduction of a new idea; there are no new ideas. Or if there are new ideas, they would not cause the least irritation if they were introduced into political society; because the world having never got used to them there would be no mass of men ready to fight for them at a moment's notice.

While Chesterton died before the great information revolution, I think he was right in one sense. We seem to be slower to embrace new ideas in science—who was not skeptical of the round-earth proposition that Columbus set out to prove?—than reworked variations on old ideas in finance, which we often embrace with reckless abandon. In fact, it is this story of the repetitious reincarnation of financial fancy that is both the essence of this report and the nub of opportunity for those who comprehend it . . . and the bane of those who do not.

Although the following notion is both vague and utterly imprecise as to its timing, we feel that the opportunity set of "tomorrow"— ideally, although with no certainty, sometime within the next two or three or so years—may be more propitious for long-term investment in general than it is today. This might even be termed the central thesis of this report. However, we have no idea whether it will be "marginally propitious," casting doubts on why we would forgo today's relatively marginal opportunities for tomorrow's, which may not be much better—or whether it will appear as "magnificently auspicious." It has not escaped our attention that you hired us to attend to such matters! Unlike flowers, opportunities to invest in great businesses at prices that imply a generous margin of safety (i.e., high expected returns and low risks), don't always come in bunches. When we see "magnificently auspicious" investment flowers, we will pluck them one by one, in hopes of eventually presenting you with a beautiful bouquet! If investment flowers should bloom *en masse*, we will be busily plucking with both hands. Either way, we expect to reach the desired goal.

Maybe the Markets Are Not Random?

Is it coincidental that Buffett has identified two sequential bust-boom secular cycles of similar length? [For the sake of brevity, a lengthy section addressing secular cycles has been omitted here. See the section in Chapter 2 titled "Warren Buffett on the Stock Market." The original material from the 2004 annual report can be found at www.mcmadvisors .com.] More important to the present case, he uses oblique language that provokes thought but lets the reader's level of understanding determine how deep to dig. It doesn't, in my judgment, require much of a leap to conclude that in 1999 Buffett foresaw, at least in a comparative sense, another secular bust. Please reread the section "What Buffett Isn't Telling Us" in the 1999 annual report [Chapter 2]. While he carefully avoided any forecast, I doubt that the collapse in the Nasdaq index from 5050 to almost 1000 came as any great surprise to him. Although "one swallow does not a spring make," three might give a person pause. Neither Buffett, I am quite sure, nor I would be implying that 2016 — or any other date—will mark the start of the next secular upswing. History is not so neat and tidy. Parenthetically, as wealth is misallocated and thus often squandered—while simultaneously being redistributed from strong (and sometimes dishonorable) hands to weak ones during these apparent sweeping cycles—it's not a stretch to argue that such cycles are as natural as the seasons. To be sure, the economy would be much more efficient over time if it could be cycle-free, but such an outcome is inconsistent with the nature of humanity . . . or perhaps the nature of nature. Excess capacity and low prices are the very conditions indigenous to the bust that makes the season ripe for sowing. The wise crocus sticks its neck out before the last snow. It instinctively knows the seasons. On the other hand, booms result in reckless spending and high prices, begging those who have sown wisely to harvest while fools plant. Neither booms nor busts are inherently bad if viewed in the larger cyclical context; the same could be said for rainy or sunny days. The trick is understanding the order of the seasons.

Buffett: One "HelluvAnomaly"

Before I continue with any more "slanging" (yes, it rhymes with the appropriate word "hanging")—with a title like the one above, surely I can turn a noun into a verb—on Buffett's philosophical coattails, it's time for my annual disclaimer. Trusting that those who know me well don't consider me a shameless sycophant (is there a reason why I would, or even could, curry Buffett's favor?), might it be argued that my apparently slavish devotion to Warren's World is nothing more than blind imitation, showing no originality? I'll not attempt to answer my own question—or the question others may have on their minds that they have yet to articulate to me. I'll present the evidence and let you be the jury. I'm comfortable and trust you are, too.

To be sure, opinions on Buffett run the gamut, largely depending on how long and how well someone has known him. Bill Ruane, among Buffett's many longtime friends and one of the original 1950s "Superinvestors from Graham-and-Doddsville" whom you'll meet in the paragraph following, climbed out onto the thin branches of the heretic's tree when he uttered: "[Graham] wrote what we call the Bible, and Warren Buffett's thinking updated it. Warren wrote the New Testament."

Nassim Taleb, in his provocative yet vituperative book, *Fooled by Randomness—The Hidden Role of Chance in Life and in the Markets*, is not so willing to buy into Buffett, whom he dubs a "random statistical anomaly." My reaction is to match fire with fire, igniting my response with statistics of my own. Nowhere does Taleb mention, let alone attempt to reconcile, the six-sigma records of the other "Superinvestors from Graham-and-Doddsville," all nine of whom studied under Benjamin Graham at Columbia in the early 1950s. In a speech at the university in 1984, Buffett turned to statistics himself to refute the generally held claim that his performance record was a random occurrence, comparing coin flipping with the benchmark-beating records of his fellow superinvestors as proof. As an aside, I was instantaneously attracted to the logic of Buffett's price-versus-value philosophy years ago after studying Graham's famous textbook as an undergraduate at Northwestern in the mid-1960s. Buffett has said, "I've never seen anyone who became a gradual convert over a 10-year period to this approach. It doesn't seem to be a matter of IQ or academic training. It's instant recognition, or it is nothing." Equally important, the "Superinvestors from Graham-and-Doddsville" gave me adequate empirical assurance that I have picked a mentor who's *not* a statistical anomaly. Three of the superinvestors ended up at two geographically far-flung firms: Tweedy, Browne Partners and Ruane, Cunniff & Goldfarb, Inc. We keep track of both of these fine organizations, exchanging ideas on occasion with Bob Goldfarb, managing partner of Ruane, Cunniff & Goldfarb. The company's stellar records remain intact. If you don't take the path of least resistance in this exciting and challenging profession, if you can shake yourself free of the almost irresistible pull of conformity, the logic of the best teachers will find you. As this report and others before it make abundantly clear, I never stop learning from those who never stop teaching. It's no more than the application of common sense: If I wanted to learn how to hit baseballs, I'd buy a copy of Ted Williams' *The Science of Hitting* long before I picked up a bat.

Despite Taleb's off-putting and condescending style, as well as wrong-headedness regarding Buffett on several fronts, his observation that past events will always look less random than they were (the "hindsight bias") should not be dismissed out of hand. While I think it not true (at least insofar as it might apply to me!), he prefers to look at people in the investment world as if they were "deranged subjects." He argues that much of what appears as someone's discussion of the past is nothing more than just "backfit explanations concocted *ex post* by his deluded mind." Taleb's book will sit on my desk throughout the writing of this report as a constant reminder to be vigilant in seeking to discern the difference between skill and chance.

Back to Buffett. A few years later, in the 2002 Berkshire Hathaway annual report released in late February 2003, he lamented:

> Despite three years of falling prices, which have significantly improved the attractiveness of common stocks, we still find very few that even mildly interest us. This dismal fact is testimony to

the insanity of valuations reached during the Great Bubble. *Unfortunately, the hangover may prove to be proportional to the binge* [emphasis added]. The aversion to equities that Charlie and I exhibit today is far from congenital. We love owning common stocks—if they can be purchased at attractive prices. . . . But occasionally successful investing requires inactivity.

Twenty months later—November 5, 2004, to be exact—in a *Bloomberg News* article that hit the wires just prior to the release of Berkshire's hurricane-depressed third-quarter earnings, reporter David Plumb reasoned that low returns on the company's growing cash hoard that was $40.2 billion as of June 30 would contribute to the disappointing results. The company's later SEC filing indicated the cash balance was $38.1 billion, but the comparison may not have been apples to apples. Regardless of a paltry return of approximately 2 percent on liquid funds languishing longingly for a permanent and productive resting place, Buffett said he was "willing to wait years for an opportunity," according to an August interview to which Plumb referred in the article. In that same interview Buffett allowed that the $19 billion in foreign currency forward contracts that Berkshire owns serves as a hedge against a dollar weakened by the ballooning U.S. budget and trade deficits. This reflects a long-standing apprehension about the continuing exportation of claims on America's wealth. "That's a long-term position," Buffett said. "I have no idea what currencies are going to do next week or next month or even next year. *I think I know over time*" [italics added to place additional emphasis on this unusually prophetic sentence]. The SEC filing showed the contracts worth $20 billion at the end of the third quarter. Buffett is seldom seen running with the herd—and for good reason. "Madness is the exception in individuals but the rule in groups," observed Friedrich Nietzsche, the nineteenth-century German existentialist philosopher.

A "Robbing Peter to Pay Paul" Macro Policy

Is it any wonder that Warren Buffett continues to sit on his hands? My guess is that he sees both the Fed's action and the Bush tax cuts, as discussed a page or so hence, as no more than a futile attempt to fore-stall the inevitable—to rob Peter to pay Paul.

The investment community may not have taken Buffett's words of reality seriously in 1999, but it is doubtful that Fed Chairman Alan Greenspan turned a deaf ear. And, going full circle, when the world's most influential central banker unsheathes his mighty sword, Buffett, intent on keeping his head, does not turn a deaf ear either. This long aside into the secretive world where trade-offs are constantly being weighed and macro policy is formulated is essential for understanding why Buffett, despite the passage of time, is yet loath to place an unmistakably bullish bet, indicating that we have come upon the once-in-a-generation barrel stocked with fish. By way of background, and thanks to various articles in the *Wall Street Journal*, in 1998 Greenspan was feeling intense pressure within and without the Fed to prick the stock market Bubble. He demurred, reluctant to second-guess millions of investors on the right value for stock prices. Moreover, it is believed he was concerned that permanently ending a bubble required rates so high they'd also wreck the economy. Those who think Greenspan's job includes direct intervention to rescue investors from their periodic episodes of lunacy have studied neither the man nor his job description.

The Bubble began to deflate—perhaps too many people had taken the English fairy tale "Jack and the Beanstalk" literally—in the spring of 2000. According to the *Journal*:

> When the economy weakened, the Fed cut rates sharply, following Greenspan's analysis of what the Fed did wrong in 1929. It cut rates twice in January 2001 and five times more through August. After the September 11 attacks, it cut four more times, and did so again in 2002 after corporate scandals undermined investor confidence. In 2003, when the Iraq war and threat of deflation hung over the economy, the Fed cut rates again. By June 2003, the Fed's key rate was at 1 percent, the lowest in 45 years.

This time, however, debate still rages over Greenspan's strategy. For now, it appears to have worked. The United States escaped with a mild recession instead of a 1930s-style Depression or Japanese-style stagnation.

According to the *Journal*, tax revenue, which for 50 years had usually fluctuated between 17 and 19 percent of GDP, surged to 21 percent in 2000. Greenspan apparently didn't appreciate how much of that would reverse once the stock Bubble burst. Shortly after the first Bush tax cut passed in May 2001, which Greenspan supported based on the above miscalculation, tax collections fell short of projections. Still quoting the *Journal*:

> By 2004, after a recession and three rounds of tax cuts, tax reve-nue fell to a 45-year low of 16 percent of GDP. In the past three years, the budget swung to a projected 10-year $2.3 trillion def-icit from a projected surplus of $5.6 trillion with no prospect of a turnaround.
>
> Greenspan's grasp of economic data and his political instincts came up short this time. Instead of accelerating productivity growth acting as the main driver of higher tax revenues, the most significant contributor was the 1990s stock bubble, which pro-duced a tidal wave of [capital gains] taxes from stock-trading profits, Wall Street bonuses and [taxable] withdrawals [liquida-tions] from retirement savings plans.

Greenspan also may have miscalculated the gap between himself and Republicans in the White House and Congress over the deficit's significance. Republican politicians embraced Greenspan's endorse-ment of tax cuts but ignored and sometimes undermined his nag-ging about the deficit. Greenspan has repeatedly urged Congress to renew a rule first implemented under Bush's father that required tax cuts be offset with spending cuts. It expired in 2002. Greenspan's fel-low Republicans defeated his renewed efforts on a party-line vote. In a statement that may haunt Republicans for years, Committee Chairman Jim Nussle, an *Iowa Republican*, rationalized: "We don't believe that you should have to 'pay for' tax cuts." (Until I read that statement, I always thought there could be no one more conservative than a corn-fed Iowa Republican. George W. Bush, irrespective of the true extent of his commitment to federal budget deficit reduction and the presumed power of a congressional majority, will have an uphill fight in making Greenspan's job, as well as that of his succes-sor, easier.)

The U.S. Current-Account Deficit

Finally, in a speech on November 19 in Frankfurt, Germany, Greenspan joined his central-bank colleagues in appraising an increasingly important issue—the globalization of trade *and finance*. He noted that "the volume of trade relative to world gross domestic product has been rising for decades, largely because of decreasing transportation costs and lowered trade barriers. The increasing shift of world GDP toward items with greater conceptual content has further facilitated increased trade because ideas and services tend to move across borders with greater ease and speed than goods."

Greenspan framed the U.S. current-account deficit in the following context:

> Foreign-exchange trading volumes have grown rapidly, and the magnitude of cross-border claims continues to increase at an impressive rate. Although international trade in goods, services, and assets rose markedly after World War II, a persistent dispersion of current-account balances across countries did not emerge until recent years. But, as the U.S. deficit crossed 4 percent of GDP in 2000, financed with the current-account surpluses of other countries, the widening dispersion of current-account balances became more evident. Previous postwar increases in trade relative to world GDP had represented a more balanced grossing up of exports and imports without engendering chronic large trade deficits in the United States, and surpluses among many other countries.
>
> So far, foreigners are willing to lend the U.S. money to finance the current-account imbalances. The worry, however, is that at some point foreigners might suddenly lose interest in holding dollar-denominated investments. *That could cause foreigners to unload investments in U.S. stocks and bonds, sending their prices plunging and interest rates soaring* [emphasis added]. Moreover, the persistence of bloated U.S. trade deficits over time can pose a risk to the thus-far-resilient U.S. economy.

In short, Warren Buffett's vision of the world is not as narrow as some think. His actions speak volumes about his awareness of both the micro and the macro environments.

Never Lose Sight of the Forest for the Trees

Standing amid the giant sequoias, one can easily lose one's bearings, unlike the eagle soaring and surveying overhead. As an earthbound creature, I must depend on my trusty compass. Moving from the forest to the sea (and mangling a metaphor en route), if the tide truly is ebbing, the overarching tidal wave of macro stimulus seems to have lifted the spirits of the majority, at least until (or if) it crashes on the beach. Excluding the drag of the still-way-down-in-the-dumps Nasdaq composite index companies, the inclusive Dow Jones Wilshire 5000, defined below, is at or near all-time highs. But Buffett's not buying, so to speak. Steering clear of "mindless imitation of others" has kept him out of harm's way many times in the past. How will we judge his actions five years from now? (Though it may be dated, we at MCM, along with our clients, owe him more than a debt of gratitude for the insights he shared five years ago. When you wonder if you're way out in left field, a smile from the consummate coach in the stands can make all the difference. While many of the conclusions reached in the 1999 MCM annual report were not directly attributable to Buffett, his imprimatur was clearly in evidence.)

Returning to an earlier utterance in 2003: *"Unfortunately, the hangover may prove to be proportional to the binge."* Buffett suspects, as I believe the last sentence confirms (and made all the more certain by his interpretation of the last-trump-card-played desperation implied by the monetary and fiscal policy initiatives outlined above), that the tide has turned, that the game may once again come to those who are patient, those who know the market's herdlike psychological proclivities and its tendency to regress to the mean and beyond. What we do know is that he will take advantage of the waves of investor sentiment from which occasional short-term (but presumably long-term for capital-gains-tax purposes) opportunities arise, but he never takes his eyes off the stage of the tide. His foray into $8 billion in junk bonds in 2002 and his flirtation with silver a number of years ago are but a few examples. What Buffett really longs for, though, are times like 1974 when he can throw caution to the winds and fill his plate to overflowing with bargains. To switch metaphors, those who know the difference between wheat and chaff will likely reap harvests an order of magnitude greater than will those to whom stalks (or "stocks") of wheat all look alike. The seeds that Buffett planted in the dark days of the take-no-prisoners bear market of 1973–1974 later grew to heights unimaginable as the sun, as it always does, overcame the darkness—about the time the clouds of despair became so pervasive that nobody cared anymore. For those already beaten and bloody, the dog days of the fall of 1974 conjured up many images, none of which looked like opportunity. Is Buffett perhaps finding cause to prepare for what might lie ahead?

Who knows whether a defining moment awaits just beyond a bend in the road? It appears that Buffett, ever-rational and ostensibly devoid of greed and avarice, has, at least for the moment, concluded that the risk of loss is greater than the opportunities forgone. That isn't a forecast—rather a nonspecific, tacit reference to the stage of the tide as he sees it. Unlike a forecast, there is no time dimension. Earlier in this section he used the same logic in explaining his bet against the dollar: "I have no idea what currencies are going to do next week or next month or even next year. [But] *I think I know over time.*" Money, as Buffett proves time and again, seems to find its way to the pockets of those who are its worthy masters. Either you rule your money or it rules you; there is precious little middle ground. If you're not sure, you already know the answer. A wag wiser than I once proclaimed: "Money is a good servant but a poor master."

Buffett's for*bear*ance is not new. He had not been seduced by the rally that followed his exit in May of 1969. From 1969 through 1973–1974, while the bear played with investors' hopes as a grizzly toys with a landed salmon, Buffett hibernated, passing on the one-decision-growth-stock "Nifty Fifty" craze. In a radical turnabout in his long-standing policy of "holding forever," in an October 27, 2003, *Barron's* interview he publicly lamented not selling Coke and Gillette at 50 plus times earnings in the late 1990s, when (I presume) they had become so expensive that they could no longer be considered "one decision" growth stocks, even though they were charter members of his sacrosanct "Sainted Seven." Whether Buffett also thought that both companies had lost some of their long-term luster is a question for another time. As a "value" investor, committed to buying low and selling high, "Buffett understood that everything depends on the price you pay when you get in" [and apparently now at extremes, when you get out]. Loosely paraphrasing Maggie Mahar, author of *Bull! A History of the Boom, 1982–1999*, a value investor stops buying at the end of the cycle, when prices are the highest. Flashing back, in Buffett's view prices were still exorbitant in the early 1970s, six years after the broad market began its long and jerky 180-degree barrel roll. Again quoting *Barron's*: "While most investors are motivated by a desire to make money, Buffett focuses first on not losing money."

An Investor's Unheralded Virtue: Patience

Let us now respectfully pause to consider an uncommon trait that is common among many great achievers: patience. In *Patience: How We Wait Upon the World*, author David Baily Harned attempts to resurrect this lost virtue, one that has served Buffett so well. Harned laments the popular disregard for waiting. Most of us do not consider cooling our heels as occupying a place "at the core and center of human life." In the world as many of us would want it to be, there should really be no "time wasted" at all (my words, but think of the irony of the phrase in this context). Gratification should be instant. Images of cell phones, Palm Pilots with Internet access, and the aggravation of long lines in airports following 9/11 raced through my consciousness. Moreover, we are unable to equate waiting with "doing anything." Harned observes that what now counts in life is "activity, agency, getting things done." As an antidote, Harned defines four dimensions of patience, upon which one might reflect in a report such as this, taking a few seconds to customize the message as it might be applied by an investor, so as to grasp for one's own benefit its everlasting and practical relevance: "endurance (suffering without discontent), forbearance (bearing with the faults of others), expectancy (a willingness to wait), and perseverance (constancy)." We can understand the virtue better by reflecting on its four polar opposites: "Impatience and apathy (the extremes of which patience is the mean), boredom, and displacement (loss of touch with one's purpose in life)." A meaty mouthful, best consumed in small bites. . .

The Interdependence of Patience and Pitches

In a quick transition to allow your overheated cerebral cortex to cool down, we will take another quick trip to the ballpark. No serious conversation about baseball would be complete without reference to the two most prodigious sluggers of all times, Babe Ruth, whose record of 714 home runs stood for 39 years until broken by Hank Aaron in 1974, and Ted Williams, whose career began shortly after the "Babe" retired, earned a lifetime batting average of .344 and hit a total of 521 home runs, despite time away from baseball defending his country in two wars. Nicknamed the "Splendid Splinter," Williams was one of the greatest natural hitters of all time. Buffett, who frequently uses Williams' "sweet-spot" analogy in explaining how he decides when to swing his golden bat, has drawn upon the techniques of the great ballplayers, as well as the great executives. Michael Lewis in *Moneyball* describes the atypical way Billy Beane, general manager of the Oakland A's, acquires players, along with the results his approach has produced in recent years. The A's have sported the second-best record in the Major Leagues the past four years (just one win behind the Seattle Mariners), with salaries a mere one-third of what George Steinbrenner, an obvious proponent of "financial determinism," has been paying the New York Yankees. Beane learned the secret of why so many rich men cannot buy success in baseball: "In professional baseball it still matters less how much money you have than how you spend it." In Buffett's league, having too much money actually reduces the likelihood of outsized success. (Beane is Buffett in baseball cap and spikes.) That Buffett takes the mound to throw out the first pitch at Omaha's Rosenblatt Stadium, home of the AAA Omaha Royals, before each year's Berkshire annual meeting is perhaps more symbolic than it appears on first blush.

In any event, Buffett was selected as the leadoff "hitter" because he is the investor's equivalent of Babe Ruth and Ted Williams, rolled into one. (It also doesn't hurt that he, Walter Scott, and the Union Pacific Railroad own the team!) Taking what appears to be a reasonable swing at an old adage, if you really want to learn how to hit a baseball, don't start by asking a rookie. In fact, avoid a rookie even if you have no alternative. Bad advice is worse than no advice at all. On the practical side, unlike any others to follow, Buffett doesn't sell advice but rather takes his own, for which he is in every sense accountable. His batting average is measured with the same precision as Williams'. He is the spirit and soul of Berkshire Hathaway—the storied history of the name even implying that in the right hands a silk purse can come from a sow's ear ("He that hath a will *hath a way*")—a holding company with some $150 billion in assets, second only to General Electric in that metric. Since the mid-1960s Buffett has allocated an ever-growing capital base with unparalleled skill and unequaled results. His 31 percent stake in Berkshire, approximately 99 percent of his net worth, is invested at absolute parity with outsiders, such as you and me.

Buffett's salary, so paltry as to make him unworthy of an invitation for membership to any CEOs club, is $100,000. Perhaps even more off-putting to members of the club is that he would be, to inject a Buffett aphorism, as out of place as a "belch in the boardroom." Having never received a bonus or a stock option, what possibly could he contribute to the boardroom blather? Buffett exudes integrity in a business world where duplicity, incrementally but insidiously, has become the *de facto* standard. From my perspective, what makes him so unique is his willingness to share his wisdom with all who will listen, his sagacity so valuable that were he not incredibly charitable with his most valuable asset, people would pay a king's ransom to sit at his feet. Figuratively, we do. Each year a growing throng of us, a standing-room-only 19,500 or so last May, make the pilgrimage to Omaha to soak up the folksy, commonsense wisdom that is so deeply ingrained in the mental framework of Buffett and his sidekick, Charlie Munger, that it flows effortlessly and consistently as they subtly use six hours of questions from shareholders as a springboard to expound on their philosophy. It's like a Little Leaguer having Ted Williams as a coach. Buffett is, no fizz intended, the "Real Thing."

What about Other Major-League Iconoclasts?

While admittedly stepping down a rung on the credibility ladder, I have chosen not to neglect the facts, and opinions, of several admittedly self-selected independent thinkers whom I respect, but whose batting averages are not as well known. An erudite maverick, Marc Faber, whose contrarian philosophy I largely embrace, warns investors when worldwide investment themes have become widely accepted and are, therefore, highly priced and risky.[1] He, meanwhile, continuously

---

[1][2006, *Speculative Contagion*] Generally, I am most comfortable with investors where our shared fundamental beliefs include the positive correlation between price and risk, as well as the negative correlation between risk and return. "One of the many unique and advantageous aspects of value investing is that the larger the discount from intrinsic value, the greater the margin of safety and the greater

and assiduously searches for opportunities in unloved and depressed markets. While most of us are just waking up to the sleeping giant, Hong Kong-based Faber is way ahead of us on the curve: He has been managing money for wealthy Chinese investors for years.

Faber, like Buffett, finds secular-cycle significance in the 80-year relationship between GDP and the market value of all publicly traded securities (first chart, Figure 7.1). Applied to an individual company, it would equate to the market-price-to-sales-per-share ratio, a rough and ragged secondary valuation technique. Faber offers the graphic as a "simple quantitative antidote that investors can administer to neutralize their often emotional "availability bias" assessment of the future."

By adding a second and complementary chart (bottom, Figure 7.1), along with using the same denominator, GDP, Faber compares total debt outstanding to the economy's capacity to service it. Using both tools, he points out the fundamental difference between what he describes as a "real economy" in 1982 and what he sees as the "financial economy" of today. In a real economy, the debt and equity markets as a percentage of GDP are small and their principal function is to serve as the conduit through which savings flow into investments. In a financial or easy-money economy (often encouraged by both low-cost equity and debt capital), the total market value of the equity market is far larger than GDP—and not only channels financial resources into economic investments, but the massive overflow gives rise to colossal speculative bubbles. Faber observes that malinvestments do occasionally occur in a real economy, but they are infrequent and their impact relatively insignificant. Certainly in 1982 the cost of both debt and equity capital was so high as to make most projects funded thereby appear conspicuously imprudent. Incidentally, given Federal Reserve Board Chairman Paul Volcker's willful intent to crush inflation, the high-probability bet was that interest rates would eventually come crashing down. As those for whom I worked at the time will recall, it was the bet I then made with virtually all of my investment capital, and rates

---

potential return when the stock price moves back to intrinsic value. Contrary to the view of modern portfolio theorists that increased returns can only be achieved by taking greater levels of risk, value investing is predicated on the notion that increased returns are associated with a greater margin of safety, i.e., lower risk." Thus saith the partners of Tweedy, Browne, who grew up in Graham-and-Doddsville.

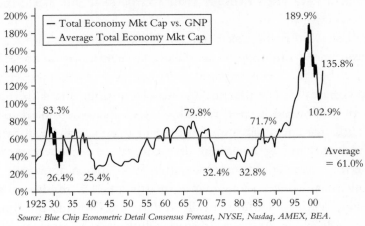

Market Cap versus GNP 12/31/24–12/31/03
Consensus Forecast for 12/31/2003

Source: Blue Chip Econometric Detail Consensus Forecast, NYSE, Nasdaq, AMEX, BEA.

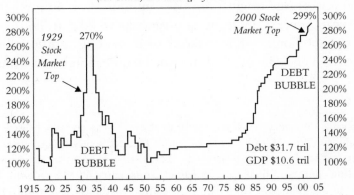

Total Credit Market Debt
(All Sectors) as Percentage of U.S. GDP

"When we are living on this much borrowed money, we are also living on borrowed time."— Paul Volcker, Federal Reserve Chairman, 1979–1986
Source: St. Louis Federal Reserve, FRED II, BEA.

Figure 7.1   "Real Economy" versus "Financial Economy"
SOURCE: *Outstanding Investors Digest*, April 30, 2004.

did fall. The pitch was clearly in my "happy zone." And the results were proportional.

Please examine these charts carefully. A picture may be worth, who knows, billions of dollars for Buffett? In 1981 domestic stock market capitalization as a percentage of GDP was less than 40 percent, and total domestic credit market debt as a percentage of GDP was 130 percent.

By contrast, at present the stock market capitalization and total credit market debt have risen to more than 135 percent and 275 percent of GDP, respectively.[2]

We believe that the link between the two charts makes their message even more ominous. Nonetheless, as persuasive as these charts appear to be, in our profession every snippet of evidence must be viewed skeptically. The practical genius of Benjamin Franklin is apparent in the following cryptic remark: "'Tis easy to see, hard to foresee." With that caveat firmly implanted in your mind, I will proceed. Net debt outstanding has risen dramatically in recent years. While an extreme example, Fannie Mae, the $950 billion mortgage lending giant that finances more than a quarter of U.S. residential mortgage debt, reported enthusiastically on its 2003 results, the "greatest year for housing in America's history. Housing sales were at all-time highs. Mortgage interest rates dropped to their lowest level since the late 1960s. Mortgage originations were up more than 40 percent from just the year before, coming in at a remarkable $3.7 trillion, as consumers bought homes or refinanced their existing mortgage." Hold your horses! This is in an $11.5 trillion U.S. economy and, compared

---

[2][2006, *Speculative Contagion*] Careful examination of year-end 2004 Government Accountability Office (GAO) and first-quarter Federal Reserve data indicates total U.S. debt outstanding of approximately $29.5 trillion. In order to avoid double counting, domestic financial companies (approximately $12 trillion) are not included. Also excluded is the GAO's calculation of the present value of Social Security and Medicare obligations, which are, respectively, $12.5 trillion and $24.6 trillion. While the Social Security and Medicare obligations are real at this point, they can be legislatively reduced at the will of Congress. We find those obligations noteworthy but, because they are not hard numbers, inappropriate to include in the total debt figures. The Dow Jones Wilshire 5000, perhaps the most representative index of all publicly traded, domestically based U.S. corporations, totaled an approximate market capitalization of $15 trillion at year-end 2004—or 128 percent of GDP. [2010 update: As of September 2010, there was approximately $40.5 trillion in total U.S. nonfinancial debt outstanding and $13.9 trillion in market capitalization (as reported by the Wilshire 5000 Total Market index)—and $14.7 trillion in GDP. Therefore, the market capitalization to GDP' ratio was approximately 95 percent, while the debt to GDP ratio was approximately 275 percent.]

with an increase in total mortgage borrowing of just over $1 trillion between 1990 and 1996, the binge in borrowing in 2003 certainly seems unpropitious if not preposterous! Frank Raines, CEO, was unreservedly optimistic. (Prone to hyperbole, Raines neglected to point out that *net* mortgages outstanding increased by a much smaller $735 billion during the year. The net figure is the result of adjustments for refinancings, mortgage principal payments, and defaults.) Following the strongest year in the history of the U.S. housing market, Raines pours it on: "The American people are unsurprisingly bullish on housing and homeownership. Two-thirds of Americans believe now is a good time to buy a home, compared with only 47 percent of Americans who are optimistic about the economy as a whole." (See the "Run for the Roses" section further on in this chapter for insights on how investors chase the "last best thing.") As a sorry postscript, a year later, on the heels of Freddie Mac's "managed" accounting scandal [see 2003 annual report: Chapter 6], Mae got her Fannie "spanked."[3]

We have no idea how much debt the economy can service. Flashing back to 1982 . . . If, for whatever reasons, interest rates rise sharply henceforth, certain borrowers (like some households overloaded with consumer credit-card, other installment, and/or mortgage debt) are likely to be stretched pretty thin. What we do know is that the

---

[3][2004, original] On December 22, 2004, the *Wall Street Journal* reported the forced departure of Frank Raines, CEO, 56, who took the blame for a shortfall in capital because of accounting changes imposed by the SEC and OFHEO (Office of Federal Housing Enterprise Oversight) that will require Fannie to recognize $9.18 billion in losses on derivative contracts, which were used for hedging interest-rate risks. A key issue for any new auditor will be whether the company's hundreds of billions of derivative financial instruments are valued properly on the company's balance sheet, given the wide latitude that companies receive in estimating the fair-market values of such instruments. Companies have been known to use the valuation of derivatives to manage earnings. Alan Greenspan is a fan of derivatives and refuses to regulate them, arguing that they reduce risk, whereas Warren Buffett warned at the 2003 annual meeting that "derivatives are advertised as shedding risk for the system, but they have long crossed the point of decreasing risk and now increase risk. As with every company transferring risk to very few players, they are all hugely interdependent. Central banks are exposed to weaknesses." Let's hope Greenspan is right, for his successor may have a tiger by the tail.

purveyors of financial-service products, including those financial institutions that deal in the black-box world of derivative products whose notional totals[4] don't appear in the above figures, have seen their earnings skyrocket, along with the debt outstanding. To be sure, money greases the skids of commerce, and easy money lubricates the engine of excess. In simple terms, financial bubbles, driven as they are by human folly, are often the result of too much money chasing too few worthy ideas, leading to overinvestment and excess supply. According to Martin Feldstein, CEO of the private National Bureau of Economic Research (and among several leading candidates to step into the shoes of Alan Greenspan in 2006), "Business spent $4.7 trillion on equipment and software from 1995 to 2000, 37 percent more than the prior six-year period. Now (2003) utilization rates of this beefed-up capacity are

---

[4][2004, original] According to FDIC data, of the $71 trillion in derivatives outstanding early last year, 86 percent were interest-rate contracts. The remaining 14 percent of the derivatives in the mentioned FDIC study are foreign-exchange contracts and equity, commodity, and other contracts. Approximately 96 percent of derivative contracts are transacted through commercial banks. The dealer J. P. Morgan Chase Bank is by far the biggest player, representing more than half the market. (Parenthetically, even more striking is the growth and use of derivatives globally. According to the Bank for International Settlements's seventy-fifth annual report, published in Basel, Switzerland, June 2005, the notional value of derivatives outstanding at year end was $320 trillion compared with $199 trillion the prior year.) [2010 update: In May 2010 the Bank for International Settlements reported that the total notional value of derivatives outstanding was $615 trillion at 2009 year end. Interest-rate contracts constituted 73 percent of the total, while foreign exchange contracts and credit default swaps represented another 13 percent of the total notional outstanding. It should be noted that collateral has grown from around 20 percent of net mark-to-market value of counterparty exposures after the benefit of close-out netting in 1999 to approximately 90 percent today.] Derivatives expose not only the holders of the contracts to the risk, but the dealer banks as well if the holders default (counter-party risk). The LTCM (Long-Term Capital Management) crisis resulted from the unexpected defaults of Russia, and the holders of the derivatives related to those defaults experienced cascading losses, resulting in defaults and counter-party defaults. Life, however, is too serious to be taken seriously, so let's end with a smile. Bob Rubin, former Wall Street banker who served as Secretary of the Treasury under Bill Clinton, assumed the Clintonesque vernacular with ease as he explained the difficulty in protecting oneself against the unexpected. "Condoms aren't completely safe," he said. "A friend of mine was wearing one, and he got hit by a bus."

the lowest in 20 years." Add telecommunications and certain regional housing markets (try to reconcile the aforementioned explosion in Fannie Mae originations above with underlying household formation growth), and you begin to get the picture.

Lest we become too enamored with money—and the grand profits that can be earned by its changers—it's helpful to remember that it is also the ultimate commodity. There is very little room for differentiation in the long run. As for commercial banks in general, their history is resplendent with the uncanny capacity to play "follow the loser," mindlessly jumping from one folly to the next. After years of miscues, have they finally seen the light? I wouldn't take that bet if the odds were 10 to 1!

If debt as a percentage of GDP should eventually shrink—which we think is probable, though we wouldn't begin to speculate about when—financial-sector earnings are almost certain to decline as a percentage of S&P 500 earnings as well. And here's the connection. With stock prices currently at a ratio of 136 percent of GDP, they might become obscenely expensive without the support of unsustainable earnings from the financial sector, *ceteris paribus*. It would appear that a sharp decline in either of these GDP ratios (debt or equity) could have a communicable and sympathetic effect on the other.

Notes another seasoned observer: "There have only been three times in the last 80 years where all elements of the stock market, the economy and debt structure have come together like they have today." Others are not so circumspect. Frederick J. Sheehan Jr., in his bold and brash "An Investor's Manifesto," pointedly presents the nightmare scenario:

> We are living at the long end—if "end" it is—of gross financial imbalances. Most people don't understand this, or won't acknowledge it. This fog of extremity and perplexity is a financial maelstrom that has been building for a generation.

We don't attempt to forecast the unknowable, nor should we discount it offhandedly as though it were not a possibility, however remote. Will we look back 10 years from now and call this the "perfect storm"?

The force behind secular cycles that can last for years seems always to be the same: human nature. Secular bull and bear cycles begin slowly because there is always a disposition in people's minds to think the existing conditions will be permanent. With this paragraph we segue into John Kenneth Galbraith's theory on cycles that is based more on the emerging science of "behavioral economics."

A Short History of Financial Euphoria

Galbraith's satirical wit makes this Canadian-born economist enjoyable to read. *The Great Crash, 1929*, considered the definitive work in some circles on the economic devastation of 75 years ago (and never out of print, thanks to new speculative episodes that would bring it back to the public's attention), has been helpful, along with other books, including *Security Analysis* (photographic reprint of the 1934 edition) and the *Memoirs of Benjamin Graham*, both quoted extensively in earlier annual reports. Graham penned his remarkable tome while in the thick of battle, when the lingering pain from the slings and arrows was the measure of his defeat—and when absolution was nowhere to be found. His intellectual detachment, his ability to rationally assess the damage and identify its proximate causes (all the while almost mortally wounded financially and deeply distraught emotionally) demonstrated extraordinary will and self-control.

Galbraith, less a warrior and more a historian, waited 20-plus years until the dust had settled. By then the public, roundly chastened, finally wanted answers. He wrote *The Great Crash* in the 1950s, whereas his *A Short History of Financial Euphoria*, published in 1990 (with a second edition in 1994), used the extravagant 1980s as a chance to revisit the inevitability of recurring episodes of financial euphoria. Prime malefactors to whom Galbraith referred—complete with accounts of their shameful falls from grace—were junk-bond king Michael Milken; Donald Trump, gambling's Tower of Babel (whose greatest virtue is chutzpah and greatest vice, bad hair); and Canadian real estate moguls Robert Campeau and the Reichman brothers, not to be confused with Rock 'n' Roll Hall of Famers the Righteous Brothers, whose "You've Lost That Lovin' Feeling" holds the distinction of being the most-played song in the history of radio. Wisdom is often found in the strangest places. Investors would be well advised to listen to the simple, six-note opening line "You never close your eyes. . . ." Though written for the 1980s, Galbraith's observations were inadvertently prophetic and poignant for the decade to follow.

More inclined toward pragmatism than prophecy, Galbraith was leery of the image that a seer rubbing a crystal ball conveyed. "There are, however, few matters on which such a warning is less welcomed," he wrote.

In the short run, it will be said to be an attack, motivated by either deficient understanding or uncontrolled envy, on the wonderful process of enrichment. More durably, it will be thought to demonstrate a lack of faith in the inherent wisdom of the market itself.

Galbraith recounted how Paul Warburg, a founder of the Federal Reserve System, and investment author Roger Babson were vehemently criticized in the 1920s; the reactions from the investment public were bitter, even vicious, regarding Warburg and Babson's warnings of ultimate collapse and depression if the speculation continued unabated in the late 1920s.

Galbraith warned that investors must resist two compelling forces if they are to avoid speculative manias, of which the late 1990s surely qualifies: "One, the powerful personal interest that develops in the euphoric belief, and the other, the pressure of public and seemingly superior financial opinion that is brought to bear on behalf of such belief." Both stand as proof of the great eighteenth-century German literary figure Johann Christoph Friedrich von Schiller's famous dictum that the "crowd converts the individual from reasonably good sense to the stupidity against which," as he also said, "the very [g]ods [t]hemselves contend in vain." As has been repeated time and again throughout these reports—and to which Galbraith lends his two cents' worth:

History may not repeat itself, but some of its lessons are inescapable. One is that in the world of high and confident finance little is ever really new. The controlling fact is not the tendency to brilliant invention; the controlling fact is the shortness of the public memory, especially when it contends with a euphoric desire to forget.

The rule is that financial operations do not lend themselves to innovation. What is currently so described and celebrated is, without exception, a small variation on an established design, one that owes its distinctive character to the aforementioned brevity of the financial memory [assumed to be around 20 years]. The world of finance hails the invention of the wheel over and over again, often a slightly more unstable version. All financial innovation involves, in one form or another, the creation of debt secured in greater or lesser adequacy by real assets.

This sameness, seldom recognized at the time as such, lends itself well to cyclical yearnings, with the rhythm rooted deeply in the human psyche. Buffett points to the facts and Galbraith to the mind; both reach the same conclusion.

Riding the Train: When to Get On, When to Get Off

As the equity market gradually got its legs after being pummeled for the years leading up to 1982, the road from despair to eventual irrational exuberance had so many detours, switchbacks, and sideshows that only a steely eye on the compass could keep one on course. Having entered the industry as a neophyte in 1966 at the age of 24, I furthered my education in the school of reality, participating fully in both cycles to which Buffett has referred. By 1982, at the age of 40, the undersigned had logged 15 years of experience in the industry. No longer a novice, I lived history in the making, every day. The market gradually picked up speed at the pace of a tired locomotive pulling a full load, huffing and puffing as it snaked its way up the mountain. Later, as the grade leveled out a bit, it traveled at an ever-increasing pace as "financial news TV" and eventually the Internet invaded our homes and offices to the point where it was nearly impossible to resist jumping aboard the train to sure riches. Unfortunately, when the rolling stock reached the crest of the mountain few realized it was time to detrain. When you don't know where you're going, it's hard to know where to get off. They don't blow the whistle for that. Once the train picks up momentum on the other side of the mountain, most everyone looks back up at the mountaintop from whence they came—and not to where they're going. By the time the passengers realize their mistake, it's too late; they've already punched their ticket at a high price. The locomotive is careening around curves, out of control, ironically down toward the valley of *opportunity* below.

As the economy evolved from real to financial from 1982 to 2000, many what now appear to have been minor bubbles occurred: IPOs in the early 1980s, Michael Milken's junk bonds, the leveraged-buyout craze in the second half of the 1980s, and the so-called (and largely forgotten) "Crash of '87" were but a few of the more obvious examples. Undeterred, the longest peacetime expansion on record chugged along, seemingly impervious to interference from the various and sundry financial episodes, with the salubrious, long-run, threefold effect of generally falling interest rates, stable commodity prices, and generally rising stock prices serving as a tailwind. According to Marc Faber, when bubbles burst in the real economy, the collateral damage tends to be limited. In a late-stage financial economy, on the other hand, investment manias and stock market bubbles often grow to be so large that, when they come apart at the seams, considerable economic fallout follows. It should be noted that in the almost four years following the Bubble of the late 1990s, the main front of economic distress that was expected to follow has yet to pass through. It appears that Greenspan may have engineered another perfectly soft landing . . . or, as mentioned earlier, has he simply robbed Peter to pay Paul?! If memory serves me correctly, Buffett took to the high ground in 1969, five years before the recession of 1974–1975, the sharpest economic setback since the Great Depression.

2005: Mirror Image of 1982?

Another prognosticator for whom I have high regard weighs in, as quoted here. [The late] octogenarian and brilliant thinker Peter Bernstein, author of *Against the Gods*, observed in the spring of 2003 that the old rules no longer apply. Bernstein was a realist.

> For now, equities aren't the best place to be for the long run. The long run here is not necessarily going to bail you out, or even if it does, the margin by which equities will outperform could be too small to compensate for the volatility. . . . The hard truth is that the market cannot grow that much faster than GDP.

Using the same data that brought Buffett and Faber to their feet, Bernstein echoed:

> In March 2000, stocks were valued at 181 percent of GDP, up from 60 percent just over 10 years earlier [and 40 percent in 1982]. Of course, an investor could gamble that dividends

would climb higher or that investors would push price-earnings ratios back to stratospheric heights, boosting capital gains. But that's not a risk I would want to take under any circumstances.

He made it clear that he was opining exclusively on the long run. "Yet," Bernstein acknowledged, "it would be extremely difficult for most investors to realize that 'the world has changed'—that we had entered a new era of investing: boom and bust." Finally, Bernstein cautioned against assuming that tomorrow will be pretty much like today.

What Have We Learned?

I hope you have learned from the evidence and arguments presented in this section that long-term "secular" cycles, like the tides, do exist. Although I don't think the timing of these cycles can be predicted, it does seem to be much easier to recognize the top of a boom or the bottom of a bust than to observe the great expanse in between. When those heady or harrowing occasions arise, there's little else you need for making rational investment decisions than to "get physical" by swinging back to the first paragraph of this section a dozen or so pages ago. Fixate on the motion and the message of the simple playground swing. The waves are relatively random and benign, unless taken for more than they are. The behavioral impetus in which cycles are deeply rooted is discussed in a later section, "Run for the Roses."

As for where we are in the long-term cycle, I turn to Benjamin Graham to frame the perspective: "If you see that a man is very fat, it makes little difference that you are able to precisely calculate his exact weight to enhance your conclusion." Synthesizing all that I have read, no other conclusion could logically follow than that the markets are likewise "very fat." How fat? We attempt next to put the S&P 500 earnings on a justly and fairly calibrated scale.

Fully Deluded Earnings: Penance (?) in the Cuff-Links Cooler

The phrase "fully deluded earnings" was coined by Jim Grant, editor of *Grant's Interest Rate Observer*. We venture into this misty landscape at the risk of being deemed delusional ourselves. Grant, with whom

I have corresponded on occasion, is a "permabear" who, in the 1990s, willingly shouldered the brunt of the abuse from those who took delight in ridiculing bearishness, like the haughty patrician Louis Rukeyser, before he was bear-clawed and summarily fired as 31-year host of the most popular financial news program ("Wall $treet *Weak*," in the opinion of this wonk, was always the more fitting moniker). "Bear" with me, but guess who got the last laugh? Michael Lewis, who wrote the Wall Street best sellers *Liar's Poker* and *Moneyball* (the latter got a nod several pages ago in "The Interdependence of Patience and Pitches"), calls Grant "one of the most interesting market analysts alive."

Lewis says there's a tendency to exaggerate the importance of bullish sentiment, even if proffered by a dimwit (not Dim*net*; see opening quotation in this chapter!), and denigrate those (some of whom are first-rate thinkers) who speak to the contrary; see the similar opinions earlier in Chapter 7 of John Kenneth Galbraith in "A Short History of Financial Euphoria." Why this phenomenon of human nature, you ask? To update Willie Sutton's alleged dictum ("Why did you rob banks?" "Because that's where the money was"), most of the money is on the bullish side of the street. Likewise, fabricated earnings became the wellspring of greenbacks galore for those for whom crossing over the ethical line was a baby step. Sutton, who actually stole the title for his book *Where the Money Was* from a reporter, was thereby handcuffed to a lie for eternity. Sutton was romanticized for his Robin Hood–like flippancy, whereas today's turnabout "robbin' hood," who deftly picks the pockets of his (relatively poor and, thanks to his actions, getting even poorer) family of shareholders to line his *own* pockets, does short, and certainly not fatal, penance in the cuff-links cooler.

It doesn't take a Harry Houdini to escape the chains of FASB (Financial Accounting Standards Board). By the same token, FASB can't hold a candle to the great magician when it comes to escaping the capricious clutches of Congress, after the politicians reach that fork in the road when they must choose between the deafening, palm-greasing, clamor of lobbyists and the squeaky but clear voice of reason. Accordingly, the game of deluding—first earnings and then those who relied upon them—became well nigh ubiquitous. In this short section, and with the help of those with whom we spoke at Standard & Poor's, along with the vast amount of data available on the S&P web site and the periodical

"HOWEVER, BY USING AN ALTERNATE METHOD OF ACCOUNTING..."

SOURCE: Copyright © 1998 Bill Monroe.

The Accounting Observer, we'll try to make some sense of how we think earnings should be determined and presented to shareholders.

The Benchmark S&P 500 Index

The S&P 500 index is the generic benchmark against which most U.S. equity performance is measured. It represents 70 percent of all U.S. publicly traded companies. Lest you think the S&P 500 is flawless, however, please refer to the 1998 annual report section titled "The Friendly Brute with No Brains" at the MCM web site: www.mcmadvisors.com ["The Friendly Brute" has been omitted from both *Speculative Contagion* and *A Decade of Delusions*].

Is the Market Cheap or Dear?

In the normal course of our reading it's not uncommon to come across substantial, sometimes shocking, variations among market commentators on the richness or cheapness of the market in general. We thought it might be useful to delve more deeply into the numbers in search of what may approximate the truth of the matter. According to Standard & Poor's, the average P/E ratio from 1935 on a *trailing four quarters, as reported, basis* is 15.63. Some market commentators have argued that with the S&P 500 at approximately the 1200 level, and since *operating earnings estimates for 2005* are close to $73, the market is valued at just over 16 times earnings, only marginally above the long-term average and thus not overly expensive.

There are two problems with this line of reasoning that makes it a comparison of apples and oranges. First, while operating earnings is an important metric that can speak to the profitability of the core business, this approach essentially treats income and expenses not directly tied to the day-to-day functioning of the business as forever irrelevant to the calculation of earnings. The most important expenses excluded from this calculation would be interest, adjusted for tax effect, and "extraordinary" charges or credits. The definition of "extraordinary" has been vitiated. That's the first example of the apples-and-oranges confusion. Second, the P/E ratio of 15 to 16 is frequently compared with one using "forward" and not "trailing" earnings. We've always believed "a bird in the hand is worth two in the bush." The (desired?) effect in using forward earnings is generally to understate the P/E ratio.

S&P's estimate for 2004 *reported earnings* is currently $58.63. The S&P 500 index closed 2004 at 1212, which puts the estimated trailing *as reported* P/E at 20.7. Using these metrics the S&P 500 P/E ratio is 32 percent higher than the aforementioned mean. Stated another way, if the S&P 500 would have closed the year at the long-term mean P/E (based on the estimate of trailing as reported earnings) it would have been 916, or 24 percent below the actual year-end close. Granted, we have no compelling argument that the S&P 500 should, forthwith or even anytime soon, regress to its long-term average P/E of 15.63, particularly with the discount rate (of which prevailing bond yields are a component) as low as it is historically. Yielding to our obligation as wealth managers to muse about future opportunity sets that may be dramatically different from today's, the possibility of both rising interest rates and equity-risk premiums, to say nothing of deteriorating assumptions regarding future earnings prospects, could put us in the most uncomfortable position of looking *up* wistfully at the "mean" P/E.

The reader may not need to be reminded that while the numerator of the P/E is calculated with exactitude every few seconds by S&P, the denominator—the earnings variable—is as malleable as the imaginations of those who concoct it. Going beyond the apples-and-oranges issues cited above, let's spend a few moments trying to further demystify earnings.

S&P 500 "Core" Earnings

In an attempt to cut through the clutter of the various (and often confusing) numbers presented as "earnings," Standard & Poor's has developed a "core" earnings figure for the S&P 500. The basic goal is to adjust *reported earnings* to get to a number that better reflects the core profitability of the 500 businesses, which in the aggregate represent the index. Here's the overview. S&P:

- Starts with the as-reported number.
- Reduces that number for the approximately 75 percent of stock-option issuance that does not appear as an expense on the income statements.
- Subtracts various pension-related expenses that have in good times often been treated like "cookie jar reserves."
- Adds any goodwill impairment charges.[5]
- Adjusts for gains and losses.
- Adds settlement and litigation expenses to get to a core earnings number.

As can be seen from the S&P 500 Core-Earnings Adjustments chart, over the relatively short time period supplied by S&P where these adjustments were made, the core earnings number has always been less than the *as-reported* number. (Reconstructing earnings prior to the 2002 FASB 142 ruling on the treatment of goodwill is a task too daunting even for S&P.)

S&P 500 Core-Earnings Adjustments

As for more details, the first adjustment—and probably the one with which most people are familiar—is option expense (see Table 7.1).

---

[5][2006, *Speculative Contagion*] As noted in an earlier footnote, in 2002 FASB ceased requiring corporations to amortize goodwill over (typically) a 40-year period, a change with which we were in general agreement. Instead, it is the responsibility of the company and its accountants to determine when goodwill is permanently impaired. It is then immediately written down to its post-impairment value. Since the goodwill-impairment charge is a noncash and presumably nonrecurring expense, S&P adds it back to arrive at core earnings. More commentary on the subject in the text later in this section . . .

Table 7.1 S&P 500 Core–Earnings Adjustments

	1996	1997	1998	1999	2000	2001	2002	2003	2004 Est.	2005 Est.
Operating EPS	40.63	44.01	44.27	51.68	56.13	38.85	46.04	54.69	67.21	73.66
As-Reported EPS	38.73	39.72	37.71	48.17	50	24.69	27.59	48.74	58.63	65.00
Option Exp PS	-.49	-1.12	-1.56	-2.5	-3.82	-5.31	-5.31	-3.92	-3.40	
Pension Int Adj.	-.12	-.05	-.33	-.14	-2.68	-5.07	-5.01	-.29	-3.98	
Other Net Pension Adj.	-.90	-1.11	-1.42	-2.28	-2.69	-2.26	-1.99	-1.71	-1.42	
Goodwill	.03	.18	.24	.16	.83	2.47	6.91	1.77	1.34	
Gains & Losses PS	-1.36	-2.50	-4.45	-4.24	-3.28	1.58	1.19	.45	-.08	
OPEB PS	.03	.05	.07	.13	-.34	-.39	-.35	-.32	-.7	
Sett & Litigation PS	-.01	.16	.47	.76	.90	.40	.83	.91	-1.73	
Reversals PS	-.01	-.03	-.11	-.14	-.06	-.10	-.19	-.08	-.06	
Core PS	35.90	35.30	30.62	39.92	38.86	16.01	23.67	45.55	52.04	

Reported earnings are reduced by the estimated amount of options expense that companies choose not to include in their reported earnings.[6] The next modifications to consider would be the pension-expense adjustments, which are not so black or white. The several pension adjustments, while important, are too complex to discuss here. We believe we understand the issues and recognize there are legitimate arguments on both sides. What is not supposition, however, is the extent to which pension funds, in the aggregate, are underfunded. That number, as of the end of 2003, was $165 billion. As of August 2004, S&P estimated that "funding should improve but at the end of the year S&P companies will still be underfunded by $112 billion." Returning to the subjective, in our judgment pension actuarial asset return assumptions are generally on the high side and, accordingly, pension expense is likely to be a drag on earnings for some time. As for the potential snake-pit promise of post-retirement healthcare benefits, we'll save that discussion for another time.

Goodwill impairment is the next adjustment to consider. While it's true that the actual goodwill impairment is a noncash charge, it is at least debatable whether this means it should therefore be added to the reported earnings and, all other things being equal, increase the core earnings number. Thought of in its entirety, an impairment charge means that there have been real economic losses. Value (cash and/or company stock) has been exchanged for an asset that is deemed now to be worth less than the original price paid. To be sure, to allocate the entire charge to any one quarter seems arbitrary when the decisions that culminated in the recognition of the loss were often years in the making. More on goodwill later . . .

Apart from the core-earnings adjustments, there are other considerations in determining the sustainability of after-tax earnings, of which the following is but one. According to the Bureau of Economic

---

[6][2006, *Speculative Contagion*] Recently about 25 percent of S&P 500 companies expensed the issuance of options, typically using the Black-Scholes pricing model. As a result of mandatory expensing beginning in 2006 and the possibility of stock market returns not matching those that gave rise to the proliferation of options in the first place, I believe that options will eventually amount to no more than a shadow of their former self in terms of their importance as a component of executive compensation.

Analysis, the third quarter's seasonally adjusted corporate profits as a percentage of GDP were 6.8 percent. Were it not for the combined effects of the 2002 and 2003 Tax Acts—amounting to corporate tax savings of $123 billion for the annualized, seasonally adjusted data as of the third fiscal quarter of 2004—the after-tax profit margin would've been a much smaller 5.7 percent. With the budgetary constraints that Congress will ultimately have to address, it may be irresponsible for an analyst to presume that the tax breaks are permanent. You do not have to take our word for this. The General Accounting Office said as much in a December 14, 2004, letter to the President, the President of the Senate, and the Speaker of the House of Representatives.[7]

Let's return briefly to the subject of "goodwill" so as not to slight the importance of historical perspective. The widely accepted definition of the value of a business is the discounted present value of all the cash you can take out of it over time. Cash expended to purchase businesses in excess of tangible assets (the bulk of the purchase price for most companies these days) is recorded on the balance sheet as purchased goodwill. If, for whatever reasons, the goodwill is later deemed to be impaired, the cash expended earlier becomes money poured down a rathole. The present value of that malinvestment of cash should logically reduce the current value of business. Likewise, cash expended to repurchase shares in the market—to offset options issued or to

---

[7][2004, original] ". . . [T]he federal government's gross debt as of September 2004 was about $7.4 trillion, or about $25,000 for every man, woman, and child in the country. But that number excludes such items as the gap between promised and funded Social Security and Medicare benefits, veterans' healthcare, and a range of other unfunded commitments and contingencies that the federal government has pledged to support. If these items are factored in, the current dollar burden for every American rises to about $145,000 per person, or about $350,000 per full-time worker. GAO's fiscal policy simulations illustrate that the fiscal policies in place today—absent substantive entitlement reform or unprecedented changes in tax and/or spending policies—will result in large, escalating, and persistent deficits that are economically unsustainable over the long term. Without reform, known demographic trends, rising healthcare costs, and projected growth in federal spending for Social Security, Medicare, and Medicaid will result in massive fiscal pressures that, if not effectively addressed, could cripple the economy, threaten our national security, and adversely affect the quality of life of Americans in the future." This is a direct quote, folks, from the Government Accountability Office. I'm not making it up.

manage earnings—at prices that are to the advantage of the departing shareholder (and therefore to the detriment of the one who stays the course) also should effectively reduce the current value of the business. Not so, according to contemporary Wall Street reasoning, where earnings, however measured, are the final arbiter of value. (Forget the cash? Not so fast. Doesn't everything ultimately get reduced to cash? Isn't it the lowest common denominator?) Sacrificing a chunk of often hard-earned shareholders' equity for past sins is deemed to give a bracing boost to profitability. Getting rid of the drag on earnings from the impaired assets with the stroke of an auditor's pen gives a lift to earnings. Similarly, the downsized shareholders' equity causes return on equity to rise. No wonder stocks rise on such public admissions of past errors. This nonsense is nothing new. See Benjamin Graham's comments on "Stock Watering Reversed" extracted from the 1934 edition of *Security Analysis*. As for the earlier iteration, here follows his summary of the same practice more than 70 years ago:

> The idea that such sleight-of-hand could actually add to the value of a security is nothing short of preposterous. Yet Wall Street solemnly accepts this topsy-turvy reasoning; and corporate managements are naturally not disinclined to improve their showing by so simple a maneuver. (Graham, *Security Analysis*, 418–419)

Where does that leave us? The preceding discussion was simply a subjective look at some of the adjustments the S&P folks make to arrive at their core earnings figure, which is their attempt to demystify earnings. There are arguments for increasing or decreasing the adjustments for several line items. For 2004 specifically, some of these arguments seem to counteract each other, and we would (netting them out) arrive at a figure very close to S&P's core earnings of $52. Putting this back into the context of valuations, the core earnings above would result in a market multiple of just over 23 times. You may scold us here for committing the same sin we accused others of committing earlier—of comparing apples to oranges—in that we are contrasting core earnings with reported earnings. Despite the difficulty in reconstructing core earnings well into the past, we don't believe the variance would be extreme. In our judgment, by any reasonable measure, the market is not cheap. You might recall Warren Buffett's statement: "We would rather be generally right than precisely wrong." As for us, if we are to err, let it be an error of excessive conservatism. You don't lose real money by forgoing opportunity. Remember also, as the dairy farmer put it, "To err is human, to forgive bovine."

Venturing a look into the future, we'll conclude this section by offering a comment or two about profit margins and earnings growth. First, after careful study, we see nothing structural that will impede the gradual regression of net margins toward their long-term mean of around 5 percent. The mean itself seems to reflect some long-held tacit acceptance of the sharing of the GDP pie among capital, labor, and government. Second, we are equally unimpressed with arguments that GDP growth will accelerate to rates heretofore unseen. Accordingly, despite all the earnings management nonsense of the 1990s, we think the historical trendline growth in earnings is the most optimistic metric to use for extrapolating earnings into the future.

As for how we cope, in our opinion, with an overvalued market and the difficulty many financially leveraged companies will have in "goosing" dividend payout ratios—particularly in light of the most favorable taxes on dividends, at least for another four years—up to the levels that support arguments of a 10 percent return from common stocks, please refer to other sections of the report.

Run for the Roses: Of Pawns, Guinea Pigs . . . and "Retail Investors"

Each age has its particular folly, some scheme, project or phantasy into which it is plunged, spurred on either by the love of gain, the necessity of excitement, or the mere force of imitation. . . . Money has often been a cause of the delusion of multitudes. Sober nations have all at once become desperate gamblers and risked almost their existence upon the turn of a piece of paper. . . . Men, it has been well said, think in herds; it will be seen that they go mad in herds, while they only recover their senses slowly and one by one.

The previous passage is from Charles MacKay's *Extraordinary Popular Delusions and the Madness of Crowds.*

Returning once again to our baseball metaphor, a "change-up" may keep you, the batter, from dozing off at the plate. Getting right into the swing of things, let's begin with the end in mind. Picking up where the 2003 annual report [Chapter 6] left off, let's take a look at the denouement (for lack of a better description) of the average retail investor as described in the next paragraph. Throughout this section we infer that the adjective "average" modifies the stereotypical characterization "retail investor," respectfully realizing that an individual outcome may fall anywhere on the bell curve, on either side of the mean, which distribution no doubt has a large standard deviation. The final resolution of the sequence of events, almost as though following a well-worn script that calls for generous improvisation, could be stated more politely, but not with more succinctness.

It might be noted that the subject appears two years running as testimony first to the writer's belief that everyone in the know should come to the aid of the least informed, like the crowd that on occasion pursues the purse snatcher. Second, though the pieces of a chessboard include the stately kings, queens, bishops, knights, and rooks, of which there are 16 in all, there are an equal number of pawns who, metaphorically, represent the "retail investor." The pawn is the chess piece of lowest value and, as chess masters know, every pawn move creates a weakness beside it or behind it. The parallels abound. Rooks (also called castles—what fun we could have with that if only we had the time!), another word for swindler outside the game of chess, are (so much for chivalry) more valued than knights. Not all is hopeless, however. While the pawn is the first line of defense to be sacrificed to protect the king, if he survives to reach the eighth rank, he can be promoted to any piece other than a king, including the all-powerful queen. Can you feel Darwin's presence in this ancient game that predates him by centuries?

One is at a loss to stereotype the so-called "retail investor" in terms of cause, but perhaps less so in effect. Those who ended up empty-handed or nearly so, who had little to show but regrets for whatever effort and savings they expended during the great "Run for the Roses," may fit the characterization of the effect.

As for cause, some retail investors of the 1990s were artless, venturing without either plan or purpose; others exhibited a credulity that impedes effective functioning in a practical world; still others were congenitally uncritical; while many were found lacking in worldly wisdom. The crafty were "too smart for their own good by half." A share was surely greedy or slothful, failing to realize that a person cannot consume more than he has produced. Wealth, many learned the hard way, is the product of an individual's capacity to think. Most regrettably, a not-insignificant number of these investors were pawns in a social/economic construct where, increasingly, corruption is rewarded and honesty becomes self-sacrifice. As for "retail investors" taken as a whole, Thomas Carlyle sardonically observed: "I do not believe in the collective wisdom of individual ignorance."

The retail investor in this drama about financial cycles is not a bit player, though in the posthumous analysis of a mania that reached bubble proportions (before its ultimate demise), he went largely unnoticed, especially in the early acts. By a series of unintended consequences—following the introduction of the self-directed 401(k) plan in 1981 and the coincidental rebirth of the mutual-fund industry—he found himself standing center stage, with a look of astonishment on his face, holding the proverbial bag when the curtain began to fall.

For purposes of this study, mutual-fund investors, as a group, are the best guinea pigs to be found. (It is not our intent to demean any participant or group of participants in the capital markets. One definition of "guinea pig" is "a person who is used as a subject for research," and that's how it's used here. In the rough-and-tumble world of investment where disciplined rationality may be the most important trait that keeps an investor and his money from being separated, the more we can surmise about the behaviors of the person on the other side of the trade, the better our chances of surviving or even prospering. For the truly patient, it is not a zero-sum game. In the short run, though, it can be brutal.) Not only are "retail investors" deemed to be among the least experienced participants in the financial markets, there is a plethora of data available on their behavior, thanks to the Investment Company Institute's (ICI) statistical and research work in quantitatively supporting the mutual-fund industry's "asset gathering" (remember the pawns?) marketing efforts. By carefully examining the data and thus gaining an awareness of this process that seems to forever migrate toward the demise of the retail investor, we will acquire another shred of evidence about the nature of financial cycles and, more importantly, gain a better understanding of whether we're closer to the beginning or the end of the run. For the retail investors who read this rather disheartening saga, may they gain wisdom as a result so that when history repeats itself they will promote themselves to the eighth rank and become imbued with a new sense of power.

While the drama begins in 1982, a prologue is necessary to set the scene. From the vantage point of today, anyone with a yen for the practical lessons history can teach will look back to that year and see it as one of the most opportune times to commit one's savings to marketable securities during the last 100 years; it was the equivalent of fishing in a stocked pond. More importantly, the rational (not to be confused with retail) investor would have reached the same conclusion—contemporaneously in 1982 when he could and sometimes did seize the moment. Stocks and bonds were so stunningly cheap that an abiding conviction about a rather understandable universal principle is all that would have been necessary to induce the wise man to throw in his lot: the natural tendency of price and value to converge (think again of the child-on-the-swing analogy). Price-value convergence? Mathematicians call it regression to the mean, and physicists, when describing the pendular movement of stock prices (thanks to Newton), note their inclination to gravitate toward the albeit vague notion of "intrinsic value," the point of the arc where they would come to rest without external agitation. Unfortunately, the retail investor was anything but rational when the opportunity arrived. He had lived through the torturous 17 years before, a long span of history, memorable for its violent shorter-term waves. While the tide, the Dow Jones industrial average, ended literally within a pathetic five points from where it began, the typical retail investor had been regularly whipsawed, often completely consumed in trying to stay afloat in turbulent seas.

Exhausted and disoriented, he eventually succumbed to despair, in his desperation thinking he had been rescued by the life raft of high, short-term nominal interest rates. Unfortunately, the raft had a slow leak. Three years into the bull market, individuals remained guarded, accounting for only 11 to 15 percent of the daily volume on the NYSE, compared with more than 40 percent in 1975, just 10 years earlier. As for household assets, according to the Federal Reserve, in 1968, when under the mattress would've been a better place, 35 percent were invested in common stocks, directly or indirectly. In 1989 by contrast, well into the next secular bull market, skittish investors had committed just 13 percent of their assets to equities. Always chasing yesterday's winner in stocks or the highest current yield in fixed-income securities, most Americans throughout the 1980s found safety initially in money-market funds and CDs, then later in bond funds. Fortunes would have been made had they simply reversed the order. Later to become ubiquitous in the 1990s, mutual funds [profiled extensively in Chapter 6]—after years in a torpid state following the abuses of Bernie Cornfeld and his gang of scalawags in the "go-go" 1960s—cycled back into favor. To be sure, mutual-fund ownership grew fivefold during the 1980s, albeit from a small base but, as noted above, for the majority of investors, mutual funds were not yet synonymous with equities.

Pension Funds: Managed for Mediocrity

Pension funds, lest you be led astray by concluding that in *all* cases money and brains are positively correlated, after throwing an average 55 percent of new money at equities during the 20 years leading up to 1982, finally chastened, collectively they timidly parceled a relatively paltry 24 percent of fresh money into common stocks when they were as cheap as they had ever been. Pension-fund managers are the institutional equivalent of the retail investor. As discussed in earlier reports, investment committees invariably oversee pension funds. Committees are small crowds and, according to my favorite book on crowd psychology [despite it being published in 1895 and out of print for years], *The Crowd* by Gustave Le Bon, when smart men and women combine their intellects to presumably optimize a solution, the result tends to be surprisingly counterproductive. Rather than being boosted by brilliance, groupthink has a perversely dilatory effect on collective reasoning. When a group is unable to foster an atmosphere of independence and diversity of opinion, which includes free-flowing exchanges of ideas, it often falls victim to the plague of the lowest common denominator. Henry David Thoreau turns the common into the eloquent: "The mass never comes up to the standard of its best member, but on the contrary degrades itself to a level with the lowest." We may be coining a new word, *un*synergism, wherein the whole is *less* than the sum of its parts, but this is not a new idea [see Chapter 3]. Mark Mobius, author of *Passport to Profits*, punches the clock: "A committee is a group of people who keep minutes and waste hours." Read on, and you'll discover how corporations have responded to this dilemma.

"Willful Ignorance"

As examined in last year's annual report [Chapter 6], under the title "The Great Abdication of Fiduciary Responsibility," the 401(k) plan was conceived and marketed ostensibly to give the individual investor more flexibility and control over his or her financial destiny, which admittedly it did in spades. Prominent on the hidden agenda, though, was the mad scramble to pass the "hot potato" of the risk and responsibility for managing the assets from the employer to the employee. U.S. sociologist Robert K. Merton's first and most complete analysis (1936) of the concept of unintended consequences helps to explain what happened. Merton would likely describe the corporate desire to cede responsibility for managing retirement assets (as noted above, the abysmal performance of the defined-benefit pension plan was increasingly becoming an albatross around its corporate neck) as "imperious immediacy of interest." By that he was referring to instances in which an organization wants the intended consequence of an action so much that it purposely chooses to ignore unintended effects. That type of willful ignorance, a root cause of unintended consequences, is very different from true ignorance, which would more appropriately characterize the plight of the worker into whose unskilled [investment-wise] hands the proverbial hot potato is summarily dropped. [The concept of willful ignorance is addressed in the Preface—as well as a couple of pages hence in greater depth.] Where the battle-weary sponsors saw risk, the newcomers envisioned the American dream. One man's garbage may be another man's (fool's?) gold . . . Please understand that such behavior is not deemed by the writer as malicious, only as shirking responsibility—"passing the buck," if you will. In the name of expediency, responsibility should be delegated as far down the food chain as appropriate but no farther. As to "how far," I suppose the question could be asked: Is the person to whom the duty is conferred able to make rational decisions on his or her own and therefore wholly answerable for his or her behavior? [For a quotation worth repeating, we turn once again to the wisdom of Albert Einstein: "Make everything as simple as possible, but no simpler."]

Although an anachronism in the codes of conduct for far too many corporate managers today, perhaps the following will serve as an admonition to the recalcitrant . . . Not one to duck the duties that came with the Oval Office, Harry Truman stood stoutly behind the famous sign on his desk that read "The buck stops here" [as also noted in Chapter 6]. Of course, feisty Harry liked the hot seat! He also purportedly said, "If you can't stand the heat, stay out of the kitchen." Are any members of corporate boards listening?

No Crime Goes Unpunished

Willful ignorance was described in the Preface as the desire for an intended consequence of an action that is so strong and overarching that one purposely chooses to ignore any unintended effects . . . to put it charitably, to reap what one has not sown. Of this ethical if not legal transgression, many were conflicted, but few were convicted. [Or, as they say in chillier climes, "Many are cold, but few are frozen."] Men and women of power and responsibility—including CEOs and their boards (the order here implying the convoluted power hierarchy), investment bankers and their research affiliates, and mutual-fund companies and their managers—willingly sold their integrity (souls?) for a disproportionate share of the spoils. (The following remarks are not directed at 401(k) plan sponsors who, for the most part, were going with the times. Several independent-minded sponsors with whom I've spoken simply felt they had no other choice.) As for those who, with willful maliciousness, have pillaged with self-enriching stock-option programs and other sleight-of-hand techniques under the guise of the doctrine of (un)just incentives and rewards, "stealth compensation" hardly characterizes the practice with the name plate of injustice that it so richly deserves. We don't quibble with "stealth," as this term befits the conduct, but "compensation" (the return for services rendered) leaves us incredulous at its audacity. In any other venue of misconduct, it would be called larceny—and on the grandest and most socially grotesque scale.

    We should not envy the moochers and parasites, nor should we conclude, regardless of the outward appearance of apparent indifference, that they are without conscience. Despite this massive redistribution of wealth, the love of money serves up its own justice for those who come by it dishonorably. Ayn Rand, in *Atlas Shrugged*, points out the true "cost" of ill-gotten gain:

> Money is your means of survival. The verdict you pronounce upon the source of your livelihood is the verdict you pronounce upon your life. If the source is corrupt, you have damned your own existence. Did you get your money by fraud? By pandering to men's vices or men's stupidity? By catering to fools, in the hope of getting more than your ability deserves? By lowering your standards? By doing work you despise for purchasers you scorn? If so, then your money will not give you a moment's or a penny's worth of joy. Then all the things you buy will become, not a tribute to you, but a reproach; not an achievement, but a reminder of shame. Then you'll scream that money is evil. Evil, because it would not pinch-hit for your self-respect? Evil, because it would not let you enjoy your depravity?

What goes around comes around . . .

Portentous or Poppycock?

Based on the study of mutual-fund data going back to 1980, a couple of conclusions seem to be driven by the facts. First, apart from the growth in popularity of mutual funds as part of a household's portfolio assets, which as warned in last year's report is subject to the law of regression to the mean, fund flows tend to follow the hottest game in town. One can logically draw certain inferences about the finality of a secular financial cycle when mutual-fund investors embrace it *en masse*. To put it bluntly, the behavior of the retail investor today is the mirror image of what we would logically expect of a seasoned, rational investor at the bottom of a secular bear market. Nobody knows how or when (the "if" is not so chancy) we will migrate from a fully priced, widely embraced, retail-driven investment environment that the wise approach with vigilance and restraint to one where the margin of safety is so great that, ironically, nobody cares. Well, almost nobody. The risk-averse investor who, by virtue of the boundless bargains, would be justified in throwing his customary caution to the winds. Buffett's comment elsewhere that "*the hangover may prove to be proportional to the binge*" is all we can bank on—and never with absolute certainty, only with high probability.

Second, the automatic cash-flow programs like 401(k) plans do not represent a commanding portion of mutual-fund cash flows into equities. Like the Baby Boomer cash cow myth, potent were it not for the fact that demand often begets its own supply, the oft-used argument that the cash flows into equities from 401(k) plans will shore up equity prices seems to be a late-in-the-game, seventh-inning credulity stretch. It also is unlikely that hoards of discretionary cash from retail investors will drive the markets upward during the next decade as they did in the 1990s. To the contrary, unless rising prices magically reappear to stimulate their instinct to play "follow the momentum," disaffection may result. Instead of providing incremental demand, they could become the proverbial wet blanket. Who will step up to the plate? Perhaps, as I suspect Buffett fears, foreign investors, loaded with dollars, will eventually assuage their currency losses by buying yet more of American business on the cheap? Congress will surely meddle, smiting those who will be characterized as "infidels" with a new iteration of Smoot-Hawley. After that, "Katie, bar the door . . ." But now I'm off on a rant!

Apparently it didn't occur to most market strategists to compare the losses of 2000 with the mauling of 1970—in what turned out to be the first cyclical bear market of several during the aforementioned 1966–1982 period when, start to finish, the Dow made as much forward progress as a jogger on a treadmill. Following the crash in 1970, the "Nifty Fifty" of the 1970s still stood tall. Those blue chips would not be decimated for another three years. Quoting San Antonio sportswriter Dan Cook (1976), former NBA basketball coach Dick Motta (1978), and countless others since, "The opera ain't over 'til the fat lady sings."

To conclude with a sober observation about the uninitiated, the behavioral propensity of financial cycles can be summed up succinctly: the accumulation by the wise when prices are low, followed by the distribution to the inexperienced when prices are high. The usually hapless *average* mutual-fund investor adds another layer of evidence to reinforce the idea of financial cycles.

What's a Hitter to Do When the Pitcher Is Throwing Junk? When "Nothing" Is More Than Something

As an "active manager" with ostensibly unlimited strategic and tactical options before us, we must discuss an "institutional imperative" that narrows, rightly or (mostly) wrongly, the range of practicable options for many in our industry. When a firm is hired to "manage money," in our harried world it is most often judged against the standard of "activity, agency, getting things done." The fearsome S&P 500 benchmark or some other index stalks them like a relentless nightmare. When stocks are moved from prime shelf space to the bargain basement, there are frequently steals galore among the discarded—though not seen as such except in retrospect—for those few who have both the wherewithal and the mind-set of a seasoned shopper on the first business day after Christmas. But what course of action do most "wealth managers" take when businesses are richly valued and opportunities scarce? They continue to swing, like the pinch-hitter in the bottom of the ninth a run down, because that's what they are hired to do. There must be a reason why most of them rarely let equities slip to less than 50 percent of their holdings, even if they fear the worst for their portfolios. At some point the shrinking percentage of equities (perceived as forgone opportunities) prompts the question that managers fear more than losing money for their clients: "Why do I need to pay you a fee when I can buy Treasury bills on my own?" Managers, whose fees are based on their ability to gather and retain assets (the standard construct, though not necessarily an indication of their capacity to preserve and enhance their clients' wealth) will do almost anything to avoid having to field that one-hop line drive.

Seth Klarman, president of the Baupost Group and author of *Margin of Safety* [published in 1991; some concepts are timeless], is anything but defensive on the subject of holding cash, regardless of the institutional imperative: "You are paying us to decide when to hold cash and when to invest it, to determine when the expected return from a prospective investment justifies the risk involved and when it does not."

We might present essentially the same idea with a different slant. Our long-standing contention is that cash, along with its short-term equivalents, is the default asset class. To the extent that we uncover enough ideas that conservatively promise five-year returns in excess of our 15 percent threshold rate, cash balances will shrink as cash flows out of safe-harbor, short-term investments toward the higher-return assets, just as water naturally seeks its own level. Conversely, when such ideas are in short supply, as they are today, cash will flow in the opposite direction, toward the default asset class. Portfolio allocation percentages are not set arbitrarily or by formula but rather by the availability of mouthwatering opportunities.

Klarman also addresses the psychological stress on the patient manager who holds cash:

> Emotionally, doing nothing seems exactly like doing nothing: It feels uncomfortable, unproductive, unimaginative, uninspired, and (probably for a while at least), under-performing. One's internal strains can be compounded by external pressures from clients, brokers, and peers. If you want to know what it's like to truly stand alone, try holding a lot of cash. No one does it. No one knows anyone who does it. No one can readily comprehend why anyone would do it. Also, believing that better opportunities will arise in the future [the optimistic bias] than exist today does not ensure that they will. Waiting for bargains to emerge may seem like a better strategy than overpaying for securities today. However, tomorrow's valuations may be higher still.

Klarman's dilemma of being "between a rock and a hard place" (like our president, who's still between "Iraq and a hard place") is credible, though it comes close to diluting if not contradicting his first straightforward assertion. One can vaguely see the ghost of the imperative shadowing the nervous manager as he makes his every move. Cash is like a burr under our saddle, a constant reminder to redouble our research efforts in search of new ideas that make their way through our filters. We're never working harder than when we appear to be doing nothing. When asked how he discovered the Law of Gravity, Newton said, "I thought about it a lot." There is a great, and often overlooked, gulf between the genesis of an idea and its fruition. The grandeur of the results often makes the enormous effort expended in between seem insignificant in comparison. Thomas Edison said that "genius is 2 percent inspiration and 98 percent perspiration." We're human, so we're also most comfortable being fully invested. But in that urge there is too often the tendency to anchor one's thinking in the limited opportunity set of today, forcing "opportunities" that don't really exist, like the parched man who mistakes a mirage for the water that will actually quench his thirst. To put it differently, the best golfers know that birdies come "as they will" as a result of good swings and good strokes; they aren't forced by obsessing about score.

"Swing, You Bum!"

To be sure, our fee structure intentionally prods us to aggressively search for ideas when we have cash, with the high-water mark acting as a governor on our enthusiasm, to check our swing unless the pitch seems headed for that part of the strike zone where, for us, a hit is most likely. If we are to retain rationality as one of our chief virtues, we must sublimate our natural inclination to keep swinging to the much more demanding calling of remaining patient, of evaluating each pitch with the idea that it's far better to walk to first base than to strike out swinging for the fences. It is no coincidence that Babe Ruth and Ted Williams were third and fourth, respectively, in career bases-on-balls statistics. While the following is an oversimplification, it helps to make the point: Ted Williams' lifetime record of 541 home runs compares with 2,021 walks (8,084 pitches went by that were "called balls"—all the while Williams was poised, at the ready, but checked his urge to swing before the pitch crossed the plate). While I would prefer using his best-ever lifetime batting average of .344 to make the point, the analysis quickly gets too complex. Rather, I roughly estimate that for each home run he hit, Williams watched patiently as at least 30 pitches he didn't like thumped into the catcher's mitt. With steely-eyed determination at the plate, oblivious to an ever-lurking hostile press and tuning out his well-intentioned fans, in a most businesslike manner he let slide by every less than acceptable "pitch" that might keep him from achieving his objectives. He approached every at-bat with the end in mind. It was diligence, determination, and discipline—not destiny—that put Ted Williams in the Hall of Fame.

Many mainstream portfolio managers, judged as they are on short-term performance, feel they must be swinging all the time. They must focus on the present, on survival. If they don't meet the relentless present demands, they'll have no corner office from which to build a great long-term record. Individual investors—or the handful of advisors, such as MCM, who are granted substantial autonomy by their clients whose focus is on building wealth—who aspire to long-term success cannot afford the luxury of impatience (though they usually think the opposite is true). Rather, they must hold their ground in the batter's box until the fat pitch comes over the plate. As Buffett says, "The stock market is a no-called-strike game. You don't have to swing at everything; you can wait for your pitch. The problem when you're a money manager is that your fans keep yelling, 'Swing, you bum!'" Even Ted Williams (or Warren Buffett, for that matter) was not exempt from those cries. He simply ignored them, though not without considerable personal cost: Throughout much of his illustrious career, Williams was pilloried by the press [and booed by a hardcore contingent of leather-lunged Boston "fans"].

The institutional imperative to "do something" does not apply to Buffett, since Berkshire Hathaway's shareholders, like those of a closed-end investment company, can neither cajole nor coerce him, they can only vote with their feet by selling their shares in the open market. In a sense, observing Buffett is an uncompromised "pure play" in rational thinking and acting. Make no mistake about it, Buffett is under a far more stringent, self-imposed imperative than the typical investment managers: to protect and enhance the value of Berkshire Hathaway on behalf of its shareholders, of which he is by far the largest at 32.7 percent. He is paid as a shareholder on performance, not promises. He knows as surely as night follows day that golden opportunities will appear with time, and he is content to stand, the bat on his shoulder indefinitely, until they appear. At Berkshire's annual meeting in 1998, he remarked, "We're not going to buy anything just to buy it. We will only buy something if we think we're getting something attractive . . . You don't get paid for activity. You get paid for being right." As noted above, we at MCM feel largely free of the institutional imperative, in part because we also are paid for being right and penalized for being wrong—both through our personal portfolios that look very similar to those of our clients (yes, we eat our own cooking!) and our performance-based fee arrangement—but also because our clients are savvy and understand the virtue of patience (of seeming to do nothing) and its positive, and seemingly counterintuitive, effect on long-term compounding.

As for hunkering down in Treasury bills . . . that may look to the casual observer in the stands like the equivalent of watching and waiting for the perfect pitch—while sitting on your *gluteus maximus* in the dugout! In reality, about the only thing you can do while standing at the plate, bat poised (if you expect to react quickly in order to take a cut at the ball that crosses the plate in your sweet spot), is be vigilant. Moreover, since the sweet-spot pitches are never telegraphed in advance (unlike batting practice), you must always be at the ready.

Returning to Ted Williams, Buffett metaphorically refers to the Splendid Splinter's swinging methodology to emphasize the importance of patience: In his book *The Science of Hitting*, Williams explains that he carved the strike zone into 77 cells, each the size of a baseball. Swinging only at balls in his "best" cell, he knew, would allow him to bat .400; reaching for balls in his "worst" spot, the low outside corner of the strike zone, would reduce him to .230. In other words, waiting for the fat pitch would mean a trip to the Hall of Fame; swinging indiscriminately would mean a one-way ticket to the minors.

The Mathematics of Patience

Having no interest in the minors, beyond throwing out the first pitch at the Omaha Royals home game during Berkshire's annual "Woodstock of capitalism" weekend, the most successful investor in the world suggests parking your money in cash equivalents and short-term bonds. He'd rather have historically low short-term returns than buy stocks or companies likely to return less than his threshold rate of return "because I'm going to be holding on to those forever . . . [E]nough acquisitions like that and you end up with a very average business. So, in this low-interest environment, we have a lot of money in bonds right now."

In responding to a question at Berkshire's 2003 annual meeting about investment hurdle rates,[8] Buffett said, "Ten percent is the figure we quit on. We don't want to buy equities when the *real* expected return is less than 10 percent, whether interest rates are 6 percent or

---

[8][2004, original] The quoted comments were not extracted from a transcript, as no recordings are permitted at the Berkshire shareholders' meeting. Relying on my own memory and the excellent notes taken by Whitney Tilson of Tilson Funds (he played court stenographer at the meeting), the quotations constitute our best approximation of what was actually said.

1 percent. It's arbitrary. Ten percent is not that great after tax." Charlie
Munger further qualified his partner's response by adding:

> We're guessing at our future opportunity cost. Warren is guess-
> ing that he'll have the opportunity to put capital out at high
> rates of return, so he's not willing to put it out at less than
> 10 percent now. But if we knew interest rates would stay at
> 1 percent, we'd change. Our hurdles reflect our estimate of
> *future* opportunity costs.

Warren finished the exchange with a specific example: "We could
take the $16 billion we have in cash earning 1.5 percent and invest
it in 20-year bonds earning 5 percent and increase our current earnings a lot, but we're betting that we can find a good place to invest
this cash and don't want to take the risk of principal loss on long-term
bonds." The MCM hurdle rate, as noted previously, is 15 percent, a
full five percentage points greater than Buffett's minimum. We think
it's appropriate for two reasons—one a strength, the other a short-
coming: First, because the assets we manage are minuscule compared
with Berkshire's, our universe of investment candidates is so much
larger that we stand a better chance of finding pricing inefficiencies
and other anomalies. Second, Buffett's finely honed investment prow-
ess gives him a significant edge in qualifying future uncertainty in an
investment. Recognizing our relative weakness in that regard, we must
insist on a higher margin of safety implicit in a higher hurdle rate.

The mathematics of waiting for fat pitches is quite compelling.
Since if you've come this far you no doubt get the gist of the concept, it doesn't seem necessary to inundate you with the numbers we
have crunched. Suffice it to say, you can earn a modestly positive return
for quite some time while waiting for fat pitches—before your average
compounded returns become lackluster. There is a counter argument
for those who, apparently unfamiliar with financial cycles, challenge
with shrill voices in their impatience, "What happens if those pitches
never come your way?" Buffett doubtless feels no obligation to take
the challenge, for to reply might dignify a question unworthy of a
response (but could have the unintended consequence of sounding
a lot like a forecast as well). A market—or an individual company's
stock price—is, in most cases, not likely to go from prince to pau-
per without plenty of price pain. Buffett believes in the tendency of

price and value to converge. Buffett's above scenario, namely, the modest return from Treasury bills, is not his worst-case scenario. The math
of patience becomes overwhelming if you factor in the possibility of
swinging indiscriminately and striking out before the fat pitches come,
a risk Buffett has made clear he is unwilling to take. Like the flowers
mentioned earlier, sometimes they come in bunches; other times they
come one by one.

"We have $16 billion in cash, not because of any predictions [about
a market decline]," he says, "but because we can't find anything that
makes us want to part with that cash. We're not positioning ourselves.
We just try to do smart things every day, and if there's nothing smart,
then we sit on cash."

As you may recall from "Buffett: One 'HelluvAnomaly'" earlier
in this chapter, Berkshire's cash hoard as of mid-2004 totaled almost
$40 billion, and Buffett had placed a $20 billion bet against the dollar. Based on what we can infer about the thinking at Berkshire since
the annual meeting in May, it would appear that he is laying up stores,
girding himself for eventual, but not necessarily imminent, action.
Given Buffett's record of snatching victory from the jaws of someone
else's defeat (for example, 1974), his cash cache, supposedly head-in-
the-sand benign, looks like enormous potential energy to me. Klarman
articulates the logic behind Buffett's actions.

> Never limit yourself to the opportunity set of today. Indeed,
> for almost any time horizon, the opportunity set of tomorrow
> is a legitimate competitor for today's investment dollars. It is
> hard, perhaps impossible, to accurately predict the volume and
> attractiveness of future opportunities, but it would be foolish
> to ignore them as if they will not exist.

The following quotation is from the notes taken by a student who
was among a group of University of Pennsylvania and the Wharton
School of Business students who spent the morning with Buffett on
November 12, 2004. When asked a question about the rich valuation of
the market he responded: "We are near the high end of the valuation
band, but not really at an extreme. . . . I suspect that stocks are too high
now. Nothing is cheap, and I am not finding a lot now, but there will
be a day when you will be shooting fish in a barrel. The important

thing is to be prepared to play heavily when the time comes, and that means that you cannot play with everybody." (The above may not be a verbatim quote from Buffett, but it seems essentially consistent with the way he sees things as interpreted by the writer throughout this report.)

Flashing back to earlier statements, these words fit "hand in glove": "Should tomorrow's opportunity [set] prove superior to today's, when presumably fear will have swept the field, and that perfect pitch finally crosses home plate, swing for the fences." Munger continues: "The wise ones [investors] bet heavily when the world offers them that opportunity. They bet big when they have the odds. And the rest of the time, they don't. It's just that simple."

Likewise, Buffett explains one reason pitches move from the outside edge of the strike zone to what Ted Williams called the "happy zone": "Occasional outbreaks of those two super-contagious diseases, fear and greed, will *forever* [emphasis added] occur in the investment community." While unsure of the timing or extent of these "outbreaks," Buffett advises investors to "simply attempt to be fearful when others are greedy and to be greedy only when others are fearful. . . . Fear is the foe of the faddist but the friend of the fundamentalist."

Marathon Endurance

The message throughout this report, summarized here, is that we are nearer the beginning than the end of the long secular transition from greed to fear, from exhilaratingly high prices to despairingly low ones, from irrational exuberance to levelheaded rationality and perhaps (I say irrespective of how remote the possibility) from a financial economy to real economy. Accordingly, we have, out of necessity, a heightened sense of vigilance, a pervasive but hopefully constructive skepticism. As always, we will focus on individual companies, constantly comparing price and value. Because of the higher-risk environment in which I think we must operate, we will be extra conservative in our calculations of intrinsic value. If, in spite of a possible ebbing tide, our convictions about the value of a company we own are high and a stock gets cheaper, we will buy more. When we're buying something of value, we want the price to keep going down. If the price gets low enough, our average cost will be well below the intrinsic worth of the business. Low prices motivate the value investor to metaphorically grab her purse and make a beeline to the mall the day after Christmas.

Having spent my entire business life in the world of marketable investments, I'm convinced that there are always pricing anomalies in the market. As mentioned in earlier reports, the spring of 2000 was a bonanza for us: We picked up the discards when the players drew from the stacked deck of Nasdaq favorites, which brings to mind the aphorism, "One man's trash is another man's treasure." The Graham-and-Doddsville investors mentioned earlier have made their mark by successfully exploiting gaps between price and value. As Buffett said in 1984,

> When the price of a stock can be influenced by a "herd" on Wall Street with prices set at the margin by the most emotional person, or the greediest person, or the most depressed person, it is hard to argue that the market always prices rationally. In fact, market prices are frequently nonsensical.

I would like to repeat from earlier reports one important factor about risk and reward as it relates to the kind of investing in which we engage. In most games of chance with which we're all familiar, risk and reward are positively correlated—that is, if you want higher returns, you must assume greater risks. The proliferation of casinos and lotteries has done wonders to embed this positive correlation in the minds of millions upon millions of Americans. So ubiquitous is this perception that to suggest otherwise often provokes an incredulous stare, if not glare.

And yet there's a rather simple explanation why Buffett's net worth is $35 billion while the fellow at the lottery window continues to fork over the last few bucks from his paycheck to voluntarily pay the most pernicious and regressive tax of all—shamefully, a tax on ignorance imposed by elected "representatives." (The irony of the lottery system is that the typical state's rake is often "pledged" to support education, of all things. The same vicious circle of catch-22 reasoning is knowingly employed by Congress, permitting Philip Morris to continue selling cigarettes to a new and nescient generation of smokers to pay the billions in claims from earlier ones.) Buffett's billions seem to suggest that the exact opposite is true with value investing. "If you buy a dollar bill for 60 cents," he says, "it's riskier than if you buy a dollar bill for 40 cents, but the expectation of reward is greater in the latter case. The greater the potential for reward in the value portfolio, the less risk there is."

By contrast, the lotteries and the casinos control the odds and therefore decide who "bears" the brunt of the risk. Is it any surprise that the odds are naturally stacked in favor of the house? It doesn't take a mathematician to understand why casinos and lotteries don't go broke, but gamblers do (as do, some may be surprised to learn, most lottery winners, but for different reasons). On the other hand, the value investor, by his understanding of the relationship between risk and return and his willingness to act independently on that insight, he *becomes* the house. He also controls the odds and (by inference) the risks; if he is skillful and patient, he stacks them in his favor. The markets are open every business day, and the prices are always fluctuating (the only certainty in the marketplace of which I'm aware). The smart investor turns a deaf ear to the crowd and listens to value instead, cherry-picking the best, purchasing them at *his* price. If he is capable of calmly awaiting his moment, unshackled from the ultimatum of the clock and unprovoked by the need to do something, time becomes his ally.

From our bottom-up perspective, the long-term challenge for us as a small shop doing battle with the New York Yankees of the investment world is to use our minds (we don't have the financial muscle) to do what Billy Beane does so extraordinarily: to find value where no one else can find value. In this picked-over supermarket where every melon has been thumped countless times (you should see the Charmin!), it seems that if, to paraphrase Beane, a company doesn't have something wrong with it, it gets valued properly by the market, and we can't afford it anymore.

Seeing the Tides through the Heavy Surf

Where some people see a dark cloud, others see a silver lining. Having cast my lot with the value camp almost 40 years ago—at the top of the last great secular cycle in 1966—I'm still amazed by how many opportunities came and went, like the waves, undulating between exuberance and despair, as the tide continued to ebb, oh so gradually and imperceptibly, until it quietly began to reverse its flow beginning in 1982. To capitalize on the post-1966 environment, you could not simply buy and hold, you had to buy cheap so that you could in the not-too-distant future sell dear. The tide was the enemy of those who became enamored with the waves. In most instances, though certainly not all, you "dated" a stock during those days, but you didn't marry it.

The opposite was true after 1982. The ever-present waves continued during the great bull market that ensued, but because of the steadily rising tide, opportunities were more plentiful, of greater magnitude and lasting longer, but also the rising water level buoyed many a less-than-enlightened idea ("a rising tide lifts all ships"). However, the concomitant comeuppance comes in the expression "Genius is before the fall" or, less poetically, "When the tide goes out, you find out who has been swimming naked." (Sadly, for many investors the relentless waves and crashing surf obscured the view of the tide until it had reached the equivalent of a river's flood stage in the late 1990s.) You may want to review the section in this chapter titled "Run for the Roses" for less-graphic details.

Beyond MCM's non-negotiable allegiance to the basic principles of rational investing as an independent and flexible firm that promotes diversity of thought, we have no other conflicting philosophical loyalties. Period. The man who often sent me a thoughtful note after he read this report, Peter Bernstein, gave his definition of a new paradigm in a public interview in early 2003. Bernstein's clients, it should be noted, were predominantly institutional managers and pension funds. He said bluntly:

> [T]he traditional institutional approach, "I will structure my portfolio in this way and make variations on the theme," won't work. So what I'm suggesting is, throw it away. You have to be much more unstructured, opportunistic and ad hoc than you have been in the past.

Later in the interview:

> . . . [I]n this looser, more opportunistic environment I foresee the abandonment of the dreadful, depressing, defaulting process of putting managers into cubbyholes—large-cap growth, small-cap value and such foolishness—along with the stifling, stupid obsession with tracking error instead of absolute returns and risks incurred.

This kind of diversity of thought is complementary to our philosophical moorings.

From the major bottom (1974) through the end of the secular regression in 1982, the S&P 500 advanced at an annual rate of 8.19 percent and at 13.7 percent with dividends[9] reinvested, while the book value of Berkshire Hathaway grew at the stunning compounded rate of 29.12 percent. Of course, back then Berkshire was the equivalent of a runabout, not a battleship. "Jack be nimble, Jack be quick . . ." and don't forget about the candlestick, or you might get burned. In 1977, quoting from the oldest annual report available on Berkshire's web site, Buffett wrote about his investment principles and the opportunities that appeared then in marketable securities:

> We select our marketable equity securities in much the same way we would evaluate a business for acquisition in its entirety. We want the business to be (1) one that we can understand, (2) with favorable long-term prospects, (3) operated by honest and competent people, and (4) available at a very attractive price. We ordinarily make no attempt to buy equities for anticipated favorable stock price behavior in the short term. In fact, if their business experience continues to satisfy us, we welcome lower market prices of stocks we own as an opportunity to acquire even more of a good thing at a better price.

Buffett is also known for having said more recently:

> Our experience has been that *pro rata* portions of truly outstanding businesses sometimes sell in the securities markets at very large discounts from the prices they would command in negotiated transactions involving entire companies. Consequently, bargains in business ownership, which simply are not available directly through corporate acquisition, can be obtained indirectly through stock ownership. When prices are appropriate, we are willing to take very large positions in selected companies, not with any intention of taking control and not foreseeing sell-out or merger, but with the expectation that excellent business results by corporations will translate over the long term into correspondingly excellent market value and dividend results for owners, minority as well as majority.

---

[9][2004, original] Dividend yields are rarely low at the bottom of bear markets. A word to the wise: The converse also is usually true.

Some principles never change . . .

Please understand, we can neither forecast the future (Galbraith sums it up by saying, "We have two classes of forecasters: Those who don't know—and those who don't know they don't know") nor expect to be as adroit as Buffett in capitalizing on the "sweet spot" pitches that will sporadically come hurtling our way. Meanwhile, in the future, as in the past, we have a decided preference for learning vicariously rather than firsthand from the school of hard knocks. As U.S. General George Patton used to say, "It's an honor to die for your country, but make sure the other guy gets the honor." Nonetheless, to quote the quixotic Don Quixote from the musical *Man of La Mancha*, from which comes the expression "tilting at windmills": "The fortunes of war [investment?] more than any other are liable to frequent fluctuations." More to our immediate need, the dreamer also is recognized for having said, "To be forewarned is to be forearmed." And because of the nature of the business of investing and our relatively diminutive size, we may be able to achieve successful results even if we find ourselves facing a headwind.

Peppered as you've been with baseballs, why not alter course briefly with a hide/tide-bound sailing metaphor? Instead of easing the sheets, engaging the autopilot, and relaxing for a gin and tonic as we would with the wind at our back, working our way "to weather" is not for the fainthearted. It's mentally and physically exhausting, requiring strength, conviction, concentration, and discipline. We must regularly tack to make headway toward our predetermined destination, "coming about" as needed to keep making progress if the winds shift even 5 or 10 degrees. A sailboat never realizes its maximum speed sailing to windward, but as the old adage goes, we have no control over the wind, but we can and do trim the sails for optimal results under the prevailing conditions. While our compass needle and ship's head (except during tacking) are pointed toward "true north," which we define in this metaphor as first protecting and then enhancing your capital, the winds are *forever clocking*. When they come around to amidships or farther abaft the beam, we'll have all of our canvas flying, and the bow wave will curl high on the prow. Then, and only then, we might grant ourselves the luxury of lacing fingers behind head and leaning back, for a few moments at least, to enjoy the ride.

Chapter 8

What History Teaches*

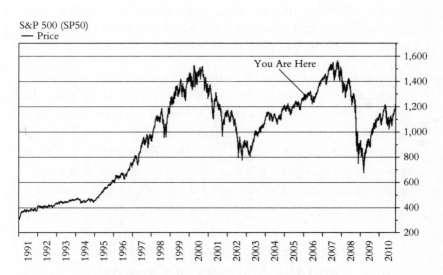

S&P 500 (SP50)
— Price

You Are Here

SOURCE: © FactSet Research Systems.

*This material is adapted from the 1998–2004 summary chapter in *Speculative Contagion*.

In the Preface [to *Speculative Contagion*], gentle encouragement to stay the course was provided for those who picked up the book, assuring readers that there are certain truisms that, if applied wisely, will allow them to "eat well *and* sleep well," regardless of the tempests of exuberance or despair that will occasionally rage outside their windows. In the following pages, there are several synthesized proverbs that you may have gleaned as you took the seven-year trek with us through time. I will attempt to list, in no particular order beyond the first one or two (which are foundational), a number of basic truths or practical precepts, in my experience-based judgment, to which you might refer should you become uncertain about which way to turn sometime in the future. The succeeding catalogue of aphorisms is by no means all-inclusive, nor are they meant to be taken at face value. Readers are encouraged to challenge every statement, extracting for themselves that which they feel will be most meaningful and reject that which they feel is superfluous or simply untrue. Perhaps before readers attempt to navigate their way through the following maxims they might reread the opening lines of Chapter 7 and arm themselves with the words of Ernest Dimnet, author of *The Art of Thinking*, an up-in-lights snippet from which is:

> Nothing is more striking than the absence of intellectual independence in most human beings: they conform in opinion, as they do in manners, and are perfectly content with repeating formulas. While they do so, the thinker calmly looks around, giving full play to his mental freedom. He may agree with the *consensus* known as public opinion, but it will not be because it is a universal opinion. Even the sacrosanct thing called plain commonsense is not enough to intimidate him into conformity.

Free Markets: Popular Delusions and the Madness of Crowds

Whether it suits us or not, the free markets will occasionally and forever respond disproportionately to external stimuli so long as they remain unfettered. The antidotes below, deduced from careful examination of this most recent speculative Bubble and the many that preceded it, begin with a lengthy discussion of a supposition that I believe, from years of personal observation, to be a bedrock truism—namely, that crowds can corrupt the capacity for individual reasoning. Much of what follows thereafter is built on that foundation. It is the reservoir of strength that comes from understanding those conditions and circumstances where the individual is mightier than the crowd from which one is able to summon the courage to keep one's head when surrounded by those who are losing theirs.

Though the market mechanism is inherently a methodical system for reconciling supply and demand, behind every order ticket to buy or sell a stock or other security is a human being, most of whom suffer from one sort of affective disorder or another. It is this temperamental link in the chain that causes the system to get downright wacky at times. Worse still, through the process of contagion—disorders like the excessive desire for more than one needs or has earned (more commonly known as greed) or fear of loss—can escalate into epidemics that sometimes spread with shocking speed according to the mathematical laws of geometric progressions, figuratively becoming a "crowd." (Although you may have heard of this before, the following simple question illustrates the power of geometric progressions. If you give someone a penny on the first day of a 31-day month, two cents on the second, four cents on the third, continuing to double your gift each day until the end of the month, how much will you have given?)

You may recall reading the section in the last chapter titled "A Short History of Financial Euphoria" from the brief book by that name written by John Kenneth Galbraith. Both *The Great Crash, 1929*, and the above booklet were written years after the fact and were no doubt more thorough and concise because the author had the full benefit of hindsight, including the capacity to research what everyone else had to say on the subject. Because Galbraith was writing from a distance—in another time, if you will—he was able to view the powerful biases that led so many astray with the clinical detachment of a pathologist performing an autopsy. Furthermore, he presumably could have maintained a leisurely pace, motivated to put the pieces of the puzzle together whenever inspiration moved him to take pen in hand. What he didn't venture to do, however, was risk opining on either the present or the future. What his scholarly efforts gained through the focused lens of reflection, they lost in failing to capture the triggering events that gave impetus to the formation of epidemics. Too, he didn't really touch on the insidious way the perception of "reality" migrated with the mood of the crowd as it grew in size and concurrently shrunk in its collective capacity for objective reasoning. Permit me to make an analogy: Subtle is the difference, but the discerning eye can spot the significant dissimilarities between a Broadway play and a movie, though they both take place in a venue somewhat related in appearance.

This effort, then, intends to leave readers with a sense that if they feel they're becoming infected by the next speculative epidemic they will have a place to turn for an antidote that was tested—not on rats in laboratories by men in white coats but by real people in the real marketplace where rampant uncertainty and high emotion are the only realities for many of the participants. What follows are certain generalized truths that may keep an investor away from the edge of the precipice over which he could easily fall into a spiral of irrationality, often leading to great financial and emotional travail—and possibly even a trip to the metaphorical pathologist mentioned above (or to the "smiling mortician" made famous by Lawrence Ferlinghetti's 1955 poem). I hope this book has conveyed how tenuous was the strand of knowledge of history and human behavior that kept us from capitulating to the cry of the crowd as it, like the cartoon of the sheep in Chapter 4, stampeded heedlessly and *head*lessly over the cliff of mindless imitation to their demise. We confess to being investment acrophobics: We fear high places. In investment parlance, we are far less anxious looking up at intrinsic value than looking down at it. Stated another way, our comfort (not to mention our confidence) is inversely proportional to the degree to which common stocks are more or less popular than the norm.

Free markets of all stripes are prone to occasional episodes of extreme detachment from reality, as evidenced by fluctuations in prices that would certainly appear to be wildly disproportionate to the underlying causes. There is little we can do to curb the innate human psyche when, collectively, it is agitated through the process of contagion to the point of irresponsible and often self-destructive behavior. But perhaps by acting independently as individuals we stand some hope of being victors and not victims through the power of knowledge, applied with wisdom. The biographies of Winston Churchill and Teddy Roosevelt would suggest that such a contention is not entirely fallacious. What can we apply that we have observed over the last five dramatic years to ameliorate the consequences of such flights of fancy in the future? Certainly man is not so inobservant that he is doomed to repeat all mistakes of the past. Wisdom is not cumulative from generation to generation, but information is. Hence, what can be extracted from the information, particularly for those who seek to convert information into knowledge? What is indigenous to all such episodes? In other words, if history is repetitious, despite each event having its own nuances that differentiate it from others, what thread of similarities connects most historical events?

Aspiring to Rationality by Overcoming Heuristic Biases

The word "rational" and its derivatives appear 180 times throughout this book. The call for rationality is found in every chapter. And yet were it not for occasional outbreaks of geometrically progressive epidemics of *irrationality*, the great incidences of speculative euphoria would likely never gain sufficient momentum to become such a force that might threaten to blow your financial house down. There is a world of difference, in terms of consequences, between a tropical depression and a Category 5 hurricane.

Warren Buffett is well known for imploring investors to be, above all, rational if they are to avoid falling prey to periodic flights of fancy and folly. Buffett himself is the model of self-control and imperturbability, a bastion of reason in the midst of a storm.

Above all other traits necessary for investment success, Buffett emphasizes *rationality*, a form of self-discipline that is part nature, part nurture. Moreover, there are a number of cognitive impediments to rational decision making that must be overcome. Several of the elementary truths are rooted in how the human mind processes information and data. While the following discussion is a little technical, it is essential to understanding why (even when we feel otherwise) we as human beings often make irrational decisions.

It all began in the 1970s with a growing field of scientific inquiry regarding how the human mind works. Our brains, it was postulated, use a strict set of compression schemes for abstracting critical features out of vast amounts of incoming sensory data. When new information is abstracted from the surrounding environment, converted into symbolic format, and archived in long-term memory, it becomes subject to certain biasing effects. Decision theorists refer to the hard-wired tendency of humans to perform abstract reasoning in cognitively economical ways as heuristics.

To be sure, heuristics save time and effort, but they often fail utterly when presented with data outside of their "domain of expertise." These failures are difficult to notice, because (1) the thinking processes responsible for judging the overall quality of one's thinking are plagued by these biases as well, (2) they are so widespread and natural that few people notice them, and (3) decisions made based on heuristics feel good; they're intuitively satisfying, regardless of their correctness.

Two of the more easily understood and related heuristics are the "above average" bias, the widespread tendency to categorize oneself as *above average*, and the "optimistic bias," the inclination to view the world through rose-colored glasses. The optimistic bias is often harmless (sometimes it is even helpful), but it's a sure road to ruin in a profession where the gullible are fodder for the occasional vultures who prove time and again that a fool and his money are soon going in opposite directions. Nowhere is the facetious application of the above-average and optimistic biases more obvious than in the ending phrase of American humorist and storyteller Garrison Keillor's widely beloved *Prairie Home Companion* radio show: "That's the news from Lake Wobegon, where all the women are strong, all the men are good-looking, and all the children are above average."

Somewhat more subtle—and clearly more insidious for investors—are the following biases:

- "Anchoring effects," for example, constitute a class of robust psychological phenomena showing that people adjust insufficiently for the implications of incoming information. We form beliefs around an anchor, and additional incoming data must fight against the inertia of the anchor, even when it is objectively irrelevant to the judgment at hand.
- The availability heuristic results in vivid recent memories overriding normative reasoning. With investing, the urge to either buy or sell is often a function of how good or bad one feels about his most recent experience. The Pavlovian association—two stimuli are associated when the experience of one leads to the effects of another, due to repeated pairing—reinforces the availability bias.

- "Base-rate neglect" effectively reduces the importance of background frequencies in favor of salient anecdotal evidence.

These biases, either singly or in combination, have the effect of inhibiting impartial judgment. As this relates to the market environment, biased investors can come to believe virtually any environment to be normative—for example, the seemingly unquestioned acceptance of the reasoning that continued to justify the Bubble months before it burst and logic that would have been rejected as absurd five years before the 2000 implosion. Bias-infected reasoning was proved to be ludicrous in the wake of the collapse. As the market proceeds in its unpredictable and asymmetrical cycles, the vast majority of investors, because of these biases, tend to accept each stage as normative. If this were not so, markets would move forthwith in the direction of what is perceived as normative. The fact that they stand pat tends to be the "pudding proof" of this phenomenon.

Today Is Not Tomorrow: Cycles and Differing "Opportunity Sets"

Seth Klarman's contention in Chapter 7 that tomorrow's "opportunity set" may be different, perhaps radically so, from today's doesn't gain much traction with most investors. And yet, to unquestioningly accept mercurial Mr. Market's judgment as the final arbiter of the fairness of the price-to-value relationship is to mistake a stooge for a sage.

History might suggest that investors anchored in today's opportunity set are a little light on the lessons of history. On the other hand, today's naysayers, including the writer, may simply have their anchors too deeply buried in a past that is never to return. Imagine how agonizing the half-century wait has been for those who still believe that dividend yields will once again eclipse those from bonds. I would counter that argument, claiming the latter phenomenon to be a once-in-a-generation change that took place at a snail's pace, whereas the manic-depressive cyclicality of markets (while unpredictable as to its timing) is still eminently foreseeable as to the inevitability of its place as a permanent feature on the investment landscape.

Those of us who presume to be investment professionals, as well as those who expect to be proficient nonprofessional investors, obviously must acknowledge the existence of biases lurking in our subconscious. One way to minimize the effect of these counterproductive biases is to "back test" our decisions in order to regularly recalibrate our thinking. The process is agonizing and humbling, for most of us tend to handle the truth badly when it conflicts with long-held beliefs. While the expression "no pain, no gain" may sound painfully trite, it is also plainly true. The golfer who disdains systematically going to the practice tee until the hands are blistered—or to the putting green with a pro—is doomed to repeat his mistakes, and thereby habituate them. If he remains steadfastly in denial, once correctable mistakes may become intractable.

Inverting the Traditional High-Risk/High-Return Paradigm

Moving from the science of the mind to the observable should be less arduous for the reader. Let's begin by attempting to demystify a seemingly inviolable concept. It is generally accepted that risk and return are positively correlated: that is, in order to earn higher returns one must take on greater risk. That principle is reinforced whenever one participates in commonplace games of chance, such as the lottery. To the extent that a stock market participant transfers that same risk/return paradigm to investment in common stocks—accepting high valuations and extreme volatility as his sole definition of risk—then the assumption of above-average risks can most logically be correlated with the expectation of above-average expected returns. This investor should be anything but venturesome in the markets for intangible assets.

But what happens if he extends his time horizons from the here and now to months or years? What if he buys stocks using the same logic he would apply to purchasing a house? Admittedly, most prospective home purchasers have a notable informational advantage over the investor in intangible assets. They are able to compare the price of a home being offered with others from the same or similar location, size, design, construction quality, and so on. Moreover, they tend to have a good idea of what they're looking for, as well as to shop in a predetermined price range that is congruent with their capacity to service the mortgage loan. The smart shoppers who, based on their own experience, think the house they're looking at is worth, say, $100,000, will become more interested if they conclude that the seller is highly motivated to part with his or her property promptly and offer the home for $90,000. If the buyers can negotiate the price down to $80,000, they may become downright ecstatic! Subconsciously, their brains must reach a logical conclusion: It's less risky to buy the house at $80,000 than it would be, on the flip side of the coin, to impulsively pay $120,000 to a clever seller. They intuitively reason that if they ever have to sell the property, the lower-cost purchase will clearly work to their financial advantage by either minimizing their loss or maximizing their profit. What should be obvious by now is that the buyer has inverted the traditional risk/return paradigm. By purchasing the house at a price deemed to be below its intrinsic worth they have reduced the amount of their risk in the event of a forced sale. On the other hand, if house prices appreciate and they choose to sell, they will have earned a greater profit. Voilà, the wonder of the low-risk/high-return paradigm. It works so well in many of our purchase decisions (the word "sale" is very effective at drawing shoppers' eyes to an advertisement) because the buyers have spent that portion of their lives as consumers accumulating information on the value of real or tangible assets.

The reason this paradigm is less effective in the stock market is because the casual investor has limited skills or experience in pricing assets that one can neither see nor touch. Evidence of ownership is but the name of a company on his brokerage statement, the value of which is wholly dependent on the uncertain proposition that it will return sufficient cash to the investor over the years ahead to justify its purchase price.

If an investor has sufficient skill and experience to first identify companies for which the determination of the range for intrinsic value is even possible and then to make that informed judgment, he has one of the pillars essential to inverting the traditional risk/return paradigm. Good fortune is likely to await this investor.

The Inevitability of Regression to the Mean

Regression to the mean, referred to frequently throughout the book, is a term that has its roots in statistics and probability theory. The example most frequently presented in this book is from physics, the central-tendency movement of a pendulum in, say, a grandfather clock, which, perhaps from personal observation, most readers find to be quite understandable.

So as to avoid unnecessary repetition, a short summary of the simple pendulum phenomenon will lay the groundwork for a number of applications of regression to the mean in the investment world. First, the pendulum will remain motionless, at its position of rest, where opposing forces are equalized, otherwise known as equilibrium. Likewise, the markets or individual stocks would never change in price were it not for the inequality of the actions of buyers and sellers. Unlike the unattended pendulum, the free markets never lacked for those doing the buying and those inclined toward the opposite, the intensity of whose motives and emotions are innumerable in their variations, as well as their capacity to occasionally aggregate. Another striking difference between the rhythmic pattern of the swinging pendulum and the irregular and unpredictable motion of the markets is that the primary force acting on the pendulum is one of the most stable physical powers, gravity.

As noted above, however, not only are markets moved at the margin by many people whose rationality is compromised by a variety of affective disorders, but the movement itself, through a feedback loop, sometimes effects and therefore exacerbates those disorders and behavioral responses to them. In this instance, "at the margin" refers only to that small minority of individuals who are actively buying or selling. Those investors who at present are neither buying nor selling will have no direct effect on the market price of anything. Up to some point, a movement can become a self-reinforcing mechanism. That point, somewhere along the extreme of the pendulum's arc, never known in advance, is where the process of regression to the mean (in mathematics it means the average, while here we're referring to the bottom of the arc, which is the same) begins. Introducing probability theory briefly . . . the farther the pendulum moves away from equilibrium or its position at rest, the greater the likelihood that it will reverse its course. Unlike the perfect symmetry of a pendulum, the mean is an ever-changing number because of the irregular movements of the market. The difference does not destroy the analogy but simply makes it a bit more complex. In simple physical terms, gravity eventually overcomes momentum. Finally, once the pendulum reaches the outer limit of its leftward or rightward arc, its course is reversed and its speed accelerates, reaching maximum velocity in the vicinity of the very position where it would be at rest without the motive force of gravity. That is why markets that have swung to extremes rarely come to rest at the mean but, rather, continue well beyond the center, once their course has been reversed by the force of a systemic change in investor sentiment equivalent to that of gravity in the physical realm.

From these observations a host of truisms follows. "This too shall pass" is an aphorism that investors would do well to keep in mind in both good times and bad. It's a reasonable assumption that today's opportunity set, if some distance from the mean, will be quite different from the figurative "tomorrows," particularly to the open-minded investor who is not "anchored" in the present. It should probably hold true as well that markets will cycle in some irregular fashion because the collective psychology of investors that drives markets tends to swing with equal unpredictability from highs to lows and back again.

There Are No Called Strikes in the Investment Ballgame

The business of investing in marketable securities has characteristics that in several ways makes it unique. First, unlike a home, a tract of land, or a private company where ownership changes hands infrequently (and, generally, in its entirety), bite-sized fractional-ownership interests in publicly traded companies are for sale every business day of the year. If a private company or a home you've desired for a long time makes a rare appearance on the market, usually at the seller's behest and price, you either swing at the pitch or head for the showers. In the public market just the opposite is true. There is no need to swing your financial bat until you see the proverbial fat pitch coming your way. Although this characteristic is one of the secondary (not primary, as in IPOs) public market's main attractions, few investors seem to take advantage of the opportunities it presents. Many who never worked through their hyperactivity in their youth might consider a heavy dose of Ritalin. Others are simply compulsive, unjustifiably feeling like a pinch-hitter once they kick the dirt off their cleats at the plate. Think of it. There are no called strikes for the rare breed known as the patient batter. Imagine what Ted Williams's statistics would've been under those rules!

Focus on the Important

Focus is a term that intentionally limits one's field of vision. Let's say we as a firm have deduced from the study of investment history that businesses possessing competitive advantages sustainable over extended periods of time tend (presuming they are well purchased) to produce the highest long-term returns. If so, we must consider everything else extraneous and irrelevant to our defined purpose. In order to avoid allowing our gaze to be distracted from that which is important, we focus exclusively on that relatively small subset of the larger investment universe. Even if a particularly compelling investment idea appears outside our subset, we will generally reject it unless we're woefully short of good ideas that fall within the confines of our field of focused vision.

Similarly, in the broader sense our portfolio management, our focus is on earning above-average investment returns over the years. Many actions that we might otherwise take in the short run suddenly appear superfluous or counterproductive, so long as we look straight ahead and keep our eyes riveted on the well-defined endgame.

The Malevolent Mathematical Mystery of Modern Money Management (a.k.a. MPT)

If you cannot understand a system, particularly one that is esoteric in its complexity, what basis do you have for placing your trust, other than blindly, in it delivering what it proposes? Academia has found a gold mine in transmuting the art of investment (that, at heart, is based on common sense) into the *science* of finance, manifested in textbooks filled with pages and pages of undecipherable equations. The idea that the intricacy of the symbolic logic necessary to solve problems is proportional to the results achieved is woefully misapplied in the world of Main Street investment. What good is the Superman wardrobe if you're not Clark Kent? Countless Nobel prizes in financial mathematics have been awarded by judges who have almost no comprehension of what they're judging. If Nobel prizes were awarded to those who have taken plain, everyday logic to incredible new heights, Warren Buffett's Nobel prizes would soon rival his billions. Buffett would no doubt take his own bounty. Is there a Nobel laureate in finance more highly regarded than the Oracle of Omaha? He makes a mockery out of modern portfolio theory (MPT) by simply proving its relative uselessness with his own results year after year. No less an intellectual authority than Albert Einstein wisely noted that "Any intelligent fool can make things bigger and more complex. . . . It takes a touch of genius—and a lot of courage—to move in the opposite direction."

Harry Markowitz introduced the concept of MPT with his paper "Portfolio Selection," which appeared in the 1952 *Journal of Finance*. In 1990 he shared a Nobel Prize with Merton Miller and William Sharpe for what has become a broad theory for portfolio selection. Concerned with the "random" risks associated with concentrated portfolios, he detailed the mathematics of diversification, proposing that investors focus on selecting portfolios based on their overall risk/reward characteristics, instead of merely compiling portfolios from securities that individually have attractive risk/reward characteristics. In a nutshell, Markowitz theorized that investors should select portfolios, not individual securities.

For many good reasons that do not include the open-ended mandate to maximize "risk-adjusted" performance, MPT has profoundly shaped how institutional portfolios are managed—and spurred the use of passive investment management techniques. The mathematics of portfolio theory is used extensively in financial-risk management and was a theoretical precursor of today's "value-at-risk" measures.

The Absurdity of the Collective Wisdom of Individual Irrationality

Several of the guiding precepts of MPT have been met with some resistance by those *long-term* investors who find them illogical, including the author. First, the efficient-market hypothesis (EMH) states that it is impossible to "beat the market" because existing share prices already incorporate and reflect all relevant information (implying that the prices set are the most reasonable approximation of intrinsic worth because all known information is rationally incorporated in the price). We say it's not the market mechanism itself that casts aspersions on the hypothesis but rather the practical asymmetry of information and the frequently biased buyers and sellers who set the prices. Fighting fire with fire, it isn't unreasonable to assume that asymmetrical information and behavioral dynamics may raise legitimate questions about the market's capacity to set rational prices. The flow of conversation among a group of drunks at the bar near closing time may be quite "fluid," but how much credence would you give to their collective reasoning power? Picture them trying to decide who is the least drunk and who, therefore, should be the "designated driver"!

To be sure, the market mechanism is frequently capable of adjudicating a price that is a fair approximation of intrinsic worth. On other occasions, like the drunks above, emotions and biases overwhelm reason, and wide gaps can and do open between price and value. Never forget "Mr. Market" and his peculiarities.

Diversification and the Myth
of Safety in Numbers

Returning to Markowitz's dubious contention that random risk demands broad diversification, simple mathematical modeling seems to have adequately proved through back testing that a concentrated portfolio with as few as 12 truly diversified companies is sufficient in breadth to reduce random risk to a more than tolerable level. One could argue that as you add companies to a portfolio that are of lesser quality and greater future uncertainty than the ones already owned, risks actually rise. So long as you choose to be invested in stocks, there is one risk for which diversification affords no protection. As you increase diversification, you concurrently and inevitably increase your exposure to market risk—namely, the tendency of your portfolio, like an index fund, to mirror the performance of the market. If you owned an index fund that mimicked the Nasdaq 500 as it fell from 5050 to just over 1000, you might begin to doubt the concept of the security of principal (or the principle of security!) that is presumed to be found in the safety of large numbers. Let there be no doubt: If you go the route of broad diversification, rest assured that you will never stand out in a crowd.

For many investors, particularly of the institutional variety, the desire to be inconspicuous in the comforting gray area of anonymity is greater than the risk of falling below the line in an effort to rise above it.

The degree to which a portfolio can be prudently concentrated among a relatively small number of companies largely rests with the skill, discernment, temperament, and experience of the investor. For most, broad diversification is the only commonsensical long-term alternative. If the layperson invests systematically—through thick and thin, which is no mean emotional feat despite its apparent simplicity—the negative portfolio effect of outlandishly high prices will to some extent be offset by compellingly low prices, such that their long-term results will be acceptably average, particularly when adjusted for the effort expended.

The appeal of a concentrated portfolio is that it is the only chance an investor has to beat the averages by a noteworthy margin. If risk is determined to be a variable, and the amount of assumed risk is a function of the relationship between the market price and the independently determined intrinsic value of the business, then please refer back to the earlier section "Inverting the Traditional High-Risk/High-Return Paradigm" to close the reasoning loop.

The New-Era Error

New eras usually ride into town on the back of a horse mistaken for a golden stallion, transformed momentarily by the brilliance of the afternoon sun. Incredulous onlookers (investors) are thinking riches, when all that's left when the illusion fades is manure. John Kay, the British economist and author of *The Business of Economics*, sums it up succinctly: "If new technologies are *generally applicable* [emphasis added], then competition means that the benefits will go to consumers. Not just most of them, all of them. New technology has always been better news for customers than shareholders."

Investment editor Jim Grant has observed that there is nothing ever really new in the world of investment and finance, just old principles dressed up in the latest fashion, often with the sole intent of making a buck from a bumpkin without making any real value. New investment principles are a contradiction in terms. Notes Warren Buffett: "If principles can become dated, they're not principles."

Chapter 9

Contagious Speculation*

S&P 500 (SP50)
— Price

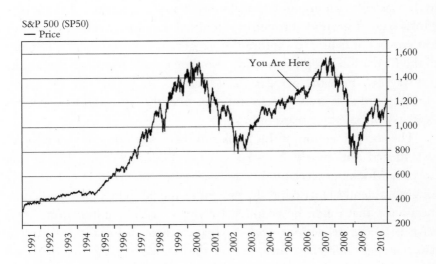

SOURCE: © FactSet Research Systems.

---

*This material is adapted from the 2005 annual report of Martin Capital Management.

Chapter 9 is composed primarily of excerpts from the 2005 and 2006 MCM annual reports. Bracketed material within the final three chapters (9–11) of the book represents 2010 comments by the author for *A Decade of Delusions*. And as noted at the start of Chapter 1, brackets also are used on occasion for clarity in quoted material. In some cases, changes have been made in 2010 for the purpose of clarity—and to avoid repetition. Not all of these changes are bracketed. In the author's opinion, such changes do not materially alter the meaning conveyed in the original annual reports and other writings. If the reader has any doubts, all original documents can be found on the Martin Capital Management web site: www.mcmadvisors.com.

Chapter 8 was the closing segment of *Speculative Contagion*. Did the journey through those seven years of real-time history unearth any nuggets of enduring insight that had practical application?

I have often wondered aloud about the utility of John Kenneth Galbraith's *A Short History of Financial Euphoria*. What he didn't venture to do was risk opining on either the present or the future. His scholarly efforts gained ground through the focused lens of reflection, but they lost ground in failing to capture the triggering factors that gave impetus to the formation of epidemics. He also didn't really touch on the insidious way in which the perception of "reality" migrated with the mood of the crowd as it grew in size and concurrently shrunk in its collective capacity for objective reasoning.

The second section of this book thus begins with a provocative and, as it turned out, timely 2005 essay, "The Perfect Storm?" Unlike the backward-looking accounts by the Galbraiths of the world, this essay sought to blend the past and the present—and all the wisdom and common sense that might be acquired by virtue of the combination. We'll leave it to our readers to decide whether their financial future might have taken a different course late in the decade if they had first read these Chapter 9 essays, which were written in 2005 and 2006. More to the moment, and perhaps the reason you're holding this book, will be whether the twists and turns of history, which includes the unknowable future, validate or impugn the cogency of *A Decade of Delusions*. Will it earn a permanent place on your bookshelf?

The Means to the End

In the next section we begin a lengthy, but we hope proportionately valuable, discussion titled "The Perfect Storm?" In it we emphasize, as we have in the past, that if one focuses on managing the risks, the returns will take care of themselves. When it comes to orienting ourselves so that we can reasonably expect to earn above-average returns over time, we approach the problem with the same mind-set: We turn our attention to the means by which we think this goal can be achieved and let the outcomes, indeed, take care of themselves. The seemingly simple statement about the preoccupation with the means, as opposed to the ends, is such an essential tenet of how we practice our profession that to leave it dangling, unexplained, would give the reader short shrift.

I have been deeply influenced by the existentialist and eminent psychiatrist Viktor Frankl, who wrote the perennial best seller *Man's Search for Meaning* (one of the most influential books I've ever read and reread) after being imprisoned in Auschwitz and other concentration camps for three years during World War II. It was while immersed in unimaginable suffering and loss that he came to believe that the most basic human motivation is the "will to meaning." Friedrich Nietzsche, the German philosopher who died five years before Frankl was born, put it rather succinctly: "He who has a *why* to live for can bear almost any *how*." Here's Frankl's take on success:

> Don't aim at success—the more you aim at it and make it a target, the more you are going to miss it. For success . . . cannot be pursued; it must ensue, and it only does so as the unintended side effect of one's dedication to a cause greater than oneself . . . You have to let [success] happen by not caring about it. I want you to listen to what your conscience commands you to do and go on to carry it out to the best of your knowledge. Then you will live to see that in the long run—in the long run, I say!—success will follow you precisely because you had forgotten to think about it.

This might be called the "means mind-set." It requires a rational, and entirely independent, assessment of the relationship between risk and opportunity. It does not preclude listening to others, so long as you are confident that their attitude toward success parallels yours. It unequivocally rules out "mindlessly imitating the crowd" at the other end of the behavioral spectrum. Following the majority, fixated as it is on success itself (while at the same time being indifferent to or unaware of the means) is a sure ticket to disappointment. It almost goes without saying that an investor who focuses on the means invariably finds himself detached from the teeming multitude of believers feverishly pursuing the illusion of easy money. The "means mind-set" is not analogous to the trembling basketball player who stands at the free-throw line with seconds remaining in the game that has gone down to the wire, making the sign of the cross, hoping for divine intervention to make up for his lack of discipline and determination during the months of practice time wasted leading up to this moment. The "means mind-set" is, by contrast, personified by Larry Bird, standing at that same line 15 feet from the basket, calm and serene—not because he knows he'll make the game-winning shot, but confident in the knowledge that having lofted the ball at the hoop 1,000 times a day for years (many of the shots from the charity stripe), he has *earned the right* to expect to make the shot.

The Perfect Storm? Viewing the Vista through the Lens of History

The panorama from the top of a mountain, a mental picture of a series of often seemingly random and disconnected events, is so much more clear and comprehensible than when one tries to gain a worldview amidst the dense foliage in the valley below. The challenge in getting to the summit is not losing one's way as one negotiates the endless switchbacks on the winding road to the peak. Without the roadmap of history, one would certainly lose sight of the summit for the trees. The circuitous and painstaking route is necessary because the slope is simply too steep for a straight-up-the-mountain ascent. Likewise, the story that is about to be told has so many interdependent elements that a straight shot to the conclusion borders on the impossible. The climb will be arduous. A friend of mine once said, "Before one can have a mountaintop experience, one must first decide to climb the mountain." Candidly assessing the temperament of the masses is philosopher Johann Wolfgang von Goethe (1749–1832): "The heights charm us, but the steps do not; with the mountain in our view we love to walk the plains." The good news is that the two charts in the middle of Chapter 7 reveal the view we have from the mountain peak.

For those who take seriously this annual foray into the facts and how they might play out in the future, the charts must seem like a recurring nightmare. The Market Cap versus GNP chart [Figure 7.1, top] first appeared in our communiqués in the 2001 annual report [Chapter 4], having been lifted from a November 1999 article in *Fortune* magazine written by Warren Buffett. He offered the graphic as a "simple quantitative antidote that investors can administer to neutralize their often emotional 'availability bias' assessment of the future." Applied to an individual company, the chart's information would equate to the market-price-to-sales-per-share ratio, a rough and ragged secondary valuation technique.

The Total Credit Market Debt chart (Figure 7.1, bottom), first appeared in the 2004 annual report [Chapter 7]. By using these two ratios, we are able to examine the association between total debt outstanding to the economy's capacity to service it and the aggregate market value of all U.S. equity securities relative to the same denominator, gross domestic product (GDP). Finally, the chart shown in Figure 9.1 and new this year [in 2005], depicts the cost of money, as well as the annual rate of increase in the consumer price index (CPI) for the same 80 years.

Notice the symmetry between the movement in interest rates and consumer prices. To be sure, correlation is not causation, so, as the story unfolds, I'll let you decide whether the relationship is (take your pick) causal, complementary, parallel, reciprocal, or mere coincidence. Intrigued? I am. Then cast your eyes back at the Market Cap versus GNP chart and observe the generally inverse relationship between interest rates and stock prices (and later, you will learn, real estate prices).[1] When you read the words of Alan Greenspan below,

---

[1][2005, original] Andrew Smithers, who heads Smithers & Co., a London-based firm that provides advice to 80 of the world's largest fund money-management

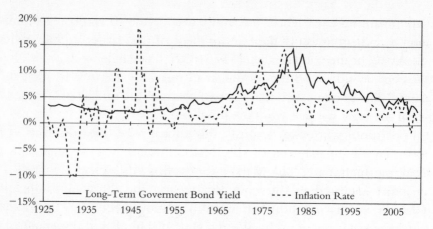

Figure 9.1   Inflation Rates and Bond Yields
NOTE: 10-year Treasury post 1953.
DATA SOURCE: www.econ.yale.edu/~shiller/data.htm.

the juxtaposition of these factors and the confusion at the Fed (a likely occurrence at the changing of the guard) as to whether it needn't worry about asset inflation when its presumed primary obligation is consumer-price stability, will become quite apparent. Combined, these illustrations make a bold statement about what appears to be an "inexplicable complacency" toward risk by so many—those words from an ever-more-incredulous and equally astute observer, Jim Grant, in the January 13, 2006, issue of *Grant's Interest Rate Observer*.

Updated information [in 2005] on both charts is calculated as follows. The market capitalization to GDP ratio uses the Wilshire 5000 index (actually 6,300 publicly traded, domestically domiciled companies) as the numerator and the trendline estimate of GDP for 2005 based on reported 2004 data. The numerator is $15.8 trillion, and the

companies, notes that interest rates and the stock prices rose during the postwar expansion between 1948 and 1968. While interest rates tripled to 6 percent, economic growth trumped the escalating cost of money, in this writer's opinion.

denominator $12.5 trillion, indicating a ratio of 126 percent.[2] We consider this information to have a high degree of accuracy.[3]

More problematic is the ratio of total debt to GDP.[4] We don't believe that a precise number can be provided because of the existence of the double counting of real estate-related debt when viewed at a point in time. For example, a homebuyer mortgages his new home at the local bank. The bank sells the mortgage to, say, Fannie Mae, a GSE (government-sponsored enterprise) commissioned to make more credit available for housing, which issues an equivalent amount on bonds to finance the purchase. The result is that there's one home creating two debt instruments: first, the homeowner's mortgage, which is counted in the total of household debt, and second, the amount of bonds Fannie Mae sells to finance the purchase of the mortgage from the originating financial institution, which is also counted in total debt outstanding.

---

[2][2005, original] If the ratio eventually regresses to the mean, or less, a variety of combinations could bring about that end. The reader is encouraged to think about what they might be. The index market value reached its peak in the spring of 2000 at $16.6 trillion and fell to a low of $9.7 trillion just before the latest Gulf War in the spring of 2003. Over half its stellar recovery to $15.8 trillion, only $0.8 trillion short of its all-time peak, occurred in 2003. In the meantime, GDP increased from $9.8 trillion in 2000 to $12.4 trillion (estimated) in 2005. Don't get too comfortable. [2010 update: As of September 30, 2010, the index market value was $13.9 trillion and GDP $14.7 trillion. The market capitalization to GDP ratio: 95 percent.]

[3][2005, original] To accommodate index funds, the Wilshire 5000 (owned by the Dow Jones Company), like the S&P 500, has reduced the number of shares used in calculating the market capitalization. Those shares not likely to be traded—like Warren Buffett's 32 percent holding of the Class A shares of Berkshire Hathaway—will be excluded. [2010 update: As a rough rule of thumb, the total market value is estimated to be about 115 percent of the float.] The so-called "float," those shares always theoretically available for sale, will be multiplied by the price to get the index value. As of December 31, 2005, the float-only index value was $1.4 trillion less than the total outstanding shares index. While I understand the practical aspects, I think this reasoning is cockeyed, and the end result will never be precise. We've encouraged them to continue publishing the aggregate data.

[4][2010] As of September 2010, there was approximately $40.5 trillion in total U.S. nonfinancial debt outstanding and $14.7 trillion in GDP. Therefore, the debt to GDP ratio was approximately 275 percent.

Returning to the home-mortgage example and carrying this thought full circle: When the bank sells a mortgage to Fannie Mae it's then free to make another loan, having sold the mortgage loan that was on its books. One gets a different perspective when viewing the goings-on as a time series. Commercial bank assets have continued to grow in spite of selling loans, such as the one mentioned above—and, as discussed in detail later, their quality is deteriorating. Likewise, Fannie Mae's (and other GSEs, such as Freddie Mac) assets grew unabated until recently, and their quality has become sufficiently suspect that the company hasn't filed a 10-K since 2003. Fannie Mae owns $1 trillion of these mortgages as assets, financed largely with borrowings and only a sliver of equity. If the Fannie Mae folks choose not to hold a loan, they can pool mortgage loans together into a mortgage-backed security (MBS); put a guarantee on it; and sell it to a third party—such as a mutual fund, a pension fund, or an insurance company. These pass-through securities can become quite esoteric. A "CMO" or "CDO" is more "derivatives like," just as a "jump Z," heavy structured finance, is much more mysterious than the GNMA (Government National Mortgage Association). (I don't speak of these instruments firsthand. My friend Mike Stout[5] is a virtual fountain of information on the inner workings of this arcane branch of finance.) In the latter case, the institutional investors end up owning the MBS, which gives them a claim on the underlying principal and interest stream of the mortgage. Thus, it's the cash from the pension fund, mutual fund, and so forth, which is going into the housing market, having been drawn into that market by Fannie Mae and Freddie Mac as issuers of MBS securities.

Approaching the debt issue from a different angle, think about what the rising debt-to-GDP ratio implies in terms of the uses to which that debt is put. It would appear that increasing amounts of debt are being incurred to finance activities that don't have the same economic impact as they did in the years leading up to the 1980s. Economists call the

---

[5][2005, original] Mike Stout, a 17-year Wall Street veteran, was a managing director with Donaldson, Lufkin & Jenrette, 1991–1997. In 1995 Stout oversaw DLJ's Residential Real Estate Group, which included subprime mortgage originations, structured finance, and securitization, among other related activities. Stout also created and managed a subprime default servicing operation that subserviced $3.5 billion of subprime mortgages.

bang you get from the economic buck the "economic multiplier."[6] This debt-financed spending doesn't become a problem until the debt-service requirements (the combination of interest expense and principal amortization) overwhelm the economy's capacity to meet that obligation. Using an example that might not be as extreme as you might think, imagine if debt service rose to 10 percent of debt outstanding. At the current debt-to-GDP ratio, a crippling 30 percent of national income (the other side of the GDP equation mentioned above) would be dedicated to debt service. If we were a closed economy, we would claim "no harm, no foul"—it's merely internal wealth redistribution among American lenders and borrowers. Unfortunately, more and more of those claims are being held by foreign entities—IOUs piling up around the world. It is reasonable to ask, "How, exactly, will these chickens come home to roost?"[7] As for those who are still concerned about

---

[6][2005, original] Those interested in the theoretical "economic multiplier" may want to refer to a basic economics textbook. Assuming the reader has some rudimentary understanding of the concept, we will argue that different types of investment spending have different multiplier effects on overall economic activity and, ultimately, national wealth. To use a simple if not silly example, assume an individual borrows $100 against his home equity. He walks out of his bank with a crisp $100 bill, rolls it into a cigar-like shape, puts a match to it, and enjoys an expensive smoke. Total debt outstanding increases by $100, with absolutely no offsetting asset being created to eventually retire it. Lest you think that example absurd, the massive overspending by the telecommunications industry in the late 1990s on, for example, utterly redundant transoceanic fiber-optic cable, led to massive asset write-downs and eventually to the bankruptcies of WorldCom and Global Crossings. In this case we're talking billions of dollars going up in smoke. As for the unfortunate investors, let's just say they are "underwater."

[7][2005, original] Not long before this report went to the printer, the *Reno Gazette* (AP) reported on a talk Warren Buffett gave to the students and faculty at the University of Nevada at Reno on January 16. Obviously, the forum was also a bully pulpit. Addressing my rhetorical question about IOUs, Buffett got right to the truth and the consequences: "Right now, the rest of the world owns $3 trillion more of us than we own of them . . . In my view, it will create political turmoil at some point . . . Pretty soon, I think there will be a big adjustment," he said without elaborating. He went on to observe that the trade deficit is running at $2 billion per day. "We are like a super-rich family that owns a farm the size of Texas. You sell off a little bit of the farm and you don't see it," he said. Without specifying a time frame, Buffett warned, "If we don't change the course, the rest of the world could own $15 trillion of us. That's pretty substantial. That's equal

double counting, would a debt-service ratio of 20 percent be that much more tolerable?

No matter how you slice it, there is an incredible amount of debt outstanding in this financial economy. Quibbling about the precise amount is the equivalent of worrying about whether you are falling from 5,000 feet or 10,000 feet when you jump out of an airplane without a parachute.

Using both tools, Marc Faber[8] has pointed out the fundamental difference between what he describes as a "real" economy, for example, 1982, and what he sees as the "financial" economy of recent years. Paraphrasing Faber in Chapter 7, I wrote:

> In a real economy, the debt and equity markets as a percent-age of GDP are small and their principal function is to serve as the conduit through which savings flow into investments. In a financial or easy-money economy (often encouraged by both low-cost equity and debt capital), the total market value of the equity market is far larger than GDP—and not only channels financial resources into economic investments, but the massive overflow gives rise to colossal speculative bubbles.[9]

----

to the value of all American stock," as is mentioned earlier in this report. Buffett said he expects the trade deficit to top $700 billion this year. That compares to a federal budget deficit that's been running at about a $400 billion rate, a burden that is not so threatening, says Buffett. While it's theoretically possible that foreign interests will eventually own all U.S. corporations, I consider it a political impossibility. At some point Congress would impose limitations on foreign ownership of U.S. equities. If all of that comes to pass, the end game seems obvious . . .

[8][2010] Marc Faber is first introduced to readers in Chapter 3. During the early stages of the bursting of the technology bubble in 2000, he opined that the excesses had reached such extremes that the Nasdaq index would give back all that it had gained in the preceding five years, during which time it had risen from 1000 to 5000. In October 2002 it reached a low of 1108. Now, eight years later, it trades around 2500.

[9][2005, original] The powerfully deflationary entry of China full-scale into the global economy has helped to put a lid on the prices of many consumer goods. How quickly, you might ask? The title of Sam Walton's best-selling biography, published in 1992, was *Made in America*. For years that was the slogan prominently posted on the side of company trucks. Today, according to one source, roughly half of the nonfood items sold in Walmart stores are made in China; Walmart is China's seventh-biggest

The primary force behind secular cycles that can (and, as you can see, often do) last for years seems always to be the same: how the human mind works. Secular bull and bear cycles begin slowly because there's always a predisposition in people's minds to think the existing conditions will be permanent. It is thus without apology that I patiently reinforce the point through repetition. It was the Dalai Lama who displayed his wisdom of the way the world works when he observed, "I learn as much from a turtle as from a religious text."

The Boys Who Cried Wolf—And How Our Fiduciary Duty Trumped Antipathy

Before we begin this journey, I must confess to finding my uncomfortable self in a state of dynamic tension as I began this essay, caught in a tug of war between antipathy on the one hand and fiduciary duty on the other. As for the antipathy, it reflects a natural aversion to dealing with unpleasant things or events. The consequences of *The Perfect Storm*, as vividly portrayed in the gripping 1996 account by Sebastian Junger (and the less evocative movie based on it) are almost too terrifying to recount.

Regarding fiduciary duty, as wealth managers for people we know as friends, it is our obligation and mission to keep our eyes on the barometer and scan the horizon for storm clouds, however far away, whose potential for widespread financial and economic damage may not be commonly understood. Moreover, we must stand vigilant, knowing that even if they hit our shores the probability is low that they will overcome embankments that the Federal Reserve and a host of other agencies have erected. Remember "Pascal's Wager" [in Chapter 6] . . . Recently bowing to Pascal, obfuscatory Alan Greenspan, who recently departed as the world's most widely recognized and least understood central banker, appeared somewhat out of his precise probabilistic paradigm when he stated a year or so ago that the consequences of certain risks, despite their low probability of occurring, are so dire as to require

---

trading partner; the others are *countries*. As Adam Smith correctly predicted, where there is free trade, there will be no (consumer) inflation. Yet with relatively tame consumer prices, with so much money sloshing around in the financial economy, far more than was needed in the normal course of business, the price of something had to rise. See Alan Greenspan's comments below on "asset price inflation."

disproportionate diligence on the part of those who might prevent their occurrence. Greenspan should know, since his actions (or inactions) contributed to the consequences about which he expresses his typically oblique apprehensions.

If not us, who? As for *ex ante* warnings, sometimes of catastrophic risks, where the uncertainty is resolved only during the course of events, the track record of the economics profession and so-called financial experts has been abysmal. Even worse, those who write laws . . . almost without exception close the legal barn door long after the miscreants are out. Government, in short, is the consummate lagging indicator. Recall that the Depression hit rock bottom in 1932, yet Glass-Steagall (1933), the Securities Act (1933), the Securities & Exchange Act (1934), the Investment Company Act (1940), and the Investment Advisers Act (1940) became law to prevent financial and economic trauma *ex post facto* that (as is the nature of such events) would likely not recur for decades. After years of egregious corporate misconduct, the onerous tax imposed largely on the good guys, the Sarbanes-Oxley Act of 2002, made its celebrated debut. One cynical but sound-thinking CEO summed it up succinctly: "As a general rule of thumb, any bill that passes the United States Senate 97–0 is probably a horrible idea." A host of new SEC rules and regulations followed mutual-fund and investment-advisor malfeasance. The long arm of ludicrous law reaches all the way to MCM. If we took the advice of advisors, we would hire a lawyer as our compliance officer. Maybe we could do society a favor by recruiting a tort attorney, as these individuals seem to be in ample supply (and demand!). Compliance with the laws and the rules is an Adam Smith-type cultural imperative: It's hardwired into the way we think about things. Will an in-house policeman make us any more vigilant? It's a no-brainer to forecast that there will be a host of new regulations and/or laws restricting the behavior of the 10,000-plus hedge funds and funds of funds, the largely unregulated repackaged replicas of the investment trusts of the 1920s (a virtual invitation to fraud and deception), once competition drives more of them over the ethical and, eventually, legal edge.

In 1998 and 1999 I found scant company among economists, the financial media (most particularly tout television), and market strategists as I sought the company of like-minded thinkers. It should be noted that Edward Chancellor, Marc Faber, Jim Grant, Fred Sheehan Jr., Robert Shiller, and Andrew Smithers were among the notable exceptions. To the contrary, the vast majority of those who were in positions where they could have made a difference maintained a shameful silence, either because they didn't know or were too conflicted between doing what was right and what was larcenously lucrative to speak. Brings to mind the question about the difference between ignorance and apathy, along with its riposte: "I don't know, and I don't care!"

A post-Enron *Time* magazine cover story by Daniel Kadlec, "You're on Your Own, Baby," advised,

> [C]hoice (in this wobbly-kneed experimental age in self-determinism) now means personal responsibility for everything from retirement funds to health care . . . The risks of inaction or unwise action are rising, even as many of the *professionals* on whom we would like to rely for guidance are proving silent, untrustworthy, and even corrupt.

Those are fightin' words, a challenge to redouble our resolve to be worthy of your trust.

"The Perfect Storm?"—Why Such a Provocative Title?

Perhaps it's to shock all of us out of our lethargy, to put us on alert for the possible confluence of disparate forces that *could* put the unprepared in harm's way. Most of us have a vested interest in the *status quo*; our anchors are set firmly in the present, and we don't typically like to be disturbed by (and seek to avoid or even deny) uncertainty or change. Furthermore, very few, if any, of us are wholly rational, that capacity compromised by mental shortcuts and biases—many subconscious— that impede the faculty for reasoning through to purely logical conclusions. If there is hope, it comes from knowing the enemy that lies within, so that, thus fortified, we can face the enemy from without untrammeled by such emotions as greed or (later) fear. It's a rare world, lest we forget, where you can have your Kate and Edith too—the country song of that title notwithstanding.

The Blossoming of the Financial Economy: The Cataclysm in the Creation of Credit

Before we launch into our examination of the causes and effects of the tidal wave of domestic (and global) credit expansion, during which the "real" economy morphed ever so insidiously into the "financial" economy and its possible (if not probable) end, let's begin our trek up the mountain by trying to define the nature and scope of the perceptions of the genie now outside the bottle. I use the plural—not because all perceptions are identical, despite the same, reasonable evidence, but because different interpreters are often intellectually and experientially ethnocentric.

Three Wise Men Opining and a Partridge in Therapy . . .

As this Old World game bird stands astride the ever-widening "parted ridge" . . . let's turn to the Three Wise Men in this "fowl" parody on the Twelve Days of Christmas. The fable in the Western church tradition begins on December 25 and ends with Epiphany 12 days later, when the Three Wise Men present gifts to the young Jesus. In secular terms, let's hope there is an epiphany (lowercase), a sudden manifestation of the essence or meaning of what in the world is going on, couched in the words that follow.

From the relatively lowly trenches, U.S. Comptroller of the Currency John C. Dugan, who attempts to contain the conduct of all national banks within the confines of prudent behavior (who seem quite incapable of circumspection themselves), calls this the "peak of the credit cycle." It's the disregard—or at least the lack of appreciation for the consequences of unchecked risk, a potentially dangerous mindset by both the lender and borrower alike (and not the flood of credit itself)—that causes Dugan to point to what's going on as "the peak."

Next, we look up at the ivory towers. Fifty-two-year-old Dr. Ben Bernanke, hailing from Princeton, New Jersey, 185 miles from the Beltway where he is still a certifiable wet-behind-the-ears new kid on the block, by a stroke of George W's pen now occupies what has become the office of the second-most powerful person in the world. Bernanke wrote recently that a "global savings glut" is not worrisome in and of itself, nor are its consequences for those who are glut-tonous, although he would prefer that the roles of the mature industrialized countries and the emerging countries be reversed. In an August 2005 speech, outgoing (now that's a stretch) veteran Fed Chairman Alan Greenspan revealed the uneasiness born of long experience[10] where

---

[10][2005, original] Despite the perils of forecasting, Greenspan remains unrepentant. In a public speech on March 6, 2000—four days before the all-time peak in the Nasdaq index and the subsequent meltdown—he was extolling the virtues

visions of the future are regularly compromised away. He lamented that Fed forecasts and policies regarding global economic activity were increasingly driven by asset price changes and the liabilities that finance them. An apparent *non sequitur* to his successor, Greenspan continued his reasoning, noting that hyperinflating asset prices often have unavoidable attendant risks. Should the newly abundant liquidity (the fuel for asset price inflation) disappear as "readily" as it materialized,

> [a]ny onset of increased investor caution elevates risk premiums and, as a consequence, lowers asset values and promotes the liquidation of the debt that supported higher asset prices. *This is the reason that history has not dealt kindly with the aftermath of protracted periods of low-risk premiums* [emphasis added].

"Risk premiums" are dissected and discussed later.

So there you have it: cameos from the trenches to the towers of the high and the mighty. The Fed chairman designee, perhaps no student of behavioral economics, is disinclined to factor nonquantifiable human inclinations into his forecasting calculus. The gatekeeper of a herd of recalcitrant bankers is trying to rein in an almost predictably episodic indulgence in risky behaviors for which there is no rational justification in terms of the end game. The ex-Fed chairman is saying farewell by cryptically pointing out the not insignificant consequences of a change in the highly unpredictable propensity of investors to assume or avoid taking a flyer. More to follow below from this same cast . . .

"Easy Money"

Way back in September 1999, Doug Noland,[11] who writes "The Credit Bubble Bulletin" weekly for David Tice & Associates, gave a speech at the Credit Bubble Symposium. Having been a fan of Doug's writing, as well as discussing the state of affairs with him on the phone on a number

---

of the new era in technology. In 2004 he sang the praises of adjustable-rate mortgages three months before the Fed began jacking up the Fed funds rate.

[11][2005, original] Doug Noland, financial markets strategist at David Tice & Associates, has 16 years of investment experience as a trader, analyst, and portfolio manager. His analytical focus has been on the financial system and the crucial role of credit. For three years he was an analyst and contributing writer for *The Richebacher Letter*, an international economics and financial markets newsletter.

of occasions, I find him to be extremely well read, astute, rational, and thus justifiably firm in his convictions. In that speech he made a statement with which I fully agree: "The Federal Reserve . . . has lost control of the financial system." As a result, we are experiencing an "unprecedented explosion of credit, particularly financial credit—or borrowings made to finance the holdings of securities—leading to endemic distortions throughout both the financial asset markets and, importantly, the almost forgotten real economy."

Excessive credit creation, beyond what the economy needs to finance a sustainable pace of real investment spending, interferes with the market's pricing mechanism, leading to pricing bulges not related to the underlying value of the asset, resulting in misallocation of resources and a misaligned economy or, as noted earlier, Marc Faber's "financial" economy.

The story of how we migrated over the decades up the risk ladder from the hard-money gold standard (Greenspan's sentimental but politically untenable favorite), to fractional reserve banking, to the completely unrestrained easy-money financial system in which we now find ourselves . . . reads like an intricate novel with more plots, subplots, and characters than most writers could imagine. With the bailout of the banking system in the early 1990s, the rate of change turned exponentially upward. *One can take a crash course in that period's history by studying Fannie Mae from 1990 to the present to appreciate the enormity of the systematic liberalization that has insidiously ripped the financial-services industry from its conservative moorings. The trillion-dollar mortgage giant is in several respects the poster child of the era of breakneck asset and liability growth, with little or no regard for nurturing the equity-capital base that stands as the only buffer between asset deterioration and financial Armageddon—unless the ultimate guarantor, Uncle Sam, elects to invoke the "too big to fail" doctrine* [emphasis added].

While rarely discussed, the two sides of the balance sheet differ greatly in character, even though double-entry bookkeeping requires that they sum to the same total. The value of assets other than cash is at best an approximation, whereas most liabilities are precise to the second decimal point. Shareholders' equity is the margin of safety for those who hold contractual IOUs issued by the entity. To those who find the unfolding account of the financial economy intriguing, I say the following with the utmost seriousness: "If you don't know from where we've come, you will know relatively little about where we are." Terms (to name just a few) like the "carry trade," asset-backed and mortgage-backed securities (structured finance), hedge funds, all manner of derivatives, monetizing mistakes, and payment-option ARMs (adjustable rate mortgages) are among the buzzwords of the mutating financial economy. If you don't know them, please read on.

Continues Noland: "And with an asset bubble creating the perception of endless wealth, it is forgotten that real economic wealth is created only through saving and sound investment—not by borrowing and consuming, not by massive credit creation and not by asset inflation. Today, credit excesses have fueled overheated domestic demand, with an historic consumption binge feeding both malinvestment and ballooning trade deficits that imperil the dollar." So much for the good news. . . .

Fast-forward to April 2005 to an interview of Noland by Kate Welling, the consummate former managing editor of *Barron's*. Noland assesses that the ascendancy of unfettered credit creation has been evolving for more than 20 years. Wily veteran bond guru Henry Kaufman foresaw the sea change in his 1984 book *Interest Rates, the Markets, and the New Financial World*, stating: "Securitizations are the future. Forget bank loan officers. Now we can just package up loans and sell them. Finance is changing." As but one of many examples, in the process of liberalization to which Kaufman referred, Glass-Steagall was shattered. It was enacted in 1933 by a reactionary Congress and repealed in 1999. After 63 years there was probably no sitting congressman who could remember the nature of the conflict of interest that gave rise to the separation of commercial and investment banks in the first place. Had the Congress of yesteryear been prescient, the law would have been put in place in the mid-1920s. Weakened by loopholes resulting from a relentless barrage of political potshots, its repeal was inevitable—at the very time it probably should've been staunchly enforced. Lobbyists are the hired guns for special-interest groups, not all of whose agendas are in conflict with the common good. As for Glass-Steagall, or attempts to thwart the abuse of stock options, in this observer's opinion the effect on the common good was essentially an afterthought. When the bulls are running the streets of Pamplona, it's best to stay out of their way.

Adam Smith, so notes Noland, wrote that free-market capitalism is dependent upon its various components working smoothly together, including the financial mechanism. Should it get out of control the process that normally results in stable prices becomes distorted, and the system itself becomes imperiled. Concludes Noland: "That is what you are observing right now. Nobody has any incentive to slow down this runaway train. Everybody has every incentive to play this game as hard as they can, and it is a self-reinforcing mechanism."

According to Pulitzer prize-winning author Doris Kearns Goodwin's *Team of Rivals — The Political Genius of Abraham Lincoln*, it was the sixteenth president's "extraordinary ability to put himself in the place of other men, to experience what they were feeling, to understand their motives and desires" that gave him the edge over his three more privileged and accomplished rivals in winning the nomination for president at the Republican National Convention in 1860. Zipping forward 120 years, few readers (let me know if you are an exception) are likely to be aware of the rarely discussed "motives and desires" that were in part responsible for the liberalization of interstate banking laws in the 1980s and the massive wave of consolidations that continues to this day. What is new in this financial economy is the prevalence of generous stock-option allotments in an industry that heretofore used them rarely, if at all. The first of Gandhi's *Seven Deadly Sins*, "Wealth without Work," proved to be no moral obstacle to the allure of "free" money as a major reason why investors have profited so handsomely over the decades from investing in financial institutions, hitching their wagons to the Gold Rush train driven by executives hell-bent on getting rich, as the financial economy came of age. Among the biggest issuers of stock options have been Fannie Mae and Freddie Mac, whose eagerness to acquire home mortgages has backstopped banks in their charge to boost home mortgage and home-equity lending. Surely others besides Warren Buffett must have considered the possible unintended consequences when the larcenous Ponzi scheme reached epidemic proportions? Perhaps they were simply too consumed with their own self-enrichment? History teaches that whenever virtually all the banks run in the same direction to boost loans and profits, that is when the next disaster will occur. Read on for an inkling of what that might be.

Dr. Bernanke on Call

Doug Noland quotes from a March 2005 speech by Dr. Ben Bernanke, new Federal Reserve Board chairman:

> Over the past decade, a combination of diverse forces has created a significant increase in the global supply of saving—a

global saving glut—which helps explain both the increase in the U.S. current account deficit and the relatively low level of long-term real interest rates in the world today.

Although I found Bernanke's reasoning to be in a theoretical sense plausible, it had the noticeable academic imprimatur of being too neat and tidy for the real world. Noland was not that politically correct! In short, Bernanke concluded that many emerging nations have undergone financial or other crises in recent years that have resulted in their becoming net exporters of capital, whereas the major industrialized nations, excluding Japan and Germany, have attracted those savings and put them to work in the stock market, personal consumption, and real estate investment. The mechanism is much more complex than that just described, but I hope you get the point. Because of mature economies and aging populations in the industrialized countries, the natural flow of savings should be in the opposite direction. Bernanke's proposals for redirecting the flows appear myopic, in my judgment.

Also, his suggestion that the twin deficits (trade and budget) are only slightly connected appears disingenuous in that it fails to account for the lack of political will that, at least in terms of the budget deficits, must be considered a root cause even to lesser mortals than professors of economics and public policy. Moreover, the technology Bubble and Bust proved that the American capital markets are not as efficient as some might believe in allocating investment dollars to the highest-return projects—but rather, in the opinion of this observer, in this most recent episode in our "financial" economy toward capital-squandering speculative excesses. Further, the spending on consumption and residential real estate, essentially nonproductive assets from a rebalancing of the trade-deficit perspective, will produce little if anything to repay the IOUs that are piling up, plus interest, around the world. Warren Buffett's earlier sizing up of the implications of the ballooning trade deficit has the same commonsensical quality to it as his capacity to expose the motives behind stock options for what they really are. He also has an uncanny ability to see through the maze of complexity to the threat that derivatives pose to financial stability at the very time when the former chairman of the Federal Reserve Board is publicly heralding their virtues as a means to reduce systemic risk.

Worse, according to Noland,

> [A]n evidently large but unknown portion of these IOUs are held—or hedged—by highly leveraged speculators, which potentially creates what Hyman Minsky (the well-credentialed economist and professor who explained, in path-breaking research, how lending patterns and mood swings can push an economy into speculative booms or steep declines) called "acute financial fragility."
>
> It was incredibly liberating to shake off the shackles of Regulation Q (the prohibition against Federal Reserve-regulated banks paying interest on demand deposits was repealed in April 2003) to march to the beat of the market, instead of fussy old regulators. But somewhere along the line, the rewards got separated from the risk-taking.

What frustrates Noland "is that no one ever asks, what's the end game?"

To be sure, as unstable as America's economic, financial, and political machines might appear to us, they are far superior to many others on the planet. Stability, after all, is a relative term.

Still, the "end game" to which Noland refers is a reality that won't go away simply because we wish it to. In a later disquieting reference to Japan, we're reminded that low interest rates and easy money are not the only ingredients in this witches' brew. Japan has been practically giving money away for 15 years to resurrect its ravaged economy, with little success until recently. Absent an occasionally voracious appetite for risk, consumers and businesspeople alike will not take a bite out of the otherwise golden apple of cheap money. In this country, our urge for gratification by "betting the ranch," to hell with the consequences, remains rapacious . . . at least for the time being.

(Don't) Read My Lips . . .

Bernanke took office after Greenspan stepped down on January 31, 2006. The new Fed chairman had responded November 15, 2005, during the Senate banking committee hearings to a question by saying fiscal policy is none of his business. Highlighting their scope-of-responsibility differences, lame-duck Greenspan in a December 5, 2005, speech less than a month later continued to harp on an old theme that he has long considered within his purview—fiscal irresponsibility: "If . . . the pernicious drift toward fiscal instability in the United States and elsewhere is not arrested and is compounded by a protectionist reversal of globalization, the adjustment process could be quite painful for the world economy."

In a rambling late-summer speech (August 26, to be precise), "Reflections on Central Banking," Greenspan, ever politically erudite, continued to narrate his own place in the history books, taking great pains to explain that the Federal Reserve is, metaphorically [my words], no Hercules in battling Hydra, the many-headed monster from Greek mythology. While he applauded the step-up in globalization and the technological changes of the 1990s, he lamented the uncertainty of adjusting to events without the comfort of relevant history as a guide. Macroeconomic management has become a persistent Hydra that simply cannot be eradicated by a single effort. If it was an unlikely *mea culpa* of sorts, rest assured that Greenspan had no intention of laying the blame anywhere but with the system. "I do not intend this brief and necessarily incomplete review of events to illustrate how far we have come or to despair of how far we have to go. *Rather, I believe it demonstrates the inevitable and ongoing uncertainty faced by policymakers.*" Paging Dr. Bernanke . . . Please pick up the white courtesy phone. Are you listening, Ben?

According to Greenspan, a risk-management approach has gained greater acceptance in recent years that was initially probabilistic in its design. It quickly evolved to "separate mathematics from intuition," putting to use the lessons of Bernoulli (1730) and the cleverness of Pascal's Wager [see Chapter 6]. Explained the former Fed chairman: "In the summer of 2003, for example, the Federal Open Market Committee viewed as very small the probability that the then-gradual decline in inflation would accelerate into a more consequential deflation. But because the implications for the economy were so dire should that scenario play out, we chose to counter it with unusually low interest rates. The product of a low-probability event and a potentially severe outcome was judged a more serious threat to economic performance than the higher inflation that might ensue in the more probable scenario."

Now, I note with no surprise, we have probabilities that are modified by subjective judgments about the weight of consequences. As you will read below, Daniel Bernoulli introduced the concept in 1730.

In an observation that strikes to the core of my acute apprehensions (about the reverse wealth effect, asset bubbles, and the "financial" economy), Greenspan chose his words carefully when he said: *"The determination of global economic activity in recent years has been influenced importantly by capital gains on various types of assets, and the liabilities that finance them. Our forecasts and hence policy are becoming increasingly driven by asset price changes"* [emphasis added]. The Hydra sprouts another head. Continued Greenspan:

> The steep rise in the ratio of household net worth to disposable income in the mid-1990s, after a half-century of stability, is a case in point. Although the ratio fell with the collapse of equity prices in 2000, it has rebounded noticeably over the past couple of years, reflecting the rise in the prices of equities and houses.

Searching for an answer as to whether the currently elevated level of the wealth-to-income ratio will be sustained in the longer run, he reasoned (yielding to his obligatory optimistic bias) that "the growing stability of the world economy over the past decade may have encouraged investors to accept increasingly lower levels of compensation for risk."

The cause-and-effect linkage between rising prices of stocks, bonds, and, more recently, homes and consumer purchasing power is obvious. The recently departed chairman again:

> The uptrend in prices gave rise to a large increase in the market value of claims which, when converted to cash, are a source of purchasing power. It is the business of financial intermediaries, of course, to routinely convert capital gains in stocks, bonds, and homes into cash for businesses and households to facilitate purchase transactions.

Greenspan mused aloud in a recent speech:

> Thus, this vast increase in the market value of asset claims is in part the indirect result of investors accepting lower compensation for risk. Such an increase in market value is too often viewed by market participants as structural and permanent. To some extent, those higher values may be reflecting the increased

flexibility and resilience of our economy. But what they perceive as newly abundant liquidity can readily disappear.

Reinforcing what was said above, Greenspan continued:

> Any onset of increased investor caution elevates risk premiums
> and, as a consequence, lowers asset values and promotes the
> liquidation of the debt that supported higher asset prices. This
> is the reason that history has not dealt kindly with the after-
> math of protracted periods of low-risk premiums.
>
> In fact, the performance of the U.S. economy in recent
> years, despite shocks that in the past would have surely produced
> marked economic contraction, offers the clearest evidence that
> we have benefited from an enhanced resilience and flexibility.
>
> We weathered a decline on October 19, 1987, of a fifth of
> the market value of U.S. equities with little evidence of sub-
> sequent macroeconomic stress—an episode that provided an
> early hint that adjustment dynamics might be changing. The
> credit crunch of the early 1990s and the bursting of the stock
> market bubble in 2000 were absorbed with the shallowest reces-
> sions in the post-World War II period. And the economic fall-
> out from the tragic events of September 11, 2001, was limited
> by market forces, with severe economic weakness evident for
> only a few weeks. Most recently, the flexibility of our market-
> driven economy has allowed us, thus far, to weather reasonably
> well the steep rise in spot and futures prices for crude oil and
> natural gas that we have experienced over the past two years.

I have long felt that Greenspan—in offering the above anecdotal evidence to support his contention that our economy's "enhanced
resilience and flexibility" makes it relatively impervious to exogenous
shocks—may well have committed what scientists call a Type 1 error
where, in this case, he assumed a relationship where none existed.

· The retiring chairman appears to be on thin ice when he argues that
the economy's ability to withstand external shocks is based on the aforementioned improved resilience and flexibility. The counterargument
is that the economy, and the financial system on which it depends, is
ever-more-fragile and rigid, weaknesses bought off with easy and cheap
money, a process that cannot go on indefinitely. The first three events

mentioned by Greenspan above never spread to the "real" economy because the floodgates of easy money were opened immediately and forestalled a reckoning. (See Greenspan's argument on disproportionate probabilities and a doomsday scenario above.) Greenspan has passed not only the baton but the hot potato. Even more to the point is a recent *Economist* cover showing Greenspan dressed in a track suit passing a stick of dynamite to his successor.

Nowhere in his speech did Greenspan mention the "global savings glut" as the primary impetus behind the discontinuities mentioned above, nor, for that matter, did he bring up the name of Ben Bernanke. When comparing the careers of Greenspan, 79, and Bernanke, 27 years younger, it would certainly appear that their time and experience perspectives, if not their ideologies, could be worlds apart. Bernanke's biography seems comparatively short, having served as an economics and public policy professor at Princeton from 1985 (no doubt relatively soon after he earned his PhD in economics at MIT) until 2002. For approximately three years he sat on the Federal Reserve Board before being appointed to the President's Council of Economic Advisers last summer. Perhaps they didn't speak about each other because they barely knew one another—for during their short overlap on the Federal Reserve Board, Greenspan was the king, and Bernanke merely a member of the king's court.

"Top of the Credit Cycle," Says a Straight-Talking Head Banker

Several months after being appointed Comptroller of the Currency and a director of the FDIC in August of 2005 by President Bush, John Dugan pulled no punches when he addressed the OCC (Office of the Comptroller of the Currency) Credit Risk Conference of his investigators in Atlanta. He began with breathtaking understatement. Calmly and coolly, Dugan related to his audience of bank inspectors that this is the "top of the credit cycle . . . where stresses and weaknesses typically appear, so what we are seeing today should not surprise anyone." Although new to the post of the organization that supervises national banks, which constitute more than 50 percent of the assets of the commercial banking system, the Harvard-educated lawyer is an impressively seasoned veteran from banking's highest ranks during some of its most tumultuous recent times. He is an experienced and wise man with something important to say to lenders, mortgagees . . . and, indirectly, to Martin Capital Management and its clients. As a ranking member of the Department of Treasury, 1989–1993, Dugan had extensive responsibility for policy initiatives involving banks and financial institutions, including the savings and loan cleanup, Glass-Steagall and banking reform, and regulation of government-sponsored enterprises. In 1991 he oversaw a comprehensive study of the banking industry that formed the basis for the financial modernization legislation proposed by the administration of the first President Bush. In elaborating on the sources of rising credit risk Dugan noted:

> One of the striking findings in our 2005 underwriting survey was the breadth and extent to which banks had relaxed their lending standards. With liquidity pouring into the market, we would expect to see increased competition for loan customers— and we are. With competition intensifying, we would expect to see underwriting standards easing—and we are. And we would expect to find emerging concentrations in some loan categories, such as commercial and residential real estate. We are most definitely seeing that.

Because of space limitations, my attentions have been directed primarily at residential mortgage lending. But in his challenge Dugan revealed some disconcerting statistics about commercial real estate lending practices that provide further corroboration of the pervasiveness of the propensity to incur bigger and bolder risks—and add fuel to my fire:

> Commercial real estate concentrations are everywhere: in large cities and small, on the coasts and in the heartland. Over the past decade, commercial real estate holdings have become an increasing share of total assets, so that about a third of national banks today have *commercial real estate holdings equal to 300 percent or more of Tier I capital.* Such concentrations by themselves would warrant supervisory concern under almost any circumstances.

Dugan lamented that in order to attract new business and sustain loan volume banks have bent over backward making compromises and concessions to borrowers along the way, resulting in commercial real estate credits with "structural weaknesses that go beyond discounted pricing." He warned that the regulators should be concerned when they see policies governing such metrics as loan-to-value standards and debt-service coverage being relaxed—overlaid by yet an increasing number of exceptions to those more accommodating policies. Dugan worried aloud about lenders routinely adjusting covenants, lengthening maturities, and reducing collateral requirements. He considers these signs of lender laxity as worrisome as the commercial real estate concentrations themselves.

Getting closer to home, Dugan turned to an equally important subject: the rapidly changing market for residential mortgages. "It seems like only yesterday when a 5/1 ARM was considered a risky mortgage product," he said. The risk, however, consistent with the essay in the 2003 annual report [Chapter 6] "The Great Abdication of Fiduciary Responsibility: The Defined-Contribution Plan" was floated downstream much the same as the 401(k) investment management uncertainty moved from the boardroom to the factory floor. The end game consequences were offloaded onto the borrowers, who, in return for lower initial payments, assumed the interest-rate risk that had previously been borne by lenders. Are you beginning to get some sense of who will be left standing if and when the music stops?

Today's newfangled mortgage products—interest-only, payment option ARMs, no-doc and low-doc, and piggyback mortgages, to name the most prominent examples—are a different species of animal, with novel and potentially risky features that "dominate the mortgage originations that many of you look at every day." How prevalent, you ask? By some estimates, interest-only products constituted 50 percent of all mortgage originations in 2004. In the first half of 2005, IOs (interest only) started to decline in favor of *payment-option ARMs*, estimated to comprise half the new mortgage originations.[12] And roughly every other mortgage these days is also a "piggyback" (first and second mortgages packaged to circumvent the mortgage insurance requirement when the first mortgage exceeds 80 percent of the "value," effectively allowing the buyer to finance 100 percent of the purchase without insurance). Or it's a reduced-documentation mortgage—if the borrower

---

[12][2005, original] When the consumer chooses not to lock in a fixed-rate 6 percent 30-year mortgage—the lowest rate in more than 30 years—in favor of a teaser adjustable rate mortgage at 4 percent, then "Something is rotten in Denmark."

meets certain FICO (Fair Isaac Corporation) or other credit-worthiness tests—"which [according to Dugan] points to another development that concerns us: the trend toward 'layering' of multiple risks. There is no doubt that when several risky features are combined in a single loan, the total risk is greater than the sum of the parts."

Understanding the Motives for Reckless Real Estate Financing

Fully understanding that "Money makes the mare go," Dugan matter-of-factly explained why these new products have become fixtures in the marketplace in such a short time. When reading about the "growth at any cost imperative" in the soon-to-be-published "The Earnings Guidance Enigma" MCM essay [published in *Barron's* January 7, 2008], file away the following in your synapses:

> One reason is that they [the new and higher-risk mortgage products] have helped sustain loan volume that would otherwise almost certainly be falling, *because rising interest rates have brought an end to the refinance boom. More important, lenders have scrambled to find ways to make expensive houses more affordable*—although there's now a concern that the very availability of this new type of financing has done its share to help drive up house prices, which in turn stimulates demand for even more non-traditional financing.

Please dwell for a moment on the absolute long-term absurdity of the preceding quotation from the hapless homeowner's perspective. You may find it helpful to turn back to Chapter 7, recalling the discussion on unintended consequences and how it might apply to the morphing of the mortgage market. For those who don't have a copy next to the porcelain throne, I'll summarize. As noted in Chapter 7, U.S. sociologist Robert K. Merton would surely characterize the mortgage bankers' scramble to force more loans on the books as "imperious immediacy of interest." By that he means the lenders want the outcome of an action so much that they purposely ignore unintended effects. This pernicious "willful ignorance," a root cause of unintended consequences, is quite different from true ignorance, which would more appropriately characterize the plight of the mortgagee when the "payment-shock" chickens come home to roost.

The ARM-ed Robber

To bring this flight of irrationality to a just and proper close, allow me to return to a product (adjustable rate mortgages) mentioned several pages above that represented roughly 50 percent of originations in the first half of 2005—the payment-option ARM—best described by Dugan himself. By focusing on decision making at ground level, it's sometimes possible to make sound inferences about what goes on up the food chain.

> And then there are payment-option ARMs, which take us to another level of risk. They, too, have their defenders, of course, who argue that such mortgages are little more than the combination of a traditional ARM and a home equity line of credit in a single loan. And, borrowers can easily treat payment-option ARMs in the same manner as a traditional mortgage, simply by selecting the fully amortizing option rather than the minimum payment option each month.
>
> In practice, however, few borrowers treat them that way. Recent studies show that a significant number of borrowers are frequently choosing to pay the minimum amount possible, a payment amount that typically falls short of the interest accruing on the loan. Even more disturbing, this choice does not seem limited to high quality, affluent borrowers who may be using the product as a payment flexibility tool. The research indicates that borrowers at both ends of the FICO spectrum make this choice, with riskier borrowers resorting to it most frequently. Because such minimum payments fall considerably short of the total interest accruing each month, the unpaid interest is added to the loan principal, and negative amortization occurs. Thus, it should come as no surprise that, of the least creditworthy holders of payment-option ARMs, nearly 50 percent have current balances above their original loan amount.
>
> Depending on how much negative amortization the borrower opts to incur—and, increasingly, borrowers are incurring as much as their lenders allow—payment-option loans expose borrowers to substantially increased levels of payment shock. For example, take a typical payment option ARM at the conforming

loan limit of approximately $360,000, with an initial interest rate
of 6 percent. If the borrower makes only the minimum payment
each month for the first five years—initially $1,200—the pay-
ment shock when the loan begins scheduled amortization will
be substantial, even if interest rates remain level. In this example,
the minimum payment increases incrementally during the first
five years to roughly $1,600, and then jumps over *50 percent*—to
$2,500—when the amortization period starts at the beginning
of the sixth year. And that assumes no change in interest rates. If
interest rates should increase just two hundred basis points to 8
percent, which is certainly not unreasonable to expect, then the
monthly payment would nearly *double* on the reset date to $3,166.
By any measure, *that* is real payment shock. Of course, the borrower might be able to refinance, but what if interest rates have
increased substantially, or house prices have dropped below the
value of the loan? That would put the borrower in a far more difficult position.

The failure of the economic and financial professions, including our former central banker Mr. Greenspan, to adequately warn of
the stock Bubble was a sin of omission of extraordinary magnitude.
Apparently embarrassed by his premature warning in 1996, as a stock
market forecaster he slipped into the shadows, taking a much lower
profile. Missing the housing Bubble may be an even bigger mistake.
As recently as mid–October 2005, Bernanke told Congress that there
is no national housing bubble, even though prices had increased by
25 percent over the last two years. As quoted in an October 27 article
in the *Washington Post*. Bernanke believes that "the Fed's job is to protect the economy, not to protect individual asset prices," said William
Dudley, chief economist for Goldman Sachs U.S. Economics Research,
as stated in the same *Post* article. If weaker housing prices should push
the economy toward recession, the awkward truth is that America's
policymakers will have much less room to maneuver than they did
after the stock market bubble burst. Short-term interest rates of only
4.25 percent leave less scope for cuts. In 2000 the United States had
an unanticipated capital-gains-tax-driven budget surplus. Today it has a
large deficit, ruling out big tax cuts. Good golly, Ben, I hope you,
along with the Senate that recently confirmed your nomination, prove

me a fool. Dear reader, given the aforementioned abysmal reactionary legislative record of the always-behind-the-curve lawmakers, and the often reactionary response of the Fed, I'd think twice before placing your bets.

Truth or Consequences?

"Merrily We Roll Along" was the most *apropos* theme song for the long-running TV quiz show hosted by Ralph Edwards in 1951. We might use that jingle today if we added ". . . toward the precipice." There may be an unavoidable aftermath for a system characterized by increasingly relaxed standards of discernment, perhaps dating back to the early 1980s. Perish the thought, but recall the aphorism "once burned, twice shy" as it applies to Japan. When an expansion continues seemingly without end, the propensity to incur ever-more-outlandish risks, the inclination justified by the oxymoronic phrase of secular righteousness, must be the inseparable companion of a world awash with plentiful credit. But flip the coin over and look at Japan after having been "once burned." Here the "pushing on the string" analogy applies: The very easy money policy that gave rise to the problem has proved to be impotent in solving it absent the above animal instinct, the predilection to embrace uncertainty with verve.

Closer to home, I've written on occasion of listening to stories from those scarred by the trauma of the early 1930s who vowed never to take a chance on equities again in this lifetime. If the venturesome spirit wilts from the heat of irrational exuberance, its polar opposite, crippling risk aversion, may suppress creativity and growth just as it has in Japan. By withholding the truth, those in positions of power have stymied the periodic and cathartic, albeit painful (and unpopular in the short run), cleansing process. A dangerous illusion of invulnerability gradually becomes an unintended side effect of a surfeit of financial excesses that, as a result, threaten to destabilize the economy or financial markets. How long would the Depression of the 1930s have gone on were it not for tooling up for the demand for war materials by our allies as Hitler, who appointed himself Führer in August 1934, began to inflict his diabolical ideology on Europe. I wonder if this is what Warren Buffett was thinking when he warned that actions often have proportional consequences. I sincerely hope Ben Bernanke, born smack dab in the middle of the Baby Boomer generation of

1947 to 1964, has seen the recently released movie "Cinderella Man," directed by Ron Howard and starring Russell Crowe as the early-1930s, Depression-era pugilist James Braddock. While it's a story of one man's uncommon courage and selfless devotion to his family in the depths of the Depression, it's also an account of the widespread suffering in the Hoovervilles all around the country (unemployment reached its peak at 25 percent) for which the blame for such a pervasive social and economic tragedy can, in part, be laid at the feet of those in high places who should've known better. My wish is that the good Dr. Bernanke understands the enormity of his responsibilities—and that his bedside manner with an ailing patient (named U.S. Economy) at least approaches that of his predecessor.

Bubbles Are Indigenous to the Financial Economy

Popular songs have a way of poetically capturing the tenor of the times. "I'm Forever Blowing Bubbles" was a major Tin Pan Alley hit in 1919—debuting ironically on the cusp of the boom in Florida real estate in the 1920s. [While the waltzy music style may no longer seem relevant in the age of Eminem and Justin Bieber, the title and lyrics certainly are—especially for the investor or investment manager for whom bubbles have become an increasingly common occurrence.]

John Dugan, the aforementioned Comptroller of the Currency, piqued my curiosity with his bottom-up look at the banking industry's latest attempt to prove once again that some bankers should simply not be allowed to handle other people's money. If there's good news it's that bankers tend to learn from their follies, so they add a degree of excitement to an otherwise moribund commodity business by making brand-new mistakes in each cycle. As reported on January 9, 2006, banks continue to lobby their regulators for permission to expand their reach—in this case into the risky non-bank-occupied commercial real estate development arena. Bank of America, the *Wall Street Journal* hinted, plans a 150-room, 15-story Ritz-Carlton hotel as part of its headquarters complex in Charlotte. The OCC said it approved the plan, "largely because the bank says that eventually it will account for 50 percent of the annual hotel occupancy." (Mr. Dugan, console yourself that there is no lasting cure for stupidity.) "It's a situation warranted by the need for a quality hotel to house bank visitors, clients and vendors adjacent to the headquarters," said bank spokesman Terry Francisco. For those who have flown into Charlotte, feasting their eyes on the landmark edifice complex known sardonically as the "Taj Ma-Coll,"[13] this latest ritzy concession to the gratification of towering egos should come as no surprise. How much anecdotal evidence do we need to confirm that the financial economy continues to reach recklessly for new extremes of brashness? The "Perfect Storm" section reached beyond my traditional grasp by thinking outside the box, which means thinking about the "(housing) box," to dissect what appears to be a house pricing anomaly. Of what relevance are levitating real estate prices, or the schemes to finance the boom in housing, to a firm that does not invest in other than marketable securities? We believe that the argument we will propose forthwith is an essential part of an interdependent larger mosaic that requires some familiarity with multiple disciplines—and feel we would be remiss in not disclosing housing's role in this increasingly interconnected financial and economic world. The following snippet from Charlie Munger brings this circuitous venture to a just and proper close: *". . . [A] curious mind . . . loves diagnoses involving multiple variables."*

First, what constitutes a housing bubble? By way of background, I return again to Robert Shiller, whose scholarly book *Irrational Exuberance* was published near the market peak in 2000. Capitalizing on the success of his first book, Shiller published *Irrational Exuberance*, Second Edition, copyrighted in 2005. In the latter he has amassed impressive evidence in support of his belief that the recent housing-market boom bears

---

[13][2005, original] Hugh McColl was the mastermind behind the merger in 1998 of BankAmerica and NationsBank (renamed Bank of America), the biggest prize in a serial acquisition binge dating back to when McColl took control in 1982. Given the storied history of Amadeo Giannini, the Italian founder of the modern-day Bank of America, who, after the 1906 San Francisco earthquake became a leader of the San Francisco banking community by providing loans to those struck by the disaster, it's some testimony to the behind-the-scenes persuasive powers of McColl that the headquarters was relocated to Charlotte. Lord Acton is known for his warning, "Power corrupts, and absolute power corrupts absolutely." The concentration of power in the banking industry will not, I say with nigh-unto-total confidence, end well.

many similarities to the stock market Bubble about which the earlier book was written. To start off, Shiller, rather effectively, in my judgment, dismisses the traditional glib explanations for housing booms, including the shortage of land, rising building costs that depart from past patterns, and low interest rates.

Examining the graphically presented history of *inflation-adjusted* U.S. home prices, building costs, population, and interest rates from 1890 to 2004 (Figure 9.2), it may be possible to make several observations of significance. Beginning with an index value of 100 in 1890, *real* home prices zigzagged gradually downward to about 70 until they shot up to around 115 during the easily understood post-World War II housing boom, driven by the parents of what was later to be known as the Baby Boom generation. It then remained relatively stagnant until 1997. Without any conspicuous precipitating impetus, and based on more up-to-date data from the Federal Housing Finance Board, house sale prices have risen by 55 percent, after adjusting for inflation, over the last eight years, compared with an average annual real rate of increase going back to 1890 of just 0.4 percent. There is no precedent for this sort of run-up

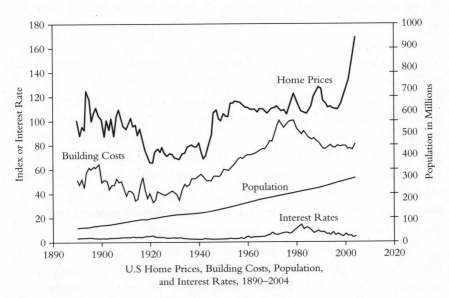

U.S Home Prices, Building Costs, Population,
and Interest Rates, 1890–2004

Figure 9.2   The Real Estate Market in Historical Perspective

DATA SOURCE: www.econ.yale.edu/~shiller/data.htm.

in home prices. Any number of commentators have opined on its huge impact on the economy and people's personal finances. The value of family-owned residential housing is estimated at $18.5 trillion, eclipsing the value of all publicly traded stocks of approximately $15.8 trillion, with more than $6.5 trillion of that total coming from the post-1997 surge in existing home prices, as well as new construction. The spike in real housing prices has led to near-record rates of housing construction. At the current rate of housing construction, there will have been 2 million units built in 2005, an amount exceeded only by the 2.4 million annual rate in 1972 as the Boomers were starting to move out of their parental homes. The pace of housing construction over the last three years is more than 40 percent higher than the average construction rate in the 17 years prior to the run-up in house prices. It's worth noting that few economists were arguing that there was serious pent-up demand nation-wide or a housing shortage due to a lack of construction during this long 17-year period. The average annual rate of housing construction from 1980 through 1996 was 1.4 million units. By some estimates, the housing sector accounts for 25 percent of all activity in the economy, with construction nearly 5 percent by itself. Thus, the combination of spending unleashed by the rising prices of existing homes and the economic multiplier-effect stimulus from the multi-year high level of spending for new construction may have propped up an otherwise ane-mic economy.

According to the Mortgage Bankers Association, inventories of new and existing homes set records for the year ending November 2005, rising 20 percent and 16.4 percent, respectively. The month's supply (inventory/sales ratio) for existing homes was 5. For condos, inventories rose by 24.8 percent from a year earlier, with the month's supply increas-ing to 5.9 from 4.8 a year before. The number of new homes built for speculation (without having a buyer in hand) continued to set records, reaching 500,000 units in October, 4.3 months' supply, the highest since December 1996. All inventory/sales ratios are skewed upward because of the high rate of sales, which is beginning to soften noticeably.

Not surprisingly, existing home price gains continued to be very strong, according to the MBA. The median price of single-family homes jumped by 16.6 percent from a year ago—the strongest year-over-year increase since July 1979, when inflation was rampant. New-home-price appreciation has continued to be softer than appreciation for existing homes. The median price for new homes increased by only

0.9 percent from a year ago. The MBA again: "The Census Bureau revised new home price data back to June, however, showing a firmer trend in the median house price appreciation in recent months than previously reported." Longer term, as one might expect from a trade organization, the MBA remains quite bullish. In 2008 it expects the 30-year mortgage loan rate to be 6.1 percent, slightly lower than it is today. It forecasts the median home price to increase from $215,000 to $265,000.

To be sure, most homeowners are sheltered from the risks of rising interest rates on their first mortgages. The proportion of mortgages locked in at a fixed rate has increased from about 60 percent in 1990 to more than 75 percent today, no doubt due to the heavy refinancing activity as interest rates fell. However, as noted elsewhere, new buyers have switched toward adjustable-rate mortgages and existing homeowners have moved over to home-equity loans, which are tied to the prime rate. The current spread between 30-year mortgage rates and the one-year mortgage rate of about 230 basis points has a pronounced impact on monthly payments—and a shocking longer-term impact if buyers finance their purchases with one of the popular, exotic, reverse-amortization loans of which Dugan speaks disparagingly above.

The problem for the credit markets (most free markets, for that matter) is the marginal buyer. This buyer is the most susceptible to the risks of higher interest rates or a downturn in the economy. The cascade effect could be enormous.

It is important to note that housing is a major source of household wealth. For more than half of all households, their home is by far their largest single asset, and its value is growing. According to the National Association of Realtors, the national median existing single-family home price was $215,900 in the third quarter, up 14.7 percent from the third quarter of 2004 when the median price was $188,200.[14]

---

[14][2005, original] The distribution of wealth in the United States has a large positive skew, with relatively few households holding a large proportion of the wealth. For this type of distribution, the median, the mid-point of the sample, is the preferred measure of central tendency because it is less sensitive than the average (mean) to extreme observations. The median is also considerably lower than the average—and provides a more accurate representation of the wealth and asset holdings of the typical household. For example, more households have a net worth near the median of $55,000 than near the average of $182,381.

Ninety-seven MSAs (metropolitan statistical areas)—two-thirds of the total—experienced price increases greater than the U.S. historical average of 6.4 percent.

By rough comparison, since the following data represent both rental (one-third) and owner-occupied housing (two-thirds), according to the most recent Census Bureau data the median household[15] net worth in 2000 was $55,000, with 32 percent in home equity, 18.5 percent in 401(k) plans, IRAs and other tax-deferred accounts, 15.6 percent in stocks and mutual funds outright, and 9 percent in interest-bearing accounts at financial institutions. We can make certain representations from the 2000 U.S. Census Bureau report about the demographics of those households that rent and those that own. Based on the statistics I studied, the 70 million owner-occupied homes (two-thirds of the total of 105.5 million units for 281 million Americans) are owned by older (87 percent are age 35-plus) heads of families, empty nesters, unmarried couples, and widows and widowers. As for rental units, no doubt apartments constitute the largest class. Less than 25 percent of Americans who rent have earned a bachelor's degree, and less than one in 10 have earned a master's degree or higher. Based on the statistics, most rental units appear to be occupied by people who can't afford a home: young people, primarily individuals, and lower-income individuals and families of all ages.

So far, however, long-term interest rates are holding steady. So, is there a bubble? Many say, no, there is no bubble. Until it bursts.

Worth noting is the fact that price increases differed dramatically from region to region, or city to city, depending on incomes and desirability. In Florida, California, Nevada, Hawaii, Maryland, and Washington, D.C., the average price rose more than 20 percent. And in Palm Beach County, Florida, the median price of an existing home shot up 35 percent in just the past year. Areas where job growth is strong or the weather and amenities appeal to retirees seem to be doing the best. Rust Belt cities are . . . well, rusting. Not surprisingly, then, it's a buyer's market in South Bend-Mishawaka, Indiana, according to the National Association of Realtors data. The median single-family house price is $101,600, up 3.1 percent in the four quarters ending

---

[15][2005, original] Household includes rental and owner-occupied housing.

September 30, 2005. The Fort Wayne area was $106,000, rising 6.8 percent over the last year. Among many other areas where housing prices have been comparatively low and growing little are Danville, Illinois; Elmira, New York; Decatur Illinois; Topeka, Kansas; and Youngstown, Ohio. The "hot spots" in terms of price appreciation the last four years were Cape Coral/Fort Myers where prices have more than doubled to $277,600 and appreciated 42.5 percent last year alone. In fact, price increases in Florida generally exceeded 30 percent statewide for the 12 months of 2005. Honolulu also doubled to $611,000, with a 31.1 percent rise last year. The same metric for San Francisco-Oakland areas is an astounding $726,900, although the rate of growth in price increases slowed to 11.7 percent last year. Los Angeles and surrounding areas was $553,200, rising another 22.3 percent in 2005. The Northeast also is strong. Housing prices in Washington, New York, and Boston—followed by the rate of increase for the last four quarters—are: $441,400 (26.3 percent); $533,600 (16.2 percent); and $430,950 (5.8 percent).

Shiller contends that after the stock market Bubble burst the asset of choice for channeling much of the available liquidity coursing through the financial economy was housing, resulting in surging real estate prices domestically and around the world. He thinks the consequence will be declining home prices for years to come.[16] While certainly no apples-to-apples comparison, The Economist notes that Japanese property prices have fallen for 14 years in a row, by 40 percent from their peak in 1991, and consumer spending has been weak. The Economist concludes: "Americans who believe that house prices can only go up and pose no risk to their economy would be well advised to look overseas."

While we Americans are most interested in the surge in house prices in certain regions of our country, The Economist pointed out in June that the flight of fancy is global. The current worldwide boom in residential real estate prices is "the biggest bubble in history," according

---

[16][2005, original] Shiller's comprehensive and exhaustive study of the real estate market from a historical perspective is only superficially summarized in this report. While every effort was made to condense his work without altering his conclusions, those interested in more detail are encouraged to refer directly to the book.

to a disturbing new report in the esteemed biweekly British magazine with a global perspective:

> The International Monetary Fund analyzed home prices in a number of countries from 1970 to 2001, and found 20 "busts"— when real prices fell by almost 30 percent. All but one of those busts led to a recession. The price of a home should reflect the future benefits of ownership, in the form of rental income for an investor or rent saved by an owner-occupier. When the price-to-rent ratio is high, property is overvalued.
>
> House prices in relation to rent have hit all-time highs in the U.S., Britain, Australia, New Zealand, France, Spain, the Netherlands, Ireland and Belgium.
>
> In the U.S., the ratio is 35 percent above its 1975–2000 average. A drop in home prices is more likely today than after previous booms for three reasons, according to *The Economist*: Homes are more overvalued, inflation is much lower, and many more people have been buying homes as an investment.
>
> Consumer spending and residential construction have accounted for 90 percent of the total growth in the American GDP over the last four years, and more than 40 percent of all private-sector jobs created since 2001 have been in housing-related sectors, including construction and mortgage brokering.

The common impulse in these episodes of exaggerated and wide-spread exuberance—near or far, tangible or intangible assets—according to Shiller and the undersigned, is the apparent willingness of individuals to surrender their semirational inklings to the impulsive, agitated, and often reckless will of the crowd, which falls under the purview of the relatively new science of behavioral economics in which I am (and have been for years) a staunch believer.

If Housing Prices Roll Over

The economic consequences of deflation in the housing Bubble, should it occur, may prove to be as misjudged and unanticipated as to its repercussions as was the (relatively benign) economy's reaction to the most recent stock market swoons, those of October 1987 and the collapse of the Nasdaq stock Bubble in March 2000. It is my contention, as noted earlier, that Greenspan may have drawn a faulty conclusion in implying that the economy, because of newfound "resilience and flexibility," is no longer easily derailed. Even Greenspan says the steep rise in the ratio of household net worth to disposable income beginning in the mid–1990s, after a half-century of stability, has had a salutary effect on consumers' propensity to spend. *A central thesis of this essay is that a diminution in that ratio is likely to have a more deleterious effect on the economy if the shrinkage in the numerator is predominantly from the decline in the value of one's home as contrasted with one's 401(k) plan or other portfolio of marketable securities.*

First, there's the matter of financial leverage. Unjustifiably high financial leverage has been the cause of more investment failures than any other variable. It allows you no wiggle room, no slip 'twixt the cup and the lip. For purposes of comparison, the typical homeowner's marketable securities portfolio is not financed with borrowed money. New York Stock Exchange Member Firms Customers' Margin Debt of $212 billion as of October 2005 was a mere pittance relative to the total value of all U.S. stocks, which is estimated at $15.8 trillion at year end.[17] By stark contrast, thanks to the panoply of creative real estate financing options discussed above, the surge in prices since 1997 has converted homes into two-, three-, or four-bedroom ATMs. Homeowners use the equity in their houses to pay off credit card debts (home-equity loan interest rates are much lower and are deductible for tax purposes) and to finance personal-consumption expenditures at a time when real earnings growth has been negligible. By some calculations, roughly 60 percent of consumer spending is financed through those down-home

---

[17][2005, original] Up from $130 billion at the market lows in the fall of 2002. The New York Stock Exchange Member Firms Customers' Margin Debt is a highly reliable coincidental indicator for stock prices as a whole. Moreover, don't take this relatively smallish number lightly. As discussed later in the section on housing, it's the marginal buyer or seller who sets the price. Those speculators, therefore, who have used margin accounts to leverage their returns are likely to exacerbate a market sell-off as they respond to margin calls. Visit the New York Stock Exchange's web site, www.NYSE.com, for details. For those interested in history, compare today's stock margin requirements with those of the late 1920s. Leveraged speculation then was in stocks; today it's in real estate.

ATMs. As for the other newly created jobs, they're concentrated in the likes of McDonald's, KFC, Starbucks, Walmart, temporary and contract jobs, and those consumer-unfriendly security jobs in airports and office buildings. In a June 16, 2005, article, *The Economist* averred that, as a result of such borrowing, "housing booms tend to be more dangerous than stock market bubbles, and are often followed by periods of prolonged economic weakness."

Second, the wealth in the form of the housing stock is much more broadly dispersed than the wealth held in the form of intangible assets, and it's generally held directly in the name of the owner, and not held by a trustee in a 401(k) plan or such. Again by contrast, for a broad demographic (probably not much different from that which owns much of the owner-occupied housing) intangible assets—stocks, bonds, and mutual funds—are held at comparatively inaccessible arm's length. When equity prices rise there is no doubt that many people rationalize the increase in the market value of their securities as a substitute for a conscious act of deferring consumption, otherwise known as savings. There is little evidence to support the notion that holders of financial assets, particularly those invested in tax-deferred 401(k) plans, profit-sharing, and other such plans, who felt, at least temporarily, less wealthy as a result of the recent bear market in stocks, stepped up their savings to compensate. The impact of rising or falling stock prices on spending is indirectly proportional to the extent that the savings are invested in tax-sheltered plans because of the practical inaccessibility of the assets and the financial penalties on monies withdrawn prematurely. Moreover, just as folks' 401(k) plan was shrinking in value, their house price was going the other way.

Third, housing bubbles, when the process of purging of excesses takes place, follow a pattern similar to that of a stock bubble, except they're in slow motion. The majority of homes are owner-occupied. Think about the many factors one must take into account when a family moves from their house to other housing. The markets are geographically, topographically, and climatologically diverse. Arbitrage (derived from *arbitrate*: to settle or reconcile differences) doesn't work effectively because of these dissimilarities (how would you compare Naples, Florida, with Baltimore, Maryland, if you were actually so inclined!) and because there are no centralized markets like the NYSE or Nasdaq, and trading costs are enormous, compared with a few cents a share for common stocks.

Confirming the points above with empirical evidence, I quote work done by the International Monetary Fund (IMF). The IMF published an in-depth analysis of equity market and real estate crashes in its April 2003 edition of *World Economic Outlook*. The average real decline in prices in a housing market crash (30 percent after four years) was found to be less than for a stock market crash (45 percent decrease in equity prices, on average, after two and a half years), but at the end of each of those periods, GDP (or "output") had fallen 8 percent after a housing bubble burst, compared with 4 percent after a stock market bubble burst.

Residential Housing: "To Everything There Is a Season"

On December 20, 2005, Fannie Mae predicted that U.S. home *sales* are set to decline by as much as 10 percent in 2006 as higher interest rates and housing-market worries reverse a five-year run that was the key impetus behind consumer spending and economic growth. Mortgage bankers are likely bracing for a drop-off in originations and refinance activity, which are predicted to fall 2.3 percent, to $1.45 trillion, and 51.6 percent, to $653 billion, respectively.

"Despite a surprising jump in new home sales for October, the housing market likely has peaked," Fannie Mae economists David Berson and Molly Boesel said in a semiannual housing survey. Residential real estate speculators take note: Home *price* gains are expected to "slow sharply" in 2006, down to about 3 percent after a couple years of double-digit growth, according to the economists. *The Economist* was even bolder: "With prices looking overvalued in more states than ever in the past, average American prices may well fall for the first time since the Great Depression."

Because of pending earnings restatements, Freddie Mac and Fannie Mae have not published audited financials since year-end 2003. Two years ago Freddie remained optimistic, saying that outstanding residential mortgage debt totaled $7.8 trillion at year-end 2003 and was expected to increase to $17 trillion by 2013. That assumes an 8.25 percent growth rate, of which 5 percent is from price appreciation, as we discovered in the fine print.

[As most readers know, Fannie Mae and Freddie Mac were judged insolvent and became wards of the state in September 2008. The federal government placed them into conservatorships, acquiring 80 percent of the equity of each. Under government ownership, both are continuing to hemorrhage at the time of this writing in late 2010. Of course, by making or guaranteeing 90 percent of the mortgage loans made today, the government (as agent for the taxpayers) and its many housing finance appendages, such as FHA, Fannie, and Freddie, are on the hook in a very difficult market. Fannie and Freddie were emblematic of—and a tragic segue into—the story of risk management that already in 2005 was running wild.]

A Remarkable Story of Risk Management—Run Amok

Recurring throughout *A Decade of Delusions* is the following theme: "Manage the risks, and the returns will take care of themselves." Any look at the prospect for all types of investments would be grossly incomplete without a careful examination of the risks that one would have to assume to be in the game. As Alan Greenspan lamented above, the systematically diminished aversion to risk is the great facilitator of many economic or financial anomalies that end badly. Sometimes intuition leads us astray and other times to enlightenment, never making the decision-making process any easier by providing some inkling of the direction toward which it nudges us. In recent years, anecdotal tidbits from virtually every front have inundated my consciousness that are in clear conflict with the watershed concept of risk management so skillfully articulated by a man I held in the highest esteem, the late Peter Bernstein, in the oft-cited book *Against the Gods— The Remarkable Story of Risk*.

Please think of the next interlude as a delightful diversion, as we turn the clock back through time, with an important purpose as we wend our way up the mountain of wisdom. Bernstein did precisely what the title suggests: He made the study of the evolution of risk into a fascinating story that spans hundreds of years. Bernstein postulated that the probability theory upon which mathematically based risk-management techniques were developed was "one of the central ideas that distinguishes modern times from the more distant past." Instead of existing for centuries as the helpless, hapless victims of the whims of the gods of fate, through mathematical advances modern man discovered the means of quantifying uncertainty, turning from the suffocating fatalism of his ancestors to the spiritual renaissance that liberated his "free will" to make reasoned choices among alternative courses of action.

Daniel Bernoulli, one of eight precocious Bernoullis, in 1730 introduced the idea that an infinite variety of human expectations and preferences play a crucial role in the decision making process (and perhaps the forerunner of behavioral economics?). Bernoulli took issue with the cold mathematical calculation of expected values by arguing that what individuals value differs from person to person and therefore what should be measured is expected *utility*. He proposed that satisfaction resulting from any increase in, for example, wealth "will be inversely proportional to the quantity of goods previously possessed," explaining why there is a tendency for wealthier people to be more risk-averse than those who are less wealthy. Bernoulli advanced one of the most profound ideas in the history of thought in one page by allowing the introduction of subjective considerations with uncertain outcomes that cannot be counted in the theretofore staid mathematics of probability calculations. Separating mathematics from intuition, he turned his focus away from rote decision theory to an attempt to delineate the idiosyncratic proclivities of the risktaker himself.

This concept is so important that further elaboration will help embed it in our minds. Continued Bernstein: "The probability of being struck by lightning is tiny but many people are excessively terrified when they hear thunder." Then he makes a critically important statement: "[F]ear of harm ought to be proportional not merely to the gravity of the harm, but also to the probability of the event." Here is another major innovation: the idea that both gravity and probability should influence a decision. We could turn this assertion around and state that a decision should involve the strength of our desire for a particular outcome, as well as the degree of our belief about the probability of an outcome. The strength of our desire for something, which came to be known as utility, would soon become more than just the handmaiden of probability. Utility was about to take its place at the center of all theories of decision-making and risk-taking . . .

Bernoulli's thesis stood as the dominant paradigm of rational behavior for the next 250 years, roughly from 1730 to 1980, a time span longer than America's history as an independent nation, and became the foundation for modern principles of investment management. Perhaps the paradigm began a cyclical shift in the early 1980s as the cost of money saw-toothed downward over the next 20 years from 20 percent to 1 percent . . . From our perspective as wealth managers, we remain tethered to Bernoulli's world, the school of thought that acknowledges some correlation between wealth and risk aversion.

The Irreconcilability of Probability Theory and Irrationality?

Returning to my apprehensions voiced in the first paragraph of "A Remarkable Story of Risk Management—Run Amok," evidence abounds of these conflicts that logic argues should be extinct in the "age of the enlightenment." One can begin with the irrational acceptance of enormous and disproportionate risks that fomented the technology Bubble to its ultimately self-destructive mass, then move laterally to the use and eventual flagrant abuse of derivatives and other exotic so-called risk-management mechanisms that have brought the once-proud icon of creative finance, the moneymaking mortgage machine, Fannie Mae, to the point where it may someday have to lean on its benefac-tor, her ever-less-rich Uncle Sam. The LTCM (Long-Term Capital Management) crisis resulted from the comeuppance of unchecked arro-gance that blindsided "no bell" laureates in the fight to push the enve-lope, as the holders of the derivatives related to unexpected defaults in Russia experienced cascading losses, resulting in defaults and counter-party defaults, thereby requiring the Fed to reluctantly deploy its "too big to fail" parachute.

How, we wonder, with the advances in meteorological science and the long-held belief in the probability of a doomsday scenario that would make the Big Easy end up more like Atlantis than the home of the Mardi Gras, could Hurricane Katrina wreak such unimagina-ble havoc, no less in America and during the ascendancy and eventual preeminence of the information age at the dawn of the twenty-first century?[18]

---

[18][2005, original] Read about the "Black Swan" events as described in *Fooled by Randomness: The Hidden Role of Chance in the Markets and in Life*, First Edition, by Nassim Taleb.

How do we explain the proliferation of gambling, the fastest-growing industry in America, according to the *New York Times*—in a piece dated more than a decade ago, showing the longevity of this trend—despite the reality that the deck is forever stacked in favor of the house? Gambling draws more customers than baseball parks and movie theaters combined. Why doesn't the appalling statistical improbability of winning the lottery deter the millions of Americans who pony up obliviously, waiting in line weekly (and meekly) to voluntarily pay a tax on ignorance—supposedly the very ideas that "distinguish modern times from the more distant past"?

With the notional value of the latest iteration of risk-transference mechanisms, derivatives, growing worldwide at a breakneck pace and now totaling over $300 trillion (yes, that's *tr*, not *b*), will they, as Alan Greenspan argues in refusing to regulate them,[19] function like property and casualty insurance, proving to be a palliative in dispersing the consequences of uncertainty? Or, as Warren Buffett warned in the Berkshire Hathaway 2003 annual report, in the hands of many men and women whose motives are rooted in a five-letter word that begins with *g*, do they take on a seductive character that occasionally drives their handlers to madness?[20] "Derivatives are advertised as shedding risk for the system," writes Buffett, "but they have long crossed the point of decreasing risk and now increase risk. As with every company transferring risk to very few players, they are all hugely interdependent. Central banks are exposed to weaknesses."

The contest here is between the theorist and the pragmatist. Of course, Greenspan didn't have the benefit of Buffett's agonizing

---

[19][2005, original] The global credit glut and the burgeoning worldwide market for derivatives have emasculated America's central bank, the lord over the great credit creating machine. The genie is out, and the best efforts of men and governments are likely to be powerless in bottling him. Risk management has—for the time being, at least—returned to the hands of the gods.

[20][2005, original] According to Mike Stout, derivatives traders are paid on the "present value of their book at year-end. Derivatives are complex and extremely difficult to price, often leaving the trader with that responsibility." Thus, the fellow whose compensation is based on an estimate of the present value of a portfolio at a point in time, "marking to market" in industry parlance, is the same person who makes the determination. Need I ask, is there any incentive to *mis*mark? So much for checks and balances.

experience in unwinding the General Re (a Berkshire Hathaway sub-sidiary) derivatives book. Buffett could, as a consequence, be biased by a run-in with a narrow slice of reality. Don't bet your life's savings on the assumption of Buffett's limited exposure. Moreover, Buffett lives by a record that is both public and precise to the penny. Perhaps Greenspan had an epiphany when he realized that at the Fed there is no "box score," no irrefutable accountability. At last, the master of obfuscation had found his niche.

Is There a Chink in the Armor?

Far too wise to accept any notion, no matter how brilliantly devised, Bernstein sought out explanations as to how this system of mathemati-cally based risk-management techniques might go awry. Almost 300 years ago German scholar Leibniz observed: "Nature has established patterns originated in the return of events, but only for the most part." Leibniz's conditional phrase "but only for the most part" gave permanence to the presence of risk. Resorting to reverse reasoning, in a world where every-thing is predictable, no change would ever occur.

Bernstein continued to question his own thesis, acknowledging that:

> [T]he mathematically driven apparatus of modern risk manage-ment contains the seed of a dehumanizing and self-destructive technology. Harvard economist and 1972 Nobel laureate Kenneth Arrow has warned, "[Our] knowledge of the way things work, in society or in nature, comes trailing clouds of vagueness. Vast ills have followed the belief in certainty." In the process of breaking free from the past we may have become slaves of a new religion, a creed that is just as implacable, con-fining, and arbitrary as the old.

Adam Smith, according to Bernstein, a masterful student of human nature, defined the motivation for assuming outlandish risks as those defined above: "the overweening conceit which the greater part of men have of their own abilities and their absurd presumption in their own good fortune." Today we call such biases heuristics. While Smith was fully aware that economic progress was advanced because of man's pro-pensity to take risks, he feared that "society would suffer when that propensity ran amok." A century and a half later, English economist

John Maynard Keynes agreed: "When the capital development of the country becomes a byproduct of the activities of a casino, the job is likely to be ill-done." As I survey the scene, I can only imagine that both Keynes and Smith are rapidly rotating in their respective graves.

Suspension of Disbelief: Actions without Consequences

We all know that actions have consequences. Of course, Newton's Third Law, "Every action has an equal and opposite reaction," applied to tangible objects. Outside of Newton's physical realm, think of the ongoing consequences of the terrorist attacks of September 11, 2001. Earlier it was noted that sociologist Robert K. Merton divided unintended consequences into willful ignorance or true ignorance. Like a stone thrown in the pond, who knows how far the ripples will spread before they dissipate? The genesis of all this craziness is no doubt deeply rooted in the global credit glut, showering down cheap and easy money like a spring rain that turns into a torrential downpour, which short-circuits the rational decision-making process, putting most individuals on an equal and lowly footing, tempting them to mindlessly swing at sucker pitches. This easily transmuted into the age of materialism where success and the presumed "good life" are measured almost exclusively in financial terms. Could it also be envy as we allow television to invade our minds below the threshold of awareness, marinating our minds with countless stories of stock-option billionaire executives, a strange new world where work and reward bear little relationship? Flashing back to the first of Mahatma Gandhi's *Seven Deadly Sins* . . . does such subliminal conditioning evoke Pavlovian responses, exacerbating our discontent with comparatively modest standards of living and insidiously, akin to the ringing bell, cause us to salivate when we see images of our "entitled" slice of the American Dream pie, however unlikely the notion? Was it ignorance or envy that led hordes of 401(k) investors down the garden path to the technology stock-mania trap?

It seems we have suspended a fundamental law of nature: Actions have consequences. While examples abound, no couple is as devoid of contrition for their misdeeds and flippant disregard for consequences as pop-culture icons Donald Trump and Martha Stewart, the king and queen of insolence, improbity, and bad hair as they shamelessly fight for the limelight in look-alike "reality" shows, both named, rather appropriately, *The Apprentice*. (The Donald seems to be winning the battle of unmitigated gall but admits that Martha's likely-to-be moth-balled copycat version has cost him ratings points.) While Trump's ongoing troubles with the banks are generally negotiated off camera, Stewart's ups and downs are in the public domain. As a proxy for her mercurial popularity and the madness of crowds, Martha Stewart Living Omnimedia went public in late 1999, hitting $50 before crashing to $5 in late 2003. Once the uncertainty of her fate was resolved, the stock zoomed to $37, only to settle back to around $20 as the true colors of the diva of duplicity became more vivid to the slow learners. When she invoked the name of Nelson Mandela, South Africa's long-imprisoned and persecuted anti-apartheid hero, saying, "Many, many good people have gone to prison," she effectively indicted herself, exposing her true character like no grand jury ever could.

Obviously, the problem is much more deeply seated; these carica-tures of reality are a mere convenience. The message from the leader-ship of our nation reveals the depth of the intentional denial of the ultimate consequences of politically expedient actions or inactions.

"I CAN'T GET THE LEFT SIDE OF MY BRAIN
TO SHUT UP LONG ENOUGH TO LISTEN TO
WHAT THE RIGHT SIDE IS TELLING ME."

SOURCE: Copyright © 1997 Bill Monroe.

What is "my fellow American" to take away from Uncle Sam's reck-lessly irresponsible behavior in taxing too little or spending too much; condoning if not facilitating runaway trade deficits; and talking about but never actually taking remedial responsibility for the toxic Medicare and Social Security time bombs, cobbling together quick fixes so they will blow up on someone else's watch?

S&P 500 Earnings Dissected

Beginning in 2003 we at Martin Capital Management started taking a close look at the makeup of the most commonly used benchmark index, the S&P 500, the one against which we compare our equity performance annually. As you may recall, earnings were presented in so many different ways that S&P took it upon itself to attempt to define a new standard: core earnings, which we examined with a fine-tooth comb in 2004. While obfuscation still rules the day, I think the U.S. economy is heading in the right direction, albeit grudgingly.[21]

Again, as you might recall, the 50-year history that we at MCM used as a basis for projecting future earnings was predicated on answer-ing the question: Is there any compelling reason to change our assumptions about long-term growth rates in GDP, net profit margins of businesses, the percentage of earnings that are reinvested in the busi-ness? Apart from a prolonged business slowdown on the dark side or a sustainable increase in productivity on the bright side, we concluded that the 6 percent growth rate is the most supportable extrapolation factor at this juncture.

Since the S&P 500 represents 71.5 percent of the value of all domestic common stocks ($11.3 trillion out of a total of $15.8 trillion),

---

[21][2005, original] We'll let you know next year the extent of chicanery involved as corporations try to outfox the regulators by finding ways to minimize the impact on earnings from new rules in 2005 that require expensing stock options in accordance with FAS 123(R). After reading the rules, it's clear that there's lots of wiggle room. For example, companies can choose among lattice models, such as the traditional Black-Scholes or the Monte Carlo simulation model. How sig-nificant is the issue? According to Standard & Poor's, the accounting rules would have reduced reported 2004 earnings among the S&P 500 not insignificant 7.4 percent.

Table 9.1   S&P 500 Sector Breakdown

As of 6/30/2005	Market Weighting	Approximate Percentage of S&P Earnings	P/E
S&P 500 Composite	100%	100%	18.8
Energy	8.8%	13.8%	12.0
Materials	3.0%	3.8%	14.6
Industrials	11.2%	10.3%	20.4
Consumer Discretionary	11.4%	6.3%	34.4
Consumer Staples	10.1%	9.9%	19.1
Health Care	13.4%	9.9%	25.3
Financials	20.3%	29.3%	13.0
Information Technology	15.1%	11.4%	24.9
Telecommunication Services	3.2%	2.0%	29.3
Utilities	3.5%	3.3%	19.8

you might find it interesting to see how the index data appear when broken out into sectors (Table 9.1).

Of most concern is the financial sector. Whether it's the explosion in the use of derivatives or the proliferation in the progressively more risky forms of mortgage lending to finance the residential housing boom (and corresponding house-price Bubble), among others, the eventual unwinding of the financial economy will likely have a severe impact on financial sector earnings.[22] The derivatives-related write-offs at Fannie Mae and Freddie Mac, likely to exceed $10 billion by some

---

[22][2005, original] Unlike manufacturing, current finance and insurance company earnings are estimates. Until loans have been collected or insurance policies are no longer in force, the adequacy of the reserves (a noncash expense) deducted from current revenues will be unknown. Reserves are estimated based on past experience. Given the concentrations in the financial-services industry, past loss experiences could well be a poor indicator of future losses. As for derivatives, we have insufficient experience to quantify their risk profiles. They could become the black hole in the financial-services galaxy.

margin, are just the tip of the iceberg. While we don't have histori-cal S&P data on financial-sector earnings, we do have data from the Bureau of Economic Analysis on the National Income & Products Accounts (NIPA) going back to 1929. Apart from massive losses in 1932–1933 that included the Bank Holiday, financial earnings repre-sented around 15 percent of corporate profits during the 1930s; mid-single-digit percentages during the 1940s; between 10 and 15 percent in the 1950s and 1960s; and the high teens during the 1970s and 1980s, hitting a low of 12 percent in 1984. During the 1990s financial earn-ings averaged roughly 25 percent, ranging from 20 to 30 percent. The percentage jumped dramatically as the new millennium began: 2000, 27.5 percent; 2001, 40.2 percent; 2002, 41.2 percent; 2003, 38.7 per-cent; and 2004, 33 percent. Now with the financial sector comprising almost a third of S&P 500 earnings, how can one not conclude that the money changers are running the game? It should be noted that the financial sector doesn't include the earnings from the huge finance sub-sidiaries of such companies as GE and GM but does include substantial earnings from the insurance industry.

To be sure, bank consolidations mentioned above may have con-tributed to a larger number of financial-industry companies that are included in the S&P index. To the extent that those consolidations have had a greater impact on S&P earnings than the combinations within manufacturing, S&P earnings would be skewed in favor of the finan-cial-services sector. However, the NIPA data referenced above are from all companies, public and private, in the financial-services indus-try and are, therefore, unaffected by consolidations within the industry. Besides, liberated from restrictions on size because of interstate dereg-ulation and the handcuffing of Glass–Steagall, the industry that has a reputation for lemming-like behavior is now in a position, as you can infer from John Dugan's comments above, to do monumental damage. Lest we become too enamored with money—and the grand profits that are being earned by its handlers—it's helpful to remember that it also is the ultimate commodity. There's very little room for differentia-tion in the long run. As for commercial banks in general, their history is resplendent with the uncanny capacity to play "follow the loser," mindlessly jumping from one folly to the next. How, we wonder, can such a cutthroat industry earn so much money? After years of miscues,

Table 9.2 S&P 500 Core–Earnings Adjustments

	1996	1997	1998	1999	2000	2001	2002	2003	2004 Est.	2005 Est.	2006 Est.
Operating EPS	40.63	44.01	44.27	51.68	56.13	38.85	46.04	54.69	67.68	76.64	85.38
As Reported EPS	38.73	39.72	37.71	47.17	50	24.69	27.59	58.74	58.55	69.69	76.80
Option Exp PS	−.49	−1.12	−1.56	−2.5	−3.82	−5.31	−5.31	−3.51	−3.3	−3.36	0
Pension Int Adj.	−.12	−.05	−.33	−.14	−2.68	−5.07	−5.01	−1.4	−1.41	−2.25	−1.94
Other Net Pension Adj.	−.9	−1.11	−1.42	−2.28	−2.69	−2.26	−1.99	−.91	−.46	−.7	−.58
Goodwill	.03	.181	.24	.16	.83	2.47	6.91	1.13	2.32	2.62	1.51
Gains & Losses PS	−1.36	−2.5	−4.45	−4.24	−3.28	1.58	1.19	−.79	−1.2	−1.56	−1.10
OPEB PS	.03	.05	.07	.13	−.34	−.39	−.35	−.62	−.68	−.75	−.81
Sett & Litigation PS	−.01	.16	.47	.76	.9	.4	.83	1.47	1.37	1.40	1.12
Reversals PS	−.01	−.03	−.11	−.14	−.06	−.1	−.19	−.05	−.04	−.14	−.18
Core PS	35.90	35.31	30.61	9.91	38.86	16	23.66	44.04	55.16	64.95	74.82

have they finally seen the light? I wouldn't take that bet if the odds were 10 to 1!

As an aside, asset returns in banking are around 2 percent or less, but profit margins, interest, and non-interest income less all expenses average somewhere in the low teens, favorably skewing the average profit margins for the S&P 500 upward. Not only that, the low price/earnings ratios from the financial sector—particularly if those earnings prove to be unsustainable at current levels—cause the S&P 500's price/earnings ratio to be understated. The same could be said for the energy sector.

Standard & Poor's estimates that 2005 trailing core earnings will approximate $65 (Table 9.2), resulting in a price/earnings ratio of 19.2, with the S&P 500 index at almost 1250 at year end. Looking forward, we should anticipate negative pension-fund adjustments to the core earnings calculation if the market stays flat or heads downward—in addition to the eventual reduced contribution from the financial sector. Of course, if an implosion of the housing Bubble occurs, and recession follows, we once again must hearken back to the "perfect storm" scenario.

Rather than writing in generalities, it may be instructive to carefully examine the list of industries that constitute the industrial sector and compare that list to those industries that make up the financial-services sector. Think about each industry and its contribution to your economic well-being.[23] Need more be said . . . ?

----

[23][2005, original] The industrial sector includes the civil or military aerospace and defense industries, building products from cement to lumber; nonresidential construction and engineering industry; electrical components and equipment; heavy electrical equipment; industrial conglomerates; construction equipment, farm machinery, heavy trucks, and non-military shipbuilding; industrial machinery; air freight and logistics; airlines; marine transportation of goods or passengers, ports, and services; railroads, including owners and operators of roads, tunnels, and rail tracks; trucking; airport services; trading companies and distributors of industrial equipment and products; commercial printing services; providers of commercial electronic data processing services; diversified commercial professional services to businesses and governments, including commercial cleaning services, consulting services, correctional facilities, dining and catering services, document and communication services, equipment repair services, security and alarm services, storage and warehousing, and uniform rental services; human resource and employment services related to human capital management, including employment agencies, employee

We end this analysis with the beginning in mind (in an admitted reversal of Stephen Covey's dictum, "Begin with the end in mind"). Why are stock prices 126 percent of GDP when the 80-year average is 61 percent? If we think of the post-1990 period as the historical anomaly that it appears to be, the average ratio is more like 45 percent. Trendline earnings growth rates have been slightly better than 6 percent,[24] albeit with dramatic short-term deviations. Profit margins, as noted above, are likely artificially inflated by the financial-services industry. On the other side of the coin, those information-services companies that are not subject to cutthroat competition—for example, the better software companies, including the likes of Microsoft, Google, and many others—do have superior margins. As of July 2005, however, information technology and telecommunications combined represented only 13.4 percent of S&P 500 earnings. Of course, the productivity benefits ripple throughout the economy. The question then becomes: Do they trickle down to the bottom line, resulting in

---

training, payroll and benefit support services, retirement support services, and temporary agencies; environmental facilities services, including waste management, facilities management, and pollution control services; office services, supplies, and office equipment.

By contrast, financial services include diversified banks; thrifts and mortgage finance, including government-sponsored enterprises like Fannie Mae; consumer finance services, including personal credit, credit cards, lease financing, mortgage lenders, travel-related money services and pawn shops; specialized finance, including credit agencies, stock exchanges, and specialty boutiques; asset management services and custody banks, including mutual funds; financial institutions primarily engaged in investment banking and brokerage services; insurance brokers; insurance and reinsurance brokerage firms; property and casualty insurance; life and health insurance; and real estate investment trusts and real estate management and development.

[24][2005, original] In terms of the GDP, if we choose as our starting year 1991 when nominal growth slowed to 3.2 percent and conclude in 2005, economic growth averaged a compounded rate of almost 5.4 percent. That number includes the slowdown in 2001 and 2002 where nominal GDP growth dropped down to the 3 percent–plus range again. During that same span of years, S&P earnings grew by almost 11 percent, compounded. Earnings in the long term cannot exceed the growth rate of GDP. Please note that we are comparing nominal GDP growth with S&P earnings per share. As pointed out elsewhere, it's our opinion that share repurchases in the aggregate did not dramatically increase earnings per share vis-à-vis the underlying nominal earnings growth.

a permanent improvement of profit margins? For myriad reasons, we think that unlikely. With regard to 20-year U.S. Treasury bond yields, averages mean nothing. In the interval between 1926 and 1964, yields remained under 4 percent. From the mid-1960s until 2005, interest rates tracked a relatively symmetrical but jagged inverted V, reaching a peak of almost 14 percent in 1981. Overall, the fall in bond prices from 1964 through 1981 and the subsequent rise from 1982 through 2005 (which rather precisely, and not coincidentally) parallels the movement in stock prices in the two major secular market cycles that Buffett describes above. There is, however, nothing one can glean from the study of the history of interest rates. It also would be difficult to take into consideration where interest rates might be five years from now, from which one could make a strong case that stock prices should not regress toward the average ratio of total market capitalization to GDP.

A Short Ending to a Long Story

In summary, we have written this reasoned, dissenting minority opinion, in contrast to the prevailing majority view, believing we have probable cause and substantial grounds to argue against the case of a resumption of the general rise in stock prices that investors have come to expect by simply extrapolating (mindless mathematics) the experience of the 1980s and 1990s, the common but illogical practice of viewing the future through the rearview mirror. We began by piecing together the publicly disclosed insights of the "three wise men": Alan Greenspan, Ben Bernanke, and John Dugan. If nothing else, they should convey some sense of the imbalances created when cheap and easy money bring about an environment where the fundamental economic law of supply and demand has been abrogated in the credit markets. In an unfettered market, interest rates fluctuate in the direction of the "clearing price" (interest rate) that achieves a balance between the supply of and the demand for credit. Atypically, the price of credit remained low and did not rise because the glut of supply satiated, if not incited, exaggerated demand. We also have observed that benign consumer price inflation is not so much the product of a vigilant Fed as it is a salutary consequence of low-labor-cost global competitors, most conspicuously China, saturating U.S. markets with cheap imports. Parenthetically, if ours were a closed economy, few would argue that the fiscal and monetary policies of the last three or four years would have been highly inflationary on the consumer-price front.

The easy-money "financial" economy, rather than promoting consumer-price inflation, has, like squeezing a balloon, precipitated asset inflation instead. We've observed the malinvestment consequences as the technology stock market Bubble, and the illogical and eventually ill-fated investment spending spree in telecommunications, came to a costly end as the new millennium began. As for the epidemic of speculation that has metastasized to residential real estate and other asset classes—the fallout looms as a threat of unknown proportions. History leaves us no choice but to conclude that the "financial" and "real" economy consequences will almost certainly be anything but pleasant.

Going from the general to the specific, we see no evidence that the price of the S&P 500, the benchmark against which we measure ourselves, reflects an adequate margin of safety. The price-earnings ratio, given the risk scenario, is on the wrong side of the long-term average. To be sure, the future is always uncertain. It's how little heed the market currently pays to these uncertainties that gives us pause. All we need to know is that the opportunities forgone today are likely to be less appealing than the opportunities that may appear in the future. We believe that a rational man must conclude that the odds are, in the main, unfavorable, that patience is a virtue and that you only have to swing mightily at a few fat pitches in a lifetime to make the financial Hall of Fame. In the meantime we are busily stockpiling investment ideas that have every attribute we consider essential—except a purchase price that compels us to make the capital commitment now. That critical variable is not under our control, and it is a formidable test of our patience to await its arrival, particularly without any assurance that it will come. For some securities it's common for prices to change by 50 percent or more in a year. Price changes of this magnitude simply do not occur in other fields such as farming, real estate, energy, and so forth. If we are ready, the opportunities can be huge.

■ ■ ■

The Perfect Storm Redux[*]

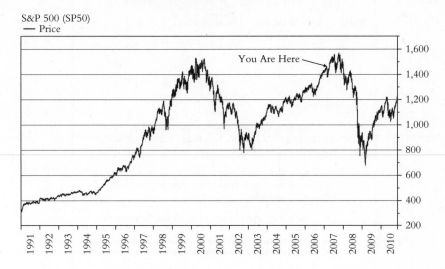

SOURCE: © FactSet Research Systems.

The late, irrepressible Peter Bernstein, introduced above, was one of my heroes, a man of great intellect, courage, and conviction. As you will recall, I quoted extensively from *Against the Gods — The Remarkable Story of Risk* earlier in this chapter in "A Remarkable Story of Risk Management—Run Amok." The following was excerpted from a *Money* magazine interview with Bernstein in October 2004 and provides additional insights into the depth and breadth of this most extraordinary man:

> In Wall Street's herd of narrow and twitchy minds, [Bernstein] is patient wisdom personified. Over the vast sweep of his long career, he has probably learned more about more aspects of investing than anyone else alive. Even a summary of his career puts most "experts" to shame: classmate of John F. Kennedy at Harvard, intelligence officer during World War II, researcher at the Federal Reserve Bank, economics professor, money manager, pioneer in investment analysis, historian, expert on risk and author.

---

[*]This material is adapted from the 2006 annual report of Martin Capital Management.

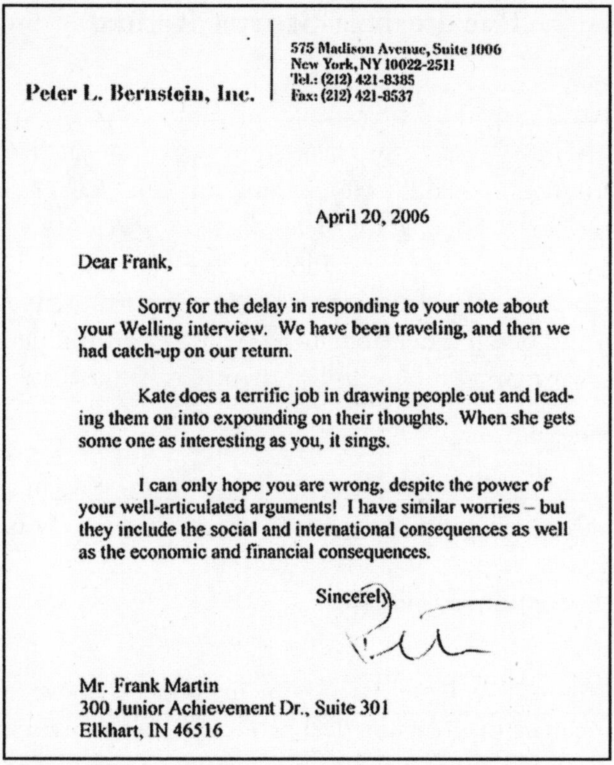

Peter L. Bernstein, Inc.

575 Madison Avenue, Suite 1006
New York, NY 10022-2511
Tel.: (212) 421-8385
Fax: (212) 421-8537

April 20, 2006

Dear Frank,

Sorry for the delay in responding to your note about your Welling interview. We have been traveling, and then we had catch-up on our return.

Kate does a terrific job in drawing people out and leading them on into expounding on their thoughts. When she gets some one as interesting as you, it sings.

I can only hope you are wrong, despite the power of your well-articulated arguments! I have similar worries – but they include the social and international consequences as well as the economic and financial consequences.

Sincerely,

Mr. Frank Martin
300 Junior Achievement Dr., Suite 301
Elkhart, IN 46516

Figure 9.3   Letter from Peter Bernstein

After reading my friend Kate Welling's piece on "The Perfect Storm?" Bernstein sent me the note shown in Figure 9.3.

Bernstein's note left me in a quandary. As usual, his field of vision was much broader than mine and instead of giving me some encouragement that I was barking up the right tree, he reminded me (in effect) that word *tree* was meant to be plural. My initial reaction was cerebral overload as I hearkened back to the sign posted outside the Springfield Retirement Community (from an archive of *The Simpsons* TV show), "Thank you for not discussing the outside world." My immediate afterthought is the immensely "helpful" word of caution from a subway station sign, "For your safety, please do not exit the tram while it is in motion." Thus you have "The Perfect Storm Redux" . . .

Stuck on the tram, I returned to *Money* for further direction from Bernstein:

Markets are shaped by what I call "memory banks." Experience shapes memory; memory shapes our view of the future. In 1958, younger people were coming in who had a different memory bank [when bond yields first rose above stock yields and have remained so for almost 50 years]. That's also what happened [in 1999] when tech stocks were enormously exciting; most of the new participants in the market had no memory of what a bear market is like, and so their sense of risk was muted.

Bernstein went on to say:

Understanding that we do not know the future is such a simple statement, but it's so important. Investors do better where risk management is a conscious part of the process. Maximizing return is a strategy that makes sense only in very specific circumstances. In general, survival is the only road to riches. Let me say that again: Survival is the only road to riches. You should try to maximize return only if losses would not threaten your survival . . .

For those who exude confidence in their perspicacity today, Bernstein might look them straight in the eye and inquire:

Can you manage yourself in a bubble, and can you manage yourself on the other side? It's very easy to say yes when you haven't been there. But it's very hot in that oven. And can you save your ego, as well as your wealth? I think I might have just said something important. Your wealth is like your children—the primary link between your present and the future. You should try to think about it in the same way. You want your children to have freedom but you also want them to be good people who can take care of themselves. You don't want to blow it, because you don't get a second chance. When you invest, it's not your wealth today, but it's your future that you're really managing.

How vivid is your memory of the inflationary nightmares of the 1970s? Bernstein contended that nobody under 50 really experienced it, as they were then too young to be accountable decision makers. The historian that he was, Bernstein thought sustaining that distant memory was more important to the future than all the fresher memories of the tech Bubble and its aftermath.

Seth Klarman is another kindred spirit whom I visited in Boston in 2005 and who was kind enough to write a testimonial for *Speculative Contagion*. By way of pedigree, Klarman, president of the Baupost Group, averaged about 20 percent per year for 24 years with only one negative year. Like Peter Bernstein and the undersigned, Klarman is fanatical about managing risk in this environment—or any environment for that matter. The following is an excerpt from the September 2006 issue of *Superinvestor Digest*:

Focus on Risk before Focusing on Return
Seth Klarman's foremost principle of operation is to maintain a high degree of risk aversion.

- Rule #1: Don't lose money. Rule #2: Never forget Rule #1.
- Klarman believes that the primary goal of value investors is to avoid losing money.
- There are three key elements of Klarman's value-investment strategy:
  - A bottom-up approach, searching via fundamental analysis
  - Absolute-return strategy
  - Pay attention to risk

Cash is the ultimate risk aversion. But clients are uncomfortable. Why should people pay a money manager to hold cash? They are paying the manager to wait for the opportunity to invest.

Think of the assets under management as if it is your own money. What other people think doesn't matter . . . Ignore questions like "How does it look to our clients and peers?"

Peter Bernstein's and Seth Klarman's warnings about the hazards of disregarding, underestimating, or denying risks left me no choice but to revisit the subject nobody wants to talk about: a possibility that the confluence of different forces from different directions could, sometime, somehow, somewhere result in an financial and/or economic storm so unexpected and devastating as to be called by the unusual name "perfect."

Finally, another wag who eschews slavish adherence to the established doctrine and whose record of remarkable secular forecasts (because he's always thinking far ahead of the crowd) puts him among the visionary elite—for example, the forecasting of the "crash" of 1987, the incredibly prescient peak-of-the-market declaration of the end of the Japanese Bubble economy and market in 1989, the iconoclastic advocacy of purchasing gold in 2001 before it doubled, among others . . . Marc Faber, who also lent his good name in an endorsement for *Speculative Contagion*, is not nearly so oblique as the rest of us! During a January 8, 2007, Bloomberg Television interview Faber unabashedly advised that global assets are poised for a

> severe correction, and it's time to sell. In the next few months, we could get a severe correction in all asset markets. In a selling panic you should buy, but in the buying mania that we have now the wisest course of action is to liquidate.

Please rest assured that at MCM we are prepared for virtually any eventuality—except for a stock market that goes through the roof. Although we don't think we, or anyone else for that matter, can consistently forecast with precision (and we know of some other calls that Faber made that did not materialize) we listen nonetheless.

Capitalism: When "Financial" Overwhelms "Commercial"

Hyman Minsky was a twentieth-century American economist and prolific thinker and author whose genius, like that of Sir Isaac Newton, was exceeded only by his humility.[25] Neither man allowed egocentric preoccupations to stymie his precocious intellectual development. Two remarkably self-effacing insights were attributed to Newton: "If I have seen further [than certain other men] it is by standing upon the shoulders of giants" and "If I am anything, which I highly doubt, I have

---

[25][2010] Recall the reflections from Ernest Dimnet (see opening quotation of Chapter 7), to say nothing of Charlie Munger and the importance of vicarious learning (most of us fail to follow the simple adage: "Life is too short not to make every effort to learn from the mistakes of others").

made myself so by hard work." Similarly, Minsky was self-deprecating in assessing his far-reaching contributions to the world of economics and finance, admitting (in terms remarkably similar to Newton's) that he stood taller because one foot was on the shoulder of John Maynard Keynes and the other on the shoulder of Keynes' occasional ideological rival, Joseph Schumpeter.

In 1974 Minsky observed a fundamental characteristic of our economy that linked finance and economics: "The financial system swings between robustness and fragility, and these swings are an integral part of the process that generates business cycles." Moreover, the prevailing financial structure is a central determinant of the behavior of the capitalist economy, according to Minsky. Likewise, the dynamism of profit-driven motives (which George Soros calls the "principle of reflexivity" in his book *Alchemy of Finance* and which sociologist Robert K. Merton defined as a self-fulfilling prophecy) influence economic activity within the context of a given institutional structure in that the structure itself changes in response to profit seeking. Resonating with Schumpeter, Minsky emphasized that:

> [F]inancial markets will not only respond to profit-driven demands of business leaders and individual investors but also as a result of the profit-seeking entrepreneurialism of financial firms. Nowhere are evolution, change, and Schumpeterian entrepreneurship more evident than in banking and finance, and nowhere is the drive for profits more clearly the factor making for change.

Think about Minsky's prescience . . .

The financial system takes on special significance in Minsky's theory, not only because finance exerts a strong influence on business activity but also because this system is particularly open — or, as some might claim, prone — to innovation, as is abundantly evident today. Continues Minsky: "Since finance and industrial development are in a symbiotic relationship, financial evolution plays a crucial role in the dynamic patterns of the economy."

In addition to emphasizing the relations between finance and business, Minsky identified progression through at least five distinct stages of capitalism. The five stages can be labeled as follows: merchant capitalism (1607–1813), industrial capitalism (1813–1890), banker capitalism

(1890–1933), managerial capitalism (1933–1982), and money-manager capitalism (1982–present). Charles J. Whalen, introduced subsequently, also refers to the latest iteration, "global finance capitalism," beginning in 1994. The broad historical framework that Minsky developed in the last years of his life has gone almost unnoticed. According to Minsky, money-manager capitalism "became a reality in the 1980s as institutional investors, by then the largest repositories of savings in the country, began to exert their influence on financial markets and business enterprises." The *raison d'être* for money managers, and basis by which they are held accountable, is the maximization of the value of the investments made by fund holders. Not surprisingly, business executives became increasingly attuned to short-term profits and the stock-market valuation of their firm.

The growing role of institutional investors fostered continued financial-system evolution by providing a ready pool of buyers for securitized loans, structured finance products, and myriad other exotic innovations about which you will read presently. It also fueled the trend toward mergers, acquisitions, corporate restructurings, leveraged buyouts, and stock buybacks—since fund managers have a strong incentive to support whatever initiatives promise to boost near-term portfolio value. In the 1980s these managed-money funds often provided the resources that corporate raiders (remember T. Boone Pickens, Ivan Boesky, and all who followed?) needed to secure corporate control. Money-manager incentives—often in combination with the force exerted by growing international competition and rapid technological and product/market changes—also encouraged corporate downsizing and reengineering. Consider comedian Ben Stein's observation, "If the laws say you are responsible, for heaven's sake change them," and it's clear that masters of the private economy left little to chance as they provided their own incestuous encouragement to the evolution of the financial system by removing many regulations imposed during the New Deal in the 1930s.

Tax-law changes also have encouraged takeovers, buyouts, and other types of corporate restructuring. While the impact on labor varied considerably, the rise of the defined-contribution 401(k) plan that has systematically displaced the defined-benefit pension plan communicates volumes. Workers must now shoulder responsibilities for their own financial welfare for which they often are ill-prepared. The "age of empowerment" may prove to be a tragic mistake. Authority without responsibility is the equivalent of a handgun in the grasp of a minor.

A decade ago [now 15 years ago] Minsky prophesied that money-manager capitalism would become increasingly global and that further international economic integration would take place in the years ahead. Here's a brief sampling of his comments on these matters: "Managed money capitalism is international in both the funds and the assets of the funds. *It has rendered obsolete the view that trade patterns determine the short-run movement of exchange rates*" [emphasis added]. *Voilá!* At last an explanation for the dollar's stubborn, though perhaps temporary, resilience.

Minsky: A Prequel?

In what could be a prequel to that which may someday lie ahead, Minsky (who was only 10 years old in 1929) reflected on the years leading up to the Great Depression. The following excerpt [emphasis added at several points] is from a paper, "Hyman Minsky's Theory of Capitalist Development," by Charles J. Whalen, Institute for Industry Studies, Cornell University.

Although the years between 1908 and 1929 were not recession-free, they were depression-free and generally prosperous—a sharp contrast with the American experience from 1866 through 1908. Because the U.S. capital market was free from any significant policy constraints prior to 1933, any regulation had to come from within the financial community. But the relative stability and prosperity attracted not only new investors but also new investment bankers to the industry (many commercial banks, for example, formed investment banking affiliates in the 1920s). While the older firms were more conservative in their practices, the new firms were "aggressively engaged in expansion of their business." Moreover, close ties between some investment companies and speculative interests meant that their policies contributed more to market instability than to stability.

According to Guilio Pontecorvo's [another eclectic economist and a professor at Columbia] landmark study of the 1920s, investment-banking firms had become victims of their own success. Pontecorvo writes that the effect of entry into investment banking in the 1920s "was to reduce the relative importance and the leadership role of the original firms. Furthermore, the industry developed a large competitive fringe. This fringe of highly competitive firms had a considerable effect on the behavior of the industry." He concludes: "The overall impact of these changes was the elimination of any internal controls that may have been present in the earlier period. The instability in the structure created by the rise of new firms was a factor in the *security inflation* that followed." In classic Minskian fashion, success bred daring—and when the speculative Bubble burst, not even the nation's great investment banking houses could contain the collapse. It was at this point that Minsky turned to the insights of Schumpeter. In a 1986 essay, Minsky wrote:

> The task confronting economics today may be characterized as a need to integrate Schumpeter's vision of a resilient intertemporal capitalist process with Keynes' hard insights into the fragility introduced into the capitalist accumulation process *by some inescapable properties of capitalist financial structures.*

Minsky believed that such integration was possible because Schumpeter and Keynes had a common perception of the task of economics: "[T]hey each define the problem that economic theory must explain as the path of development of an accumulating capitalist economy through historical time." From this perspective, the economy is a complex, time-dependent system. Society is an "evolutionary beast," changing in response to endogenous factors, not an equilibrium seeking and sustaining system.

The Depression made manifest the need for public action to stabilize economic activity in the face of business downturns. *Due to the divergence between individual and collective rationality*, it was nearly impossible for individual bankers, businessmen, and farmers to do anything except cut loans, slash prices, reduce employment, and increase agricultural yields—all of which made matters worse in the aggregate. Franklin Roosevelt's answer was the New Deal, a series of policies and reforms that ushered in the next stage of U.S. capitalist development.

On financial innovation, in 1993 Minsky wrote:

> To understand the short-term dynamics of the business cycle and the longer-term evolution of economies it is necessary

to understand *the financing relations that rule, and how the profit-seeking activities of businessmen, bankers, and portfolio managers lead to the evolution of financial structures* . . . Consumer sovereignty is subordinated to the vision of entrepreneurs and the critical analysis of bankers in determining the path of the economy.

Drawing on Schumpeter, Minsky noted that the banker/financier is the "ephor" (controlling figure) of a market economy, and that the central bank is the ephor of the ephor. Since *policy interventions in the economy are the product of political processes,* Minsky stresses that the path through time of an economy is a *political economy phenomenon.*

Further, Minsky calls merchant capitalism and banker capitalism "commercial capitalism" and "financial capitalism," respectively. Marc Faber, my friend mentioned earlier who calls Hong Kong home, refers to the same phenomenon but by more prosaic names: the "real" economy and the "financial" economy, as described in the 2004 and 2005 annual reports [Chapter 7 and the first two-thirds of this chapter, respectively].

The Evolving History of Economics and Finance: Reflections

The current liquidity-induced stock market rally should be of interest only to those whose perspective is short term. Not drifting from our investment mandate, our ever-evolving portfolio posture continues to run counter to the prevailing sentiment. We've become especially focused on liquidity, as ready access to cash in what may be a radically different and profoundly attractive opportunity set ahead is of paramount concern.

Careful readers of this volume have no doubt committed the two charts, which appeared in the middle of Chapter 7, to memory (!), so they will not reappear here. The first chart, the historical trend in the ratio of the market value of all publicly traded U.S. equities to GNP/GDP, serves as a rough measure for the ebb and flow of the valuation of common stocks in general. The second chart displays the trend in the ratio between total debt and GDP.

Information on both charts is calculated as follows. The data for the aggregate market cap to GDP ratio use the Wilshire 5000 index as the numerator and the trendline estimate of GDP for 2006 based on actual 2005 data. The numerator is $17.7 trillion (including $1.6 trillion owned by "insiders"), and the denominator is $13.2 trillion, indicating a ratio of 134 percent. We consider this information to have a high degree of accuracy. The range for the 70 years ending in 1995 was from our market lows of below 30 percent to bull-market highs around 80 percent. The average is 60 percent. By this crude measure, domestic common stocks, in the aggregate, are selling at more than twice the 80-year average.

Equally problematic is the ratio of total debt to GDP. We do not believe that a precise number can be provided because of the existence of the double counting of real estate-related debt when viewed at a point in time. We estimate the Total Credit Market Debt to GDP ratio to be 330 percent. The ratio reached 270 percent in the depths of the Great Depression, only to fall back to between 120 and 140 percent for the almost 50 years leading up to the early 1980s, where once again it began its long ascent to record highs.[26]

No matter how generous you are in interpreting the above big-picture data, it corroborates the details that Doug Noland and others have provided. Fred Sheehan Jr., whom I quote in Chapter 7 and introduce in the following paragraph, adds his own interpretation of the growing debt relative to GDP. "Between 1920 and 1980, every dollar of growth was supported by about $1.40 of new debt. The ratio is $7 of borrowing to a dollar of growth today. This," he notes with a touch of sarcasm, "is economically unproductive but financially remunerative." The connection between the financial and the real economies, as Faber or Minsky would avow, is ultimately inseparable. Either a greater share of GDP is dedicated to servicing the burgeoning debt, or the assets (phantom or otherwise) are liquidated in distress—and the creditors end

---

[26][2010] As of September 2010, the market capitalization to GDP ratio was approximately 95 percent, while the debt to GDP ratio was approximately 275 percent, essentially the same as in 2006. Calculation of this ratio is most difficult because of double-counting issues, to which even the most sophisticated seem unaware.

up using the then worthless "certificates of confiscation" to paper their crumbling walls.

According to my aforementioned Bostonian friend and collaborator Mr. Sheehan, who often writes erudite essays for Faber's publication *The Gloom Boom, & Doom Report*, the "financial markets owe much to illusion." In a December 2006 historical essay, "War of the Nerds," Sheehan laments the complacency toward risk among most investors and the attendant nonchalance toward the possible consequences. In a particularly compelling story, Sheehan recounts the several unheeded warnings by a prominent central banker who described the economy as:

> living on the edge of an abyss if taxes and spending were not addressed. [The banker] then observed that if nothing were done, the first trouble would be some basic questions about convertibility of the dollar . . . the government will be forced to consider imposing direct controls over wages, prices and credit.

Federal Reserve Chairman William McChesney Martin issued these and similar warnings in speeches in 1965 and later in 1968. Martin's warnings came to fruition on that fateful day in August 1971 (not to be confused with the fateful August day three years later, the culmination of Watergate) when President Nixon opted off the gold standard and imposed temporary wage and price controls.[27] Parenthetically, it was in the evening following that Sunday afternoon presidential announcement

---

[27][2006, original] By the early 1970s, as the Vietnam War accelerated inflation, the United States as a whole began running a trade deficit for the first time in the twentieth century. The critical turning point was 1970, which saw U.S. gold coverage deteriorate from 55 to 22 percent. This, in the view of neoclassical economists, represented the point where holders of the dollar had lost faith in the ability of the U.S. to manage its budget and trade deficits.

In 1971 more and more dollars were being printed in Washington, then being shipped overseas to pay for government expenditures on the military and social programs. In the first six months of 1971, $22 billion fled the U.S. In response, on August 15, 1971, Nixon unilaterally imposed 90-day wage and price controls, a 10 percent import surcharge, and most importantly "closed the gold window," making the dollar inconvertible to gold directly, except on the open market. Unusually, this decision was made without consulting members of the international monetary system or even his own State Department and was soon dubbed the "Nixon Shock."

that, in utter disgust, I took pen in hand and began writing essays on the capital markets and the economy. It must've been the tipping point [see next chapter]. I've kept on writing ever since. So let me make this perfectly clear: Feel free to blame my penchant for purple prose on Richard Nixon!

Sheehan's essay begins (as this essay concludes) with a repeat-for-emphasis reiteration of the thought-provoking quote from George Eliot's tragic story, *Silas Marner*:

> The sense of security more frequently springs from habit than from conviction, and for this reason it often subsists after such a change in the conditions as might have been expected to suggest alarm. The lapse of time during which a given event has not happened is, in this logic of habit, constantly alleged as a reason why the event should never happen, even when the lapse of time is precisely the added condition which makes the event imminent.

[Dear reader, it is hoped that Chapter 9 was as intriguing as it was arduous! In the grand scheme of things, 2005 and 2006 were both pivotal and momentous. The perfect storm—the confluence of so many forces, potentially destructive when aggregated—was taking form.

The chapter attempted to identify some of the more diverse factors, as pernicious as the cause and effect of the well-above trendline advance in housing prices to a monetary policy that led to a distortion in asset prices, and as subtle as the progressive disregard for risk in critical areas of the economy and financial system that made it possible for the storm to grow unchecked. Whether looking at the unsustainable innovation in the financial system by examining the composition of S&P earnings or examining the conflicted regulatory environment in the reorganization of investment banks to transfer risks away from their partners, the financial sector of the U.S. economy was certain to be a key driver of the inexorably accelerating doomsday machine.]

Chapter 10

The Tipping Point

S&P 500 (SP50)
— Price

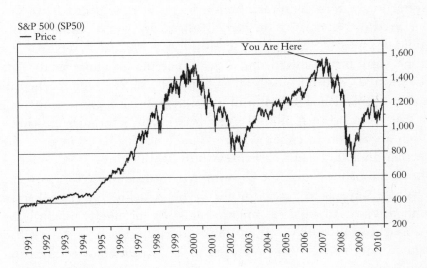

SOURCE: © FactSet Research Systems.

Chapter 10 begins with a brief excerpt from Martin Capital's Quarterly Capital Markets Review, July 2007, followed by the draft of a letter dated the same month in which I proposed to explain to MCM clients a potential "put option" hedging strategy. The next section, "What's Up, Doc?," was published as part of an ongoing sequence of Quarterly Capital Markets reviews, this one in October 2007. The chapter concludes with the 2007 annual report, published in February 2008.

When, the reader might wonder, did the vague notion that had been germinating in my mind for some time—the sum and substance of Chapter 9—about "things ending very badly" become sufficiently concrete in my thinking that I actually took action to capitalize on it?

On May 5, 2007, I was a man with a mission among an otherwise teeming throng of Buffettites, a potpourri of 25,000 mostly Berkshire Hathaway shareholders, at the Qwest Center in downtown Omaha, Nebraska. Almost as a coincidental indicator of the popularity of common stock investing since the early 1980s, the crowd had grown exponentially from the several hundred who were present when I first journeyed to Nebraska in the early 1980s to lay eyes on the man who would become my "mentor in absentia." My attendance was sporadic in the years that followed, but I again became a regular in the late 1990s as the crescendo in the popularity of risk assets approached its peak—a coincidental indicator of my ever-growing apprehensions.

For several years running I had woven my way through the queue to put a question to either Warren Buffett or Charlie Munger at the meeting. In 2007 I had a particularly burning question to ask, one that I knew probably could not be answered forthrightly. My query did not cause anyone to reach for his or her Blackberry. Had Warren responded as I thought he might, but knew he likely couldn't, the financial world would've turned. The quotation below is what I had written. I don't recall how closely my spoken words followed the script tucked away in my pocket.

> Warren, having read and reread your (2006) chairman's letter, I was particularly struck by your "help wanted" ad for an eventual successor to you and Lou Simpson to oversee Berkshire's investments in marketable securities.
>
> Instead of advertising for a Ted Williams, the Hall of Famer to whom you often refer because of his rational approach to

becoming a hitting legend, you proposed to recruit the consummate defensive player. Here are your words, and I quote: "We therefore need someone genetically programmed to recognize and avoid serious risks, *including those never before encountered.* Certain perils that lurk in investment strategies cannot be spotted by use of the models commonly employed today by financial institutions." In a world where everyone's talking about return, you talk about risk.

What I inferred from this job description, your warnings on derivatives, the dollar, executive compensation, the Gotrocks family and its "handlers," your preference for private deals over publicly traded stocks, among others, is that in general since 1999 your assessment of the investment environment in marketable securities does not appear to be radically different from how you felt exactly 30 years ago, when you more or less took a multi-year hiatus from marketable securities because you simply didn't like the odds. Am I reading you correctly? I would hope that Charlie might give his two cents' worth as well.

Excerpt from Quarterly Capital Markets Review, July 2007

As expected, neither Buffett nor Munger answered my question directly. What Warren did say, according to my notes, while being obligatorily obtuse, was: "When I closed the Buffett Partnership, I felt (and wrote to my investors) that the prospective return was about the same for equities and municipal bonds over the next decade, and I was roughly right. It's not the same today. I'd have 100 percent of bonds in short-term bonds. *Forced to choose* between owning the S&P 500 vs. 20-year bonds, I'd buy stocks—and it would not be a close decision. But I wouldn't have an equity investment with someone who charged high fees. We don't have the faintest idea where the S&P or bonds will be in three years, but over 20 years we'd prefer to own stocks."

Fortunately, we at MCM are not forced to choose between two extremes, nor are our fees high! Nonetheless, throughout the Berkshire Hathaway 2006 annual report (the aforementioned chairman's letter) and the answers at the annual meeting on May 5, Buffett's and Munger's mosaic of responses resembled the composite picture I had in my mind's eye: *"The key to long-term investment success is to avoid wealth-destroying catastrophes."*

[Excluded are several pages of my notes on comments from both Buffett and Munger during the four- to five-hour hour Q&A on which the above italicized conclusion was based.

I returned from Omaha with my own assessment confirmed by reading the tea leaves in Omaha. While the number of weak links in the world's financial phantasmagorical chain was multiplying, I narrowed my focus to the more aggressive U.S. investment banks and soon prepared the draft of a letter to clients explaining my action plan. At least in the financial sector, the tipping point was at hand. The three-page letter follows.]

Draft of Letter to MCM Clients, July 2007

At a recent meeting of Martin Capital's five-member Kitchen Cabinet, all of whom are clients, I presented a rather unconventional strategy that I am using in my personal accounts. (It is separate and apart from the use with many of you of S&P 500 LEAP put options to at least partially protect our equity positions against catastrophic risk.) Recall the Keynesian quotation from the Quarterly Capital Markets Review you just received: "Worldly wisdom teaches that it is better for reputation to fail conventionally then to succeed unconventionally." Much to my surprise, the cabinet members were interested in learning more and suggested that the strategy be shared with all clients.

To begin, the strategy employs the use of the most common derivatives, stock options, and yet it is still sufficiently complex in its entirety that many may find it difficult to evaluate the risk/return trade-offs. In addition, the imperturbable temperament essential to be able to tolerate the losses (and possible gains) with equanimity—however moderate they are relative to your portfolio size, until or even if events cause the strategy to appear farsighted—is relatively uncommon. In effect, you will be placing your trust in my understanding of the complexities and interdependence of the various components that must come together fortuitously to make the strategy a success. This particular situation has not arisen during my 40-year investment lifetime and it's quite possible that I have misjudged or misevaluated one or more of the critical elements. Finally, timing is critical to the optimal success of this strategy. Unfortunately, I could easily be months, if not years, early.

In the context of my overall portfolio I think the strategy is well within my tolerance for risk, the definition of which is articulated in any number of MCM annual reports. Equally surprising, I would judge my risk tolerance to be lower than many of our clients. Unconventional behavior can be quite conservative just as conventional behavior can be terribly risky. For example, one of the main reasons we are so under-invested in common stocks vis-à-vis other managers in this market is because, in my judgment, we are currently grossly underpaid for the risks we thereby assume. Our more conventional brethren are either impervious to the risk/return imbalance, see it as the price they must pay to be in the game, or are in denial.

Those who do not feel comfortable at this point should probably stop reading here!

If you're still with me, I'll break the strategy down into its two primary components. First, a combination of factors has given rise to some huge but so far largely disregarded risks in the financial services sector, as addressed in the [July 2007] Quarterly Capital Markets Review [excerpts above]. Unprecedented technology and communications developments, copious amounts of leverage made possible by sometimes fleeting liquidity, and the increased complexity in financial innovation and "tight coupling" have created a *Demon of Our Own Design—Markets, Hedge Funds, and the Perils of Financial Innovation*, the title of the book by Richard Bookstaber that captures poignantly the systemic nature of the risks. The reality that they are woven together informally but with an unavoidably tight interdependence among similarly constituted firms, particularly in times of crisis, can result in highly irrational behaviors. These excitable emotional responses, exacerbated by the self-perpetuating nature of informational feedback loops, can have potentially dramatic effects on the prices of those securities. The companies about which I am writing are the major investment banks on Wall Street: Goldman Sachs (Figure 10.1), Bear Stearns (Figure 10.2), Lehman Brothers (Figure 10.3), Merrill Lynch (Figure 10.4), and so forth. Unlike the portfolio insurance scheme of 1987, an unwinding of the above may not impact the security markets as a whole as they did in 1987. It's hard for me to imagine, however, that the major players on

Goldman Sachs Group (GS-US)

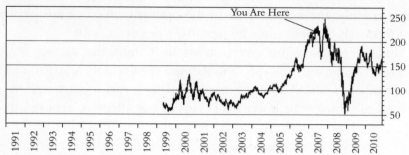

Figure 10.1   Goldman Sachs Group Stock Price History
SOURCE: © FactSet Research Systems.

Bear Stearns Companies (BSC. 1)
— Price

Figure 10.2   Bear Stearns Companies Stock Price History
SOURCE: © FactSet Research Systems.

Lehman Brothers Holdings (LEH)

Figure 10.3   Lehman Brothers Holdings Stock Price History
SOURCE: © FactSet Research Systems.

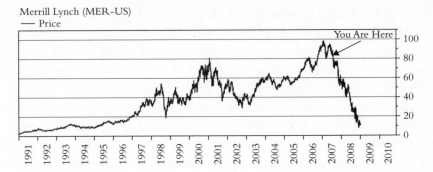

Figure 10.4 Merrill Lynch Stock Price History
SOURCE: © FactSet Research Systems.

Wall Street can avoid a body blow to their balance sheets and income statements should the system under which they are operating malfunction in unison. Should that occur, I would expect their shares to drop dramatically.

If you're curious, read everything you can on the Bear Stearns subprime mortgage funds debacle. It's a telling example of the systemic risk that, through contagion, could have the same effect on the major Wall Street houses as it had on the market in 1987. The thesis is that there is enormous risk, most of which is undisclosed and even covered up, at these highly leveraged institutions of which the public is unaware. Whether a "normal accident" becomes an extraordinary one—like Long-Term Capital Management—cannot be forecast. And whether, should a meltdown occur, it infects the broader market is unknowable. While very important, it is not germane to this particular strategy.

The second component is the means by which one capitalizes on such a meltdown, if and when it occurs. Most of you have been exposed to put options, which are exchange-traded derivatives, quite unlike the more exotic over-the-counter variety that are subject to serious mispricing risk by the counterparties and their traders whose incentives to acquiesce to "moral drift" are extremely high because of the mega-bonus money at stake. In any event, I am purchasing deep-out-of-the-money six months or so put options on these companies.

Let's examine the strategy from a worst-case/best-case perspective. For the sake of argument, assume your annual capital commitment to the strategy is the equivalent of what you earn if all your assets were invested in Treasury securities at 5 percent. A $5 million portfolio would thus commit $250,000 per year. If all the put options purchased every six months over a two-year period expire worthless, your loss from the strategy will be 5 percent of your portfolio per year or $500,000 in total dollars. While the best case is impossible to know in advance—and is highly dependent on adroit purchases and sales—it could be substantial. If the options appreciate 25 times, your total pretax gain is $6.25 million.[1] Your rate of return will depend on whether a meltdown occurs soon, after you've invested $125,000, or later, after investing $500,000. Keep in mind, always framing everything in the worst-case scenario, two years from now you could be $500,000 less wealthy with nothing to show for it. That, of course, is what keeps 99.9 percent of the investors on the sidelines. As for me, since that reluctance keeps option premiums low, that's why I'm in the game.

Referring to the second sentence in the introduction to the 2006 annual report [not excerpted in this book], please read the following:

> To paraphrase, Munger advises that one should continuously search and wait for conspicuous, logical, and simple investment opportunities that will be recognizable as such. They will be few and far between, but if one bets heavily when the odds are highly favorable, "using resources available as a result of prudence and patience in the past," one's lifetime investment results will be improved dramatically.

---

[1][2010] Readers may be curious about how the 25-times number was derived. Using a hypothetical example, assume the shares of an investment bank were selling at $100 when the put options were purchased. The strike price, 40 percent out of the money, was, therefore, $60. In economic terms, the share price had to fall to $60 before the options were "in the money," and therefore had any "intrinsic" value. (While too esoteric for the short discussion, changes in the "implied volatility" of the option contract could—and in fact did—cause the prices of the contracts to increase manyfold, well before the stock price declined below the strike price.) For the sake of simplicity, let's focus on intrinsic value alone. If the stock declined 45 percent, the options would be $5 in the money (the $60 strike price less the market price of $55). If the purchase price of the option on a per-share basis was $.20 (a close approximation of the low premiums that existed at the time), by simply dividing the $5 by the $.20 cost of the option, one arrives at the 25-times payback. Not wishing to overstate the case in the letter, it isn't difficult to calculate the payback if the stock fell 50 percent or more.

Whether what I am doing meets Charlie's criteria is open to question. Although nominally I'm not committing large amounts of my portfolio capital, by using options and the leverage that they provide I am creating the same effect. The difference is that I know precisely what my maximum loss could be.

I've only begun to establish my positions. I will complete them when and if option prices provide an appropriate risk/return trade-off. If a meltdown should occur before the positions are completed the gains will be much less than hoped for. Should you decide to join me, I will, to the best of my ability, purchase options for you at prices equal to or more attractive than the purchase prices for my own account.

Almost all of my own portfolio replicates that of our "typical" client. (As noted earlier, at MCM we like to say, "We eat our own cooking.") Throughout my investment life I have lived by the rule Charlie Munger espouses above. At the time of each commitment it always looks extreme, at least relative to everyone else. Often the payoff is extreme, at least relative to everyone else! Who said making money was easy?![2]

—Frank Martin, CFA

---

[2][2010] Because of the complexity of the transaction and the absence of any identifiable catalyst—and the fact that my dire concerns about the nature of the risks in and among the investment banks were not widely embraced (at least in terms of degree)—the rest of the MCM research team was understandably reticent to present the idea to clients. For similar reasons, the members of the Kitchen Cabinet opted out. As noted in my letter, I was far more convinced about *if* than I was *when*. Time is money. So the letter remained a draft; it wasn't sent out. Errors of omission occur in our profession every day, and it serves no purpose to cry over spilled milk. I have many such errors (of omission) to my name as well. While, for obvious reasons, specifics will not be provided, I feel an obligation not to leave the reader hanging. In my own personal accounts where I purchased the put options, the return exceeded even the best-case number presented in the letter. The timing was perfect, if not actually a little early. Lest you form the wrong opinion of my perspicacity, it wasn't until I read *The Quants* by *Wall Street Journal* reporter Scott Patterson, published in 2010, that I discovered just how close to the abyss the banks were in the summer of 2007. Truth be told, the trade of a lifetime was probably about 20 percent skill and 80 percent pure luck. Please do not interpret that statement as false modesty. If I had been truly prescient and steadfast in my convictions, I would have purchased 18-month options and held them through thick and thin on the way to Armageddon.

[By the fall of that year, more evidence that we were reaching the tipping point came flooding in. Following is the quarterly letter to clients distributed in October 2007.]

Quarterly Capital Markets Review, October 2007: "What's Up, Doc?"

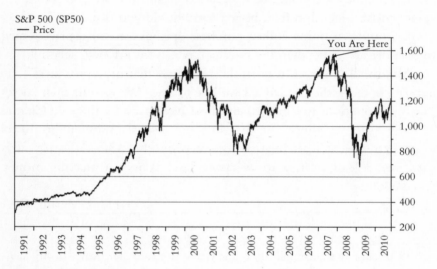

SOURCE: © FactSet Research Systems.

The title could be a catch-all rhetorical question for a flummoxed investment advisor—or a quizzical one for Ben Bernanke, PhD, or any of the Goldman Sachs alums who, like puppeteers, really pull the strings behind the curtain of the financial economy. The title also could be a chance for you to practice your Bugs Bunny imitation if the reading gets tedious or, simply, an allegory depicting the folly and farce that constituted the prelude to what became the 1972 hit comedy by that name. Take your pick! As for the detail provided, chaotic times require more of an explanation than stable ones. For those who prefer thumbnail sketches, you need not tread beyond the following bullet points. For those who desire a little suspense, skip the thumbnails.

- Using the analogy of waves and tides, to the trained eye there seems to be a once-in-a-generation tectonic shift in pricing risk under way, obscured temporarily with the ambient noise associated with a credit crisis and the headline-grabbing regulatory response.

- Writings emanating from MCM are designed to exhibit continuity from one to the next so that these easily overlooked sea changes don't go undetected until it's too late to react.
- At this point the epicenter of the crisis is Wall Street and its environs, and it is there that we have found the fissures that triggered and will likely continue to exacerbate the crisis.
- The "Minsky Moment" provides a great but obscure economist's philosophical framework for what is happening in the day-to-day world.
- Was the Fed's double-barreled 50-basis-point cut in rates also double-barreled in attempting to stave off recession, as well as shore up asset prices? Probably, also proving that, public utterances notwithstanding, the Fed is not always rational and reflective in times of crisis.
- What will be the second- and third-order effects (unintended consequences) of the Fed's actions? Will the cut in rates have its desired effect? We think not.
- Given everything that we have read, studied, and (in part) assimilated, we have concluded that more financial and perhaps economic headwinds—separated by tempting respites—lie in wait. While this is hardly a forecast, such an environment will not likely treat overall common-stock prices kindly.

"WHAT WE NEED AROUND HERE IS A POSTIVE CASH FLOW."

SOURCE: Copyright © 1996 Bill Monroe.

Cyclical or Secular? The Current Crisis in the Larger Context of Cause and Effect—Connecting the Dots through Time

Readers who have paid close attention to the annual and quarterly reports received from Martin Capital Management over the years have no doubt observed that there is a continuity or flow to them—like chapters in a book still being written. This communication approach is intentional. As decision makers on your behalf, this type of disciplined, reflective, benchmarked thinking helps us maintain equanimity throughout the inevitable ups and downs in the financial markets and to remain focused and rational when others, less grounded, may allow emotions to get the upper hand. Even though we all live in the present, in our role as investors we must think like futurists: We must always try to visualize the environment in which we will reap so that, in the here and now, experience-based rationality will determine when and where to sow. Many corporate annual reports we read are discrete (though hardly discreet), marketing-oriented documents, written by PR people, with predominantly a one-year, rearview-mirror time horizon. It's unsettling to read five consecutive years in one sitting, all the while wondering if it's the same company as you go from one report to the next. That's a literary luxury that makes no business sense and one we seek to avoid at all costs.

The July 2007 Quarterly Capital Markets Review [written in late June 2007 and excerpted above] is a telling case in point. You may be well-served by rereading it carefully. Sometimes it's easier to understand where you are by looking back at your footprints in the sand to see your route. This is particularly true when you find yourself in a crisis: shifting the metaphor, to see more clearly in what has, within a few short months, become a confusing, smoke-filled room. Is it little more than overcooked food on the stove (reminding me of the all-too-common announcement, "Dinner will be ready when the smoke alarm goes off"), or is the eye-burning, toxic signal more ominous? If at this moment you think the smoke has cleared, we strongly urge you to hasten to the nearest exit. What should be clear to everyone at this point is that nobody who's pushing products or ideas on or from Wall Street, as broadly defined, wants to see prices go down or a recession follow . . . under any circumstances. It wouldn't hurt to pass everything you read—and see/hear in the media—through that filter.

Of Waves and Tides (and the Crucial Difference Between)

To clear the air, at least in terms of the previous subhead, *cyclical* refers to events that recur in irregular patterns. In the economic context, business expansions and contractions are often referred to as *cycles*. Their patterns are unpredictably asymmetrical and, though cause and effect are linked, the connection is tenuous at best. *Secular*'s most common definition connotes worldly, as opposed to spiritual, happenings. In the economic vernacular, *secular* refers to a very long-term trend. If cycles are the waves, secular trends are the tides. The action of the waves is discernible to anyone in a beach chair at the ocean's edge. The tides, on the other hand, are as surreptitious as they are powerful: undetectable unless you sit patiently and watch by the hour as the waves ever so subtly creep toward you or away from you. That is precisely the perspective from which we write. It may become dangerous to your financial health to allow yourself to become enamored with the waves if this predilection causes you to lose sight of the tides.

Most of us are "anchored in the present," with the future being viewed as little more than simple extrapolation of the past. Business cycles have occurred with enough frequency in years gone by that most investors and business people are aware of their existence, if only with the benefit of hindsight. It's the tectonic shift of the secular trends that often go unnoticed until it's too late, and then the apparent cause-and-effect relationship appears shockingly disproportionate: to wit, the Asian tsunami of December 2004. It is the tsunami effect that Warren Buffett expects his successor as manager of Berkshire's marketable-securities portfolio to not only *under*stand but to be prepared to *with*stand.

Quoting Seth Klarman (Baupost Capital's brilliant manager), we have often challenged those who find it too arduous to think beyond the present with the notion that tomorrow's "opportunity set" may be shockingly different from today's. If you compare this report to the one written three months ago, there should be no lingering doubts about the practical relevance of Klarman's observation. For those looking for the philosophical underpinnings of that concept, please return to the opening lines of Chapter 7.

The Misalignment of Incentives and the Opaque World of High Finance

The epicenter of the current financial crisis is and remains Wall Street—and is therefore a good place to start in divining whether what we're seeing is an entire iceberg or only its tip. Hardly without precedent, the same can be said about the crises in 1987 and 1998, about which more is written below. Wall Street, long prophesied to become the mad financial alchemists of today, made the subprime-mortgage, hedge-fund, and private-equity overindulgence possible. [Hyman Minsky, introduced in the last chapter, once again appears center stage below. While there will be some repetition, Minsky's message is so profoundly relevant that adding emphasis through reiteration is intentional.]

Recently reporting third-quarter results were the large investment banks, originators and benefactors (at least until lately) of unprecedented and what have proven to be profoundly risky innovations in structured finance and other esoterica. Given the turmoil in the credit markets, including but not limited to the blight of subprime mortgages, the results appeared relatively benign, perhaps suspiciously so. Let's mention how they keep score because there's a world of difference between your portfolio with MCM and those of the "financial titans." Virtually all the securities you own are actively traded, and access to up-to-the-minute market-price information is instantaneous. Tangentially, any individual client can turn his or her portfolio to cash rather immediately and with modest concession to the prevailing market price. Of course, as Keynes noted, there is liquidity for some but not for all.

Under a new accounting rule, the titans live under different rules from the likes of you and me. The titans are required to distinguish between financial assets that have real market prices (Level 1) versus those based on models (Level 2) and those that are little more than management guesses (Level 3).[3] The bulk of the titans' financial assets

---

[3][2007, original] The firms began breaking down their financial assets into these "levels" at the start of their current fiscal year, which began in December, when they early adopted a new accounting standard related to fair, or market, value measurement. All U.S. companies will have to begin using it for financial years starting November 15.

fall into the mark-to-model category—or Level 2. The survival instinct manifests itself in times of financial turmoil. The panicking, drowning man is so singularly consumed with filling his lungs with air that his rescuer may himself become the second victim of the first victim's fear of suffocation. In like fashion, mark-to-model becomes mark-to-myth concurrent with a certain but unquantifiable migration in asset classifications from Level 2 to 3. Asset values thus become murkier as a financial crisis worsens. Not surprisingly, the short-term incentive to realize gains on whatever assets are above water in Level 3 assets (and to defer losses) justifies any means if there's an end that appeals to the most basic of instincts: survival. Postponing the probable in hopes that the winds will shift so that it won't become the inevitable is the kind of doomsday-deferral reasoning that permeates much decision making in times when rationalism is temporarily suspended. Complicating things is the effect of mushrooming financial leverage over the last four or so years, amplifying the effect of good and bad choices.

Finally, the hundreds of trillions of dollars in notional value of over-the-counter derivatives are not included in Level 3 asset totals. Thus far the sleeping giant, the one that dwarfs all others, has avoided being infected with the liquidity virus. Earlier dispatches have warned of what has come to pass. This one, peering into an always uncertain future, remains resolutely cautious, suggesting that the eye of the storm has yet to pass.

A "Minsky Moment"

Returning to Hyman Minsky,[4] a sequence of financial events can foment a "Minsky Moment," often enveloped in the fog of uncertainty. The stage is first set by "a prolonged period of rapid acceleration of debt" in which more traditional and benign borrowing is increasingly replaced by borrowing that depends on new debt to repay existing loans. Then the "moment" occurs, "when lenders become increasingly cautious or restrictive, and when it isn't only over-leveraged structures

---

[4][2007, original] References to Hyman Minsky are attributable to my friend and Minsky cohort, Charles Whalen, PhD.

that encounter financing difficulties. At this juncture, the risks of systemic economic contraction and asset depreciation become all too vivid."

Minsky's reading of John Maynard Keynes rests on Keynes' appreciation of the distinction between risk and uncertainty. According to Keynes, a situation involving risk is one where probabilities can be assigned with confidence, whereas a situation involving uncertainty is different—in that there are no precise probabilities to rely on. In a situation characterized by uncertainty, said Keynes, our knowledge is based on a "flimsy foundation" and is "subject to sudden and violent changes." Increasing financial leverage faster than means to service it can turn risk into uncertainty. Such an unstable environment is anathema to orderly investment in the pursuit of accumulation of wealth. Keynes' notion of uncertainty does not support the efficient-market hypothesis, but rather its opposite, which Minsky dubbed the financial-instability hypothesis (FIH).

According to Minsky's theory, the financial structure of a capitalist economy becomes more and more fragile over a period of prosperity—evolving from borrowers being able to pay back interest and principal when due right down the slippery slope to the terminal phase (Ponzi finance) when debtors must borrow even more to make interest payments on their existing liabilities. During the buildup, enterprises in highly profitable areas of the economy are rewarded handsomely for taking on increasing amounts of debt, and their success encourages similar behavior by others in the same sector (because nobody wants to be left behind due to underinvestment). Increased profits also fuel the tendency toward greater indebtedness by easing lenders' worries that new loans might go unpaid.

Concurrent with the growing demand for credit is that its suppliers begin to see lending as an innovative, profit-driven business. Minsky writes that bankers and other intermediaries in finance are "merchants of debt, who strive to innovate with regard to both the assets they acquire and the liabilities they market." Both the evolutionary tendency toward Ponzi finance and the financial sector's drive to innovate are easily connected to the recent situation in the U.S. home-loan industry, which has seen a rash of mortgage innovations and a thrust toward more fragile financing by households, lending institutions, and purchasers of mortgage-backed securities.

The expansionary phase of the financial-instability hypothesis leads eventually to the Minsky moment. The starting point is when it becomes clear that a high-profile company or a handful of companies have become overextended and need to sell assets in order to make their payments (read: Bear Stearns et al.). Then, since the views regarding accepted liability structures are subjective, the initial shortfalls of cash and forced selling of assets "can lead to quick and wide revaluations of desired and acceptable financial structures." Not Minsking words, the renowned economist writes, "Whereas experimentation with extending debt structures can go on for years and is a process of gradually testing the limits of the market, the revaluation of acceptable debt structures, when anything goes wrong, can be quite sudden."

Without intervention in the form of corrective action, usually by the central bank, the Minsky moment can engender a meltdown, involving asset values that plummet from forced selling and credit that dries up to the point where investment and output fall and unemployment rises. This is why Minsky called FIH "a theory of the impact of debt on [economic] system behavior" and "a model of a capitalist economy that does not rely upon exogenous shocks to generate business cycles."

If left unchecked, the Minsky moment can become a "Minsky meltdown," a spreading decline in asset values capable of producing a recession. Still the question remains unanswered: Has the moment "Ben" checked by the Fed to avoid a meltdown?

Understanding the Fed's Motives: Shore up Assets or Stave Off Recession?

In times of crisis, decisions are often made by selecting the least immediately threatening alternative among multiple evils. Think of it as a financial triage. In remarks on September 22 at a conference in Frankfurt, Germany, marking the fiftieth anniversary of the Deutsche Bundesbank, Federal Reserve Vice Chairman Donald Kohn defended the central bank's aggressive interest-rate cut, saying it was driven by concerns about the broader economy rather than an interest in protecting investors or the value of housing. Trying to disabuse investors of the notion that the "Greenspan put" (that the Fed would react to falling asset prices by slashing the discount rate as it did in the bear market of 2000–2002) would become the "Bernanke put," Fed Governor Kevin Warsh reiterated that the Fed's next move depends on economic events, rather than on financial markets. "The goal of our policy . . . is not to look at any particular asset class" but instead is to watch "what's happening in the real economy." Rhetoric notwithstanding, Bernanke looks more and more like a Greenspan with facial hair.

During a September 6 talk at the Brookings Institution, former Chairman Greenspan seemed to echo the case for a rate cut—but for a more esoteric reason:[5]

> Business expansions are driven by euphoria and contractions by fear. While economists tend to think the same factors drive expansions and contractions, the contraction phase of the economy is quite different, [with] fear as a driver, which is going on today, is far more potent than euphoria. What strikes me about the current period is it's wholly consistent with my generalized view of how important innate human characteristics are in sustaining the business cycle.

Greenspan questioned the prevailing notion that the housing-wealth effect is, in fact, symmetrical on the upside and downside. Citing academic literature (remember Daniel Bernoulli?), Greenspan confirmed his belief in the idea that, for most of us, the pain of a dollar of loss is far greater than the pleasure of a dollar of profit:

> Fear is the driving force on the downside. Elements of wishful thinking and euphoria form the upside. When we look at the external world it's very obvious. Fear is a far more dominant projector of action than is euphoria or anything like that. The division of labor . . . essentially creates competition and specialization and hence rising productivity and growth. Fear invariably

---

[5][2007, original] On several occasions in the past Greenspan has departed from a straightforward probabilistic approach to decision making, as he is doing now. Because of the asymmetry of outcomes, particularly in these times, Greenspan (and Ben Bernanke) fear the consequences of consumer-price deflation more than they do incipient inflation. By erring on the side of excessive accommodation, they risk triggering another asset bubble, a crumbling dollar, and other second- and third-order effects.

and universally induces disengagement, and disengagement is negative division of labor.

On that occasion Greenspan also shifted his commentary from the economy to the markets, saying the current market turmoil is in many ways "identical" to what occurred in 1987, the infamous "Black Monday" crash, and 1998, when the then giant[6] hedge fund Long-Term Capital Management nearly collapsed:

> The behavior in what we are observing in the last seven weeks is identical in many respects to what we saw in 1998, what we saw in the stock-market crash of 1987, I suspect what we saw in the land-boom collapse of 1837, and certainly [the bank panic of] 1907.

The euphoria in human nature takes over when the economy is expanding for several years, leading to bubbles, "and these *bubbles cannot be defused until the fever breaks.*"

Bubbles can't be deflated through incremental adjustments in interest rates, Greenspan suggested. The Fed doubled interest rates in 1994–1995 and "stopped the nascent stock-market boom" but, when stopped, stocks took off again. "We tried to do it again in 1997" when the Fed raised rates a quarter of a percentage point, and "the same phenomenon occurred."

"The human race has never found a way to confront bubbles," he said. *What Greenspan neglected to advise was what, if anything, the central bank can or should do when the fever breaks . . . and the day of reckoning approaches? With the free markets reacting by pushing long-term bond prices down (and yields up), no doubt in response to fears of rising inflation and escalating uncertainty simultaneous with the Fed calling for the presses to print more money, how can this bode well for home or stock buyers?*

Sounding eerily Greenspan-esque, Mr. Kohn, while acknowledging that the Fed's actions—through low interest rates early this decade—helped fuel the start of the latest housing boom, he deflected the cause

---

[6][2007, original] Eight years later the commodity hedge fund Amaranth lost $6 billion—or 75 percent of its value—in the month of September 2006 alone. While eclipsing Long-Term Capital Management in size, the event was soon to be relegated to afterthought. Conditioning helps take surprise out of the unexpected.

(appropriately, in my opinion) to the workings of crowd psychology. Said Kohn:

> I suspect that, when studies are done with cooler reflection, the causes of the swing in house prices will be seen as less a consequence of monetary policy and more a result of the emotions of excessive optimism followed by fear experienced every so often in the marketplace through the ages.

The Cheap Money chart (Figure 10.5) depicts credit spreads, how risk is priced for different-quality debt securities over time. When the spreads are narrow, lenders demand less of a premium in interest rates from less-credit-worthy borrowers and, according to Minsky, later in the cycle, from progressive relaxation of standards to overnight tightening, the opposite is true. As you examine the chart, the question that could immediately come to mind is: "Has the pendulum started to swing and, if so, when will it gain enough momentum to crush any resistance and run its course?"

Second- and Third-Order Effects of Central Bank Intervention

Far more interesting are the second- and third-order effects—those unintended consequences of the Fed's discount-rate cut, along with the

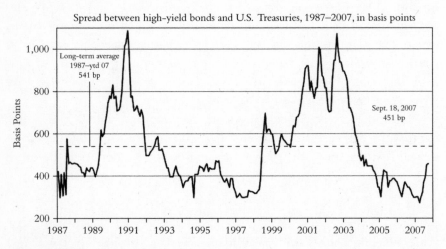

Spread between high-yield bonds and U.S. Treasuries, 1987–2007, in basis points

Figure 10.5   Cheap Money
SOURCE: JP Morgan Chase.

Open Market Committee's parallel action that often has a more powerful impact on human behavior, the financial markets, and the economy
than the more obvious first-order changes.

Friend Jim Grant summed up the relative strength of the dollar
(compared with what it would be on a trade-weighted basis) in one short
sentence: "The twenty-first-century dollar is a miracle of suspended
disbelief."

"Without financial failure," the governor of the Bank of England
adjured on September 12, "genuine financial success is impossible." He
went on to warn that if "wayward banks and their careless depositors
could always depend on their hovering governments for timely succor,
the world would be impoverished." Moreover, he continued, "the provision of large-liquidity facilities penalizes those financial institutions that
sat out the dance, encourages herd behavior, and increases the intensity
of future crises." Five days later the British Treasury moved to squelch
an old-fashioned run on Northern Rock, the United Kingdom's fifth-
largest mortgage lender. That UK depositors were acting a bit squirrelly
likely reflects their lack of experience with such uncertainty. A day later
the Fed announced its 50-basis-point reduction in each of its twin target
interest rates. Given the global nature of what seems to be unraveling,
perhaps it's not only a flight from the dollar but a flight from money in
general, the aforementioned Jim Grant opines. The 6.5 percent year-
over-year change in consumer prices in China has not caused a ruck-
us . . . yet. Continuing debasement of currency may be one of the most
pernicious second-order effects.

Lest we forget, in a zero-sum game one person's gain is another's
loss. By reducing the cost of short-term money to borrowers, the Fed,
in exact proportion, cuts income of savers, including foreigners financing our twin deficits. Think about the second-order effects of that
on both parties. What will be the effect on economic activity if the
income to savers is reduced at the same time the rate cut does nothing
to cause the lenders to trust their recalcitrant borrowers any more than
they did before? If lending contracts at the same time that income to
savers falls, the scenario begins to look a lot like Japan in the 1990s. In
a similar vein, although gross debt outstanding has increased dramatically worldwide, there has been no change in net debt. For every borrower there must be a lender. What will be the second-order effects of
engaging in activities that shore up the market value of damaged assets

on the lenders and borrowers alike? See the admonition of the governor of the Bank of England previously.

It's common knowledge that the consumer is financially stretched, but it's still a dirty little secret that corporate America is not as flush as it appears. Far too deep a subject for this report, it's mentioned only to caution you from thinking that the business sector—both public and private—has the wherewithal to stem the tide. I'll leave you hanging with a teaser. Because real assets are carried at cost less depreciation, whereas financial assets (equal to just 30 percent of tangible assets and net worth in the United States back in 1952, they represent more than 80 percent of them today) are marked to market, financial accounting and the Bureau of Economic Analysis (BEA) national-income accounting differ importantly in determining how corporate earnings are calculated. Incidentally, the BEA doesn't count the profits on the trading of financial assets because no real value is created.

Publicly traded companies account for just 20 to 33 percent of corporate debt as defined in the national-income accounts but earn two-thirds or more of corporate profits. Do the math on the private companies and ponder this: The risk of bankruptcy isn't just a function of the total amount of debt, it's about the distribution of debt.

Here's a little more information. The U.S. national-account data show that nonfinancial companies have been paying out more than 100 percent of their profits in dividends and share buybacks. Until 1984 a combination of retained earnings and new issues allowed a steady rise in quarterly net worth. Since then, however, buybacks have overwhelmed retained earnings to the extent that net reductions in equity have averaged more than 3 percent a year. And with investments in plant and equipment exceeding depreciation by $400 billion a year, the United States' national-account data point to rapidly rising leverage.

Edging toward the Precipice

If the inflationary and all the other derivative effects of the Fed's actions don't perplex you, recall what happened after the Fed embarked on a series of rate cuts to blunt the potential economic effects of a fall in asset prices almost seven years ago. On January 3, 2001, the Fed surprised the markets with a half-point rate cut. The markets soared on hopes the tech Bubble would deflate only a bit, not burst. In actuality, the lows wouldn't be reached for nearly two years. Comparison with 1998, when the Fed flooded the markets with liquidity to bail out Long-Term Capital Management, is so fraught with dissimilarities on many fronts as to render it irrelevant.

While not as suspenseful, think of this report and its predecessors as reading the book before you see the movie. If it's suspense you're looking for, lay the book aside. Even though we're human and enjoy excitement (and even a little levity), when it comes to managing your money we become deadly serious. Following the lead of Keynes, we drill down wherever possible to reduce the element of uncertainty and replace it with something more quantifiable and statistically predictable, getting as far beneath the surface as possible for what Keynes called risk. In times like the present, when emotions have outsized influence on decisions, we return to our understanding of crowd psychology until rationality returns.

The "Simple" Question Why?*

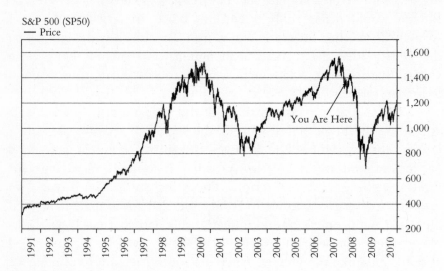

S&P 500 (SP50)
— Price

SOURCE: © FactSet Research Systems.

My preparation for this annual exercise has had the most amazing unintended consequences. Abraham Lincoln summed up what was required: "Give me six hours to chop down a tree, and I will spend the first four sharpening the ax." In the solitude of the early-morning hours I have, indeed, sharpened the ax. At that time of day nothing intrudes on my time for reading, thinking, and (applying "healthy" skepticism) constantly inquiring and asking the burr-under-the-saddle question *Why?* During the daylight hours, when the normal world stirs, whether by the miracle of the Internet, the telephone, or face-to-face dialogue, the search for answers to earlier musings becomes all-consuming. The quest for what *Why?* reveals, often the source of wisdom, has, over the years, resulted in encounters with some of the most interesting and fascinating people, past and present, in the disciplines of business, finance, and macroeconomics. The names are too numerous to recite here; you will see a few of them sprinkled throughout the report. This, then, is not truly my report; it is a composite of some of the best thinkers extant. I'm merely the messenger.

---

*This material is adapted from the 2007 annual report of Martin Capital Management.

It isn't only coincidence that an inordinate number of references are made to John Maynard Keynes and Benjamin Graham. Not surprisingly, these intellectual giants wrote their greatest works in the years immediately following the Great Depression: Keynes, *The General Theory of Employment, Interest, and Money* (1936) and Graham, *Security Analysis* (1934). Analogously, one wouldn't ask a lifelong Floridian how to survive Alaska's winters. Rather, we would seek out Jack London of "To Build a Fire" fame—and, on the financial front, Keynes (from afar) and Graham, who weathered the most cataclysmic economic storm in this country's history.

An Early Epitaph for the First Decade of the New Millennium

Being fiercely independent and congenitally skeptical, and thus often appearing annoyingly unconventional, please indulge me for a moment as I step back to reflect on the first eight years of the new millennium. After all, sometimes we get so caught up looking at the pieces— worrying about an impending recession or what the Fed might do at its next meeting—that when the last piece is placed we are "puzzled" by what's before our eyes.

Despite the big interim rally in the S&P 500 (the Nasdaq was not so lucky), the roller-coaster decade that began with the much-hyped nonevent, Y2K, has thus far not been kind to U.S. stocks. It's hard to believe, but U.S. Treasury notes have trounced them, and even mundane cash equivalents have done better.

With 2008's poor start, things are looking even worse. As of January 22, the S&P index's annual average total return, capital growth plus dividends, was less than one-quarter of 1 percent from what it was at the end of 1999. To put it in dollar terms, $100 invested in the S&P 500 eight years ago is worth $102 today. When the final chapter of this decade is written, the epitaph for many asset classes may read: "So much risk, so little return." For all the action, anxiety, and wealth-gobbling frictional costs, such as fees and commissions (which would have thrown actual results well into negative territory), most investors would have been far better off in every sense of the phrase parking all their money in U.S. Treasury securities and municipal bonds eight years ago. When it's all said and done and they look down at the ground, they'll discover they've been on a . . . (not so) merry-go-round. Of course, only a few can step off the carousel because, by the nature of the asset ownership construct, stocks cannot simply be put on the shelf in nobody's name pending a better opportunity. For better or worse, depending upon who's name is on the certificate, they must be somebody's property all of the time. The investment management industry was paid hundreds of billions of dollars taking tickets from those who chose to ride in circles. At least somebody got rich.

For students of stock market history, the shocking sub 1 percent total return since the beginning of this decade, before inflation's purchasing power loss is factored in, is really not so startling. The 1982–2000 bull market was the biggest in history and the excesses it fomented will take a long time to purge. Given what follows in the pages ahead, it's myopic, in this writer's judgment, to think that the cleansing is complete. For the record book, without a significant recovery in stocks relatively soon, the decade could finish as the worst in annualized total equity returns in the last 100 years, irrespective of whether measured in nominal or inflation/deflation-adjusted terms. The S&P 500 returned −0.1 percent in the Depression-era 1930s. When including gains or losses in purchasing power, the 1930s actually registered a return of a positive 1.9 percent because deflation averaged 2.0 percent. The 1970s still hold the record as the only negative total return decade in purchasing power terms: −1.5 percent. Records, however, are made to be broken.

How Many Pieces Are Necessary . . .

. . . before you visualize how a puzzle must look when completed? Benjamin Graham spoke volumes with the following statement: "If you see that a man is very fat, it makes little difference that you are able to precisely calculate his exact weight to enhance your conclusion."

Clear-thinking Dietrich Bonhoeffer, the German Lutheran pastor and theologian, penetrated the mist surrounding the propaganda and Adolf Hitler's charismatic oratory to the evil that lurked within the madman's mind. Bonhoeffer was able to visualize consequences that most non-Jewish Germans, to say nothing of Neville Chamberlain, Britain's prime minister, failed to see. Bonhoeffer was part of the German Resistance movement against Nazism for which he was ultimately hanged by special order of youngish Heinrich Himmler (44), founder and officer-in-charge of the Nazi concentration camps who held final command responsibility for annihilating "subhumans" whom the Nazis deemed unworthy to live. In the saddest of ironies, Bonhoeffer was executed on April 9, 1945, just days before liberation by Allied forces. Himmler himself committed suicide six weeks later. The following insights into the nature of wisdom from Bonhoeffer are all the more poignant because of the price he paid to acquire them.

> To understand reality is not the same as to know about outward events. It is to perceive the essential nature of things. The best-informed man is not necessarily the wisest. Indeed, there is a danger that precisely in the multiplicity of his knowledge he will lose sight of what is essential. But on the other hand, knowledge of an apparently trivial detail quite often makes it possible to see into the depth of things. And so the wise man will seek to acquire the best possible knowledge about events, but always without becoming dependent upon this knowledge. To recognize the significant in the factual is wisdom.

Warren Buffett would appear to have Dietrich Bonhoeffer's rare capacity to parse seemingly random details "to recognize the significant in the factual." In the Berkshire Hathaway 2006 annual report, published in March 2007, the Oracle of Omaha ran what was ostensibly a "routine" advertisement announcing the beginning of a search for a successor for himself and Lou Simpson (who is only six years his junior) as manager of Berkshire's marketable securities portfolios. [It was to the following ad that I made reference early in this chapter as part of a question asked at the annual meeting in Omaha. Though somewhat repetitious, my occasionally irritating inclination to ask *Why?* about almost everything left me no choice but to ponder whether there was more meaning to Buffett's statement than was immediately obvious.]

> Picking the right person(s) will not be an easy task. It's not hard, of course, to find smart people, among them individuals who have impressive investment records. But there is far more to successful long-term investing than brains and performance that has recently been good. Over time, markets will do extraordinary, even bizarre, things. A single, big mistake could wipe out a long string of successes. We therefore need someone genetically programmed to recognize and avoid

serious risks, *including those never before encountered*. Certain perils that lurk in investment strategies cannot be spotted by use of the models commonly employed today by financial institutions. Temperament is also important. Independent thinking, emotional stability, and a keen understanding of both human and institutional behavior are vital to long-term investment success. I've seen a lot of very smart people who have lacked these virtues.

Why did Buffett choose to make public a need that he could have satisfied with dispatch in private? No investor is better known or knows better. A few well-placed, quiet inquiries would have generated a short list of eminently qualified candidates and avoided all the hoopla—and that assumes Buffett doesn't already have his list of diamonds in the rough. Is it consistent with his behavior that he will actually screen the reported 1,000 applications received? Just perhaps his motives were more subtle . . . ? Could it be that he was obliquely sounding a ringing note of caution to those readers who are "thinkers" [as Ernest Dimnet defined them in the excerpt from *The Art of Thinking* that begins Chapter 7]? All of Buffett's earlier warning bells (for example, the long-term consequences of persistent trade deficits) came from the mind of a man who *thinks* about long-term consequences, and his utterances were designed to provoke thought, not action. None, as best I can recall, triggered an emotional market response. Buffett, Bernanke, and others in high places are keenly aware of the adage "No love is lost on the bearer of bad tidings."

Roger Babson's[7] bombastic speech on September 5, 1929, was as prescient as it was ill-considered: "Sooner or later a crash is coming, and

---

[7][2010] Roger Babson (1875–1967) is probably best remembered for founding Babson College in Massachusetts. Of more interest to the author was Babson's interest in economics and investment, subjects on which he authored more than 40 books. According to biographer John Mulkern, "Babson attributed the business cycle to Sir Isaac Newton's law of action and reaction . . . His pseudoscientific notion, that the laws of physics account for every rise and ebb in the economy, had no more validity than [astrology or alchemy]. But just as astrology gave birth to astronomy and alchemy to chemistry, so, too, did Babson's efforts to explain the economic cycle . . . lead to the economic breakthrough that revolutionized the business of economic forecasting." The more I learn about Babson, the more I like him!

it may be terrific!" Unfortunately, Babson's warning was the equivalent of screaming "Fire!" in a crowded theater, and the panic that ensued was clearly an unintended side effect. [My only criticism of Babson is that he didn't "whisper." Were I in such a theater and happened to be the first to see an early-stage fire, I would hope that I'd quietly urge people toward the exits. To scream "Fire!" is to condemn many to death by unnecessary suffocation.] The events that followed in the fall of 1929 surely contributed anecdotally to Keynes' contention five years later that there is "liquidity for some, but not for all." [Of course, even if Babson had whispered, the forces that brought on the Crash and Depression were aligning themselves that autumn, Babson or no Babson.] As historical accounts have made abundantly clear, Babson was roundly denounced for his doomsday prognostication. The prominent Yale professor, Irving Fisher, equally infamous for stepping in front of the freight train of shifting sentiment, personalized his attack on the messenger of imminent mayhem. Wall Street's (conflicted) power brokers sneered at Babson's "intemperate predictions. The advance will continue as before—despite such 'gratuitous' forecasts." Whether Buffett "whispered" in his chairman's letter—or the undersigned read far more into his message than was intended—will be known only in the fullness of time. Were I to personally attempt to reach Buffett by phone, it's unlikely that I would learn anything more than I already know. Benjamin Franklin observed: "Three may keep a secret, if two of them are dead." I don't like what that implies!

Yet it is possible, in this writer's judgment, that Buffett may have whispered. And if his words are ever turned against him in an effort to make him the scapegoat, he can always quote Alan Greenspan: "If I have made myself clear, you must have misunderstood me." [I'm reminded of the variation on the opening line of Kipling's famous poem: "If you keep your head when all about you are losing theirs . . . perhaps you've misunderstood the situation."]

Those who perused the extensive essays in Chapter 9 should not be surprised by the current goings-on in the credit and housing markets. If the text is analogous to a screenplay, the early scenes of the movie are playing in theaters around the world as this report is being written. A year or two ago we didn't need to know all the precise causal details, for which the credit pandemic is now the effect, in order to draw rational conclusions.

Unlike the labors required to plow through the 2005 and 2006 annual reports [Chapter 7], I'll not drag you through all the reasoning in 2007 that led me to conclude that the odds convincingly augur that it's better to be safe than sorry. Unlike Buffett, I live in the luxury of relative anonymity, and my words have the same effect on markets as they might on the dozing patron in the final act of a Verdi opera. Such a somnolent sort is not stirred in the least from his stupefaction by the crescendo of superb drama, harmony, melody, and counterpoint. I'll hearken back to the wisdom of Bonhoeffer and present an apparently trivial—only insofar as it's not commonly understood or appreciated— fact that "quite often makes it possible to see into the depth of things." If the gist of what follows in the pages ahead doesn't hit you like a blindside tackle from Brian Urlacher, you may want to think of yourself as the patsy at a table of card sharks.

Benjamin Graham said if you don't have an intimate knowledge of the chronic behavioral anomalies of "Mr. Market," the imaginary manic/depressive who personifies the emotional impetus behind the actions of the "crowd," you're doomed to mediocrity or worse. Singer Kenny Rogers put it a different way in his hit tune "The Gambler." Bringing all your intuitive capacities into play, you must read the faces around the table and the cards in your hand to draw an inference on the basis of admittedly insufficient data whether it's time to hold 'em, fold 'em, walk away, or run.

To be sure, we're referring to markets, not individual stocks. There are wonderful exceptions to the rule, but the workings of arbitrage (the preoccupation of speculators in finding, capitalizing upon, and therefore neutralizing pricing anomalies among and between similar securities) in a crowded marketplace renders them as scarce as hen's teeth. Of course, the arbitrageur's perspective is short term, still leaving plenty of opportunity for the investor who can look forward a few years . . . and whose clients will permit him to do so.[8]

---

[8][2007, original] A market index is an average, however configured and weighted. Within the "averages" there are industries and companies whose prices are anything but reflective of the average. The question an independent analyst must ask is: How does today's stock price compare with what may be the intrinsic worth of the company five years hence, properly discounted to its present value?

As you've seen so often on these pages, in this age of unfathomable advances in technology, financial developments remain archaic and stubbornly cyclical. The latest iterations are little more than a new mask on the face of reincarnated bad judgments and misaligned incentives. John Stumpf (CEO) of smartly run Wells Fargo summed up the plight of his peers: "It's puzzling why bankers have come up with these new ways to lose money when the old ways were working so well." Warren Buffett, singing from the same hymnal, addressed the challenges of remediation:

> . . . [A] plan by some large banks to create a fund to buy tarnished mortgage securities is unlikely to cure what ails the financial markets. . . . You can't turn a financial toad (into a prince) by kissing it or by securitizing it or by transferring its ownership to somebody else.

Both men were obliquely making references to one element, man's proclivities, and their rippling effect on the whole of things. Mixing Christianity and Islam—first from Ecclesiastes: "There is nothing new under the sun." Second, as Muhammad observed eons ago: "Believe, if thou wilt, that mountains change their place, but believe not that man changes his nature."

Just a Few (Pieces) Will Do

The alchemists in structured mortgage finance, operating in a tailwind economic environment of low interest rates, rising home prices, and well-below-average defaults, mixed a potentially fresh toxic concoction of low average-quality securitized mortgages. Repackaged again as a plethora of exotic structured finance securities, meagerly overcollateralized so that many tranches carried the AAA imprimatur, massive amounts of leverage were added to the bubbling brew. With complexity growing exponentially so that it became nearly impossible to find the beginning if you started at the end, the system edged toward its breaking point, hinging precariously on a single model assumption: that future defaults would be in line with recent experience. When the first signs of softening in real estate prices surfaced, lenders quickly learned that the default assumptions—mechanical extrapolation of the abnormally favorable delinquency experience of recent years into the future—proved that mortgage bankers had been fatefully optimistic. Lenders had grossly underestimated and therefore underpriced risk; they were goaded on by animal spirits and asymmetrically inflammatory incentive arrangements ("Nothing is quicker at changing a man's moral outlook than cash in large sums"). The brass ring and corporate competition for market share blinded players of all stripes to the ultimate consequences. So engaged were they in the battle that they lost sight of the war where sea changes were occurring. Semirational lenders were easily blown from their moorings as the contagion spread. By collectively taking on far more risk than any one lender realized, the aggregate losses, once they began to snowball, couldn't be easily contained.

The severity of the subprime debacle[9] may be only the prelude to the main act yet to take center stage, a tragedy of grander scale playing off Broadway in the equally Byzantine corporate credit markets. The generally unanticipated (though not for my faithful readers) and unprecedented decline in housing prices[10] may have been the catalyst in bringing the subprime mortgage markets to their knees, but it may be a recession that is necessary to expose the "under the radar" reckless abdication of fiduciary duty in the corporate credit markets. Over the past decade, the exponential growth of credit derivatives has created heretofore unequaled amounts of financial leverage in corporate credit.

---

[9][2007, original] Based on the current price of the ABX subprime credit-default swap (CDS) index, admittedly only an approximation, losses are expected to total $300 billion, with $80 billion announced before year end by some of those left standing when the music stopped.

[10][2007, original] Home prices in 10 major U.S. metropolitan areas in October were down a record 6.7 percent from a year earlier, according to the S&P/Case-Shiller Home Price Index. To put the decline in context, the index jumped 74 percent in the six years through 2006, while U.S. median household income rose just 15 percent. At press time the *Wall Street Journal* announced that December year-to-year new-home sales were 41 percent lower than the level in December 2006. The median price of a new home decreased by 10 percent to $219,200 in December from $244,700 in December 2006. Obviously, price trends in new homes have an impact on price trends in used homes. Although unprecedented in magnitude in recent history, the boom/bust cycle in housing could well follow a typical, though painfully elongated, self-correcting pattern.

Similar to the growth of subprime mortgage structured finance products, the rapid rise of corporate credit innovations required ideal economic conditions and separated those who evaluated risk from those who bore it.

I'm not suggesting that the consequences of the subprime mortgage fandango are behind us. Blundering legislative intervention, interest-rate resets, and foreclosures are likely to cause great suffering for hundreds of thousands if not millions of Americans over the next couple of years. In daily financial press accounts, we're reminded that lenders can postpone the day of reckoning only so long. Citigroup and Merrill Lynch, serial disclosers, announced on January 15 the infusion of another $19.1 billion, dripping with irony and soon likely to be followed by political backlash, from Sovereign Investment Vehicles. The remediation process has been obstructed by contrite lenders who, like in the 1930s, live by the adage: "Once burned, twice shy." When the system is crying out for looser credit, the bankers respond by tightening. They exacerbated the problem and are now stymieing the orderly resolution. Still, this "demon of our own design" is no longer lurking in the shadows.

Credit-Default Swap Alchemy: Transmuting Junk into Gold

Today's commercial bank is not your grandfather's bank. Unfortunately liberated from the straitjacket of Glass-Steagall and other post-Depression Era safeguards, the once prosaic corporate credit market advanced in just a decade like General Sherman's 1864 march to the sea through such a mind-boggling, easy-money-enabled series of incarnations that it metaphorically may resemble the fairy tale "Rumpelstiltskin" from the collection of the Brothers Grimm (any resemblances are purely coincidental). The mythical dwarf possessed the power to spin straw into gold. Alas, as if coauthored by Ayn Rand a century later, the fictitious little fellow proved that "no man may be smaller than his money."

In this heretofore unimaginable environment the investment banks saw fertile soil (read: fees booked immediately that approximated 8 percent of the premium). In the mid-1990s Wall Street gave birth to *credit-default swaps* (CDS),[11] the basic contract from which all credit derivatives emanated, in order to meet the need for a more fluid trading vehicle. The CDS is an innovative financial instrument that revolutionized the way credit instruments change hands. It is a financial agreement between two parties where liability is transferred to a counterparty for value. Simply put, it is a marketable, radically nonstandard insurance pact that is virtually devoid of the safeguards indigenous to traditional property and casualty insurance with which we're all familiar. [Some say CDS were created to avoid being classified as insurance so that issuers would not have to deal with pesky insurance regulators and the traditional underwriting requirement.] The standard contract is for five years, though they're selling in the secondary markets like hotcakes. Bank loans or marketable corporate debt are the underlying assets. The buyer of CDS pays the periodic premium to purchase credit protection on a specified, notional amount of exposure. In the event the corporate debtor faces, in the parlance of the trade, a "credit event"—typically a bankruptcy, failure to pay, or restructuring—the owner of credit protection receives payment for the amount of the loss. In terms of exposure, a buyer of CDS is "short" the credit risk of the debtor. He may have purchased the CDS as a hedge to protect a portfolio asset or, more likely, to speculate that the value of a loan or a bond would become impaired. Conversely, the writer of protection assumes a risk comparable to owning the loan or bond, receiving a premium payment in the presumed

---

[11][2007, original] Thus far having no direct experience as buyer, seller, hedger, or speculator in the murky world of credit-default swaps (CDS) derivatives, I set about learning as much as I could vicariously so that a vague threat could be reduced through familiarity to something less mysterious. As it happened, one of the most incisive investigative financial journalists extant, my friend Kate Welling (with whose keen intelligence, insatiable curiosity, and literary excellence most of you are by now familiar), led me through the maze. Attribution for what follows in the text above starts with Ms. Welling and ends with a host of other unnamed sources to whom my research led me. Framing all this in the context of a possible systemic conflagration would not have been possible without an understanding of the financial innovation infrastructure provided by yet another friend, Rick Bookstaber, PhD, author of the must-read *A Demon of Our Own Design: Markets, Hedge Funds, and the Perils of Financial Innovation*. Sometimes it's not what you know (particularly if you hail from little ol' Elkhart, Indiana) but who your friends are—and what *they* know—that makes all the difference . . .

value-for-value exchange. Thus, the CDS market is a zero-sum game between the buyers and sellers of default protection.

The introduction of CDS coincided with a favorable economic climate for creditors and debtors. Since the nadir of the last credit cycle in 2002, creditors had a uniformly positive lending experience with defaults running at about 1 percent, well below the historical average. The CDS market blossomed in the era that may be known as "casino capitalism," and the issuance of credit and credit insurance continued apace, unrestrained by considerations of risk. From a modest infancy a dozen years ago, the notional value of CDS today is so large that it surpasses the amount of actual bonds or loans issued or granted by an order of magnitude. That is to say that a company may have issued $1 billion in bonds and yet have $10 billion of CDS contracts outstanding concurrently. If the debt were to default with eventual recovery of 40 cents on the dollar, then the loss to investors holding the bonds would be $600 million—but the loss to credit-default-swap sellers would be $6 billion. In addition to spreading risk, credit derivatives, in this case, also amplify it dangerously. Leverage comes in many forms.

A candidate for the title of Godzilla[12] of potentially catastrophic derivatives, CDS contracts now total a mind-boggling $45.5 trillion[13] of outstanding credit risk, swelling an astonishing ninefold the last three years alone. Putting such a large number in perspective, it's almost five times the U.S. national debt and more than three times the U.S. GDP.[14]

---

[12][2007, original] Godzilla is one of the most recognizable symbols of Japanese popular culture. The early Godzilla movies—there have been 28—constituted a filmographic metaphor for the United States, portraying the Tyrannosaurus rex–like dinosaur as a frightening nuclear monster, embodying the fears that many Japanese continued to hold about the nuclear attacks on Hiroshima and Nagasaki, as well as the nightmarish dread of recurrence. Godzilla's character changed over the years, making him more heroic and thus more appealing to children. Today's Godzilla has fallen somewhere in the middle, from protector to harbinger of destruction. The metaphor lives, and it morphs . . .

[13][2007, original] According to the comptroller of the Currency's Quarterly Derivatives Report . . .

[14][2007, original] The total risk will be mitigated to an unknowable extent because many of the players hedge their bets. However, given the huge losses disclosed thus far by commercial and investment banks, their "hedged books" were not so well hedged after all. Hedging is typically based on historical risk experience. When risks escalate, hedges often prove woefully inadequate.

While a recession would almost certainly knock the CDS market into a cocked hat, this feat of financial legerdemain is so ill-constructed, with only the slimmest margins for error, that it may fall of its own weight even without the help of a stumbling economy. Credit-default swaps taken as a whole are really little more than a thinly disguised unregulated insurance instrument without the conventional insurance underwriter's obligation to maintain statutory loss reserves or minimum regulatory capital, to say nothing about minimum ratios of liquidity on their balance sheets. Not only do the incentives encourage the taking of helter-skelter risks, the underwriters have shown a propensity to grossly underprice it in their haste to put revenues on the books and, lest we forget all-powerful incentives, accrue gargantuan bonuses. Since few firms have "claw-back" compensation provisions (once paid, the Wall Street middlemen for CDS sellers and buyers typically have no recourse against the salesmen), a mispriced distant potential claim carries almost no ethical weight *vis-à-vis* this year's bonus. Grossly misaligned incentives in the subprime lending industry played no small part in pushing the mortgage-backed security (MBS) market, along with all its many stepchildren, over the edge into insanity. Any system that is structured so that a large premium payment is collected up front while a claim of indeterminate amount—actuarial benchmarks are virtually nonexistent—due months, if not years, hence will often encourage "moral drift." Imagine the consequences if $45 trillion of insurance policies experience a natural loss of 5 percent, and there are no reserves set aside to make good on the $2.25 trillion in policy claims (or, even $1.35 trillion, assuming recovery rates of 40 cents per dollar on defaulted debt). No matter how you slice it, the late Senator Everett Dirksen's wry observation (which he purportedly denied), paraphrased and multiplied by a factor of 1,000, is *apropos*: "A trillion here and a trillion there, and pretty soon you're talking about real money!"[15] A paltry $300 billion in possible subprime mortgage write-offs seems trivial by comparison.

---

[15][2007, original] The following comment Everett Dirksen did not deny. It is offered at this point to break the barrage of depressing numbers and bring a smile to your lips: "When I face an issue of great import that cleaves both constituents and colleagues, I always take the same approach. I engage in deep deliberation and quiet contemplation. I wait to the last available minute, and then I always vote with the losers. Because, my friend, the winners never remember, and the losers never forget."

The moneymaking machine has hummed at ever-increasing velocity as long as companies received cheap financing (or refinancing if primary obligations could not be met), borrowers repaid lenders, and expectations remained cheerful. Given their subordination in the capital structure, junk bonds (or, euphemistically, high-yield bonds) are a logical place to look for the first signs of trouble. Statistics of high-yield issuance reveal relaxed lending standards in a marketplace where risk was benign and therefore ignored. In each year since 2004 more than 40 percent of all new debt scooped up by investors garnered ratings below investment grade. For perspective, the amount of new paper of poor quality issued in each of the last four years far exceeded the amount of such issuances in any year since the late 1980s.[16] The stars were aligned: Cheap money, strong economy, and default rates that were so abnormally low as to be analogous to the perfect sucker pitch—and, *voilà*, CDS issuance blossomed like an outfield full of dandelions in springtime. Under such idyllic conditions, the need for default insurance to hedge or to protect seemed slight. At the end of the day it's all about monetary incentives, pure and simple. Most people are motivated by self-interest, and they'll behave accordingly. With all the fees to be generated on both sides of the trade—and with risk of default appearing to be *de minimus*—$45 trillion in the CDS have been written to date, many of which were probably priced to "perfection" rather than to reality.

High-yield bonds are dubbed *junk* for good reason. Here's a brief synopsis of the "junk-bond cycle":

> Corporate mortality tables indicate that defaults of high-yield bonds within five years of issuance occur 28 percent of the time for those just below investment grade and 47 percent of the time for those with the lowest ratings. Past instances of high default rates lagged periods of strong cash junk issuance by 4 to 5 years, coinciding with recessionary periods in the economy. In good times, issuance is high, underwriting standards are low,

---

[16][2007, original] Payment-in-Kind (PIK) instruments, much like the negative amortization mortgage, which flourished in the 1980s, have enjoyed a renaissance in recent years. In the simplest of terms, PIKs appear when the financial fabric is stretched so tightly that borrowers cannot pay in cash, so they pay in promises of future cash. When PIKs surface, the sharks aren't far below.

and investors forget that risky credits may actually default. A few years later, the economic cycle turns and junk bonds reveal their flawed character.

A disproportional amount of low-grade paper hit the market in recent years, but that was not all. Investors also received meager compensation for taking risk. High-yield spreads over Treasury yields have hovered around historical lows for nearly four years, indicating that investors have paid little attention to the real possibility of loss.[17]

Counterparty Risk

At one time Alan Greenspan actually applauded derivatives as a means of dispersing risk. Warren Buffett, who is both practitioner and visionary, famously described derivatives bought speculatively as "financial weapons of mass destruction."[18] In Berkshire Hathaway's annual report to shareholders in 2002, he wrote:

> Unless derivatives contracts are collateralized or guaranteed, their ultimate value also depends on the creditworthiness of the counterparties to them. In the meantime, though, before a contract is settled, the counterparties record profits and losses—often huge in amount—in their current earnings statements without so much as a penny changing hands. The range of derivatives contracts is limited only by the imagination of man (or sometimes, so it seems, madmen).

As the movie rolls on, Buffett appears more and more prescient. Greenspan is writing books, coaching from the bleachers, and, just as this report was going to press, he took a position as advisor to hedge-fund manager John Paulson, whom you'll meet later in this chapter. According

---

[17][2007, original] Presentation by Dr. Edward I. Altman, "Current Conditions in Global Credit Markets," October 2007.

[18][2007, original] Despite Buffett's reference to derivatives as WMDs, he owns them. Unlike many 30-something hedge-fund managers recklessly selling CDS insurance, few people in the world are better equipped, through long experience and the most rational of minds, to transform the risk inherent in derivatives in his favor.

to the aforementioned Comptroller of the Currency's *Quarterly Derivatives Report*, the concentration of risk is trending upward, with the top 10 institutions providing 89 percent of the total notional amount bought and sold. The perennial top four are household names: Morgan Stanley, Deutsche Bank, Goldman Sachs, and JP Morgan Chase. Counterparty concentration appears to remain a feature of this market; JP Morgan is at the bottom of the mortgage derivatives list but at the top of the corporate creditor derivatives list. In its defense, the company has an enormous edge in that the insider information it legally possesses as underwriters for the companies that issue the debt in the first place is asymmetrical. When the expert with whom you deal has superior knowledge and inferior scruples, Google the lyrics of "The Gambler" for what to do next!

Who May Be Left Holding the Bag?

Banks are the primary sellers of CDS, totaling 40 percent of all written CDS. Banks claim to run hedged books, effectively serving as a market-maker in the CDS market. As should be evident from the events in subprime, even the most sophisticated systems are often unable to fully hedge risks of this size, degree of complexity, and changing character. If printed materials are any indication, banks may be asleep at the switch. The "Counterparty Considerations" section in the Credit Derivatives Primer of market-share leader JP Morgan is a single paragraph on the last page of the volume, which proclaims "the likelihood of suffering [counterparty default] is remote."[19]

It's estimated that hedge funds have sold about $15 trillion of CDS, which suits their avaricious fee structures to a tee. Like clipping coupons, they collect premiums that are likely run through the income statement without adequate set-asides for future claims. There will be no fireworks until someday somebody presents a claim against that insurance sold for which there are no reserves. If the industry experiences a 5 percent loss ratio, that would just about wipe out the investors' equity in hedge funds. That's what we call counterparty risk. One imponderable is the concentration in the hedge-fund industry: It's estimated that

---

[19][2007, original] JP Morgan Credit Derivatives and Quantitative Research, "Credit Derivatives: A Primer," January 2005, 25.

some . . . 200 firms control 80 to 85 percent of all hedge-fund assets. In terms of systemic risk, it's probably a forlorn hope that the sellers of unreserved insurance are more broadly dispersed.

Coming Full Circle

As the above idiom implies, perchance we have ended up in this essay precisely where we started. To paraphrase Ben Graham, do we need to know the fat man's exact weight to know he's obese? Can we infer critical features about the whole by simply comprehending an apparently trivial detail that quite often makes it possible to see into the depth of things, as Dietrich Bonhoeffer did? Did Warren Buffett not tie together in one paragraph the random warnings from "black swan"[20] events hiding in the shadows to admonitions about system-imperiling runaway greed and avarice in his chairman's letters in recent years?

Rather than detailing the risks that abound—including some that defy description—summing up, in "an apparently trivial detail" (e.g., the CDS market, heretofore likely unknown to most readers), the consequences of denying the existence of those risks drives the point home. The following is an immutable, and what should be perceived as sobering, law of compounding: A single 100 percent loss can wipe out an entire lifetime of cumulative gains. Compounding is not an equal-opportunity mechanism. Its rewards and penalties are asymmetrical.

We conclude this section with one real-time story that, parenthetically, parallels a similar concurrent experience by the undersigned, albeit on an infinitesimally smaller scale. In this moment of travail, the story begs the question "Whose advice do you heed?" Who are the [Ernest Dimnet] thinkers? There are two men with the surname Paulson, one widely known (Henry) and the other (John) obscure until recently. Goldman Sachs alum (aren't they all?) Treasury Secretary *Henry* "Hank" Paulson mouthed the party line of denial until the crescendo of facts exposing

---

[20][2007, original] *Fooled by Randomness: The Hidden Role of Chance in Life and in the Markets* (2005) and *The Black Swan: The Impact of the Highly Improbable* (2007) were written by Nassim Nicholas Taleb, a pioneer in the field of complex derivatives, now turned scholar and essayist. A black swan, according to Taleb, is a high-impact, hard-to-predict, and rare event beyond the realm of normal expectations. Prospective readers take note: The books are erudite, but his style on occasion can be off-putting.

the subprime debacle drowned out his hollow words. Concurrently, *John* Paulson, 51, was betting against Henry, conventional wisdom, Wall Street's talking heads, and the subprime market myopia. While a bit early and despite his first bets being losers, his obsession with the emerging facts, which he consumed voraciously, only strengthened his conviction.

"I've never been involved in a trade that had such unlimited upside with a very limited downside," John Paulson is quoted as saying. Pure Buffett . . . At root, John's story is one of dogged perseverance in the face of relentless pressure to conform. And John is unquestionably a Dimnet thinker. His reward as a hedge-fund manager: $3 billion to $4 billion for himself—believed to be the largest one-year payday in Wall Street history. Beginning in 2005, he and his analysts shorted risky CDO (collateralized debt obligation) slices and bought credit-default swaps that complacent investors seemed to be pricing too low. As his profits mushroomed he began to worry about counterparty risk. Thanks to the wrong bets of some big banks and Wall Street firms—his counterparties—and the first-leaver advantage, his concerns were assuaged for the time being.

John Paulson is a man from humble beginnings and not without compassion. He has kept a low profile, saying he's reluctant to celebrate while housing causes others pain.

As for what's ahead, according to the *Wall Street Journal*, Paulson has taken profits on some, but not most, of his bets. He remains a bear on housing, predicting it will take years for home prices to recover. He's also betting against other parts of the economy, such as credit-card and auto loans. He tells investors "it's still not too late to bet on economic troubles."

While his prose is not as elegant as the British statesman who follows, perhaps Paulson was framing today's problems along the same time continuum and in much the same way as one of the greatest thinkers in the twentieth century did some 65 years earlier . . . "Now this is not the end. It is not even the beginning of the end. But it is, perhaps, the end of the beginning."[21] Who's to know in advance? One simple little adage

---

[21][2007, original] So observed Winston Churchill after the Allied victory in the Second Battle of El Alamein over Erwin Rommel's forces in 1942 after a series of earlier defeats in World War II.

has served me well over the years: "The early bird may get the worm, but the second mouse gets the cheese." The differences are as subtle as they are significant.

■ ■ ■

[Thus ends Chapter 10, "The Tipping Point." It covers the nine months from May 2007 through February 2008. While no one knew at the time how the future would unfold, it was enough to know that the point of inflection had arrived. It is my hope, based on what you have read in this and the preceding chapter, that you may have reached the same conclusion.

If so, that prompts the obvious question: Why did those in authority, those who could have at least "whispered" a warning, remain silent? Could forethought have resulted in 2008 being remembered as the year in which the air of excess hissed out of the Bubble in something short of a chaotic process rather than the year in which the Bubble burst in utter chaos? The answer to that counterfactual inquiry is, of course, unknowable. *The earlier* Why? *question, of course, provokes another of more immediate concern: Given what has been written on these pages about the still fragile financial system and the flagging economy, and the less than stellar attempts to resuscitate them, what should you, as you read this sentence, be thinking about? Should you not be wondering about what warnings morally responsible leaders should be whispering, but aren't? Should you not be thinking about the myriad unintended long-term consequences of the* ad hoc *measures taken to postpone what could be the inevitable?* I am.]

Chapter 11

The End or
the Beginning?

S&P 500 (SP50)
— Price

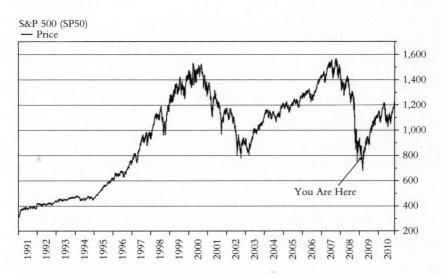

You Are Here

SOURCE: © FactSet Research Systems.

The 2008 annual report was published in February 2009, less than a month before the S&P hit a closing low of 677 on March 9. The United States was in the midst of a migrating global financial maelstrom and enveloping Great Recession. As noted in the Preface, when disasters hit, natural or man-made, individuals and institutions instinctively turn to the paternal arms of Uncle Sam. Those in power tend to reflexively reciprocate in kind. However ill-conceived the governmental actions, however ineffective the experimentations, however costly the ultimate consequences, the political and social imperative is to intervene. Centralization of control has enfeebled the once free(r) markets. The Great Recession began in December 2007 and, apart from an easy-money-induced huge rally in risk assets, the economy remains largely unresponsive. Some observers in the months and years ahead will argue, understandably, that letting markets clear unimpeded—however terrifying in the short run—would have resulted in a deeper but far shorter V. Interfering with the Darwinian process of natural selection, where the strong survive at the expense of the weak, invariably creates a host of unwanted consequences. Japan is a prime example. The point, however, is moot. To quote the current chairman of the Federal Reserve Board, "There are no atheists in foxholes and no ideologues in financial crises." Believing at the time that the economy, and perhaps the capital markets, were in for a long siege, the 2008 report began by reminding readers, almost with a sense of relief at having dodged what could have been a fatal bullet, of what it took to preserve wealth during the most cataclysmic crisis since the 1930s.

> Every generation or two the true value of "wealth management" is revealed. Being aware that a single, big mistake can wipe out a lifetime of successes, a wealth manager must be hardwired to recognize and avoid grave risks, including those never experienced before. Fierce independence of thought and action, equanimity of temperament, abiding rationality and a keen understanding of human nature are essential. History doesn't repeat itself, but the passions of men do.[1]

---

[1][2008, original] Throughout this report many references are made to the lessons learned from history. The following quotation—from the 2006 annual report (but not included in Chapter 9 of this book)—attempts to build a bridge of understanding between the events of which history is the effect and the human behaviors that

[Toward the end of the summarized 2008 report, we offered a glimmer of hope.]

At Martin Capital Management, our long-term wealth management record affirms the efficacy of the belief that if you can't find a dollar for 50 cents you should pass. As our written record reveals, we have a keener nose than some for both danger and opportunity. In earlier missives, we warned of impending peril when it was largely invisible. With this report we are alerting the rational investor to opportunity, without yet being able to see to the other end of the tunnel of despair.

[Later in this chapter, at the beginning of excerpts from the 2009 annual report, the record of Martin Capital Management's investment performance will be discussed in detail. The means by which we avoided the carnage in 2008 (MCM total account, −7.8 percent; S&P 500, −37 percent) and still managed to participate in the rally of 2009 (MCM total account, 21.6 percent; S&P 500, 26.5 percent), without exposing portfolios to more than a modest amount of risk, should make for interesting reading. Most of the report, however, was devoted to diagnosing the origins of the crisis, proposing a survivor's mind-set similar to that which enabled Admiral Stockdale to survive the "Hanoi Hilton" in Vietnam—and accepting the harsh realities of the snowball effect.]

---

are often their cause, to wit: "As to the relevance of history to imagining possibilities for the future, Machiavelli observed: 'Whoever wishes to foresee the future must consult the past; for human events ever resemble those of preceding times. This arises from the fact that they are produced by men who ever have been, and ever shall be, *animated by the same passions* [emphasis added], and thus they necessarily have the same results.'"

Origins of a Crisis: Decoupling Risk and Return*

That which cannot be seen is sometimes more powerful than that which can. After lurking in the shadows for several decades, mutating risk has finally made its fearsome presence known.

In the beginning, risk and return were coupled . . .

There was a time when your local bank's mortgage lender from whom you nervously borrowed money to buy your first home had a vested interest in its repayment. The incentives were properly aligned to encourage the long view: Actions, we were told from our earliest days, have consequences. If your coat-and-tie mortgage lender made enough bad loans, you might see him next wearing a hairnet, flipping burgers at McDonald's.

Over the last 20 years, risk and return have progressively decoupled. Financial innovation was to become the forbidden fruit.

"Securitization" was among the watershed developments in financial innovation. "Commercial" banks of old made loans judiciously, the dollar amount put on their books limited by regulatory capital adequacy ratios. Bundling loans and selling them to "investment" banks that marketed them as *negotiable* asset-backed *securities* (ABS), the process of securitization linked lender and investor for the first time. Like technology, no breakthrough is without its unintended repercussions. Accountability for risk got lost in the shuffle. Because the Federal Reserve did not have authority over investment banks, it soon lost control over the creation of credit as the "shadow banking system" usurped its power. Securitization enabled the credit explosion. Glass–Steagall, R.I.P., or so it was thought when President Clinton laid it to rest in 1999 . . .

Risk associated with a mortgage loan becomes increasingly opaque as it leaves the originating bank and disappears into the investment banker's sausage grinder of complexity and comes out the other end as a "structured finance product" known as a CMO, CDO, RMBS, CMBS, or some other confusing acronym. By design, as risk and return move up

---

*This material is adapted from the 2008 annual report of Martin Capital Management.

the credit food chain, they decouple. A CMO (collateralized mortgage obligation) is a legal entity wholly separate from the investment bank that created it. By slicing and dicing mortgage loans into a hierarchy of tranches, or classes, risk is parceled, ostensibly enabling investors to choose their own degree of exposure.

The rating agencies of Moody's and Standard & Poor's were no bit players in this unfolding drama. Driven by the most basic of incentives, they showered AAA-ratings like a priest sprinkles holy water after lingering a bit too long at the altar. To the discriminating eye, the assumptions in their models didn't hold water, but no one seemed to care at the time.

Moody's and Standard & Poor's charged into the unknown on the backs of credit default risk models that didn't compute if house prices started falling, spurred on by the dubious assumption that a slightly overcollateralized portfolio composed largely of subprime frog-like loans could, by some miracle of financial alchemy, morph into a prince. Bingo. The game was over, and the meltdown that started in the mortgage markets on a single faulty premise began its migration throughout the financial system . . . and then on to the real economy. Nobody is minting money nowadays . . . except the U.S. Treasury, but that's tomorrow's problem.

Wall Street, the epicenter of the crisis, convulsed into a money-making, risk-taking, and, most important, risk-creating colossus by an alteration so simple and subtle that it went largely unnoticed. For generations, investment banks were partnerships where risk-conscious owners played with their own chips. Then in 1980 industry bellwether Salomon Brothers transformed itself into a publicly owned corporation. Salomon made the trade of its lifetime: It sold off responsibility for its actions to its new shareholders for a relative pittance in dividends. The Pandora's box of risk shuttling was opened wide. The incentives and penalties of the game changed with the stroke of a pen, and investment bankers of every stripe jumped aboard the gravy train. OPM, which sounds and acts like opium, is a crude Wall Street acronym for "other people's money." OPM forever shifted the culpability for risk. Not so many years later, when risk untrammeled by accountability finally brought the Street to its knees, the former partners had the loot and the shareholders the loss.

The devil once again is in the details. Hank Paulson, whose brief tenure as Secretary of the Treasury will not likely mark him as the Alexander Hamilton of the twenty-first century, was nonetheless *Time* magazine's runner-up for its Person of the Year in 2008. In September 2008 *Newsweek* dubbed him King Henry in a cover story. Paulson's earlier, less visible work included serving as chairman and CEO (formerly senior partner) of Goldman Sachs. In 2004 the SEC bowed to the powers that be,[2] unanimously agreeing to release the major investment houses from the net capital rule, the requirement that their brokerages hold reserve capital that limited their leverage and risk exposure. Goldman Sachs, then headed by Paulson, was among them. Is there reason to wonder just how Paulson was able to amass a nest egg estimated at $700 million? Thus the rich irony of Paulson self-righteously thrashing the very shareholders who bore the risks supporting his own great wealth accumulation. If asked to define a conservative, Paulson might have responded, *When you have something to conserve, you'll know.* According to that definition, if the shareholders were conservatives several years ago, they no longer are. As so often happens, pride goeth before a fall. Amid the rubble Goldman Sachs and Morgan Stanley are the two majors still standing, but on shaky legs. Paulson helped raise the golden goose and then offed its head. King Henry *VIII?*!

The Hot Potato of Risk

From the earliest securitizations, the hot potato of risk has been tossed everywhere. The commercial banks thought they were flipping it to investment banks who thought they had offloaded it to their customers, with the rating agencies looking a lot like thus-far-unindicted co-conspirators. For reasons too intertwined to attempt to unravel in this relatively brief report, suffice it to say: "What goes around comes around." When the music stopped, the shareholders of the commercial and investment banks, along with the investors who had purchased toxic products, were the first to fall. While many individual investors suffered, the heaviest toll was taken by the mutual funds, pension plans,

---

[2][2008, original] Ben Stein—lawyer, actor, critic, and son of economist Herb Stein—once called Goldman Sachs the "real government of the United States."

endowment funds, hedge funds, and others.[3] You know, those financial intermediaries who oversee what is, directly or indirectly, our money. In case no one asks, conspicuous by its absence is the name of a single executive of any of the failed institutions who shared a similar personal financial fate. Of course, if failing means a reduced bonus or dramatically reduced net worth, there finally were a few. And no, Bernie Madoff, a smoke-and-mirrors charlatan who reportedly "made off" with an almost unfathomable $50 billion, was not overlooked.

Back to the Age of Innocence?

There is hope for "re-pairing" risk and return. Left solely to the monetary and fiscal devices of government intervention, the intention of which is to ameliorate the consequences of excessive risk-taking, recoupling is unlikely. The reality that no government edict, policy, or infusion of money has thus far brought a stop to snowball declines in asset prices or economies does not bode well for the process of recoupling. Few lasting lessons are learned when the law that actions have consequences is circumvented.

The much-maligned free capital markets are doing their job, thank you, in downsizing the demon of risk despite the countervailing force of macro policy intervention. If risk is indeed not a constant but rather a function of the relationship between the price of something and its underlying value, what holds for individual investors might apply to investment markets as a whole. The decoupling of risk from the risktaker enabled the creation of hugely disproportionate amounts of synthetic and ultimately systemic risk. The flight from risk also exhibits the characteristics of a very large snowball. In the process, about $7 trillion of shareholders' notional (paper) wealth in U.S. companies—the gains of the past six years—was wiped out in a year of violent market swings. Globally, including the United States, stocks lost 42 percent of their value in 2008, as calculated by the MSCI (Morgan Stanley Capital International) world index, erasing more than $29 trillion in value and all of the gains made since 2003. What the interventionists are trying to

---

[3][2008, original] Overlaps occur. Endowment and pension funds own hedge funds as do fund-of-funds and so on.

cover up with a few trillion dollars of taxpayer money, the thus-far-free capital markets are exposing with nominal losses of tens of trillions of dollars in shareholder wealth. Just for good measure, tack on another 10 percent decline in the S&P 500 during the first three weeks of 2009.

Since we often think of risk in terms of the likelihood of loss, it stands to reason that an asset priced at zero is risk-free to the buyer. It logically follows then that, relative to the recent past, worldwide the risk of loss has been reduced by $29 trillion. Though many risks persist, the risk of loss in the capital markets around the globe is at least nominally much lower than it was a year ago. While exacting much pain and bucking interventionism, the capital markets sure as shootin' are relentlessly pushing prices down toward realignment of risk and return. Markets are, lest we forget, little more than scoreboards. They flash the ever-changing prices at which buyers and sellers exchange liquidity for shares of stock. Market participants are sometimes extremely emotional, exhibiting bouts of manic-depressive behavior. Indeed, the pendulum alternates between despair and euphoria—and every emotion in between.

Although the world's stock markets fell dramatically in 2008, in some measure they reflected the temporary or permanent impairment of the underlying assets themselves. Not surprisingly, the free market process of purging financial risk is nearly impossible to contain and compartmentalize. It is contagious. It has infected the economy. Economic output is declining at the cost of 2.6-plus million jobs lost last year and many more likely this year.

The Question on Which the Future of Investment Hangs

Will the migrating financial and economic consequences of the decoupling of risk and return prove to be so traumatic that the current risk aversion exhibited by consumers, lenders, investors, and others will become as deeply embedded in our psyches as it was following the Great Depression? Or will it all subside soon after the crisis atmosphere abates, as more optimistic pundits believe? Momentous social issues notwithstanding, *the future of investment for a generation hangs in the balance*. If the former, "Bubbles" will become a distant memory, and the foundation for low-risk, long-term investment will be laid. *If the latter, instability and crises will persist, and speculation will continue to displace invest-ment* [emphasis added].

Like it or not, the momentum of the snowball effect is huge. The absence of either credit or confidence can precipitate an economic collapse. Recovery, to paraphrase John Maynard Keynes[4] as he wrote in 1936, requires the revival of both. In the current episode, the credit crisis preceded the crisis in nonfinancial sector confidence. This was quite different, it should be noted, from the experience of the 1930s. As Ben Bernanke has ruefully discovered, low-priced credit hasn't been a sufficient palliative to jump-start the credit machine. Once risk crashes to the fore, like Godzilla before a terrified crowd, the legs of confidence get wobbly. *Perish the thought, but if recoupling risk and return are prerequisites for renewing the confidence of true investors, the long road, the one Washington will likely spend trillions of dollars to avoid, may be the only route back to innocence* [emphasis added]. . . .

If indeed it is to be the long road, it will be arduous. Period. We, however, have been preparing for the journey. Read on to see what it takes to survive. Also, take heart: Thinking in terms of rainbows, we expect to find a pot of golden opportunities along the way.

The Stockdale Paradox: What Do Survivors Have in Common?

The difference between investment victims and survivors can be most subtle. Especially today, there is a mindset that POWs and survivors of natural disasters share that current long-term investors would be advised to adopt.

---

[4][2008, original] *The General Theory of Employment, Interest, and Money* (1936), John Maynard Keynes. Keynes was a pioneer in the theory of full employment and made his reputation in the 1930s by encouraging fiscal stimulus. He had a great deal of influence on Franklin Roosevelt. Keynesian economics has been used frequently in the post-World War II period and is being embraced by President Obama. Were Keynes alive today, I wonder if he would be employing the strategies associated with his name. Long an advocate of letting circumstances dictate responses, his spend-your-way-out-of-trouble prescription, used repeatedly in the post-World War II era, may not be the shoe that fits in 2009.

Jim Collins, in his best seller *Good to Great*, describes what is known as the Stockdale Paradox, recounting the courage of Vietnam POWs who survived deprivation, uncertainty, and loneliness while in captivity. According to Admiral James Stockdale, a Congressional Medal of Honor recipient, these prisoners of war were able to accept the brutal facts of their reality while maintaining an unwavering faith in the endgame.

When Collins asked Stockdale which prisoners didn't make it out of the "Hanoi Hilton" alive, the admiral gave a quick and surprising response: "the optimists." They were the prisoners who refused to accept their reality, clinging to the hope that they would soon be released. When those hopes were dashed, they eventually died, many of broken hearts.

What separates those who persevere until the end and those who do not, according to Stockdale, is not the presence or absence of adversity but how one deals with the inevitable misfortunes of life. Unremitting optimism that doesn't lend full credence to the harsh realities is likely to give way to eventual despair.

The analogy to the uncertain financial times ahead breaks down, of course, in relation to what POWs suffer in times of war. Short of social disorder, we are not likely to be in any physical danger, nor be deprived of the basic comforts of life. Although the menace to today's investor is opaque and abstract, its reality nonetheless must be accepted if one is to survive.

Know Thyself

Before you become too sure of your capacity to endure, consider Laurence Gonzales[5] and his best seller *Deep Survival: Who Lives, Who Dies, and Why*. Gonzales recounts stories of those who actually went looking for risk. The book's appendix, "The Rules of Adventure," is a misnomer. Gonzales' message between the lines is really about developing survival skills applicable to any threatening situation that might be unexpectedly encountered—from fighter pilots who find themselves

---

[5][2008, original] *Deep Survival* is among the growing collection of books in my library that focus on behavioral economics.

involuntary guests at the Hanoi Hilton to investors trapped in roiling financial markets like whitewater kayakers in a narrow chute.

Ever vigilant, Gonzales' first rule is to stay out of trouble. So far we at Martin Capital Management have managed to avoid making wealth-threatening choices during this adventure. Investing is a journey fraught with temptations for the overconfident or ill-prepared. As we envision the difficult road ahead, the greatest risk to be encountered in getting from here to investment Nirvana will not be determined by the threats from events and circumstances in the world around us but rather from the *insidious enemy within*.

In an earlier age fear was the emotion essential for survival. And yet in modern times much of brain functioning is still reptilian when it comes to money. Money is symbolic. As a store of value, it is proxy for the most basic of risks and rewards that are important to our survival in the modern world. Recall your state of mind from 2003 to 2007. Making money has the same euphoric effect as a mood-enhancing narcotic. As 2008 evolved, however, notice how quickly euphoria gave way to fear. The threat of loss of money evokes immediate responses from the emotional centers of the brain. Emotional responses were the tools of survival eons ago. They are antithetical to deep investment survival in the twenty-first century.

The vast majority of investors actually think risk won't bother them until they feel the pain of loss. Having observed market participants for more than 40 years, I must conclude that myopia can be as counterproductive as fear. Gonzales' book is chock full of stories of adventurers whose confidence was untested. Although the sound is the same, real bullets evoke a different response than blanks. James Montier, like Jason Zweig,[6] has studied the irrational behaviors of investors when the emotion of fear of loss dominates the cognitive process. Montier discovered that even when the odds are 50-50, past losses diminish the willingness to take current risks. Paradoxically, instead of learning from their mistakes,

---

[6][2008, original] Jason Zweig is author of *Your Money and Your Brain* and writes a weekend column for the *Wall Street Journal*. A convenient source for some of the material in this report was a May 2007 interview Zweig had with Kate Welling, whose subscription-only web site, Welling@Weeden, is a treasure trove of interviews with the *crème de la crème* of the investment community.

additional losses, expected with such odds, caused participants to become increasingly risk-averse over time.[7]

Warren Buffett's discipline ensures that his higher-order cognitive capabilities dominate the more reptilian responses. It prepares him for the demands of the modern world by allowing his higher-order skills to prevail where emotions would fail. Investors like Buffett tend to emanate calmness, an imperturbability that transcends the crises of the moment. They exist in a state of not being bothered by things that bother most people. Of course, eons ago Buffett would have been some prehistoric creature's lunch.

It's not that Buffett and fellow iconoclasts are without emotion. Zweig coined the term "inversely emotional," giving academic credence to Buffett's aphorism: "I am greedy when others are fearful— and fearful when others are greedy." Almost sociopathic in his response to what others see as threatening, Buffett actually feels better the farther prices fall. Decades of observation have led me to conclude that most people are proportionately emotional: The fear factor declines as prices rise and increases as prices fall.

Zweig came across another intuitive and complementary insight. The emotional part of the brain is highly active in short-term decision making, understandable if one thinks in terms of pain avoidance. Many people experiencing disturbing symptoms still avoid a trip to the doctor

---

[7][2008, original] James Montier, a gifted strategist who writes a bimonthly essay under the title "Mind Matters" for the French bank Société Générale devised a simple, sequential, coin-tossing experiment with rewards that were conspicuously biased to encourage the participants to bet on every toss. That notwithstanding, when participants experienced loss after a flip of the coin, they were less likely to bet on the next toss. Moreover, what he learned from the process, as illogical as it may seem, is that the aversion to uncertainty actually increased over the course of the experiment. If players were rational and learned from their experience, the longer the game progressed, the more they would have been expected to figure it out. Surprisingly, or perhaps unfortunately, the greater their experience the less they decided to invest. They were getting worse at the game as time went on. By contrast, a control group that had a very specific form of brain damage that limited their capacity to feel fear significantly outperformed the group of normal brain functioning participants. [2010 update: Mr. Montier continues to write a periodic investment commentary; however, he has done so since 2009 as a member of investment manager GMO's asset allocation team.]

because of the fear of pain or uncertainty. Case in point: A thirty-something attorney practicing in my county of residence several years ago died of heart failure. A few days prior to the heart attack that killed him he had told a colleague about a recurrence of chest pains. His friend said, "You need to see a doctor." The lawyer replied, "I know, but if I go, I probably won't like what I hear."

To be sure, the future is very abstract and provides little in the form of near-term emotional rewards. I've spent 40 years surrounded by people who watch the prices of the stocks they own as they fluctuate on a daily or, heaven forbid, hourly basis. Speeding through time on an emotional roller-coaster that ends where it starts is like envy: Nothing good comes from the expenditure of enormous energy.

The uncrowded thinking space in the time dimension is the future. Once focused on that space, the short-term, pain-avoidance syndrome is kept at bay. The harsh reality is that we will be destined to be average if we think and act like everyone else.

"All We Have to Fear Is Fear Itself"

The FDR-style "Fireside Chats" posted to the MCM web site during the course of 2008 had two purposes. First, we sought to keep you apprised of the emerging harsh realities. Second, thus forewarned you could be emotionally forearmed, forestalling the emergence of the insidious fear of the unknown. In this writer's judgment myriad risks still loom on the horizon, risks that few investors have encountered before. As alluded to above, the most threatening are not external. They are cerebral, the tricks our minds play on us. Notwithstanding all the physical threats, Stockdale's greatest enemy was not his Vietcong captors. It was the only facet of the experience over which he had any control—his attitude. The Hanoi Hilton was really a test of his perseverance, his mental toughness. "I never doubted not only that I would get out, but also that I would prevail in the end and turn the experience into the defining event of my life, which, in retrospect, I would not trade." Stockdale was remarkably victorious in the battle of mind over matter. While on a far lesser scale, will we be able to rise above the harsh realities and ultimately echo the sentiments of the only naval officer ever to wear both aviator wings and the Congressional Medal of Honor? Fear will test us like we've never been tested before. That's why the dais will not be crowded . . . We expect to remain standing . . . if we have the courage to accept the harsh realities.

Harsh Realities and the Snowball Effect

The harsh reality is snowballing down upon us. To survive we must know that the enemy is fear, the product of ignorance or denial, not the circumstances themselves.

It is no mean feat to look harsh realities full in the face. Few people do.

We humans are hardwired to avoid discomfort and pain. Thus the foolish reward the courtiers who tell them what they want to hear; the wise bestow their gratitude on those who struggle, however futilely, to reach them with the truth.

The following observation bears the stamp of humility on the diploma from the school of hard knocks: People who are fascinated by complexity and intrigued by uncertainty are likely to be the ones who have something worthwhile to say about the future.

As you try to understand the scope and breadth of the harsh realities in which we find ourselves mired, remember the famous retort from Jack Nicholson in the movie *A Few Good Men* as he responded to the entreaty from the military prosecutor played by Tom Cruise. Cruise: "I want the truth!" Nicholson: *"You can't handle the truth!"* My assumption is that you desire the truth; my hope is that *we* can handle it. It is unlikely that it will be found in the mindless reassurances of the Hank Paulsons of the world.

In one of his last interviews before leaving office, Treasury Secretary Paulson elucidated as only he can:[8] "We've done all this without all of the authorities that a major nation like the U.S. needs." Is the reader to accept "We've done all of this" as self-affirming or self-condemning? It sadly appears the secretary still sees himself as Superman overcoming the insurmountable. "We're dealing with something that is really

---

[8][2008, original] *Financial Times* interview with Hank Paulson, the outgoing U.S. Treasury Secretary, December 30, 2008.

historic and we haven't had a playbook," he continued. "The reason it has been difficult is first of all, these excesses have been building up for many, many years. Secondly, we had a hopelessly outdated global architecture and regulatory authorities . . . in the U.S." Paulson concluded by saying any future regulatory overhaul should emphasize "better and more effective" regulation. Reform also "needed to make sure that infrastructures and powers were robust enough to allow large institutions to fail."

The formidable avalanche-like power of a giant snowball rolling down the mountainside conjures up a graphic mental image of the destructive force of the global meltdown in the financial markets. As is the nature of such events, no one can ever predict with precision when the increasingly daunting efforts to push the ever-larger ball of snow up the incline will eventually prove no match for its burgeoning mass. What one can say with some certainty is that when the spherical mound of snow is thundering down the mountainside it will flatten everything in its path. The bigger the snowball, the broader and longer is the swath of destruction. Even though its pace has slowed somewhat, the financial snowball thus far has been unstoppable despite heretofore unprecedented efforts by the Treasury and the Federal Reserve. Through the process of contagion it has migrated from the financial system to the real economy. Virtually all contemporaneous and leading indicators of economic activity are in a state of free fall. It's no surprise that conditions have forced President Barack Obama to frantically package an estimated $1 trillion economic stimulus program, which he launched soon after taking office January 20.

The imponderables are endless in this no man's land. There's at least a kernel of truth expressed in the earlier lamentations of Paulson. We are floundering in uncharted waters. Although it's widely presumed that a Keynesian demand-pull fiscal stimulus program is the most appropriate remedial action, there is room for doubt among reasonable observers. Even Keynes noted that consumers are far from Pavlovian in their response to stimuli. As one of the preeminent scholars of the Great Depression, Keynes posited that an investment spending cycle generally begins with "spontaneous optimism" and "animal spirits." But now consumer confidence is snowballing downward in conjunction with a dysfunctional financial system and a slumping global economy. Is it logical and responsible to expect that throwing money in its path will be sufficient to rekindle spontaneous optimism and animal spirits?

It should be noted that the proposed massive fiscal stimulation program is the chosen strategy by default. With Fed funds rates near zero percent, monetary policy may have played its last trump card.

A rational concern regarding when the tide might turn is the future of securitization, a key mechanism of modern banking that enables banks to bundle loans and bonds into securities for sale to investors (as discussed in detail earlier). This crucial market is moribund now that many of its creations are selling for a fraction of their carrying value. Three decades ago, banks supplied $3 out of every $4 of credit worldwide. Today, because of securitization and the "shadow banking system," that share has dropped to about $1 in $3. Unless what remains of the investment banking industry is able to securitize—which, in turn, depends on investors' willingness to buy the bundled loans—credit will remain tight, even if banks resume lending.

Households, whose spending constitutes 70 percent of GDP, have thus far not answered the bell, refusing to step back in the ring. Consumers have become more circumspect about their spending and saving decisions. They no longer view them casually in the gristmill of the new harsh reality. Such behavior has a name. It is called the "thrift paradox." What is prudent behavior for the individual may be antithetical for the economy at large. Referring once again to Paulson's remarks, one of the long-expanding excesses to which he referred is America's gradual emergence as the world's largest debtor nation. As if to pour salt on the wound, research[9] has shown that when the ratio of public debt to GDP is already high, the multiplier effect of fiscal stimulus is likely to be low. Even more worrisome, in extreme cases fiscal expansion can be counterproductive. Not surprisingly, the sheer size of the combined monetary and fiscal stimulus programs—reflected in the mirror of a worldwide loss of confidence in the dollar—may have the unintended side effect of further depressing consumer confidence.

Adding to the malaise, the thus-far-cheap financing of ballooning budget deficits should not be taken for granted. It will not bode well for

---

[9][2008 original, revised] Carmen M. Reinhart and Kenneth S. Rogoff, 2008. "Banking Crises: An Equal Opportunity Menace." National Bureau of Economic Research Working Paper 14587. Draft dated December 19, 2007.

the prospects of recovery if what consumers have learned about the limits to their indebtedness proves to be applicable to governments as well. If the United States runs short on foreign creditors willing to finance the budget and trade deficits at less than confiscatory interest rates, our policy options begin to narrow dangerously. A ruinous inflation or even heretofore unthinkable currency devaluation should not be ruled out.

In realistic summary, it is little more than restating the obvious when I note that the restorative efforts that have been and will be employed by the new administration are figuratively robbing Peter to pay Paul. Apart from the looming long-term consequences of Band-Aid therapy, the process will surely be remembered as one tarnished by wastefulness, bureaucratic bungling, political patronage, and (yes) corruption. Even deeper down in the behavioral realm are F. A. Hayek's contentions—namely that social science, including economics, has been built up on the pretense that it's possible to gain "scientific" mastery over complicated social problems. Such intellectual ambition (*hubris?*) is inherently Icarus-like, he argued. It is "the fatal conceit."[10] Sadly, a fiscal stimulus program that defers the burden on the taxpayer at the cost of higher marginal tax rates in the future does little to instill long-term incentives to work, invest, and innovate. The financial crisis has been blamed on deficient risk management. The proposals for a large fiscal stimulus suffer from the same weakness.[11]

Those, dear readers, could be the harsh realities of the snowball effect. Do not give up hope. The process is cathartic and, ultimately, can be liberating.

---

[10][2008, original] *The Road to Serfdom* is listed among the 25 books the *Washington Monthly* proposed as a reading list for President Barack Obama. Author Friedrich Hayek, of the Austrian school, won a Nobel Prize in economics.

[11][2008, original] The idea that boom causes bust—and that great busts are self-reinforcing—originated in the Austrian school of economics, with its chief protagonists being Friedrich Hayek and Ludwig von Mises. "The main tenets of Austrian business-cycle theory can be summarized as follows: (1) the boom causes the bust; (2) the bust is proportionate to the boom; (3) major intervention is likely to cause major unintended consequences; and (4) sound money is the best policy in all environments." (Let there be no mistake, Austrian business-cycle theory has been harshly criticized by such influential economists as John Maynard Keynes and Milton Friedman. Of no minor significance, Hayek and Mises both predicted the upcoming crisis in 1929.) [Walter Deemer et al., "A Way Forward"]

Can Harsh Realities Be Quantified?

Not to leave those hungering for the tangible hanging on a clothesline of dangling prepositions and metaphors, I've attempted to put a little meat on the bones of conjecture. There are reasonably understandable explanations of four different methodologies for roughly valuing common stocks in the aggregate—and over many decades.

1. The first compares the total market value of all U.S.-domiciled companies annually with GDP. It has been featured in a number of earlier annual reports.
2. The second, a model originated by Ben Graham and updated by Bob Shiller, traces the 10-year trailing deflated price-earnings ratio from the early 1920s.
3. The third, Tobin's q-ratio, compares the market value to the replacement value of corporate assets over the same time frame.
4. Finally, a name out of the past, Edson Gould, attempts to use dividend yield as a measure of valuation.

These four different ways of looking at the same thing provided not only similar conclusions as to when major market lows occurred but, with reasonable accuracy, how depressed valuations were on those occasions. Common stocks were most out of favor in the early 1920s, the early 1930s, and the early 1980s, the last episode being the only instance of double-digit inflation and interest rates. If the current malaise continues, and those same low valuations are eventually realized, the S&P 500 could decline further to somewhere between 400 and 550, the Dow Jones industrial average, 4000 to 5500. From year-end prices the further erosion in total market value could range between 30 and 50 percent.

You'll be making a big mistake if you take the above to be a forecast. As indicated in the preceding section, you'll be making an even bigger mistake if you don't make adequate mental provision for what could be a worst-case scenario.

I'm all the more hesitant to opine with specifics on the real economy. First, anything I might offer is little more than the warmed-over forecast from someone else. Moreover, forecasters seem to come from two camps. First are those who draw their paychecks from a for-profit enterprise. Given the obvious incentives, there must be a presumption that if they have a bias it will most likely lean toward the optimistic side. The other cohort comes largely from the academic community. The work of these folks has its own biases. Of all the many opinions I have read over recent months, one from Martin Wolf of the *Financial Times*[12] seemed the least infected with common biases and was based, for better or worse, on the antecedents of other banking crises in advanced economies since World War II—in addition to two prewar developed country episodes: the Great Depression in the United States in the 1930s and in Norway in 1989.

The academic sources Wolf quoted[13] from a year ago showed that standard indicators for the United States, such as asset price inflation, rising leverage, large sustained current account deficits, and a slowing trajectory of economic growth "exhibited virtually all the signs of a country on the verge of a financial crisis—indeed, a severe one." So far, on point. In a January 2009 paper, the academics cited by Wolf focused on the comparative historical analysis of the aftermath of systemic banking crises.[14] According to them, such crises tend to be protracted affairs, with three characteristics in common.

1. First, asset market collapses are deep and prolonged, with real housing price declines averaging 35 percent and stretched over six years. On average equity prices took 3 and a half years to fall 55 percent.
2. Second, the crises were followed by profound declines in output and employment. Unemployment rose on average by seven percentage points over the contraction phase of the cycle, which averaged more than four years in duration. Peak-to-trough declines in output averaged 9 percent, although the duration was two years, half that for unemployment.

---

[12][2008, original] "Choices Made in 2009 Will Shape the Globe's Destiny" by Martin Wolf. Published January 6, 2009, *Financial Times*.

[13][2008, original] Reinhart, Carmen M., and Kenneth S. Rogoff. See earlier footnote 9 regarding the same authors.

[14][2008, original] While I thought the research was sound, the statistical support could've been much better—for example, simple use of standard deviations with averages.

3. Third, the real value of government debt exploded, rising an average of 86 percent. Interestingly, the bailout spending related to recapitalizing the banking sector was not the main driver of the mushrooming debt. *Rather, the culprit was the inevitable collapse in tax receipts resulting from the contraction in economic output, as well as the countercyclical fiscal policies aimed at mitigating the downturn.*

No matter what course the financial and economic crisis takes, the not-so-harsh reality is that, as stated, "This too shall pass." By exposing you to hypothetical worst-case scenarios based on the repetitious nature of human behavior, along with somewhat similar episodes from the past, we hope we have helped you form the kind of expectations that will set you up to be a survivor, not a victim. One point bears repeating, however. Long-term stability is predicated on recoupling risk and return. Government macro policies are, in the name of social stability, aimed almost exclusively at stopping the bleeding. To the extent that the consequences of risk indulgence are thereby ameliorated, long-term stability is in jeopardy.

The Future of Risk Aversion

There are profoundly positive consequences from the harsh lessons investors and consumers are in the process of learning. The significance cannot be overstated. As observed earlier in this chapter, *"[T]he future of investment for a generation hangs in the balance."* The wisdom to be gleaned from older men is a sure way to steepen the DIY (do it yourself) learning curve. Peter Bernstein, to whom I last referred in Chapter 9, I shamelessly do again. (You can never learn too much from a great man.) Bernstein lived the history about which he wrote.[15]

Based on Bernstein's shared recollections and our mutual belief in the predictable irrationality of human behavior, we envision a future that closely parallels the acute risk aversion mind-set that framed the

---

[15][2008, original] Peter Bernstein, "How Far Away Is the Past? How Near Is the Future?" in CFA Institute, *Conference Proceedings Quarterly* (December 2008), 3.

attitudes of investors turned savers[16] for several decades after the Great Depression. The man who saw so much and who reflected endlessly on what he observed said:

> The new environment will be slow to develop excesses, especially in the credit area, and this result will last for a long time. So, we can be patient, seek out opportunities calmly and quietly, and not worry because nobody will be in a hurry. Secondly, liquidity derived from trust and not from the central banks will not be in unlimited supply because trust itself will be limited in supply for a long time. The word awash will vanish from the vocabulary. This result means that if you have liquidity, you have a precious asset and can achieve high returns.

There will be a revolution in expectations and priorities. Savers were so risk-averse after the war that most business school graduates went into business instead of off to Wall Street to make their fortunes. Bernstein recalled that only two of his fellow 1947 graduates from Harvard migrated to Wall Street, and one of them was named J. P. Morgan III.[17] After graduation Bernstein began teaching money

---

[16][2008, original] Not finding a suitable definition of the difference between savings and investment, I'll offer my own. Savings is the conscious act of deferring consumption, of setting aside a portion of one's disposable income so that it might be expended in the future. Investment is what you do with the money set aside. There is no place one can put money that has been set aside that is entirely immune from risk (money tucked away in a lockbox as a store of value may buy less in the future because of inflation in the price of goods it will be used to purchase). Cautious investors may seek out the asset classes that have historically been the safest: savings accounts at banks: CDs, U.S. Treasury bills, and so forth. More enterprising investors will assume greater uncertainty in terms of future payback. They may invest in real estate, mutual funds, and so on. Intelligent investors (which is also the title of one of the greatest books written on the subject) attempt to reconcile expected return with risks incurred.

[17][2008, original] Two Harvard economists, Lawrence F. Katz and Claudia Goldin, have long studied the career choices of Harvard undergraduates. In recent years 23 percent have entered banking and finance, six times the percentage of the 1960s. Money has been the lure. Compensation was triple that of their nonfinance contemporaries. Far more significant in terms of recoupling risk and reward, a National Bureau of Economic Research working paper by Thomas Philippon of

and banking at Williams College in Massachusetts. Bernstein had his students study the financial statements of a local bank—Williamstown National Bank—where most had deposited their money. He pointed out with apparent dismay that 75 to 80 percent of the bank's assets were invested in bonds and only a small amount in loans. Soon the bank president summoned the greenhorn, admonishing him: "Bernstein, you don't understand a thing about running a bank. We have all these depositors who could ask for their money at any time, and I have to remain liquid." The Williamstown bank president's preoccupation with risk aversion was an apt proxy for the cautious outlook of bankers in the late 1940s and beyond, a convex rear-view mirror perspective on the future in which the image of the Depression was magnified out of proportion with reality. [Will history repeat itself?]

The time to embrace opportunity is when everyone else is focused on shunning risk. There were two risks that experience had told Depression-era Americans to avoid: market and business (or credit) risk. The stock market crash-induced trauma was seared into investors' psyches for a generation. The business depression that followed sealed the demise of confidence, obliterating the Keynesian urge toward "spontaneous optimism" and "animal spirits." With the propensity to recklessly embrace risk in pursuit of return (that marked the 1920s) purged from the minds of all those who bore the scars of the Depression, assets sold at prices that were stripped of "blue sky." Although the Depression

New York University and Ariell Reshef of the University of Virginia found that the difference in pay between finance and the rest of U.S. industry was slight, if any, *except in the late 1920s and then again from the mid-1990s to 2006.* With total bonus payments on Wall Street reaching $18.4 billion last year, a sea change could be in the offing. The harsh reality is that high pay on Wall Street is an episodic phenomenon. If history repeats, the pay for top bankers could fall into line with pay for other professions, like doctors and lawyers. Maybe the best minds will once again be employed creating things of lasting value?

Wall Street also set the tone for other industries, as the compensation of senior managers rose far faster than for most workers. In 2007 the total compensation of chief executives in large U.S. corporations was 275 times that of the salary of the average worker, estimates the Economic Policy Institute in Washington. In the late 1970s CEO pay was 35 times that of the average U.S. worker. Overdue compensation restitution, as appears to be occurring in 2009, reduces the risk of social revolution.

lingered through the 1930s, the giveaway prices at which businesses sold reflected the sorry state of affairs. It was the exogenous stimulus from the Lend–Lease program that began in March 1941, more than 18 months after the outbreak of war in Europe that began to slowly stoke the fires of recovery.

Two critical concepts introduced at the outset of the report are worthy of repetition: Risk is not a constant, nor can it be avoided. Investors often fail to realize what modern portfolio theory dogma refuses to embrace: that risk is variable, that it is functionally related to the price paid for an asset. A junk bond portfolio, to use an extreme example, is less risky at a yield of 20 percent than at a yield of 4 percent. In the last 18 months junk bonds traded at both extremes. To use a hypothetical example, if 10 percent of the portfolio defaults and the recovery rate on the defaulted bonds is 50 percent, the current yield falls to 12 to 17 percent. If the default rate turns out to be 20 percent, the yield is still 7 to 12 percent.

Investment risk can never be avoided because the very act requires investing now with the expectation that more than what has been ventured will flow back in the sometimes capricious future. The greater the apprehensions about the vagaries of tomorrow, the less an investor is likely to pay for a given asset. When the perception of uncertainty is profoundly influenced by past experience (where assuming risk resulted in losses), the price investors are willing to pay for an asset is likely to be more influenced by fear of risk of loss than opportunity for gain. The antithesis of investors' irrational willingness to be undercompensated for the risks assumed in euphoric times—the equally unreasonable insistence by "once burned, twice shy" investors that they be overcompensated for the risks assumed in troubled times—is manna from heaven for the courageous, value-driven, long-term investor who is not without fear but is not controlled by it either.

Price Is What You Pay, Value Is What You Get*

S&P 500 (SP50)
— Price

SOURCE: © FactSet Research Systems.

As the guidepost "You Are Here" chart reveals, the end of our journey through the Decade of Delusions is nearly complete. Appropriately, a full account of Martin Capital Management's investment performance history during these turbulent years may be seen in Tables 11.1 and 11.2, excerpted from the 2009 annual report. As made clear in the Preface, the primary purpose of these numbers is not to promote but rather to reconcile words and actions, theory and reality.

The difference in rate of return between MCM Equities and the Total Account depends on the percentage of Total Account assets committed to equities (Figure 11.1). The S&P 500 market value is the irregular horizontal bold line. Apart from individual client account constraints, generally the percentage of assets allocated to equities is a function of their availability at prices that provide an adequate risk-adjusted margin of safety.

In terms of dollars (Figure 11.2), $5 million invested with Martin Capital Management January 1, 2000, is now worth $9.5 million, after fees but before taxes. The same amount of money hypothetically invested in the S&P 500 would be worth $4.5 million, with no fees and no taxes.

---

*This material is adapted from the 2009 annual report of Martin Capital Management.

Table 11.1 MCM Annual Investment Performance

Year	MCM Equities*	MCM Total Account (1)	S&P 500 (2)	Relative Performance (1)–(2)
2000	29.3	21.3	−9.1	30.4
2001	22.7	16.4	−11.9	28.3
2002	−13.6	−11.5	−22.1	10.7
2003	33.0	25.1	28.7	−3.6
2004	4.8	3.5	10.9	−7.4
2005	−.2	−.07	4.9	−5.6
2006	5	.8	15.8	−15.1
2007	1.5	3.2	5.5	−2.4
2008	−21.5	−7.8	−38	29.2
2009	51.4	21.6	26.5	−4.9

*Net of fees.

Table 11.2 MCM Multiyear Compounded Investment Performance

Period ending 12/31/09	MCM Equities*	MCM Total Account (1)	S&P 500 (2)	Relative Performance (1)–(2)
Ten Years	9.3	6.5	−.9	7.4
Five Years	4.8	2.9	.4	2.5
Three Years	6.4	4.9	−5.6	10.5
One Year	51.4	21.6	26.5	−4.9

*Compounded annually, MCM data are net of fees.

Disclosure: The MCM Equities Composite shows the performance of the equity investments in all discretionary fee-paying accounts managed by MCM. Historical returns include accounts that may no longer be under our management. The MCM Total Account Composite shows the performance of all assets held in fully discretionary fee-paying accounts who have given us authority to invest 100 percent of the account in equities and are managed per our model portfolio. Because we began presenting the Total Account Composite in 2008, it contains only accounts that were actively managed on December 31, 2008, plus accounts that have since been added. MCM believes that because the fully discretionary accounts are, and historically have been, so similarly managed in terms of types and proportions of securities, survivor bias—if any—is not material. Both MCM composites are net of all management fees and include the reinvestment of all income but do not reflect the effect of taxes. The composites are compared with the S&P 500, an unmanaged market capitalization-weighted index of 500 common stocks chosen for market size, liquidity, and industry group representation to represent U.S. equity performance. S&P 500 returns do not include consideration for fees or taxes.

Due to client nuances—including equity allocation constraints, start date, and cash-flow differentials (derivatives, constraints, tax issues, etc.)—an individual's account performance may differ materially from the composite. *Past performance is no guarantee of future results.*

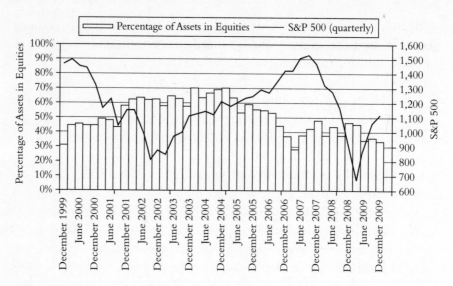

Figure 11.1   MCM Aggregate Allocation of Client Capital

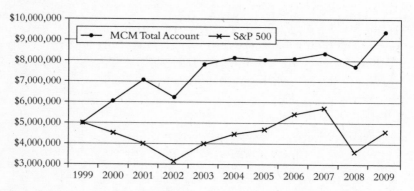

Figure 11.2   Ten–Year $5 Million Investment: MCM versus S&P 500

2009 Investment Performance: Discussion and Analysis

While 2009 is but the last annual leg in the worst decade, market-wise, in more than 100 years, this report is written annually and will, therefore, review the year just past first. In terms of the S&P 500 it was shaped like a "check mark"—down until March 9 and up at a decelerating rate thereafter. Our total account performance was up 21.6 percent; the S&P 500 rose 26.5 percent. The "Aggregate Allocation of Client Capital" table indicates we spent most of the year with more than 60 percent of your assets in short-term U.S. Treasury securities and the highest-quality municipal bonds, ending with only one-third of our typical client's assets invested in increasingly expensive equities.

No doubt you are wondering how we earned such Total Account returns with so few equities and so much of your money hunkered down in short-term, highly liquid assets yielding less than one-half of 1 percent? When the markets went into a free fall in September 2008 we had to make a choice about what to do with all the cash in our coffers. How were we going to ride out what looked more and more like the 1991 nor'easter about which the book *The Perfect Storm* was written (and after which the featured essay in the MCM 2005 annual report was named)? We could favor the traditional blue chips—that throughout the bear market never sank to anything approaching the fishing-a-stocked-pond valuation lows of the other major secular bear markets of the past—or we could safe-harbor major portions of portfolios in U.S. Treasury securities and place smaller bets on less-than-blue-chip companies whose market prices had been trashed and would likely spring back faster in the event of a contra-trend rally. We opted for the latter—and our bet paid off: Stocks that were on the bargain rack largely because of financial risks exposed by the crisis rallied by a factor of two or more compared with those that were conservatively capitalized.

Volatility has been our friend throughout the last several years. While modern portfolio theory (MPT) thinks of it as a measure of risk, we think it's a measure of opportunity. Although comprising a relatively small part of portfolios, our equities were up over 50 percent for the year. Nothing like this sentence will appear in next year's report.

As to whether the financial system and the economy will follow the V-pattern lead of the financial markets, which increasingly is the consensus view, the undersigned remains doubtful.

The Lost Decade

The first decade of the new millennium will be recorded by historians as the most shocking and widespread reversal of fortunes since the 1930s. It began when the giant wealth-imploding sound rumbled through the

408   A DECADE OF DELUSIONS

markets in March of 2000. The technology/telecommunications/dot-com Bubble burst, with the tech-laden Nasdaq composite plummeting nearly 80 percent from 5000 to 1100 by 2002. Badly crippled, it languishes seven years later just above 2200. The S&P 500, much more broadly based but still well represented with the likes of Microsoft and Intel, along with many highly priced, large-cap growth companies and a host of lesser exotica, fell nearly 50 percent from peak to trough. Then, after a four-year, easy-money-driven respite from 2003 to 2007, the second leg of this epic saga—this time led by the financial sector that had grown rich and reckless exploiting financial innovations—got under way in earnest in October 2007. The S&P 500 surrendered 57 percent of its index value to fall to the prevailing low-water mark reached in March 2009. Despite 2009's impressive rally, at year end the S&P had regained only half the ground lost since the October 2007 peak (remember this sentence when reading Einstein below). As for the decade as a whole, the benchmark S&P 500 index, including dividends, declined 1 percent on a compounded annual basis.

During the decade the boom-bust cycle spread to residential real estate, aided and abetted by an easy and cheap money central bank policy and financial innovation run amok that ultimately brought a broad swath of American households to its metaphorical knees. The real estate debacle has been the stuff of headlines since 2007 and little needs to be repeated about the Sasquatch-sized footprint on the homeowner's backyard. Suffice it to say, 1 million homes were foreclosed upon in the third quarter alone. The trauma and suffering visited on families across the land, as well as many other developed nations of the world, is incalculable and ongoing.

The most damaging blow, in terms of the breadth of its destruction, was still to come. In December 2007 the country haltingly entered the worst financial crisis and economic contraction since the Great Depression. While there are many ways to describe the carnage, nothing reveals the human toll quite like the following statistics: 10 percent of the workforce is unemployed, with another 7.5 percent "underemployed." Those statistics are even more unsettling when one considers that the average working American has less than 60 days' worth of savings put away for a rainy day—and one-fifth have no savings at all. That's a lot of people stretched dangerously thin.

In attempting to salvage the financial system and brace against the flood tide of unemployment, massive doses of Keynesian-style fiscal, as well as unprecedented monetary stimuli, were thrown willy-nilly at the crisis. Whether they will have the desired effect has not yet been determined but, regardless, the future burden of trillions of dollars of fiscal stimulus debt (and other bubbles fermenting because of zero interest rates engineered by the Fed) are all but guaranteed.

Investment Performance, 2000–2009: Discussion and Analysis

As for the 10 years that most everyone would like to pretend didn't happen, and consistent with our annual commitment to full disclosure, we will explain how it was that we were able to paddle our little canoe upstream. Illustrations and explications will be laced throughout the discussion that follows. Equally, if not more important, we will expand on the various risks we took in eking out those returns. We hope the explanations are enlightening.

The Most Powerful Force in the Universe

Let's begin with a big, little-understood idea. Albert Einstein, the unintended father of the atomic bomb, revealed the breadth of his genius when he declared: "The most powerful force in the universe is compound interest." While we refined our understanding of it through years of practice, it was apparently dismissed by most as too difficult, perhaps because the brainstorm came from Einstein, the man who expounded so effortlessly on the theory of relativity. Among its precepts, losses have a disproportionate effect on long-term compounding. Most people are generally aware that it takes a 100 percent gain to offset a 50 percent loss, but we aren't sure everyone can explain why—and what its relevance is to portfolio management. Can *you*, we ask delicately? Moving up a notch in the degree of difficulty, we pose another question while hoping not to be overbearing: If the individual year data in the table of S&P returns are arbitrarily rearranged, what effect will this rearrangement have on the 10-year compounded results?

The tables above were given to randomly selected clients who were asked to examine the data, then explain how we bettered the S&P 500 by 7.5 percent compounded annually over 10 years. The deafening silence spoke volumes about (1) how little most investors really know about the mathematics of long-term compounding and (2) how poor we investment managers are as communicators. Up to my old tricks and to make amends for imposing, $5 out of my own pocket goes to any reader who answers correctly the two questions at the end of the preceding paragraph. Cheating is encouraged. Explain your prowess to your friends so they can collect their five-spot. Despite my parsimonious, penny-pinching reputation, I would pay many times that amount to eradicate (or even minimize) the hobbling misunderstanding of this concept that is so foundational to our investment style. Feel free to call if you need help . . . but don't expect the five bucks [an offer made in the original report only!]. The greatest value investors like Warren Buffett and Sir John Templeton have a little-known companion virtue: frugality. I'm simply trying to emulate them, and my friends tell me I'm quite successful at it (cheap, to use their word)!

Another insight may steepen the learning curve. Compare MCM's total account returns with those from the S&P 500 in the preceding tables. People's eyes are first drawn to the obvious: *MCM performance trailed the S&P in every feel-good up year during the decade.* So much for making hay while the sun shines. That's six out of 10, including the ignominious five consecutive years, 2003–2007. Despite looking like dolts for longer than necessary to test most people's threshold of pain for not keeping up with the Joneses, we finished among the leaders over the most challenging investment decade in our lifetimes. (Please reread the second half of that sentence!) *Sometimes* it's not how much you gain in the good markets but how much you don't lose in the ugly ones that separates the winners from the wannabes. As you can see, going with the flow is easy. Paddling upstream isn't.

Because our overarching—and unconventional—strategy was preservation of capital in a decade during which common stocks were consistently more highly priced (and risk, correspondingly, paid far less heed) than ever before, our 10-year results eclipsed those of two of the most esteemed (by us and hordes of others) mutual-fund giants, Sequoia and Longleaf Partners, who themselves finished near the top of their group rankings. Perhaps one of the most telling stories is that of Bill Miller, legendary manager of Legg Mason's Value Trust. Miller, for whom we have the highest regard, became famous for besting the S&P 500 for 15 consecutive years ending in 2005. In 2008 Value Trust made an ill-fated bet on the financial sector, and the fund shed 55 percent of its value. Even after a solid comeback through November 30, 2009, the fund's 10-year compounded return was a 15-year, record–obliterating −3.21 percent.

Value Investors: A Rare Breed

Value investors of our ilk (likely less than 3 percent of all managers) have to be willing to patiently defer gratification and act unconventionally. Moreover, they are likely to underperform in rising markets, as noted above, demanding a higher margin of safety than their peers and forswearing the thrill of always chasing the latest, greatest idea. In an era of casino capitalism, a value investor is the ugly duckling. While Warren Buffett legitimized our style, even he believes that the number of managers who practice our craft will remain comparatively small. It simply takes too much discipline and patience—and is too difficult to market. Who wants to turn over his money to what frequently looks like a head-in-the-sand ostrich? We are pleased that we don't have much competition . . . until we think about why.

It is our belief that outlier success in the money management business does not go to people who think and behave conventionally—and are therefore statistically destined to be average. It comes at a cost: by separating from the pack and not only thinking independently but by thinking well beyond the moment. Short-term thinking is filled with counterproductive emotions; fear and greed don't carry much weight in the long term. The farther you can stretch out your horizon, the more you can engage your rational mind without emotional interference, the less competition you have and the more likely you are to do well. Not coincidentally, the long-term paradigm of the great value investors (those who compound ideas into wisdom and money into sustainable wealth) is much the same as that of the great CEOs in American business and industry. Most important to clients and prospective clients, the great value investors seem to be more capable of repeating outperformance than random luck would suggest. Buffett is simply the most conspicuous example.

Even forearmed with these presumed insights, we still found the going tough from time to time. On occasion we were surveying the forest, while the eyes of most others were zeroed in on the trees. The year 2006 was one of discontent for some of our clients and, therefore, for us. The S&P 500 racked up its second-best year in what had been to that point a lackluster decade, rising 15.8 percent, and our total account performance was conspicuous by its anemic under-performance: a paltry 0.7 percent. Some of our clients were wondering if we were out of touch with a new reality. Our equity performance was competitive, but the undersigned was the spoiler, insisting that the equity securities we wanted to own have a much greater than usual margin of safety embedded in their purchase price, resulting at one point in equities dropping to 30 percent of total assets. I had a vague but powerful notion of what could happen—always with the "perfect storm" in the forefront of my mind. But the reality is that no one knows the future. Precious compounding time is often lost when ships are berthed in safe harbor, but no storm appears. Opportunities are forgone. It was an agonizing year and a half before the financial storm of our lives hit.

There's always plenty of humble pie for everyone after the game, including us. With the benefit of hindsight, if on the first day of the new decade we had invested a hypothetical $5 million entirely in 20-year, zero-coupon U.S. Treasury securities, it would be worth $15 million today, before taxes. Gold did better but was a less certain bet. Imagine the simplicity of making one smart decision in 2000 and then going into intellectual hibernation for the next 10 years. We call this idyllic state Rip van Winkle investing.

There's a little problem, however, in the implementation: Unlike Mr. van Winkle, we can't "rip" off to the woods to escape the nagging wife (a metaphor for the "institutional investor's imperative") who refuses to let us sleep, insisting that if we're not doing something we're not adding value. Of course, on occasion it is the client who plays the role of the nagging spouse.

The Lost Decade was a case study in the trade-offs necessary to win by not losing, and that's assuming that in fact our patience and focus were eventually vindicated. The sacrifices seem so manageable in theory but become much more problematic when put to the test in the real world.

Thank you, Dr. Einstein. The decade was what it was, and we had to adapt to the circumstances. The years 2010−2019 will certainly serve up their own set of unique challenges.

Risk—Once Again a Four-Letter Word?

In the opinion of the undersigned, we'll know the present storm has passed *only* when investors' aversion to *risk* becomes irrational and well nigh indelible. Imagine irrational risk avoidance displacing irrational exuberance. Now that would be something new! Parenthetically, imposing new regulations, what we do to atone for sins not soon to be repeated, are redundant in such times; they're the equivalent of fighting the last war. If risk truly becomes a four-letter word, the need for yet more measures to contain aberrant behavior will diminish under the lingering moral weight of the malefactors' transgressions. A flurry of new laws and regulations becomes a lagging indicator, I note sardonically. When these new rules hit the headlines, we'll know at that point they won't be needed for a long time. Likewise, the capital markets tend to be more judicious allocators of capital assets in the aftermath of episodes when they performed the job badly. And when the cry for managed capitalism becomes deafening and risk taking becomes passé, logic and history would say it's time to restore the system's freedom. Of course, when the crowd roars, nothing else really matters. Don't you just love the ironies?

In the past decade, when risk was recklessly ignored, defense proved to be the best strategy even though, or perhaps because, everyone else was playing offense. The opposite is likely to be true in the years ahead if and when risk aversion gets deeply embedded in the mass psyche. Then risk as an investment criterion will be overrated and return underrated. And only then an offensive (in just *one* sense of the word!) strategy should provide superior returns at minimal risk of permanent capital loss.

Imagine the freedom if one believes that another similar episode is unlikely until memories of this one have faded. History confirms time and again the constancy of human behavior. Most people envision the future as an extension of the past. To leave the security of the pack, to wander out on your own into the unfamiliar wilderness of agonizing uncertainty and isolation, without which independence of thought is impossible, is simply too unnatural, too frightening. It is in assuming that the future will be a carbon copy of the present or near past that gets investors into deep water during euphoric times, and it's what makes them oblivious to the shallow water just under their furiously dog-paddling feet during the desperate times when survival overrides all mental (and physical) faculties and processes.

■ ■ ■

Having just reread the preceding paragraphs, I am painfully reminded of exchanges between two famous pairs—the first about writing style and the second, vanity. [I plead guilty as charged on both counts.] His prose manifesting meticulous attention to diction and cadence, William Faulkner wrote of Ernest Hemingway: "He has never been known to use a word that might send a reader to the dictionary." To which the master of understatement replied: "Poor Faulkner. Does he really think big emotions come from big words?" Next, but no less revealing, is the reported repartee between George Bernard Shaw and Winston Churchill. "I am enclosing two tickets to the first night of my new play; bring a friend . . . if you have one." Churchill's deadpan response: "Cannot possibly attend first night; will attend second . . . if there is one."

Risk Management and Its Trade-Offs

Any manager who talks about returns without mentioning risk is like the magician whose sleight of hand has you believing there is only one side to the reward/risk coin. At MCM we intentionally invert: "If you manage the risks well, the returns will take care of themselves." As I hope has been evident by now, woven throughout the recap of the last 10 years have been various references to the many faces of risk:

- Macro—the economy slumps, and your company projections are too optimistic.
- Market—along comes 2007–2008, and there's almost no place to hide.
- Valuation—the price you pay exceeds the value you get.
- Business—competitive advantages prove unsustainable.

- Management—no need to comment on the range of malfeasances possible by those intent on deceit.
- Financial—having too much debt chasing too little income.
- Opportunities lost—about which more is written below.

Although most people think about risk in terms of its most common effect, capital lost, there is also the risk of opportunities forgone. Examine MCM total account performance from 2004 to 2007. Opportunities *were* lost. That's the price of cashing in chips early. It's a delicate and potentially hazardous balancing act to try to have it both ways. In the years 2000–2002 and 2007–2009, at least in a relative sense, the tables turned, and we avoided losses of capital that others didn't. There is a difference between opportunities missed and capital lost, with which most investors, anecdotally, do not appear adequately familiar. You can miss a million opportunities in a lifetime and still become very rich. Every single asset that has risen in price that one didn't purchase was an opportunity lost. Capital losses are not so forgiving. If you lose 100 percent of your capital—just once—you're broke.

It's All in Your Head

The inner nature of most of us is inclined more toward the hyperactive hare than the plodding tortoise. Can you think of anything more boring than watching turtles race? Even the thought is oxymoronic. Absent immediate emotional rewards, the time dimension in which the long-term value investor plies his trade is sparsely populated. Having a front-row seat as 2008 unfolded, I must admit to being fascinated by the short-term orientation of market participants. They quickly responded to day-by-day news and events while appearing deaf to the ever-louder rumblings of the onrushing avalanche, the emerging crisis behind the headlines. The evidence suggests that most people actually saw Bear Stearns as a singular event, not the first domino.

Psychologists might characterize long-term thinkers of the Buffett/Graham value camp as borderline "sociopaths" (as noted earlier in this chapter): They see opportunity and danger where others don't and actually get a feeling of satisfaction from knowing they're doing the right thing while most of those around them are doing the wrong thing.

They turn frequently destructive emotions to their advantage: Again borrowing Jason Zweig's memorable phrase, they are "inversely emotional"; unlike most investors, they actually feel better the lower prices fall and worse the farther prices rise. This is the ideal frame of mind, it should be noted, for those who desire to buy low and sell high.

The long-running speculative contagion that likely ended with the post–October 2007 bear market has tested the mettle of everyone. Even if we think long term, we live in a short-term world, the world of e-mails and their ubiquitous tentacles, "crackberries." Thought is swallowed up in a warp-speed existence. Despite Martin Capital's top-decile or better investment results, maintaining our composure, as well as a long-term perspective, required tenacious (and, yes, sometimes agonizing) self-control. It would be inhuman, however, not to occasionally be beset by self-doubt. As you'll read later, today is no different. Leading up to the bear market there were signs everywhere of impending trouble [see Chapter 9], and stocks in general were both popular and expensive. The market in 2007 was in the process of recording the best year since 2003, and most investors, looking into the rearview mirror to see the future, *saw* nothing but clear skies.

Analysis and Intuition: The Yin and Yang

A recurring theme you will encounter as you read this report about the Lost Decade is that successful investing is part science and part art; the maddening yet fascinating conundrum is knowing which to apply when. It should go without saying that seeking the balanced blend between the analytical and the intuitive is as elusive as is scratch golf for the duffer. With the benefit of hindsight, at critical inflection points over the last decade it appears that the intuitive thinker was better equipped as a problem solver than the analytical one. Intuition tends to rise in relative importance when the environment is undergoing rapid and dynamic change, wherein present analytical models are suspect and, postmortem, proved obsolete.

Many of the forces that gave rise to the financial crisis were without historical precedent, at least in the lifetimes of most decision makers. The mental frameworks or models that were relied upon were not stress-tested under rigorous conditions that included the 1930s and post-1989 Japan. For example, relying on contemporary historical precedent alone it was *logical* to conclude that house prices would not experience prolonged declines. The intuitive thinker, giving full range to his mental faculties in looking both backward *and* forward in the soaking up of all anecdotal and other information like a sponge, was less encumbered by the dogma of data when viscerally sizing up:

- The potential consequences of shockingly relaxed mortgage under-writing standards.
- High-risk financial innovations offered ostensibly to facilitate homeownership for the masses (with misaligned incentives that promoted antisocial behavior and richly rewarded those not ethically encumbered).
- The artificially low cost of money.

Regarding the extreme "tails" on financial innovations, the watchdogs of last resort—the data-dependent analytical and sequential processing-oriented rating agencies like Moody's and Standard & Poor's—simply didn't get it. Friedrich von Hayek (1899–1992) summed it up succinctly: "They are measuring what is measurable, not what matters."

As for the valuation of equity securities, the same type of dynamic tension existed between the analytical and intuitive. See Shiller's "Graham" P/E chart (Figure 11.3). Although it reached an all-time-record high of 45 times earnings during the tech Bubble (by comparison,

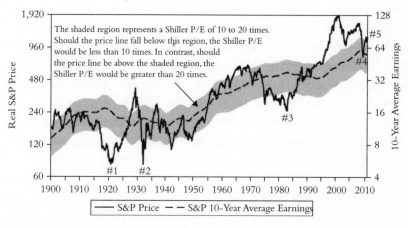

Figure 11.3   Shiller's "Graham" 10-Year Moving Average Price/ Earnings Ratio

SOURCE: www.econ.yale.edu/~shiller/data/htm.

it broached a mere 30 times briefly in 1929), it ranged between 20 and 25 times throughout the rest of the decade, except when it briefly slumped to 13.3 times at the end of March 2009 [annotation 4 on the Shiller chart]. Many otherwise intelligent analysts fell victim to the various biases that shackled them to the belief that a market multiple much greater than the long-term average of 16.3 times was the new normal. The free-ranging intuitive thinker questioned the rationale of using recent historical P/Es. Given the financial storm clouds that were looming on the horizon, why wouldn't the Shiller P/E eventually trade below its average or lower—even though it hadn't traded there since the mid-1980s? Indeed, the fact that it hadn't plumbed the depths of prior crises is, to the out-of-the-box thinker, *all the more reason why it could* [remember Silas Marner in Chapter 9?]. After all, in the aftermath of all prior memorable bubbles, the Shiller P/E fell below 10 in the 1920s, 1930s, and 1980s [represented as annotations 1 (4.8 times), 2 (5.6 times), and 3 (6.6 times), respectively]. I suspect that no more than one person in 10 today believes a sub 10 Shiller P/E is probable, let alone possible.

Why do we put so much credence in the Shiller P/E?[18] Please review the four other valuation measures earlier in this chapter. They all tell virtually the same story, but the reasoning behind the mathematical construct of the Shiller P/E is simply the most intuitively appealing to us.

Finally, the archaic approach to reversing the trend in unemployment may be the wrong remedy at the right time in that it fails to recognize subtle but significant changes in attitudes and expectations among consumers. President Obama's response to too many job seekers chasing too few jobs is to provide tax incentives as inducements for businesses to hire. What may be the fly in the ointment is the consumer himself who forgoes spending until he gets his financial house in order. This is an intuitive observation about which more is written in the final section, "2010 and Beyond."

In the future, if and when low valuations indicate that risk aversion has been priced, if not overpriced, into the debt and equity markets—and, because of arbitrage-induced correlation, into an increasing number of individual securities themselves—the intuitive thinker will take a backseat to the analytical one.

---

[18][2010] The Shiller chart is an updated and improved version of the one that appeared in the 2009 annual report.

2010 and Beyond

At Martin Capital we don't do forecasts, nor do we spend much time listening to folks dressed in gypsy garb, rubbing little glass spheres in carnival tents. All kidding aside, forecasting is a legitimate profession as long as one understands the mandate. That we even have forecasters is proof positive that they are paid to make elegant prognostications, not necessarily accurate ones. The job is beyond human analytical capacity: There are simply too many idiosyncratically moving parts. We leave it to others to engage in an activity, the end result of which is either looking stupid or lucky. As alluded to elsewhere in the report, we have only (1) vague notions that are the byproducts of many thousands of hours of reading, watching, and listening (and almost embarrassing amounts of time simply thinking about it all and asking ourselves questions like "Why?" and "Does this really make sense?") and (2) a deep aversion to losing money. That's all we've needed to get us through the last decade, and we trust that will be sufficient during the next. We might go so far to say that a detailed economic forecast in hand is not only unnecessary but potentially counterproductive. Such feckless specificity might lead to false confidence if upbeat or to cold feet if bleak.

Return again to the preceding Shiller P/E chart. Based on valuation alone, investors had one thing that should have been very reassuring

going for them whenever the P/E was in single digits—limited risk of permanent capital loss, at the very time, ironically, when further capital losses were the most widely feared outcome. We use the S&P 500 as a convenient proxy for *shorter-term* price movements for stocks in general. Without dragging you through the mathematical muck of MPT, suffice it to say that there are varying degrees of correlation between and among individual stocks in the S&P 500. Some are more volatile, some less so, and some are even negatively correlated; they go up when the market goes down—like gold stocks, generally. The Shiller P/E is relevant to us. Not surprisingly, when it's high (like now) attractively priced companies are as scarce as hen's teeth. When it's desperately low—which last occurred from the mid-1970s to the early 1980s—you find yourself in the happy state of running out of money before you run out of ideas. Of course, in the vast expanses of time in between, when financial and economic conditions are comparatively stable, the cost is simply a higher ante to be in the game. You can't change the market, but it is worthwhile not forgetting that the beam you're walking is most often more than two inches above the ground. In the long run, nothing beats great businesses, and nothing beats the satisfaction of ownership if those businesses are purchased sensibly.

Given the widespread belief that the next economic expansion is under way, that we have passed the low point in the financial crisis and economic contraction, we read of no pundits suggesting that a Shiller P/E of 10 or less is even remotely possible. Apart from the questionable credibility of economic forecasts, particularly those where a blatantly optimistic bias is rationalized as a necessary evil, we have a vague and nagging notion that all is not well. If one takes a gander at the MCM asset allocation graphic, it is clear that we are anything but sanguine. The widespread financial and economic uncertainty and despair that we consider necessary in order to justify committing large percentages of capital to equities in general is simply not there at an average Shiller P/E of 16.3, let alone at the lofty 20 where the market is now valued.

It may be easier to reconcile that disparate view with the presumed wisdom of the market if the reader accepts that most of the professional investor army goose-steps to the relative-return cadence and we, though not out of unthinking conformity, to the absolute-return one. The difference is one of perspective. In 2008 MCM's return of −7.8 percent was certainly nothing to crow about, even though the S&P 500 was down 37 percent. Quite the opposite, the relativists might strut around the barnyard a bit if their portfolios were down *only* 32 percent. On the flip side, we can tolerate, in a hoping-no-one-noticed sort of way, our conspicuous, barely in the black, relative-return shortfall in 2006, an outcome that would have caused apoplexy among the relativists. But if one prefers white-knuckle, roller-coaster rides, the relativists have much more to offer. Besides, both groups may start and end at the same place—if the relativists don't disembark, as sometimes happens, at the point of maximum pessimism.

Having declared my conviction, and therefore likely appearing disingenuous, might it be that the relativists are dangerously overplaying their hand in this increasingly valuation-rich market? After the 2008 bloodletting, the risk of falling behind in what could be a free-lunch rally might temporarily blind the relativists to our implicit Hippocratic (fiduciary in our parlance) duty. If the unthinkable happens, the relativists and, more important, their clients, might capitulate to the most destructive emotions—fear of total loss, the ultimate and decisive defeat. As one astute fellow

SOURCE: Deb Leighty.

observed: "When you're dead, you're dead for a long time"—precisely, as the history of the 1930s would suggest, the wrong time to forswear common stocks, as so many did, for the rest of one's life.

An ounce of prevention . . . requires a pound of independence. This homemade cartoon (shown on page 421) had its debut in Chapter 4 [the 2001 annual report]. It reappeared in the 2006 report [though not in Chapter 9 of this volume] for those who couldn't stomach 60 pages of prose. It is with the trepidation, much the same as I experienced during the earlier showings, that I unveiled it once again—and likely for the last time.

One foggy notion we have, a possible cog in the forecasting wheel, could be a modeling miscue similar to that which gave rise to the collapse of the subprime mortgage market and all the other dominoes that followed. The ruinous assumption then was, using backward-looking data and not forward-looking thinking, that housing prices would not experience a pronounced and sustained slump. Today's possible mistake just could be that consumers and lenders will not respond, Skinnerian-like, as they have in the past, like the human equivalents of brainwashed rats in a maze. That fiscal and monetary palliatives being applied to ameliorate the current crisis will not counterbalance what may be a yet unnoticed sea change in people's attitudes and expectations. The "dollars from helicopters" monetary policy response, employing doctrines of the past instead of relying on intuition in the present, has been geared more toward recent economic contractions: the "typical" post-war inventory recession. In a cyclical recession, private-sector balance sheets are not badly affected and people, on the most fundamental level, are still optimistic. Assets exceed liabilities by a comfortable margin. So when the Fed drives interest rates down, and people are still trying to maximize profits, there will be some response to those lower interest rates. People borrow money, they purchase goods and services, and the next expansion begins. In a balance sheet recession, which is what I believe this to be, people behave differently.

As was the case in Japan in the 1990s and the United States in the 1930s, the first priority of people in the private sector who feel acute financial stress (because asset prices have fallen and debts haven't) becomes to *reduce* debts instead of *maximizing* profits or spending. It's important to remember that the private sector cannot legally print money nor can it haphazardly and irresponsibly run deficits like Uncle Sam. Their bankers might have accommodated them a few years ago, but not now, for they have their own asset problems. If we zero in on the housing segment, the point hits close to home. Over recent years the value of the median homeowners' most important assets, their houses and financial assets, has declined whereas their debts have not. Their net-worth cushion has become dangerously thin. The balance sheet squeeze is occurring at a time when the other source of household financial security, disposable income, also is under duress. When people are worried about keeping their noses above water, even zero interest rates will not evoke the conditioned or heretofore predictable response: borrow and spend. Instead, they defer consumption to pay down debts. Needless to say, this phenomenon can feed on itself. Debt-reduction asset sales (think foreclosures) drive asset prices lower, while debt obligations do not shrink accordingly. The cycle can become vicious. It's a case of actions that are perfectly rational at the micro level turning disastrous when engaged at the macro level. In earlier writings we have referred to it as the "thrift paradox."

In theory, with the private sector pulling back its spending horns, the public sector must engage in deficit spending to take up the slack to offset the drag on GDP. The private sector savings will finance the government's largess. Intended or not, that is precisely what is happening— and what is necessary in the short run to shore up the economy. The Keynesian prescription is being widely embraced, but political and ideological partisanship will likely roadblock the effort. Something to think about . . .

As the cartoon suggests, for the moment we have cast our lot with the doubting Thomases. It is not coincidental that the December 2009 Fireside Chat was titled "Among the Last Skeptics Standing." With our high cash ratios, we're positioned to protect your capital from near-term loss. Longer term, cash may not insulate you from the following types of hazards:

- Degradation of the credit worthiness of our sovereign debt.
- Devaluation of the dollar opens a Pandora's box of risks.
- The possibility that hyperinflation will undermine the purchasing power of the dollar faster than rising yields on short-term U.S. Treasury securities will compensate.
- Punitive tax increases on the wealthy.

We think constantly about those "not-included" risks. As for the equity markets, we believe it likely that the current advance will prove nothing more than a major rally in a yet incomplete cathartic bear market. Without the purgation of the excesses built up over several decades, a solid foundation, where risk is once again relegated to a four-letter-word status, cannot be sustained.

As noted earlier, by our unconventional choices we have exposed you to loss of opportunity. If the market knows no rational bounds—not uncommon during speculative flights of fancy, occasionally for uncomfortably long intervals—and marches onward and upward from here, we will leave you standing at the gate. This is why so few investment managers step back during the "glorious process of enrichment." It's potentially dangerous to the manager's financial and career well-being. If, on the other hand, one holds firm to the educated belief that the market's reach for the stars will be truncated by the nagging realities that wishful thinking will not make go away, then it's easier to go against the grain of popular sentiment and feel good about what one's carefully reasoned, albeit vague, notion suggests is the right thing to do. If you were managing our money, that's how we hope you would behave.

We must confess to possessing one huge advantage over many of our fellow investment managers. It stems from serving a unique group of clients. Many own or owned their businesses and brought their long-term business perspective to the much less deliberate and focused world of investment in marketable securities. Sometimes we forget to mention that we also have been the students, learning patience and process from them.

Looking forward as a boutique investment advisory firm, we are encouraged by what we think may be in store for our clients. If yesterday's record is an indication of a sustainable competitive advantage in the form of a carefully calibrated, disciplined, and necessarily unconventional investment process, then we hope that, no matter what the challenges, the decade to come will be fruitful. We believe it likely that sooner or later a *BusinessWeek* cover story will proclaim the "Death of Equities," as it did in 1979. Looking backwards from the dregs in 1979 to the peak in 1966, most investors agreed that equities were dead. For the value-hungry firms like MCM, headlines like that will drive us to the fields to sow—and to sow abundantly. We have both seed and patience to wait for the eventual harvest, whenever it comes.

Since the late 1990s it has proven prudent for value investors to focus on managing risk, to win by not losing. When investors become irrational about risk (see "Risk—Once Again a Four-Letter Word?" several pages previous), it will then be the season for judicious value investors to take the opposite tack, to shift their focus away from risk and more toward calculated return, to accept quotational losses with equanimity, because of the greatly reduced likelihood that they will become permanent losses. As noted elsewhere, once investors come to irrationally fear risk (with the same intensity with which they were irrationally exuberant), they are not soon dissuaded. The defining characteristic of the next decade for value investors may be the once-in-a-generation opportunity to play offense. From 1975 through 1998, a 14-year stretch that began with risk being scorned, Berkshire Hathaway's annual increase in per-share book value outpaced the appreciation of the S&P 500, including dividends, in all but two years, or about 15 percent of the time. Value investors normally assume that over long stretches they will underperform the benchmark indices 30 to 40 percent of the time. Of course, the undersigned is no Warren Buffett! Still, we get tingly when imagining the possibility that just maybe during the next decade we'll trail only in three or four years instead of six or seven!

In what would be value investors' nirvana, those who won by not losing in the last decade and those who believe that successful long-term investing goes to those who prudently and patiently purchase superior businesses (and are willing to accept the concomitant volatility in market prices) will be one and the same.

Epilogue

"This Time Is Different"

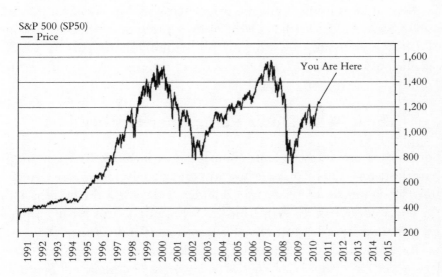

S&P 500 (SP50)
— Price

SOURCE: © FactSet Research Systems.

Seeing the future is easy when it's already past. Until now, dear reader, you've been able to critique my comments knowing how events played out. But now cast your eyes on the chart above and note how lonely and exposed the "You Are Here" dot seems to be. From this vista, the one from which I view the world every day, only the past is known. The future is not. Given the awesome responsibility of managing the life savings of others, what would *you* tell them about the days and months ahead? Several ideas in the Epilogue reflect my current thinking—or at least as current as the publishing medium allows. Although an Epilogue is obligatory, it may in some measure be redundant. As Jean–Baptiste Alphonse Karr noted in 1839, *"Plus ca change, plus c'est la meme chose,"* or "The more things change, the more they remain the same." Often adapted and reinterpreted over the years (most recently by rocker Jon Bon Jovi in "The More Things Change"), the old adage confirms anecdotal human experience. Or, as Yogi Berra might say, "It's *déjà vu* all over again."

Several ideas in this Epilogue originated with Fireside Chat No. 8, published April 22, 2010, available in its entirety in the library section of MCM's web site: www.mcmadvisors.com. Future Fireside Chats may be posted to the web site from time to time.

Those Who Don't Remember History . . .

Some ideas are transcendent. Humankind's inability to learn from past mistakes—often reappearing in cumulatively more costly iterations as memories of yesterday's blunders fade—is a theme repeated for effect several times in this book. Scholars confirm what historical anecdotes reveal. Most recently Ken Rogoff and Carmen Reinhart produced prodigious volumes of data in their 2009 work with the tongue-in-cheek title *This Time Is Different: Eight Centuries of Financial Folly.* Two years earlier the duo had hit upon another human proclivity, this time of political entities. Their December 2007 paper "Banking Crises: An Equal Opportunity Menace" (introduced in MCM's 2008 annual report) confirmed what the worldly wise already knew: Governments around the world—including our own—are no more inclined to reveal their true financial condition today than in the past.

Such collective amnesia by the governed and lack of transparency by those who govern contribute to the human suffering that ensues in crisis after crisis. That is precisely why today's fiscal and monetary damage control may be nearly as ineffective at stemming the tide as the various and sundry, and often experimental, interventions during the Great Depression. That statement is not made lightly. Early-stage fiscal policy initiatives, which produced far-less-than-advertised economic multiplier effects, have been hamstrung by political gridlock ever since. On the monetary side, Ben Bernanke, unlike many in positions of high political authority or the body politic itself, knows Depression history. The more pertinent question: Is he able to apply history's lessons to today's subtly similar yet significantly different set of challenges? Thus far, the results are not reassuring.

Moving from the trenches to the unrestricted view from the high ground, I wonder: Could it be that the very laws and regulations written in the 1930s to prevent another upheaval—and to protect citizens from having to suffer the consequences should it recur—had a most perverse and unintended side effect? Could it be that they inadvertently became the building blocks for the current crisis?

Today's financial hangover is quite unlike your grandfather's. It's bigger, more systemic, more entrenched, and ironically, as stated above, it owes its very existence to the safeguards written into law in the 1930s, for example: FDIC (deposit insurance), Glass-Steagall (separation of commercial and investment banks), which together helped pave the way for the dangerous separation of actions and responsibility ("moral hazard"), which then led unavoidably to the intrusion of the government into the private sector (the insidious "too-big-to-fail doctrine"), to name a few. Moreover, the lenders to the banks in the 1930s were known as depositors, and they bore the brunt. Because today's depositors are insured, the lenders of last resort are the Federal Reserve System and the FDIC, who are ultimately backstopped by taxpayers. Absent the personal accountability of the 1930s, this time around the banking crisis did become the equal opportunity menace.

History from the Inside Out

Thanks to electronic media (Google "News from 1930"), over the last year I have figuratively traveled back in time, each day reading 30 to 40 vignettes from the *Wall Street Journal* on dates that correspond to today's, only circa 1930–1931. In short, the experience of reading today's political, social, and economic developments and opinions alongside those of the same date eight decades ago is, in a certain sense, unnerving. A day rarely goes by without me wondering whether the "passions of man" constitute the principal constant in history. Even researchers Rogoff and Reinhart, despite their scholarly exposition—or perhaps because of it—overlook the very warning implicit in the title of their book. Like Congress, the White House, and virtually every author who has written about the crisis, they couldn't resist the folly of proposing solutions to a problem that is intransigent: the endemic predilections of humanity. I believe that we are doomed to repeat the mistakes of yesterday *if we deny the power of the primal propensities of our species;* in equal measure, we are set free *if we reason within the limits they impose.* According to the man (yes, Einstein) who claimed that compound interest is the most powerful force in the universe, "Doing the same thing over and over again and expecting different results" is insanity. Beyond the realm of science and within the murky world of human behavior, we might simply call it history!

Moreover, because people today, much as those almost 80 years ago, were on the inside of the economy looking out, and because human beings are an integral part of the very system they're trying to analyze, even regulate, those who believe that governments are in control of economies may be victims of their own illusions. Read on.

The Insidious Disappearance of Accountability

The antisocial consequences of the intended safeguards mentioned above are mirrored in the insidious abrogation of personal responsibility across broad swaths of America. Those who don't directly bear the consequences of their behaviors tend to act differently from those who do, a phenomenon known as the aforementioned moral hazard. Think of the Welfare State boomerang. In business, the slow deterioration of the common-law practice that defines the nature and extent of the relationship between a principal and his or her agent (employer/employee, owner/manager, beneficial owner/institutional shareholder), namely the "agency dilemma," has become more problematic as the chasm between the two parties widened.

I write from personal experience. Prior to the early 1980s, Wall Street investment banks were organized as partnerships (including the Cleveland-based McDonald & Co., where I, as a general partner with unlimited liability, worried more about my net worth than my net income!). Once investment banks transformed themselves into publicly traded corporations, personal liability ceased to be the constraint of aberrant behavior that it once was. The mischief that this not-so-subtle change fostered was instrumental in the collapse by 2007 of what had become a financial house of cards.

Institutional investors owned 10 percent of this country's public corporations in the 1950s; today they own 70 percent. In this era that Hyman Minsky dubbed "managerial capitalism," the investment time horizons of institutions have shrunk to the point where Keynes, were he alive, would charge them with playing casino capitalism with OPM (other people's money). Common-stock mutual funds nominally control 26 percent of American industry. Once long-term investors, they now (on average) turn over their portfolios 100 percent each year. Rather than acting as advocates for their owners—or standing tall as the last bastion against forces intent on crippling capitalism—institutional investors of all stripes are more likely to take flight than fight when trouble appears. The demanding and thankless task of policing recalcitrant CEOs and their minions is left to others who follow in the revolving door of institutional ownership. The buck usually gets passed until the music stops.

The Invisible and Irresistible Forces

Perhaps there is something else lurking behind the curtain that dwarfs even the machinations of governments. Could it be that forces in the physical world, though largely invisible in finance and economics, are at work? Is it possible that Newton's third law of motion—that for every action there is an equal and opposite reaction—may lead one to logically conclude that the forces that caused the "apple" of near-universal excess to overcome gravity and rise to such dizzying heights are likely to be counteracted by equal and opposite forces?

Nearly 200 years after Newton, philosopher and essayist Ralph Waldo Emerson appealed to the laws of physics to explain the nature of humanity in a similar action/reaction duality. He called it the law of compensation. Within every cause, Emerson reasoned, grew the seed of its own effect. Even before Newton and Emerson, Buddha identified the central law of our existence as *karma*, which in Sanskrit means *action*. For every action there is an effect; this law of cause and effect, Buddha taught, is the central law of both our internal and external world. "As you sow, so shall you reap," said Jesus several centuries later. The common thread: Actions have consequences—and those consequences, though likely quite different from the actions themselves, tend to be more or less proportional.

The Intersection of the Philosophical and the Pragmatic

Washington, collectively, doesn't think all that much about such lofty ideas; the culture there isn't philosophical, it's pragmatic. And in times of crisis it is often spontaneously reactionary and doggedly deceptive. Decision making is compressed into short-term, *ad hoc* measures. Consequences are tomorrow's problem. Analytic philosopher Bertrand Russell saw a certain transcendent utility in anecdotal wisdom, especially during times of upheaval. Firsthand knowledge that gives order and unification to complex social systems like economics—which does so by critically examining the grounds of our convictions, prejudices, and beliefs—allows one to frame issues in a broader, although admittedly inexact, context. (When explicit answers for questions can be found, the field of inquiry leaves the realm of philosophy and becomes science!) Like Newton and Emerson before him, Russell sought understanding in the midst of confusion and sometimes chaos. And so it is for us. If, by leaning toward the philosophical, by thinking longer term while critically evaluating prevailing "convictions, prejudices, and beliefs," we just might be able to see through the smoke to the fire.

The pragmatic solution to economic unpleasantness throughout the last decade has been to repeatedly inject the economy with the adrenaline of cheap and easy money. The philosopher shudders in disbelief. The ongoing attempt to put off the consequences of years of cumulative excesses by jacking up the prices of assets to levels above their intrinsic worth is itself not without potentially dire consequences. The Fed's current action of pushing interest rates down to near zero is having the effect of driving people out of the safer assets into the riskier ones, of sacrificing the prudent to save the foolish. Societies have crumbled for lesser transgressions.

That such extraordinary excesses that build up in recent decades can be contained with so little proportional consequence boggles the mind. Whatever their motives, Oz-like governments are playing Russian roulette behind the curtain, which should be ample cause for us to match such recklessness with an equal measure of skepticism.

Respect for Risk . . . Just for a Fleeting Moment

Preoccupation with risk was all the rage early in 2009. The yield differential between U.S. Treasury bonds and low-quality corporate "junk" bonds is a logical proxy for the extent to which investors in all asset classes are willing to accept risk in the pursuit of return. In March 2009 the spread between Treasury bonds and the lowest-quality corporate bonds not in default proceedings, the S&P CCC-rated "extremely speculative" category, peaked at roughly 35 percentage points. Fear quickly morphed into greed and, by the end of 2009, a new record for the issuance of junk bonds was set. In a reversal of epic proportions, yield-desperate investors drove the spread from 35 down to nine percentage points in less than one year. Junk bonds were the 1980s brainchild of Michael Milken, who, like the "shadow" bankers two decades later, was at least for a time able to perpetuate the illusion of turning a sow's ear into a silk purse. Admittedly, he and the investment bankers who followed profited mightily from selling their sorcery. Those who subscribed to the silliness, however, paid a huge price for their ignorance. That the word *junk*, as it describes a class of assets once almost universally thought safe, would assume unquestioned legitimacy in the investor's vernacular was surely an early symptom of the growing indifference to risk. It's a baby step from there to CDOs (collateralized debt obligations), especially with unregulated derivatives exploding on the scene in the late 1990s.

Whether in the debt or equity markets, savers and investors in search of return are finding it necessary to crawl further and further out on the risk limb. In their desperation they are paying huge premiums for risky assets. If the Fed's attempt to forestall deflation by this most questionable means fails, investors will be the sacrificial lambs. If the markets surprise by doing the unexpected and head south, the economy, without the fragile boost of the wealth effect, will no doubt be right behind. As if oblivious to the new risks that the Fed was injecting into the capital markets (as noted in Chapter 11), Congress meanwhile debated financial reforms to protect the investors and taxpayers against an enemy that was born of its own legislative and regulatory laxity. When risk premiums plummet—particularly when the unintended byproduct of monetary stimulus runs amok—things are not likely to end well. Markets that undervalue risk are anathema to a value investor. Dollars selling for $.50 are as scarce as World Series flags at Wrigley Field. Instead of value, we are more likely to find 50-cent pieces selling for a dollar.

I believe that the spectacular market rise currently being celebrated has underpinnings similar to the cheap-money "fools' rally" from 2003 to 2007—and that we are in both a secular bear market and an economic contraction that may not have seen its darkest days. Thinking into the future as we are inclined to do, the only development that would leave us scratching our heads would be further dramatic moves to the upside. We cannot forecast if, when, or how far the pendulum might swing, but our record suggests that sometimes we seem to be slightly ahead of the crowd in sniffing out trouble.

Just as a rising tide lifts all ships, the opposite is also true. If, as this essay suggests, today's high tide follows the rhythms of nature— this time downward—then finding attractively priced businesses will become that much easier. They are most plentiful when the market is dominated by distressed sellers, many of whom are parting with heir-looms not because they want to but because they must raise cash. In Greenspan-speak, it's known as the "liquidity preference." In the real world, as among the financial titans post–August 2007, the public denials of the need for liquidity are usually accompanied by acute private urgency. It's a buyer's market during periods of "catalyst myopia," when prices are deeply depressed, but nobody can point to a specific reason to buy anything. This is the reciprocal of today's environment.

On a personal note, it would be a mistake for readers to typecast the writer as a perennial pessimist, particularly for those who aren't famil-iar with my investment posture in the 1980s. During the first decade and more of the greatest bull market in modern history, I was rationally exuberant, finding more opportunities than I had money. I was always fully invested, sometimes even borrowing money to buy more of a good thing. If one carefully studies Shiller's "Graham" P/E chart in Chapter 11, one will discover that my optimism had a solid foundation in value. Because of my conviction that interest rates were unsustainably high, almost everything appeared cheap in those stocked-pond investment days. Next take a gander at the Shiller price/earnings ratios from the mid-1990s to the present. Most investors have been unaware of, indifferent to, or accustomed to chronically overvalued markets as the new norm. They suffered the consequences of ignorance or apathy in 2000–2002 and 2007–2009—and, just perhaps, history may repeat itself in the months or years ahead.

As a rational optimist at the core, I expect there will come a day when I will once again be miscast—likely in the midst of pervasive despair—as an irrational optimist. I will take that characterization no more seriously than I take today's. All along this journey, of which the 12 years covered in the book constitute but a passage, I've taken solace, as well as found courage for my convictions, in knowing that the road I'm taking has never been, nor ever will be, crowded.

Index